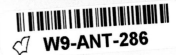

Teach Yourself Word for Windows

Gary Cornell

Osborne **McGraw-Hill**
Berkeley New York St. Louis San Francisco Auckland Bogotá Hamburg London Madrid Mexico City
Milan Montreal New Delhi Panama City Paris São Paulo Singapore Sydney Tokyo Toronto

Osborne **McGraw-Hill**
2600 Tenth Street
Berkeley, California 94710
U.S.A.

For information on software, translations, or book distributors outside of the U.S.A., please write to Osborne **McGraw-Hill** at the above address.

Teach Yourself Word for Windows

Series Design: Seventeenth Street Studios

1234567890 DOC 9987654

ISBN 0-07-882010-4

Contents

Acknowledgments, *vii*
Introduction, *ix*

I Essential Word Features

1 Getting Started with Word for Windows 6.0 . . . 3

1.1 WHAT IS WORD FOR WINDOWS 6.0?, 4
1.2 STARTING A WORD SESSION, 5
1.3 ENDING A WORD SESSION, 9
1.4 BECOMING FAMILIAR WITH THE KEYBOARD, 10
1.5 LEARNING ABOUT THE WORD SCREEN, 13
1.6 CLOSING AN EXISTING DOCUMENT TO WORK WITH A NEW ONE, 19

2 The Many Ways to Work with Text . . . 21

2.1 ENTERING TEXT, 22
2.2 INSERTION AND OVERTYPE, 30
2.3 SAVING YOUR WORK, 31
2.4 OPENING AN EXISTING DOCUMENT, 41
2.5 PRINTING AND PREVIEWING BASICS, 43
2.6 HELP, 46

3 Working Within a Word Document . . . 57

3.1 MORE ON MOVING THROUGH A DOCUMENT, 59
3.2 SELECTING TEXT, 65
3.3 DELETING AND REARRANGING TEXT, 72
3.4 SEARCHING FOR TEXT IN YOUR DOCUMENT, 79
3.5 SEARCHING FOR AND REPLACING TEXT IN YOUR DOCUMENTS, 84

4 Wizards . . . 89
4.1 WHAT IS A WIZARD?, 91
4.2 USING THE AWARD WIZARD, 93
4.3 USING THE AGENDA WIZARD, 99
4.4 USING THE CALENDAR WIZARD, 105
4.5 USING THE LETTER WIZARD, 109
4.6 USING THE RESUME WIZARD, 111
4.7 USING THE MEMO WIZARD, 115
4.8 USING THE FAX WIZARD, 117

5 Using Word to Help Your Writing . . . 121
5.1 SPELL CHECKING, 123
5.2 USING WORD'S THESAURUS, 135
5.3 GRAMMAR CHECKING, 138
5.4 USE WORD'S AUTOTEXT FACILITY, 141

II *Mastering Word*

6 Changing How Text Looks . . . 149
6.1 CHANGING HOW CHARACTERS LOOK, 151
6.2 FONTS, 162
6.3 INSERTING SPECIAL CHARACTERS, 170
6.4 ADVANCED SEARCH, REPLACE AND COPYING: SPECIAL CHARACTERS, FORMATTING, OR FONTS, 174

7 Lines, Paragraphs, and Styles . . . 185
7.1 SHAPING HOW A PARAGRAPH LOOKS, 187
7.2 JAZZING UP A PARAGRAPH, 200
7.3 USING STYLES, 208
7.4 USING TEMPLATES, 221
7.5 AUTOMATIC FORMATTING, 225

8 Laying Out a Page . . . 233
8.1 NEW WAYS TO VIEW YOUR DOCUMENT, 235
8.2 PAGE SETUP, 241
8.3 PAGE BREAKS, PAGE NUMBERS, AND GENERAL HEADERS AND FOOTERS, 248
8.4 FOOTNOTES AND ENDNOTES, 257

9 Previewing and Printing Your Work . . . 263
9.1 PRINT PREVIEW, 264
9.2 PRINTING, 270
9.3 PRINTING ENVELOPES, 276

10 Lists and Tables . . . 283
10.1 LISTS, 285
10.2 FIRST STEPS WITH TABLES, 296
10.3 MODIFYING AN EXISTING TABLE, 306
10.4 SORTING AND CALCULATING WITH TABLES, 317

III *Advanced Word*

11 Working with a Single Large Document or Multiple Documents . . . 327
11.1 OPENING AND WORKING WITH MORE THAN ONE DOCUMENT AT ONCE, 329
11.2 USING MULTIPLE DOCUMENT WINDOWS AND SPLITTING THE SCREEN, 331
11.3 DIVIDING YOUR DOCUMENT INTO SECTIONS, 337
11.4 OUTLINING, 344

12 Document Management . . . 353
12.1 SUMMARY INFORMATION, 355
12.2 ANNOTATIONS, 358
12.3 REVISION MARKS, 362
12.4 FIND FILE, 367
12.5 MASTERING FIND FILE'S SEARCH CAPABILITIES, 377

13 An Introduction to Desktop Publishing . . . 385
13.1 GRAPHICS, 388
13.2 WORKING WITH COLUMNS, 394
13.3 WORKING WITH FRAMES, 399

14 Form Letters, Envelopes, and Labels . . . 411
14.1 GENERATING FORM LETTERS, 413
14.2 GENERATING LABELS AND ENVELOPES, 432

A A Ten-Minute Guide to Windows . . . 441
MOUSE POINTERS AND ICONS, 442
MOUSE ACTIONS, 443
STARTING WINDOWS, 444
ENDING WINDOWS, 445
WINDOWS AND ITS LITTLE WINDOWS, 446
STARTING PROGRAMS FROM THE PROGRAM MANAGER, 446
MENUS, 449
DIALOG BOXES, 453
FILE MANAGER, 460
ABNORMAL EXITS FROM WINDOWS, 464

B Installing Word for Windows 6.0 . . . 465
SETTING UP WORD FOR WINDOWS 6.0, 466
INSTALLING AND REMOVING WORD COMPONENTS AFTER YOUR ORIGINAL INSTALLATION, 473

Index . . . 477

Acknowledgments

One of the best parts of writing a book is when the author gets to thank those who have helped him or her—for rarely is a book truly produced alone. In this case, words (and Word) fail me when I try to find ways to thank the team at Osborne/McGraw-Hill. Their patience, dedication, help, cheerfulness—you name it—went far beyond the call of duty. This book simply could not exist without their incredible work and equally incredible help. To Deborah Craig, Mark Karmendy, Jeff Pepper, Vicki Van Ausdall, Helena Worsley, and the Production department: Thanks!

Robert Heitzman wrote the first versions of most of the exercises and two of the chapters, and patiently pointed out many ways to make this book better. Deborah Craig's help went far beyond what an author can expect (or hope) to have from a copy editor. I'm really grateful to her!

Finally, thanks to all my friends who put up with my strange ways and my occasional short temper for lo, so many months.

Introduction

This is a book for the complete beginner. I've tried hard to make this a book that you can use to learn Word for Windows 6.0, regardless of whether you have never used a computer before or are simply making the transition to Word for Windows (and even Microsoft Windows) for the first time.

But, I've tried to help you learn Word for Windows in such a way that I don't insult your intelligence or treat you as a "dummy" or an "idiot." In particular, I've tried hard not to talk down to you. (If you find a page where you think I have, copy it and send it to me, care of the publisher. If I agree, I'll correct it and send you a free copy of the next version of this book when it comes out!)

This is a step-by-step approach to learning Word for Windows. Each chapter has an introduction telling you what that chapter is going to teach you, and is further broken down into digestible, easy-to-follow lessons. This approach lets you master the most useful features in Word for Windows without choking on unnecessary details. The text clearly specifies the steps needed to accomplish the tasks most users of Word for Windows want—and need—to know.

Every chapter (except the first) begins with a way to make sure you have mastered the previous material. These Review Skills Checks refer to the specific sections in the previous chapters that cover the material. This way you can easily go back to the referenced section if you have any trouble with the activity. Similarly, every chapter ends with exercises called Mastery Skills Checks that refer back to specific sections of that chapter, and exercises called Cumulative Skills Checks that let you check (again, with specific references) on the bigger picture. Finally, within each chapter there are lots of hands-on examples and check-yourself exercise sets to make it easier for you to know that you have mastered the material covered within the individual sections.

How This Book is Organized

This book is divided into three parts and has two appendixes. Part 1 covers fundamental Word for Windows skills like entering text, navigating around the screen, correcting spelling, and saving and printing your work.

Part 2 covers the rest of the features most users of Word for Windows will want to master in order to get their work looking exactly the way they want. You'll see ways to make text smaller and larger, and learn how to change the shape of a character, paragraph, or page. You'll see how easy it is to handle lists and tables using Word for Windows 6.0. You will probably want to read the first 10 chapters pretty much in order.

Part 3 covers more advanced topics: working with multiple documents, document management, desktop publishing, and using Word to prepare form letters, envelopes, and labels. These chapters can probably be read in any order you want if you are willing to refer back occasionally to an earlier chapter. These features are useful—often fun—but may not interest everyone.

The first of the two appendixes gives you a quick course in Windows itself. This appendix covers pretty much all you need to know about Microsoft Windows in order to use Word for Windows! The last appendix explains how to install Word for Windows and re-install part or all of it later on if need be.

Conventions Used in This Book

Special keys are enclosed in a *lozenge* so they stand out. For example, keys such as Ctrl and Home appear as shown here. Similarly, if you need to press the "right arrow" key, you'll see, "Press →." If you see bold type inside a line, it indicates text you need to enter. For example, you might see a sentence that says: Type **How are you?** and then press Enter. Otherwise, text you need to enter is set on a separate line or lines, in color in a font that looks like this:

"How are you?" This is a question that doesn't expect a serious answer.

When you need to use a combination of keys simultaneously, the keys will be separated by a plus sign. For example, "Press Ctrl+A" indicates that you should hold down the key marked "Ctrl" on your keyboard while pressing the "A" key. Similarly, when you need to use more than two keys to do something and need to hold them all down simultaneously, all the keys will be separated by a plus sign. For example, "Press Ctrl+A+B," indicates that you should hold down the key marked "Ctrl" on your keyboard while holding down the "A" and the "B" key—so all three keys are depressed simultaneously.

"Press Alt F" on the other hand means press the "Alt" key, then the "F" key—you don't have to hold down the "Alt" key while you press the "F" key (although you can). If you need to press three keys in succession, the second is separated from the third by a comma. For example, Alt F, P means press the "Alt" key, then the "F" key, and then the "P" key. You don't have to hold down the keys simultaneously.

In this book you will see a couple of ways to describe choosing an item from a menu. One may be "Open the File menu and choose Close (Alt F, C)." This means, of course, press the "Alt" key, then the "F" key, and then the "C" key. If the item rather than the menu is stressed, you may read "Choose Close from the File menu." Or you may just read "Select File, Close" (without the "Alt" key combination). This somewhat shortened instruction is found more as you progress in the book since you will become more and more accustomed to choosing menu items.

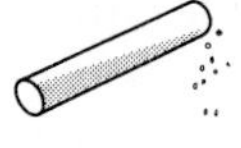

NOTE *The underlined letters you see in this book, such as "F" and "C" in the example above, correspond to the same underlined letters you see on menus onscreen. In this book, we have underlined only menu keys and their options; however, any time you see a letter underlined on a menu, dialog box, etc., onscreen, you can use the "Alt" key combination to access your choice.*

Filenames and file extensions appear in full capital letters: WINWORD, SAMPLE1.DOC, and so on. Microsoft Windows is referred to simply as "Windows" most of the time.

Review Skills Checks, Mastery Skills Checks, and Cumulative Skills Checks show the section numbers that they refer to in brackets. You can look back in those sections to quickly review the information needed.

Notes for Special Users of Word for Windows

Microsoft tried hard to make Word for Windows usable by people in unusual situations: if you have trouble seeing the characters onscreen because you either have a laptop or are sight impaired, there are ways to work around this. Similarly, if you have trouble handling a mouse or pressing keys simultaneously, Microsoft has a way around this as well.

For Laptop Users and Sight-Impaired Users of Word for Windows If you are having trouble seeing the characters that Word uses on your screen, Word allows you to increase the size of characters—without increasing the size they will be when they are printed. This is called *zooming*. Although the following directions may not make much sense yet, they will if you return to them after you have read Chapters 1 and 2; you will know how to work with the Word for Windows screen by then. To enlarge the characters that Word for Windows uses, load Word for Windows (see Chapter 1 and Appendix B), and look at the top of your screen for something that looks like this:

Type a percentage larger than 100 (the maximum is 200) at the place; Word will increase the size of the characters onscreen accordingly. To go back to the usual size, repeat the process only this time type 100 in the box.

The last thing you may want to do is enlarge the toolbars. This can be done by opening the View menu, choosing Toolbars and then checking off the Large Buttons box. (The shortcut is Alt V, T followed by Alt L. To go back to the usual size buttons, repeat these keystrokes.)

A Note for People with Manual Disabilities If you have trouble handling a mouse or simultaneous keystrokes (as are needed often in Word for Windows), contact Microsoft for their "Access Pack for Microsoft Windows" at 206-637-7098. The Access pack lets you enter key combinations one at a time or use the keyboard to replace the mouse completely. You can slow down the rate at which keys repeat when you press them or turn this feature off completely.

part one

Essential Word Features

1

Getting Started with Word for Windows 6.0

chapter objectives

By the time you finish this chapter you will be able to

1.1 Begin to understand what Word for Windows 6.0 can do for you

1.2 Start Word for Windows 6.0

1.3 End Word for Windows 6.0

1.4 Use the computer keyboard to navigate and issue commands in Word for Windows 6.0

1.5 Understand the Word for Windows 6.0 environment

1.6 Give yourself a clean screen to work on

THIS short chapter both provides an orientation to Word and gives you some of the basic skills that you need before you can move on. Don't worry if you are a beginner; this books doesn't assume that you've used a word processor before. (If you are unfamiliar with Windows, you can turn to Appendix A for a quick overview of what you need to know.) On the other hand, if you are switching from another word processor to Word for Windows 6.0, you can work through the material in this chapter that much faster.

1.1 WHAT IS WORD FOR WINDOWS 6.0?

Word for Windows 6.0 is the latest incarnation of the best-selling Windows word processor. That's the easy part. The hard part is choosing what to discuss in this section to give you a idea what this program can do! Just listing all of Word for Windows 6.0's features would take many, many pages.

For the moment, just note that Word for Windows 6.0 is probably the only software package you need to prepare printed material—whether for home, school, or business. After you've had a little experience with Word, you'll be able to prepare memos, newsletters, mass mailings, term papers, and more almost effortlessly.

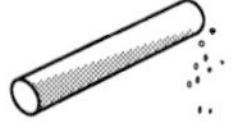

NOTE *Since "Word for Windows 6.0" is rather a mouthful, this book uses the term "Word" from now on.*

Word processors have been around since the dawn of personal computing—way back in the 1970s. Think of these early word processors as smart typewriters. With such word processors you could type (the computer jargon is *enter*) text, change it easily, and, when you were satisfied with your results, print what you had entered. All this is *much* easier to do than with an old-fashioned typewriter. Messy white out to correct errors has become a thing of the past. You can even type without needing to worry about the end of the line—because the program will automatically move text to a new line when you reach the end of a line. (This feature is usually called *word wrap*.)

Like any good modern word processor, Word can do much more than early word processors. It can check your spelling, give you access to an on-line thesaurus, and can even check your grammar. However, word processors traditionally haven't been good at handling graphics, tables, columns, large documents like books, or special effects such as different typefaces or the strange symbols used in science, engineering, and economics. Word, however, can handle all these tasks and more. For example, Word can sort, search, and do routine maintenance on the addresses used in mass mailings. (By the way, Word can also print postal bar codes to save you some money if you do use it for mass mailings.)

This is why Microsoft says, with some justification, that Word is not a *word processor* but a *document processor*. A powerful document processor like Word also makes it easy to do *desktop publishing*. Desktop publishing requires a program that can handle multiple columns, graphics, and text in different sizes and shapes. As you will see Word will meet most or all of your desktop publishing needs. Not only can Word handle graphics as easily as text, it also enables you to actually see what your document will look like when printed. This *WYSIWYG* ("what you see is what you get") feature makes Word the tool of choice for all but the most complex page layout tasks. For example, Figure 1-1 is a hypothetical memo prepared in a typography that might have been appropriate for the author. Notice how the shape of the letters (in the jargon this is called *the font*) reflect a certain time and mood. So not only does Word provide desktop publishing features—including a variety of fonts and character sizes, borders and shading, and the ability to import graphics—it also gives a fairly accurate representation of these features on your screen.

In sum, it's hard to imagine a task involving printed material that Word can't do. Most important of all, *the designers of Word worked very hard (and for the most part succeeded) in making its features easy to use.*

Perhaps the best way to end this section is to show you some sample documents prepared with Word, such as the one shown in Figure 1-2.

1.2 STARTING A WORD SESSION

First make sure that you have installed Word following the directions given in Appendix B. Since Word is a Windows program, you have to activate Microsoft Windows before you can use Word (see Appendix A). If, when you turn on your computer, you see the Windows desktop as described in Appendix A, your screen will probably look something like Figure 1-3. Double-click on the icon labeled "Microsoft Word" (it's highlighted in Figure 1-3). Windows then starts Word.

FIGURE 1-1

A typical WYSIWYG display in Word

Date: 1 January 1599

To: The backers of my latest play

From: William Shakespeare

Subject: My views

Our revels now are ended. These our actors, as I fortold you were all spirits and are melted into air, into thin air.

REMEMBER *If any terminology you see (like "double-click" above) is unfamiliar to you, you need only turn to Appendix A for a survey of what you need to know about Windows to work with Word.*

First you'll see the copyright screen, which also indicates who licensed the copy. In a moment, Word normally displays a "Tip of the

FIGURE 1-2

A sample newsletter

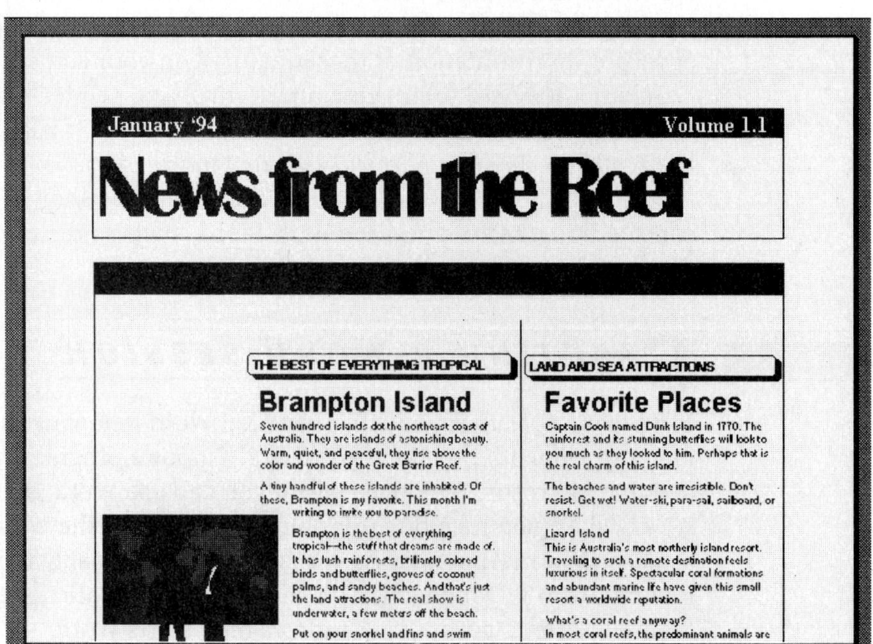

January '94 Volume 1.1

News from the Reef

THE BEST OF EVERYTHING TROPICAL

Brampton Island

Seven hundred islands dot the northeast coast of Australia. They are islands of astonishing beauty. Warm, quiet, and peaceful, they rise above the color and wonder of the Great Barrier Reef.

A tiny handful of these islands are inhabited. Of these, Brampton is my favorite. This month I'm writing to invite you to paradise.

Brampton is the best of everything tropical—the stuff that dreams are made of. It has lush rainforests, brilliantly colored birds and butterflies, groves of coconut palms, and sandy beaches. And that's just the land attractions. The real show is underwater, a few meters off the beach.

Put on your snorkel and fins and swim

LAND AND SEA ATTRACTIONS

Favorite Places

Captain Cook named Dunk Island in 1770. The rainforest and its stunning butterflies will look to you much as they looked to him. Perhaps that is the real charm of this island.

The beaches and water are irresistible. Don't resist. Get wet! Water-ski, para-sail, sailboard, or snorkel.

Lizard Island
This is Australia's most northerly island resort. Traveling to such a remote destination feels luxurious in itself. Spectacular coral formations and abundant marine life have given this small resort a worldwide reputation.

What's a coral reef anyway?
In most coral reefs, the predominant animals are

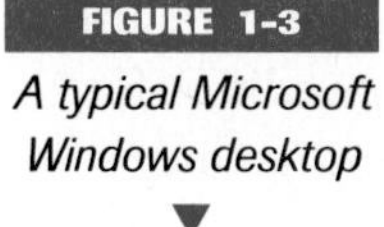

FIGURE 1-3

A typical Microsoft Windows desktop

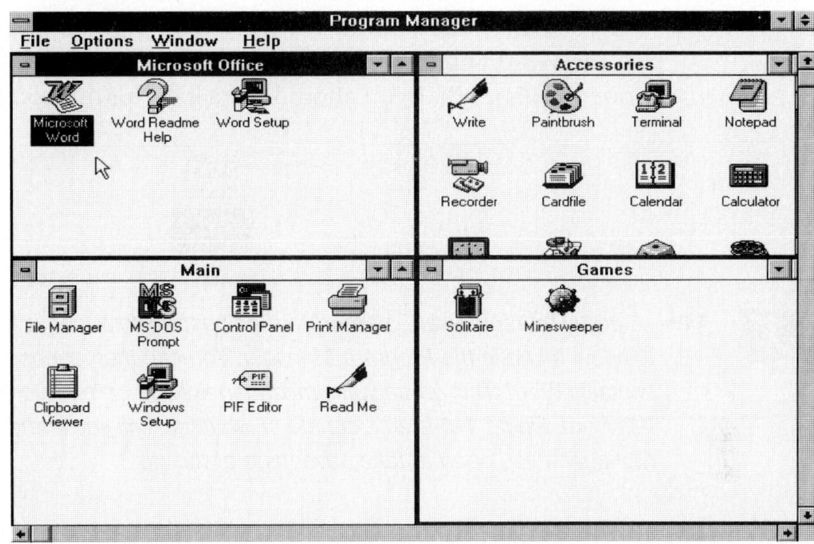

Day" superimposed on the main Word screen, as shown in Figure 1-4. These tips will become more useful as you become more familiar with Word. To make the tip disappear, press the Enter key. Now you're in Word's *editing screen*. This is where you type and edit your documents.

FIGURE 1-4

"Tip of the Day" superimposed on the main Word screen

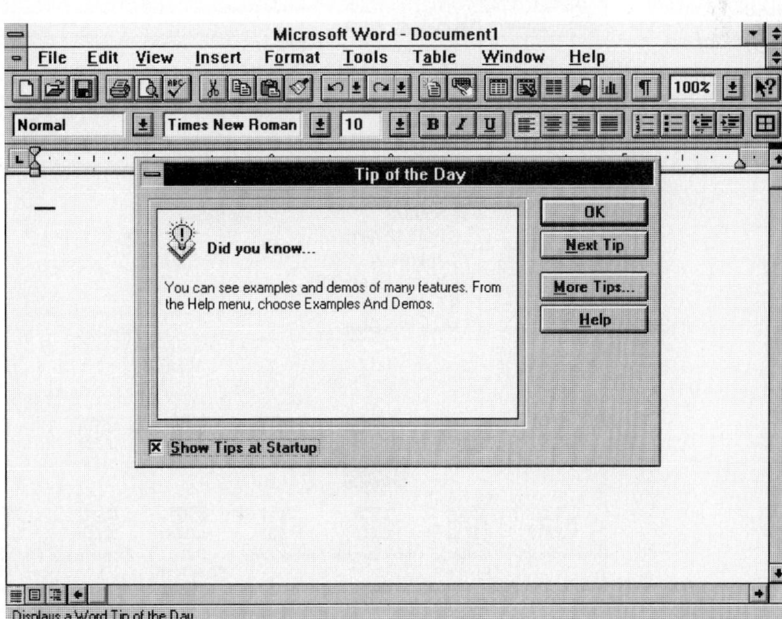

If you can't find a Microsoft Word icon like the one shown in Figure 1-3, the Word window may have been *minimized* (see Appendix A for more on this). What you should do is look for an icon like this one:

TIP *A pretty much fail-safe method for finding the Word icon is to pull down the Window menu in the Program Manager. You can then choose the group that contains Word. This group will almost certainly be called Microsoft Office or WinWord. Figure 1-5 is an example of what you will see in the Windows Program Manager if you need to take advantage of this tip.*

Double-click on this icon. This will take you to a screen resembling Figure 1-4. If what you see on your screen doesn't resemble any of these possibilities—if you can't find an icon like the ones just mentioned—please check Appendix B to see that you have installed Word properly. If need be, turn to Appendix A to make sure you understand basic Windows techniques.

FIGURE 1-5

Finding Word via the window menu

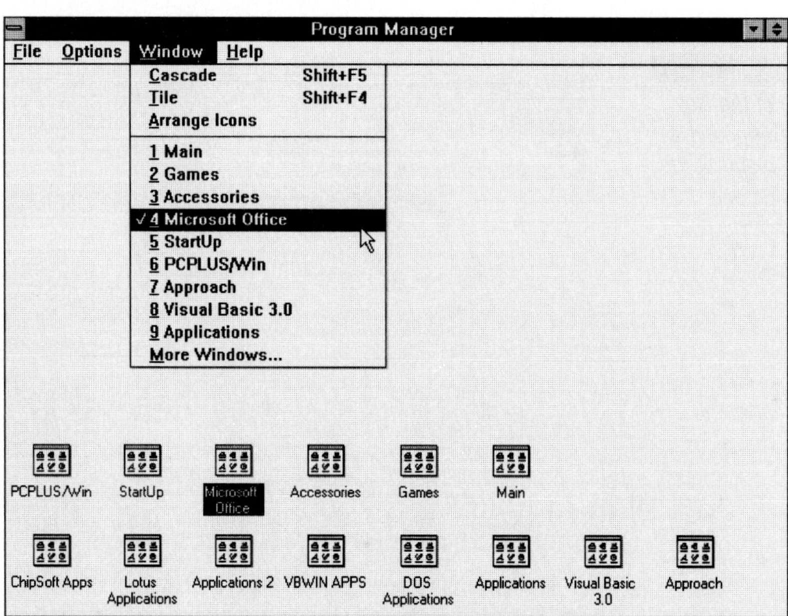

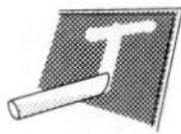

TIP *If your computer doesn't start up with Windows, then you will be at what the jargon calls the DOS prompt. It usually looks like C:>. Type the following and then hit Enter in order to try to simultaneously load Windows and Word:*

WIN C:\WINWORD\WINWORD

EXERCISE

1. Start a Word for Windows session from the Program Manager by double-clicking the Microsoft Word icon.

1.3 ENDING A WORD SESSION

You must always end a Windows program and then Windows itself—returning to the infamous DOS prompt (usually C: >)—before shutting off your computer. *This can not be stressed enough.* Just turning off your computer before closing Word or exiting from Windows can lead to major problems. (If this happens, for example, because of a power outage, see Appendix A for what to try if your computer is behaving strangely.) Without meaning to scare you (too much), not shutting down Word and Windows properly can mean:

- Work you thought you have saved wasn't really saved at all.
- Your hard disk fills up with temporary files that are not needed.

To end your Word session, choose Exit from the File menu (Alt F, X) or press Alt+F4.

If you have made any changes in the document since the last time Word saved it (or even if you have clicked in the wrong place so that Word thinks you have made a change), Word pops up a dialog box that looks like this:

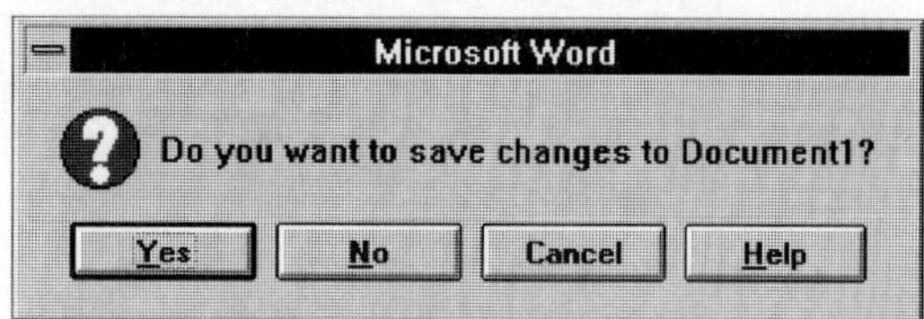

Click on the No button (or use Alt+N) to close the message box and not save your work. (If you click on Yes, Word will probably present you with a dialog box for saving your work. See the section in the next chapter on "Saving Your Work" for more on this very important topic.) Word then places you somewhere back in the Windows desktop. You can then leave Windows itself by using the Alt+F4 combination. (See Appendix A for more on the Windows desktop.)

EXERCISE

1. Begin a Word session on your computer.
2. End the current Word session using Exit in the File menu.
3. Exit Windows and shut down your machine.

1.4 BECOMING FAMILIAR WITH THE KEYBOARD

A computer keyboard is similar enough to that of a typewriter that it is easy to get started. For example, the Spacebar and text keys work much as you would expect. As you will see in the next chapter, the key marked Enter is similar but not identical to the carriage return key on a typewriter.

To make further progress with Word, you need to learn about keys that do not exist on an ordinary typewriter keyboard. For example, many of these keys move you around in a document. You can tell where text will go when you type by looking for the *insertion point*, which looks like a vertical bar as shown here. (The insertion point is the equivalent of the *cursor* in DOS-based applications with which you may already be familiar.)

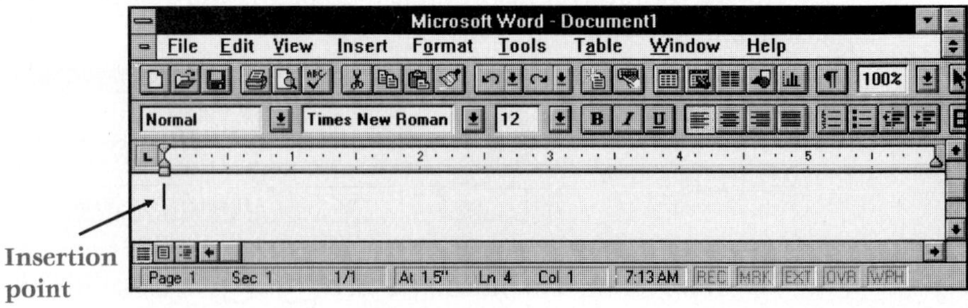

Figure 1-6 shows the location of these special keys (such as the arrow keys) on two popular keyboards. Your keyboard may be a little different, but most of the special keys should be there somewhere.

Table 1-1 lists most of the special keys that you use when working with Word documents. Although Table 1-1 is *not* something you need to memorize, you will want to know where the keys listed in the left column are on your keyboard.

Next notice the function keys that are located along the top or side (or both) of your keyboard. These keys provide shortcuts for many actions. Some of them (like F7 to activate the spelling checker) can be seen on the menus. (The most common Word shortcuts are displayed on the inside covers of this book.)

The keys marked Shift, Ctrl, and Alt are always used with other keys—often with the function keys. For example, Alt+F4 is the standard key combination for ending a program in Windows—so it is one way to end Word. In addition, Ctrl+End moves the insertion point to the end of a document and Ctrl+Home moves the insertion point to the beginning of a document. You will learn and use many of these key combinations as you go further with Word.

Key	Action Taken
Enter	Ends a short line or a paragraph
Backspace	Deletes the character to the left of the insertion point
↑	Moves the insertion point up one line
↓	Moves the insertion point down one line
←	Moves the insertion point one character to the left
→	Moves the insertion point one character to the right
Pg Up	Moves the insertion point to the preceding screen of text
Pg Dn	Moves the insertion point to the next screen of text
End	Moves the insertion point to the end of the line
Home	Moves the insertion point to the beginning of the line
Tab	Moves the insertion point to the next tab stop (possibly moving text as well)
Num Lock	Switches the numeric keypad at the side of the keyboard between numbers and the direction keys

TABLE 1-1 *Special Keys for Moving Through Word Documents*

FIGURE 1-6

The Standard and Enhanced keyboards

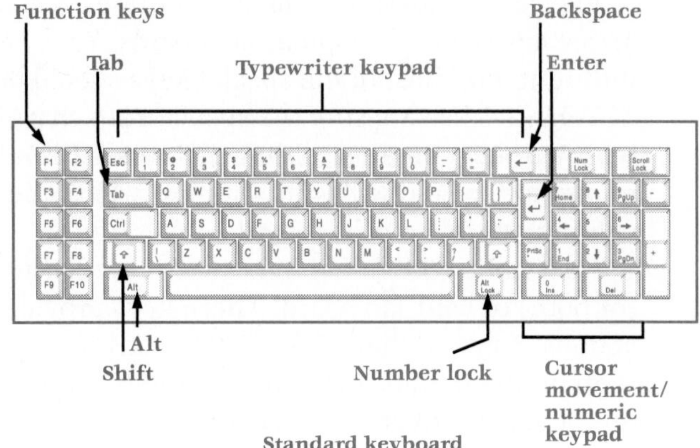

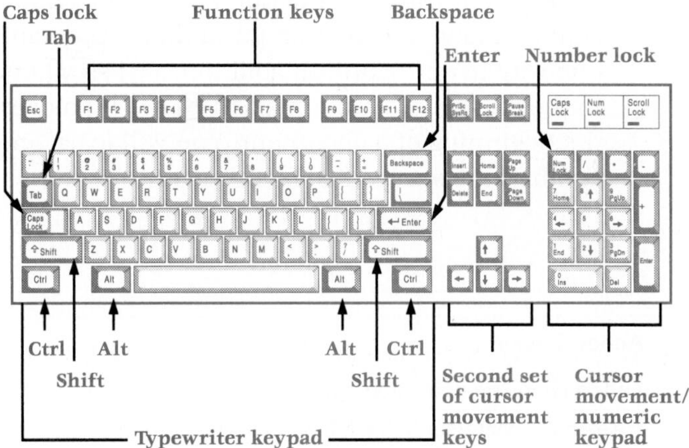

EXERCISES

The following exercise assumes that you have just started Word and have selected OK in the Tip of the Day dialog box.

1. Enter the following text. Don't use the Enter key at the end of each line; just let Word wrap the text for you. (Recall that this feature is called, naturally enough *word wrap*.)

   I just started Word for Windows and I am typing text merrily along just as if I know what I'm doing. This exercise will help show me how the special navigation keys (like the arrow keys) can be used to move around in a document. I should have about three lines of text now, enough to see how most of the special keys work.

2. Press the Home, End, Ctrl+Home, and Ctrl+End keys and watch where the insertion point goes each time.
3. Press Ctrl+Home and the ↓ to move the insertion point to the beginning of the second line. Press Ctrl+End. Press the ↑ and Home to move the insertion point to the beginning of the next to the last line again. Experiment with the other navigation keys combined with Home, and End. To challenge yourself, try using Ctrl with the arrow keys.
4. Press Ctrl+Home. Press Tab to indent the first line of text to the first default tab stop. Press Backspace to remove the tab you just entered.
5. Press Ctrl+End. Press Enter to end the first paragraph and press Enter again to enter a blank line. Turn on Num Lock and type **1234** from the numeric keypad. Turn off Num Lock.
6. Press Pg Up and Pg Dn and notice what they do in this short example. In a longer document Pg Up and Pg Dn move the insertion point one screenful at a time.
7. Press Alt+F4 and select No in the "Do you want to save changes..." dialog box that pops up.
8. Restart Word by double-clicking the Microsoft Word icon.

1.5 LEARNING ABOUT THE WORD SCREEN

Figure 1-7 shows you the main Word editing screen after the Tip of the Day is gone. This blank *document screen* is what you see after you clear the Tip of the day. This screen may look awfully complicated, but don't worry. The purpose of this section is to give you enough details to orient yourself without giving you so many that you are overwhelmed!

The top line of any Windows application is usually called the *title bar*. The title bar lists the name of the program and usually provides some information about what the program is working on at the moment. For example, as shown here, the title bar says Document1.

Microsoft Word - Document1

The big area in the center of the screen is called the *document screen* or *document area*. This area is where you enter text, graphics, and any other information that you want to include in your document.

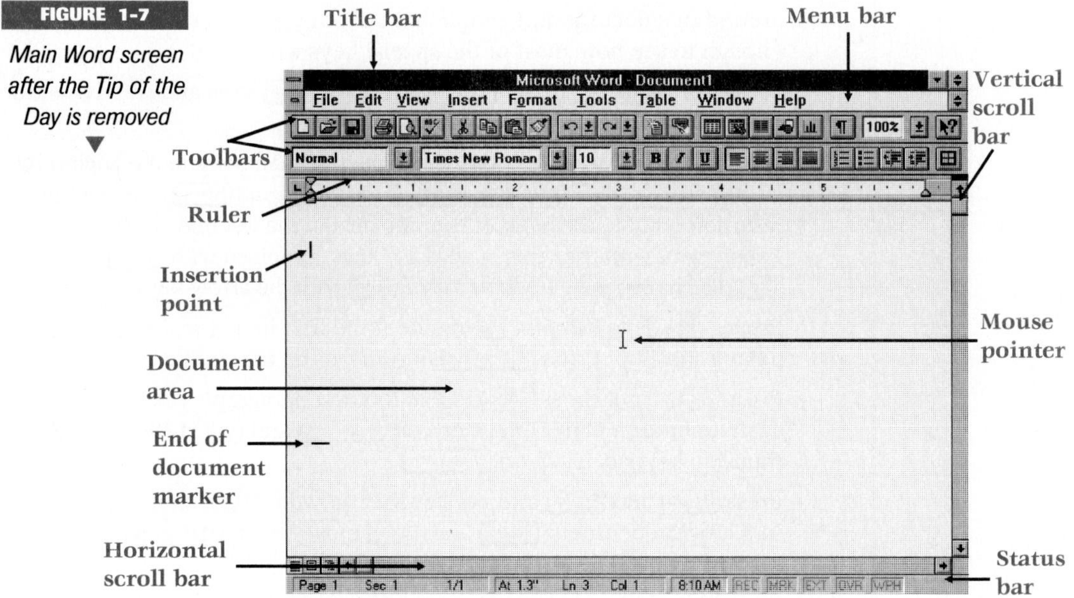

FIGURE 1-7 *Main Word screen after the Tip of the Day is removed*

MENUS

As with most Windows applications, you release the power of Word by choosing items from pull-down menus. In Word, most of these menus are listed on the *menu bar.* Word is a very well-behaved Windows application: If you are comfortable with another Windows application you should feel right at home with Word's menus. Similarly, when you become familiar with Word's menus, you will be comfortable with the menus in most other Windows applications.

The easiest way to choose an item from a menu is to click on the name of the menu that contains the item and then click on the item itself. You can also press Alt and then press the letter you see underlined in the menu. This is called an *accelerator key* or *hotkey.* For example, you can press Alt, then press F for the File menu or E for the Edit menu, etc.

The easiest way to close a menu is to press the Esc key. To return to the document screen press Esc again. You can also click inside the document area at the place you want to insert new text. If one menu is open you can move to another menu by using the ← key to open the menu on the left and the → to open the menu on the right. Some menu items also list shortcut keys like Ctrl+X for the Cut feature or F5 for the Go To feature. (A *shortcut key,* as explained in Appendix A, is a key or combination of keys you can press to activate an item without opening a menu—for example, remember that Alt+F4 is the shortcut key for ending a program in Windows.)

Figure 1-8 shows what the Edit menu looks like when it is pulled down. Notice that some of the items are grayed—indicating that they can't be chosen because they doesn't make sense in the current context. For example, the Undo item in the Edit menu shown here is grayed: If you haven't done anything, there's nothing to undo! Finally, menu items might have a three-dot *ellipsis* after their names. The ellipsis indicates that choosing the item leads to a dialog box that you will need to fill in. (Remember Dialog boxes solicit further information from you that is needed to carry out the command. See Appendix A for more information on them.) Notice that the bottom line of Figure 1-8 gives you a capsule description of the current menu item.

TOOLBARS

Word usually starts up showing these two *toolbars*.

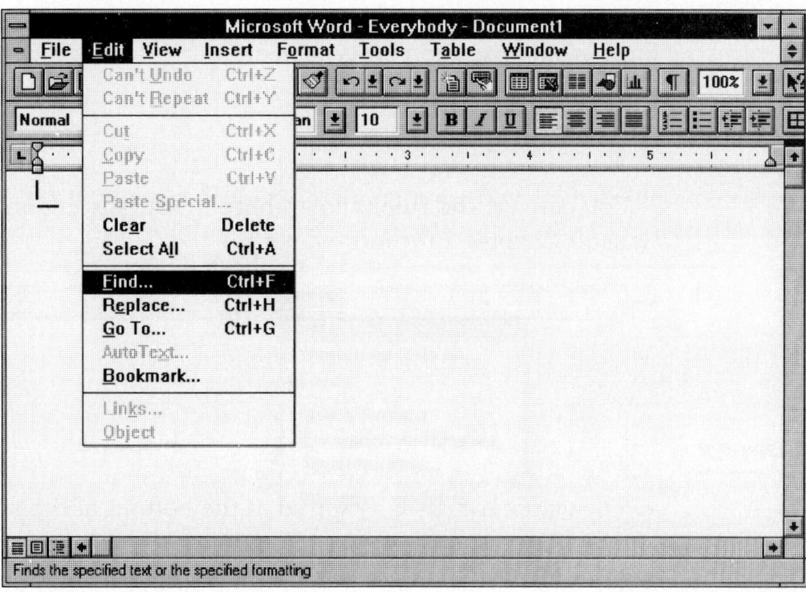

FIGURE 1-8

The Edit pull-down menu

As you can see, a toolbar is a series of icons that symbolize common tasks. If you have a mouse, clicking on one of these tools is a shortcut for accomplishing that task. For example, the scissors tool is a shortcut for cutting out text; that's pretty clear. The icon next to it turns out to be the one for copying. That one is perhaps less clear! The top toolbar is called the *standard toolbar* and the one just below it is called the *formatting toolbar*.

Because there are so many buttons on each toolbar, it is easy to forget what they're for. In fact, there are eight basic toolbars, so few people bother memorizing the purpose of all the tools they contain. There are two solutions to "icon overkill" as it is sometimes called. The first is to learn the ones that you want and forget the rest. (The author's personal choice!) The second is to use Word's built-in *ToolTip* help when you need to remind yourself what a specific tool does. To see a ToolTip, point to a particular toolbar button to display its name in a little box, as shown here.

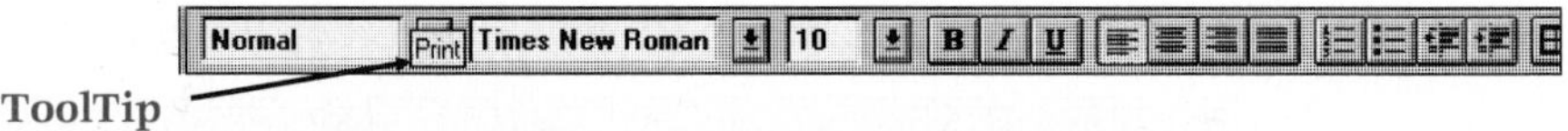

In addition to providing tools for formatting your text, the formatting toolbar (the second basic toolbar) supplies information about the text you are currently working with. For example, it lists what *typeface* and point size you are using. (Typeface is printer—not computer—jargon for the style of character used.) Please see Chapter 6 for more information on typefaces.

RULER

You can use the ruler shown here to set tabs, indents, and margins. Consult Chapter 7 for more details.

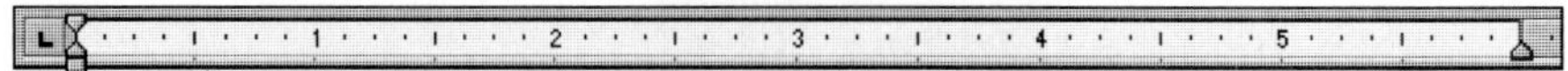

STATUS BAR

The status bar, usually found at the bottom of the screen, provides a lot of information about your document. For example, it tells you the page number you are on and how many pages there are in your document. The status bar also tells you how far down on the page you are—which line and what column and so forth. It even tells you what time it is according to your computer's clock. Finally, remember that the status bar gives a capsule description of any menu option that is highlighted, or of any tool that you place the mouse pointer over.

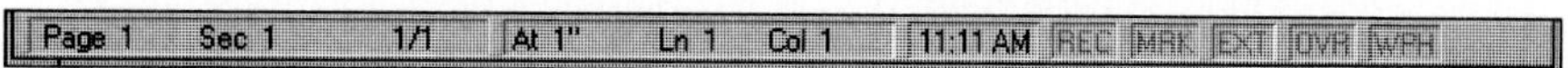

SCROLL BARS

The scroll bars shown here are used to quickly move through text. Scroll bars become most useful when you start working with long documents. You will learn more about them in Chapter 3.

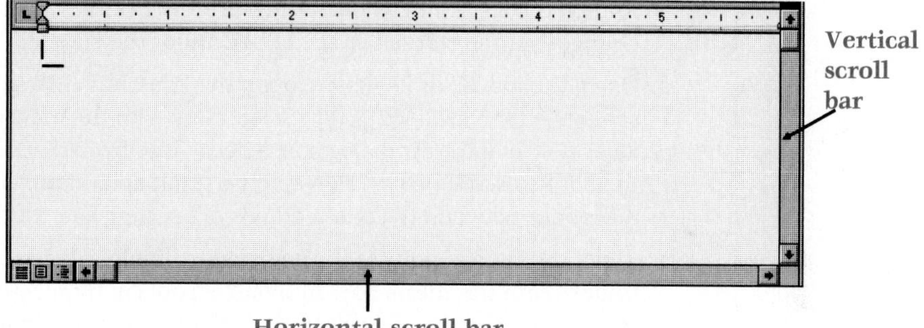

MOUSE POINTERS

There are two basic mouse pointers in Word: the ordinary Windows arrow that usually shows up when you are outside the document area and the I-beam that shows up when you are in the document area. Later chapters will discuss some other mouse pointers when you learn the task that they match up with. (At this point, if the mouse pointer takes on an unfamiliar shape just press the Esc key or move the mouse. One of these two techniques will usually switch the pointer back to one of its basic shapes.) Of course, if the mouse pointer changes, then Word is probably trying to tell you something.

EXERCISES

This exercise assumes that you have just started Word and have selected OK in the Tip of the Day dialog box if necessary.

1. Find the title bar and note the default document name Word has supplied.
2. Using the mouse, click File on the menu bar and click Close on the pull-down menu that appears. Note the changes on the menu bar.
3. Press and release the Alt key. Use the ← or the → and move the highlight between File, Help, and the control box (it looks like a dash) in the upper-left corner of the screen. Press Enter and then use the arrow keys again. Press Esc to close the pull-down menus and press Esc again to remove the highlight from the menu bar. Press Alt F to open the File pull-down menu directly. Use the ↑ and ↓ keys to move between items on the File menu. Press Esc.
4. Repeat the steps in the preceding exercise, only this time watch the changes on the status bar at the bottom of the screen.
5. Using the mouse or keyboard, open the File menu. (Note the hot key sequence for New (Alt F, N.) Select New with the mouse or keyboard. Select OK in the New dialog box. Select Close from the File menu. Use the hot key sequence to open a new default document. Note the difference between the two methods of opening a new document.
6. Move the mouse pointer to the standard toolbar located just underneath the menu bar. Activate a ToolTip by placing the mouse pointer over any toolbar button. Activate the ToolTip for the other buttons on the standard toolbar, the formatting toolbar, and the buttons in the lower-left corner of the screen.
7. To challenge yourself, select Toolbars from the View menu. Check Microsoft. Use the title bar to drag and drop (see Appendix A for what this means if you are unsure) the Microsoft toolbar onto the far left side of the screen. Using a blank area on the Microsoft toolbar, drag and drop the toolbar on the right, bottom, and top margins of the screen. Drop the toolbar on the center of the screen and click the control box or use the Toolbars dialog box to remove the Microsoft toolbar. Drag it back to its original position.
8. Move the mouse pointer into the document area in the center of the screen and note the pointer's shape. Move the mouse pointer off the document area and note how it changes shape.
9. Move the mouse pointer into the document area and click the left mouse button. Enter a couple of lines of text. Using the mouse, move the insertion point to various positions within the text. Note the

changes in the column and line readouts displayed in the center of the status bar.

10. Press Ctrl+End. Press Enter. Type **123456789** and press Enter. Press Tab and type **123456789**. Move the insertion point around in these two lines of text and notice how the column number on the status bar is reported.

1.6 CLOSING AN EXISTING DOCUMENT TO WORK WITH A NEW ONE

While working through the first part of this book, you will often want to start with a fresh screen. (Word does allow you to have more than one document open at a time; in fact, you can have as many documents open as memory permits, but you can only *work* on one document at a time. This will be covered in Chapter 11.) At first, however, you will probably want to have only one document open at a time. In order to get a clean screen you will have to *close* the old document in order to start up a new document.

To start up with a new document (a fresh screen) *without saving your work* do the following:

1. Chose Close from the File menu (Alt F, C).
2. If the following dialog box pops up, choose the No button.

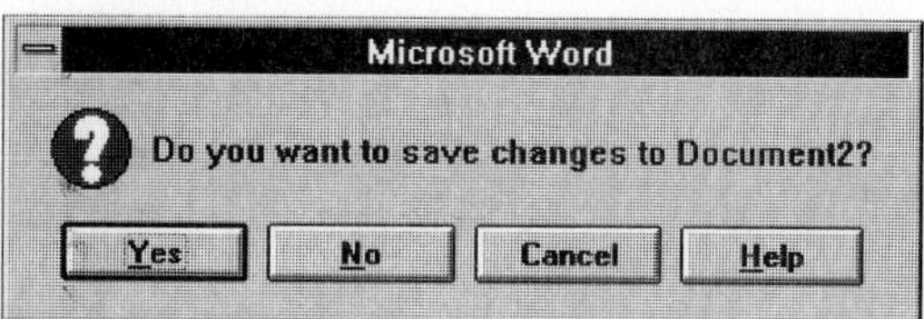

3. Press Ctrl+N for a new document or click on the New button on the Standard toolbar.

mastery skills check

1. Exit Word if it's running now. [1.3]
2. Start Word. [1.2]
3. Type a paragraph or two of text from this book into a new document. [1.4]
4. Use the End to move to the beginning of a line. Use the Ctrl + Home combination to move to the beginning of the document. Try the other navigation keys listed in Table 1-1 to move around the document. [1.4]
5. Close the current document Window without saving the changes. [1.6]
6. Using the ToolTip feature, find the New button and use it to create a new document. [1.5]
7. Exit Word. [1.3]

2

The Many Ways to Work with Text

chapter objectives

After completing this chapter, you will be able to

2.1 Enter text in Word

2.2 Delete or replace existing text and insert new text

2.3 Save your work

2.4 Retrieve previously saved work by opening files

2.5 Do basic printing or previewing of your documents

2.6 Use the help system

IN spite of Word's ability to handle graphics, page layouts, mass mailings, and what have you, most of the time you will simply be entering text. This chapter covers the basics of working with text, including how to enter text and how to make simple changes. You'll even learn how to use Word's undo feature if you decide that you don't like what you just entered. Then you'll see how to save and retrieve your work—you'll even learn how to have Word save your work automatically at specified intervals. Then it's on to the basics of printing and previewing documents.

At the end of this chapter, you'll learn how to use Word's on-line help system. People seem to be divided on the value of this incredibly extensive on-line help system. When you are first starting out, on-line help may seem overwhelming. The more familiar you are with Word, however, the more useful the on-line help system becomes. For this reason, this chapter concentrates on the mechanics of getting into and out of the help system—and doesn't try to cover all its features.

review
skills check

1. Start Word. [1.2]
2. Type a few lines of text. [1.4]
3. Use the mouse to move the insertion point around in the text you just entered. [1.4]
4. Close the current document without saving changes. [1.5, 1.6]
5. Create a new document. [1.5, 1.6]
6. Exit Word. [1.3]

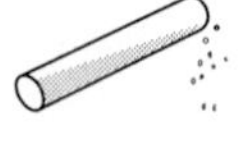

NOTE *You may want to clear the screen by creating a new document for each example in this chapter.*

2.1 ENTERING TEXT

Once you start Word and clear the Tip of the Day if necessary, you can just start typing using Word's default settings. For most purposes, these work just fine. (Chapter 8 explains how to change the default settings for things like margins.) The insertion point—the vertical bar that marks your location in the document—moves as you type. Practice this kind of typing and imagine Word and your computer as the world's most expensive typewriter. However, you don't have to listen for the bell that a typewriter uses to tell you that you are close to the end of a line. This is because Word automatically *word wraps*, moving text to the next line when it doesn't fit on the current line. Word wrap becomes particularly important when you add or delete text when editing a document: Word can automatically rewrap the text so that it lines up properly between the margins.

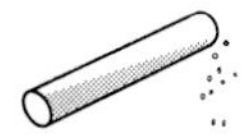

NOTE *Only press Enter at the end of a paragraph or when you need to create a blank line.*

This is because if you later edit the text, Word will not use its word wrap feature when it gets to the end of a line that came about because you hit Enter. Computer jargon actually makes this distinction clearer by means of a nice metaphor. The jargon says a line that you hit Enter to end it has a *hard return*, a line that ended because Word used its word wrap feature has a *soft return*. This metaphor stresses the extra flexibility *soft* returns give you over *hard* returns!

It is often important to distinguish visually on your screen between a new line that resulted from the word wrap feature and one that resulted from pressing Enter. Since the Word screen doesn't show this normally, to see the distinction you have to display what Word calls *nonprinting characters* on your screen. The easiest way to do this is to click on the Show/Hide button on the standard toolbar. As you will see, Word uses a nonprinting character that looks exactly like the icon shown to the left of this paragraph to indicate the end of a paragraph. If you pressed Tab to indent a line, Word inserts a nonprinting character representing a tab as well. (Tabs start out every 1/2 of an inch, see Chapter 7 for more information on tabs.)

The following table shows the most common nonprinting characters as they show up when you have clicked on the Show/Hide button.

Keystroke	Nonprinting Character
Enter key	¶
Tab key	→
Spacebar	•

Many people leave the nonprinting characters displayed all the time. If you don't like this, click on the Show/Hide button to hide them again. This button is an example of a *toggle,* which is jargon for something (like a light switch) that goes either on or off each time you select it. (It will look pressed in when it is on.)

EXAMPLE

1. Type the following lines by Aldous Huxley and press the Enter key after each one:

   A bad book is as hard to write as a good one.
   We are all geniuses—up to age 10 or so.

   Now type the following line which is also by Huxley:

   Technological progress has merely provided us with
   more efficient means of going backwards.

Now click on the Show/Hide button. The result will look something like Figure 2-1. (Notice the paragraph marker—don't worry if the size of the text seems larger than you have on your screen. We

FIGURE 2-1

Text with hidden characters showing

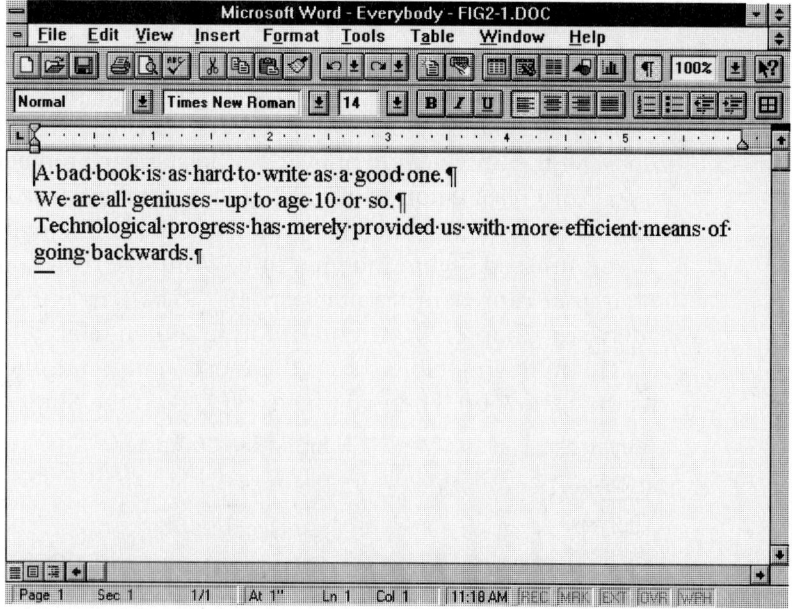

increased the size to make it easier for you to see the nonprinting characters—you'll see in Chapter 6 how to increase the size of characters as was done here.)

THE Shift KEY AND THE Caps Lock KEY

When you type text, pressing a Shift key lets you enter uppercase letters or special characters like ! and @ that are listed on top of a key on the keyboard. Once you release the Shift key, you can type lowercase letters again. To type multiple uppercase letters, you will probably want to press the Caps Lock key. However, Caps Lock *does not* work the way it does on a typewriter; instead, it only affects the letter keys. Even if you have Caps Lock on, you still need to press the Shift key to enter characters such as ! or ?. In addition, if you have turned on the Caps Lock feature, pressing the Shift key while typing results in lowercase letters. Finally, like the Show/Hide button, the Caps Lock key is a *toggle*; you press it once to turn it on and again to turn it off.

EXAMPLE

1. Enter the following text using the Shift key:

   William Gates
   Don't Overuse Capital Letters
   DON'T OVERUSE CAPITAL LETTERS

   Notice that you could have used the Caps Lock key very efficiently for the third line. Now try entering the following text using the Caps Lock key:

   TESTING 1 2 3

SIMPLE ERROR CORRECTIONS

Although you will soon discover much more sophisticated methods for correcting errors, you can always use Del and Backspace to remove characters from the screen. The Del key removes the character to the right of the insertion point and the Backspace key removes the one to the left of the insertion point.

EXAMPLES

1. Type **124**. Then press the Backspace key to delete the character to the left of the insertion point and type a **3** to make it 123.
2. Some changes are best made by combining Del and/or Backspace with the arrow keys. For example, type **12468**. Press the ← key five times to position the insertion point before the "1." Press the Del key to delete the character at the insertion point, leaving only 2468.

AUTOCORRECT

Typists make the same mistakes frequently; stock phrases come up time and time again. To take advantage of this, Word includes an automatic correction and typing feature called *AutoCorrect*, which is on by default. For example, when you type **teh** and hit the spacebar, Word will immediately change the misspelling to "the." If you accidentally type **don;t** and hit the spacebar, Word will automatically change it to "don't."

The AutoCorrect feature is controlled by the AutoCorrect option on the Tools menu (Alt T, A). Choosing this option brings up the dialog box shown in Figure 2-2. Word starts out with relatively few AutoCorrect items; you can add to the list to make Word reflect how you work. (Scroll through the AutoCorrect list box to see what items Word already includes.)

To add an item to the AutoCorrect feature:

1. Enter what you want to always be replaced in the Replace text box. It must not include any spaces and the case matters.
2. Enter what you want it replaced with in the With text box.
3. Click on OK.

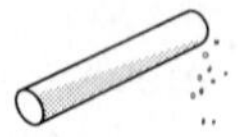

NOTE *If you do not want Word to automatically correct what you type, make sure the box marked Replace Text as You Type in the AutoCorrect dialog box is not checked.*

FIGURE 2-2

The AutoCorrext dialog box

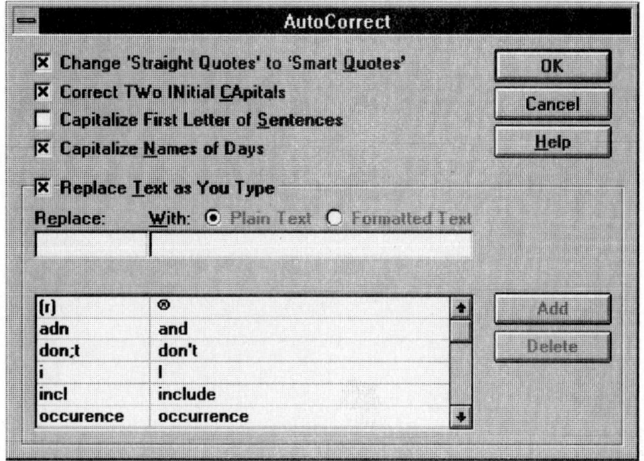

The AutoCorrect feature also makes it possible to quickly type stock phrases. For example, if you add **asap** to the AutoCorrect feature with **as soon as possible** as the correct version, you can save yourself 15 keystrokes. Whenever you type **asap** in the future and hit the spacebar, Word will automatically correct it to read "as soon as possible."

EXAMPLES

1. Type the following text with the AutoCorrect feature on; make sure to include all the spelling errors.

   My friend adn I don;t like you.
   ALl studnets recieve seperate help.
   i am seperate from the Borg

   Notice that Word corrects the double initial caps in the second sentence.

2. Add the correct spellings of "didnt," "frend," and "mistak," to the AutoCorrect list and then type

   My frend didnt make a mistak

   The text will be corrected automatically.

3. Add some stock phrases like asap (as soon as possible), IMHO (in my humble opinion), and syour (Sincerely yours) to the AutoCorrect feature. Then type the following text:

12/31/99

Dear Sir,

IMHO i think i have waited long enough. I would like an answer asap.

syour

The letter will be corrected automatically.

UNDO AND REDO

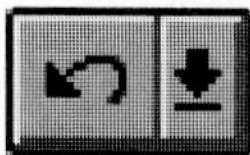

Word makes it easy to change your mind if what you just typed doesn't satisfy you. To undo your most recent typing (or most any action you may have taken with Word), choose Undo from the Edit menu (Alt E, U or Ctrl+Z). Unfortunately, Word may undo more typing then you planned on. In this case, choose Redo from the Edit menu (Alt E, R or F4) to restore the text you typed. Word will generally let you undo more than one action. Click on the downward-pointing arrows next to the Undo and Redo buttons (shown in the margin) to see a list of the 100 most recent actions taken, as shown here. (Notice that actions besides those related to typing are shown.)

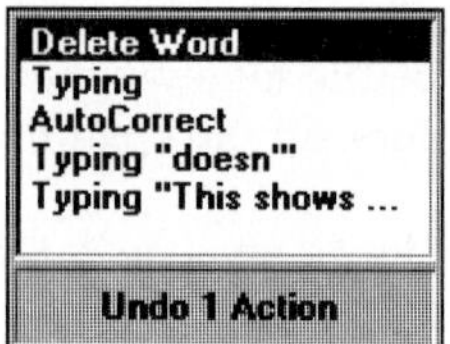

If Word cannot undo an action, the Undo option on the Edit menu will be grayed and the Redo option on the Edit menu will be replaced by Repeat. (Word can undo up to 100 actions!)

EXAMPLE

1. Start with a blank screen and then type the following comment from Disraeli. Do not press Enter.

   The author who speaks about his own books is almost as bad as the mother who talks about her own children.

   Now undo the typing to remove the text and restore the blank screen.

EXERCISES

1. Type a few lines of text into a new document, allowing Word to automatically word wrap the text, and press Enter to end the paragraph. Press Enter again to insert a blank line. Then enter a few more lines of text, including some tab characters.
2. Enter the following text using tabs to indent the author's name and the reference:

   It was we, the people; not we, the white male citizens; nor yet we, the male citizens; but we the whole people who formed the Union.

   And we formed it, not to give blessings of liberty, but to secure them; not to half of ourselves and the half of our posterity, but to the whole people—women as well as men.

   Susan B. Anthony
   Women's Right to Suffrage

3. Locate and press the Show/Hide button on the standard toolbar. Notice the changes in the document area. Press it again, notice the changes once more.
4. Use the arrow keys or the mouse to move the insertion point around in the text. Experiment with the Del and Backspace keys, noting which side of the insertion point characters are removed from.
5. Enter a blank line at the end of your text, and type **Thanks, Susan!** Press the Undo button. Press the Redo button.
6. Close the previous document and start up a new one. From the Tools menu, select AutoCorrect. Add **myphone** as an item to the AutoCorrect list using your phone number as the item into the Replace/With list. Type **You can contact me at myphone anytime.**
7. Open the AutoCorrect dialog box and delete the myphone entry.
8. Challenge Yourself! Select Options from the Tools menu and select the View tab. Under Nonprinting Characters, make a selection other than All and click on OK see the effect on the document window. Reselect All after experimenting to once again display all nonprinting characters.
9. Close the document without saving your changes.

2.2 INSERTION AND OVERTYPE

Probably the two most common editing operations are inserting new text and replacing existing text. In Word you control this feature by pressing the Ins key. By default, Word starts out in *insert mode*. In this mode, whatever you type appears to the right of the insertion point and pushes all the remaining text to the right. Use insert mode to add new text to an existing document without losing what is already there. When you're in insert mode, pressing the Ins key switches you to *overtype mode*. In overtype mode, whatever you type replaces any existing text to the right of the insertion point. From overtype mode, press the Ins key again to return to insert mode.

You can tell which mode you are in by looking at the status bar: If the OVR indicator is grayed you're in insert mode, and if the OVR indicator is black you're in overtype mode. For example, in this example Word is in overtype mode.

It's a good idea to get in the habit of checking what mode you are in. If you forget that you switched from insert to overtype mode, you may accidentally lose information by typing over it. If you want to switch modes, remember, just press the Ins key or double-click on the OVR indicator on the status bar.

TIP *If you discover that you're in the wrong mode, you can often use the undo feature to recover text you may have accidentally typed over.*

EXAMPLES

1. Type the following well-known proverb:

   Expect the unexpected.

   Now, making sure you are in insert mode, move to the beginning of the sentence, add the word **To**, and change the first "e" in "expect" to lowercase. Next move the insertion point just in front of the period, add a space, and add the following words to transform the quotation into a remark by Oscar Wilde.

To expect the unexpected shows a thoroughly modern intellect.

2. Type the following quote:

To err is human, to forgive divine.

Then change to overtype mode and use the arrow keys to efficiently change the quote to read

To err is human, to really foul up requires a computer.

2.3 SAVING YOUR WORK

A good sign to keep over the desk of anyone who works with computers is

> *Saving your work is necessary; saving it often is smart.*

Word provides many ways to save (and resave) your documents. You choose where and under what name to save a document as well as whether to keep backups of previous versions. Before you can save your work, you need to know the rules for naming files.

Every file has what you can think of as a first and last name. The first name can be up to eight letters (numbers, underscores, and a few characters such as ~ and - are also allowed) but can't include spaces. The last name, usually called the *extension,* can be up to three letters (numbers and underscores are also OK here and spaces are still forbidden). The following table lists some possible file names, mentioning whether or not they are legal:

File Name	Legal/Illegal
MYNAME.DOC	Legal
MY NAME.DOC	Illegal (a space)
MYNAME,DOC	Illegal (a comma)
FOO.BAR	Legal

File Name	Legal/Illegal
123WAS.IT	Legal
123WASN'T.IT	Illegal (an apostrophe)
123WASNTIT.NO	Illegal (name too long)

Like family members, Word documents usually share the same last name (file extension). Word automatically uses DOC as the extension unless you specifically tell it otherwise.

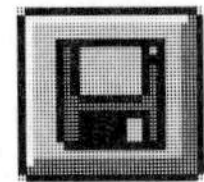

Now that you know about file names, it's time to start the all-important process of saving your work. Choose Save from the File menu (Alt F, S or Ctrl+S).

The first time you choose this option, Word opens a dialog box like the one shown in Figure 2-3. This is a fairly typical Windows dialog box for saving files. No matter how many times you choose the Save option, you see this dialog box only once. If you choose the Save As option, on the other hand, then you will see this dialog box each time. This is because the Save option saves a file with the same name, overwriting the previous version. You use the Save As option on the File menu to save a copy of an existing file with a different name—so you will need to fill in this dialog box again each time.

To use the Save As dialog box:

1. Choose the drive you want to save the file on by clicking on the Drives drop-down list box and then selecting the desired drive from the list that drops down.
2. Choose the directory you want to save the file in by moving to the Directories list box and clicking on the directory you want.

FIGURE 2-3

The Save As dialog box

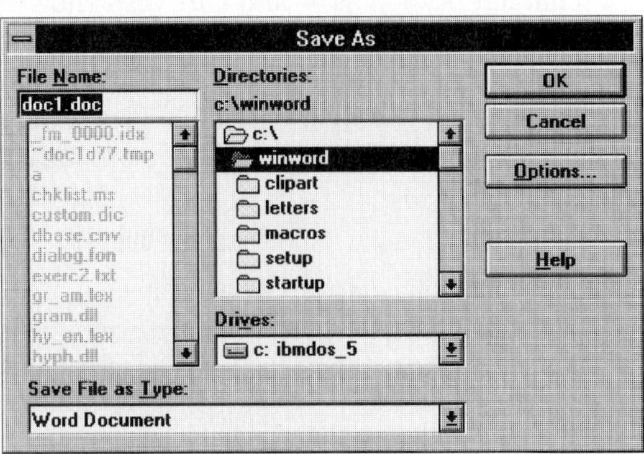

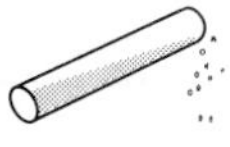

NOTE *If you can't see the directory where you want to place the file in this dialog box, you will need to move up or down the directory tree. To move up or down the directory tree you need to double-click on the parent directory. (If any of this terminology seems strange to you, please see Appendix A for more on this jargon.)*

3. Enter a file name in the File Name text box.
4. Click on OK.

Word gives you a countdown using little (blue, on a color monitor) squares on the status bar while it is saving the document.

If you try to use an illegal file name to save your file, Word warns you with a message box like the one shown here. Click on OK to make this box go away and try to figure out why your name was wrong. Click on Help to get some general information about what could have been wrong. (See the last section of this chapter for additional details on Word's help system.)

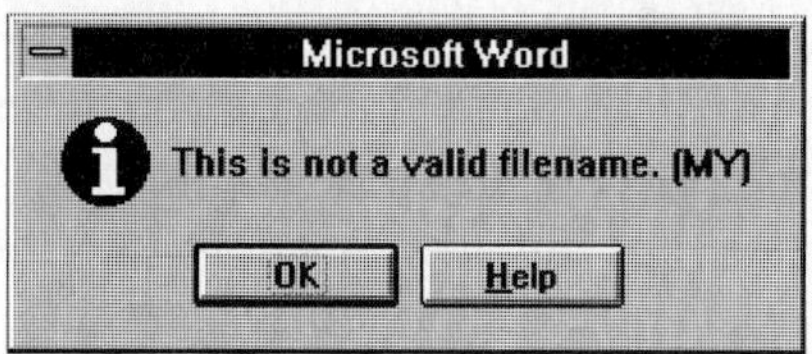

Sometimes when you go to save a file for the first time, you will inadvertently choose a file name that is already in use. If a file already exists with the name you chose, Word presents you with a dialog box that looks like this. If you click on Yes, Word replaces the previous version (see below for how to save the previous version as a backup).

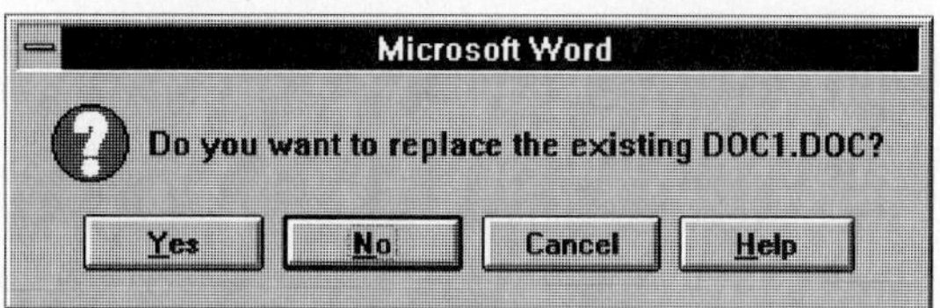

Once you've saved a document for the first time, each time you choose Save to save any changes to the document, Word automatically uses the same name—you will not need to fill a dialog box in again.

CAUTION *Each time you choose the Save option to save a document, Word overwrites the previous version.*

EXAMPLE

1. Start with a blank document and then enter the following Mark Twain sayings:

   A classic is something that everybody wants to have read and nobody wants to read.
   Get your facts first, then you can distort them as much as you please.
   Nothing so needs reforming as other peoples habits.
   When in doubt, tell the truth.

   Now, to save this file in your favorite directory with the name TWAIN1.DOC, select that directory under Directories and then enter **TWAIN1** in the File Name box and click on OK.

SAVING A DOCUMENT WITH ANOTHER NAME (THE SAVE AS OPTION)

Sometimes you want to save a document with another name, on another disk, or in another directory. Two of the most common reasons for doing this are that you might want to save a backup on a floppy or you might want to create a "scratch copy" to modify.

Anyway, when it comes to saving your work, the joke that "Just because you are paranoid doesn't mean that they are not out to get you," is the rule to go by. (As anyone who has worked with computers knows, the "they" in the joke are the gremlins that make Murphy's law work so well. You know the gremlins that kick your power cord, ruin your hard disk, cause momentary power failures ...) Always keep a backup of vital work on a floppy as well as on your hard drive.

To save a file with another name or in another location, choose the Save As option from the File menu (Alt F, A). This opens the same dialog box you saw in the previous section when you chose the Save command from the File menu to save a file for the first time. Proceed exactly as before. (If you are trying to save a file over an existing file, Word will again warn you.)

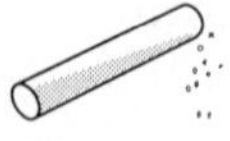

NOTE *You must keep the disk on which you last saved the file in the drive.*

For this reason, many people use the Save As command twice in succession each time they save their work: the first time to save the document to a floppy disk and the second time to save it on their hard drive before they remove the floppy for safekeeping. (The reason is that hard disks give much quicker access to your data. So by storing the data on the hard disk last, Word is always looking at the hard drive where access is fastest rather than the floppy where it is *slow*.)

EXAMPLE

1. If the file with Twain's quotes is still on the screen, follow these steps to save it with the name CLEMENS1.DOC on drive A:
   a. Choose Save As from the File menu.
   b. Type **A:CLEMENS1** in the File Name box in the Save As dialog box that pops up.
   c. Click on OK.

SAVING IN ANOTHER FORMAT

Many people have to share documents with people who use other word processing programs. (You can skip this section if this doesn't apply to you.) If you installed the necessary converters (see Appendix B), Word lets you save a document in a format that other word processing programs can read. Word is very good at saving in WordPerfect format, less good at other formats. In any case, you will probably lose some formatting information when you save in different file formats (see Chapter 6).

To save your document in a form that another word processing program can read

1. Choose the Save As option from the File menu.
2. Click on the downward-pointing arrow on the right side of the Save File as Type drop-down list box, as shown in Figure 2-4.
3. From this list, choose the word processing format you want (scroll through the list if necessary).
4. Click on OK.

FIGURE 2-4

Saving a document for use with a different word processing program

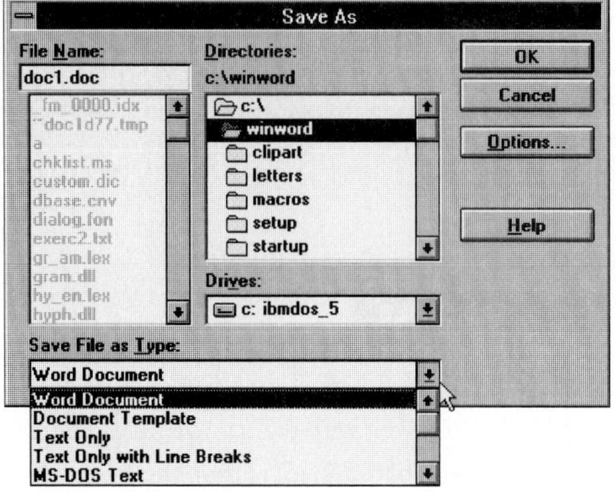

TIP *If you can't find the format you want, try to save the document in the Rich Text format. Another possibility is to call Microsoft or the manufacturer of the other word processing program to see if they have a converter for the format you need.*

There are two options in the Save File As Type list that are needed very rarely. But, if you need to give the information in your document to someone who can't use one of the standard Word formats in their program, they are absolutely necessary. Think of these methods of saving your documents as last resort options—to be used only when you have two people in your office using programs that can exchange data in no other way. (If you are never in this situation, skip this material!)

Here are short descriptions of these two Save options.

MS-DOS Text The MS-DOS Text option saves only the characters you entered; everything else is lost. In particular, all the lines that were word wrapped by Word are blended into one very long line.

MS-DOS with Line Breaks This option also saves only the characters you entered, but all the lines that were word wrapped will appear on separate lines. Use this option when you just need the text, but no formatting information—for example, if you used Word to make a list of names and addresses and want to send someone only this information.

EXAMPLES

1. To save a document with the name WP51TEST.DOC in WordPerfect 5.1 format:
   a. Choose Save As from the File menu.
   b. Enter **WP51TEST** in the File Name box.
   c. Click on the arrow on the right side of the Save File as Type box.
   d. Choose WordPerfect 5.1 from the list. (Scroll if necessary to get to this item.)
   e. Click on OK.

THE MOST USEFUL SAVE OPTIONS

The Options button in the Save As dialog box brings up a dialog box containing some useful options. Bring up the Save As dialog box (Alt F, A) and click on Options (once the Save As dialog box is on the screen) to see the dialog box shown in Figure 2-5. You can turn all of these check boxes on or off independently by clicking in the boxes associated with them.

Here are short descriptions of the most important of these check boxes along with some suggestions as to which settings are best in which situations. The next section briefly describes the remaining elements of this dialog box that are important when you work in groups.

FIGURE 2-5

The Options dialog box for saving documents

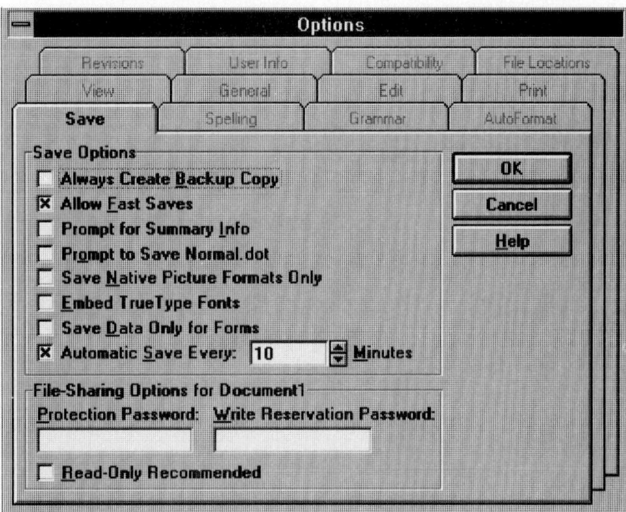

Automatic Saves When you turn this check box on, Word saves the active document automatically at the specified interval. This means the Automatic Save option is very useful, particularly if you have trouble remembering to save your work. Choose a short enough time interval that you will not run the risk of losing too much work. On the other hand, since Word becomes less responsive while it is saving work, too short an interval is no good either. The default of 10 (every 10 minutes) is fine for some people. Really nervous people (like the author) set this option to 5 minutes.

Backup Copies If you turn the Always Create Backup Copy check box on, Word creates a duplicate copy of the file (with the .BAK extension and the same "first name") each time you save a file. This is a good safety feature if you have enough disk space, since it gives you one more chance at recovering your data if problems arise.

Fast Saves The Allow Fast Saves check box (which is on by default) speeds up save operations by recording only the changes to a document. This is faster than saving the whole document but also less safe because the complete document is not stored each time.

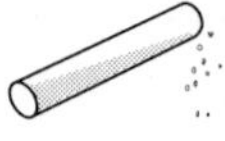

NOTE *When the Allow Fast Saves option is on (the box is checked), Word's ability to find documents containing specific text may not work perfectly. For this reason, many Word users make sure the Allow Fast Saves check box is off for all of their documents. (See Chapter 14.)*

EXAMPLES

1. To change the Automatic Save option to 5 minutes:
   a. Choose Save As from the File menu (Alt F, A).
   b. Choose the Options button.
   c. Enter **5** in the Automatic Save Every box.
   d. Click on OK.
2. To go from fast saves to full saves:
   a. Choose Save As from the File menu.

b. Choose the Options button.

c. Make sure there isn't an "X" in the Allow Fast Saves box (Alt+F is the toggle).

d. Click on OK.

PROTECTING YOUR DOCUMENTS WHEN WORKING IN A GROUP

Most of the other elements on the Save tab of the Options dialog box shown in Figure 2-5 are important only if other people may want to look at or change *your* document. In this situation, controlling access to your documents is very important. Here are short descriptions of the most important of the options that control document access.

Protection Password To prevent other people from *even looking* at your document from within Word (or at any other program), type a password under Protection Password. Only those who know the password can open the document. A password can contain up to 15 characters and can include letters, numbers, symbols, and spaces. As you type the password, Word displays an asterisk for each character that you type. When you click on OK, another dialog box pops up asking you to type the password again for confirmation, as shown here:

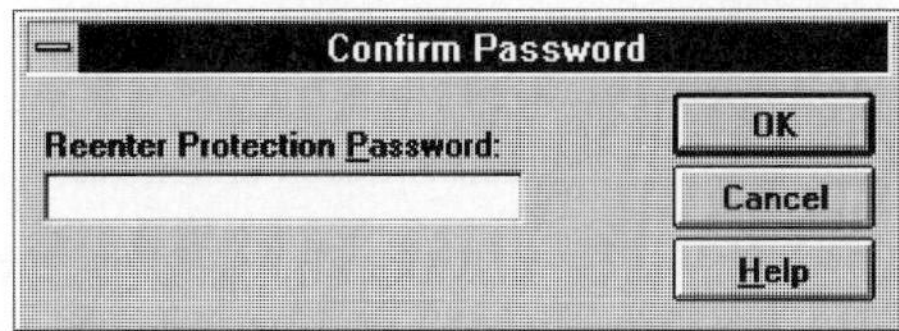

Every time you try to open a password-protected document, Word presents you with a dialog box like the one shown next. Once you assign a password, you must supply the password (using exactly the same combination of uppercase and lowercase letters) to gain access to the file.

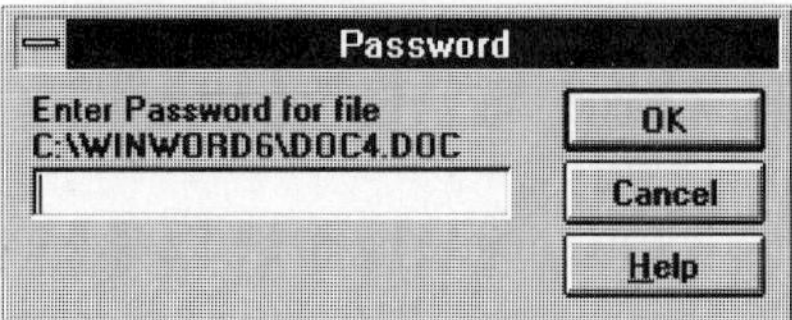

CAUTION *You cannot open a password-protected file without the password. If you forget the password, the information in the file is lost for good.*

To remove the password protection from a file, you must be working with the file. (Remember, you can't open the file without the password, so you can't remove a file's password unless you already know it.)

1. Choose Options on the Save As dialog box.
2. Erase the current password.
3. Click on OK.

Write Reservation Password If you assign a write reservation password to a document, people without the password will be able to look at the document but not make changes to it. As when entering a protection password, enter a password under Write Reservation Password, click on OK, and then reenter the password for confirmation.

Read-Only Recommended (*Read-Only* is jargon for "look but don't touch.") Read-Only Recommended is a handy option that has Word suggest to anyone who opens the document that they open it as a read-only document. (The next section explains how to open documents.)

EXERCISES

1. Create a new document. Type **Exercise Two - Three - One**. Click on the Save toolbar button and save the file as EX2-3-1. Note that Word adds the .DOC extension as it saves the file. Add a few changes to the document and attempt to close it using the Close option on the File menu. Save your changes.
2. Create a new document by clicking on the New toolbar button. Enter some text and try to save the document as EX2-3-1. Answer No to the Replace prompt and Cancel the save operation by pressing Esc.
3. Select Save As from the File menu and then click on Options. Check Read-Only Recommended for the current file. Select OK. Save the file as EX2-3-4.
4. Challenge Yourself! Close the previous document and open a new document and type **Test Document** followed by a blank line and some additional text. Click on the Save button and then select

Options. Select the Prompt for Summary Info check box under Save Options and select OK. Save the document as EX2-3-5. Note the text Word uses as the default title. You will learn more about summary information and document statistics in Chapter 12.

5. Challenge Yourself! Select File, Summary Info. Review the data and then select the Statistics button to see more information about the document.
6. Challenge Yourself! It's a good idea to store all your documents in a single directory or a series of subdirectories. When you install Word, it automatically stores your documents in the WINWORD program directory, which is not a good idea. Perform this exercise item to create a separate document directory and to tell Word to store documents in that directory from now on.

   Select Options from the Tools menu and then select the File Locations tab. Highlight the Documents line and click on the Modify button. Highlight the root of the drive WINWORD is on and then select the New button. Enter a new directory name, such as DOCS (or any other legal file/directory name). Click on OK to create the directory.
7. Close the current document, repeating this step until all documents are closed if you have forgotten to close a document that you previously opened.

2.4 OPENING AN EXISTING DOCUMENT

If the document you want to reopen is one of the last four you have worked with, reopening it is easy. If you look at the File menu shown in Figure 2-6, you can see the *most recently used list* at the bottom.

Here is how to take advantage of this feature:

1. Open the File menu (Alt F).
2. Press the number (from 1 to 4) that corresponds to the document you want.

If the document you want to work with is not one of the four you have used most recently, you need to choose Open from the File menu and then make selections from a dialog box that looks much like the Save As dialog box you saw earlier, as shown in Figure 2-7.

FIGURE 2-6

File menu with a list of the most recently used files

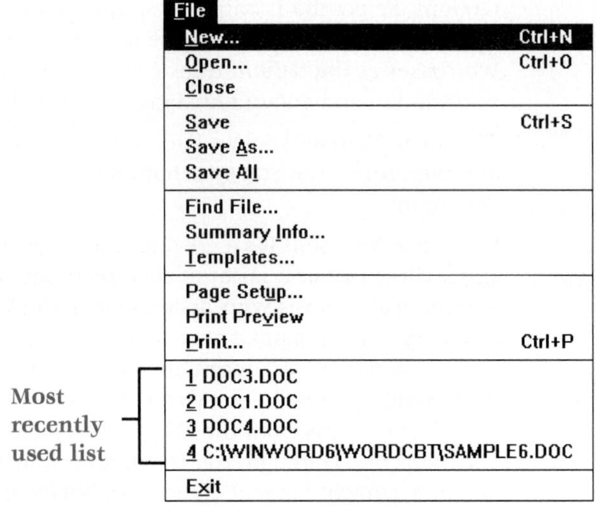

To open a document:

1. Choose the drive where the document is located by making sure the correct drive is selected in the Drives list box. Click on the arrow and choose a different drive if need be.
2. Choose the directory where the document is located by clicking on the desired directory in the Directories list box. If the directory you want is not showing up, you can move up (or

FIGURE 2-7

The Open dialog box

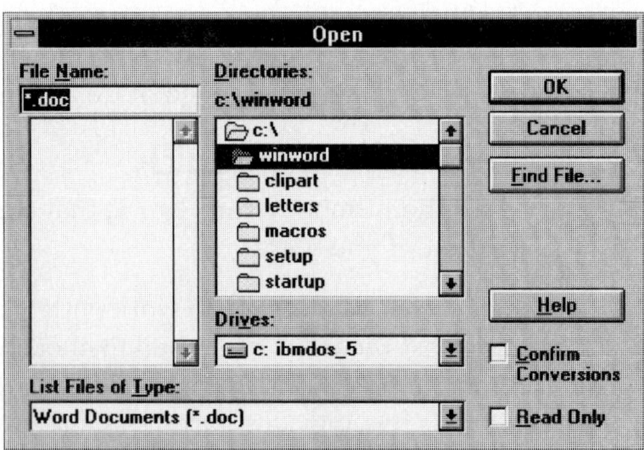

down) the directory tree by double-clicking on the directory you want.

3. Under File Name, enter the document's file name.
4. Click on OK.

NOTE *Remember, if you open another document without closing the current document, you won't bother Word in the least. You can open as many documents as your computer's memory allows. Working with multiple documents is covered in Chapter 11. Also, Word can open documents created in many other word processors automatically.*

EXERCISES

1. Open EX2-3-1.DOC from the most recently used list of files at the bottom of the File menu. Close this file.
2. Open EX2-3-2.DOC using the Open toolbar button. Note the Read-Only warning.

2.5 PRINTING AND PREVIEWING BASICS

Word uses Windows to control its printing operations. If you have already selected a printer for Windows you don't have to do much else. (If you don't know how to install a printer in Windows, consult the documentation that comes with Windows.)

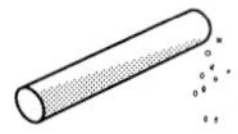

NOTE *It's always a good idea to save a document before trying to print it.*

One nice feature of Windows is that there's no need to learn arcane codes to print perfect documents. In addition, most of the time you can continue working with Word or another Windows program while Windows prints your document.

The easiest way to print a document is to use the Print button on the standard toolbar. When you use this method you won't need to fuss with any settings—Word uses the default settings—the settings you last used.

The other possibility is to choose Print from the File menu (Alt F, P or Ctrl+P). This opens the dialog box shown in Figure 2-8. Make sure that the various options (number of copies, which portion of the document to print, and so on) have the desired settings. Then click on OK. At this point, Word sends the information off to the Windows print manager and you will soon get your hard copy. (See Chapter 9 for more on this dialog box.)

REMEMBER: *The settings you have in this dialog box are used the next time you use the Print button.*

Finally, although most of the time you will need a printed copy (or *hard copy*) of your documents, with Word there's no need to waste a lot of paper and time to check that a complicated document looks just right. Instead, you can take advantage of Word's *Print Preview* ability. This feature (covered at length in Chapter 9) displays on the screen a close approximation of what the printed document will look like. You can even make last minute editing changes while previewing a document. Print Preview is also relatively fast; on most machines it will be many times faster than actually printing the document.

To start Print Preview:

- Choose Print Preview from the File menu (Alt F, V).

After repaginating, Word displays a screen that has a birds-eye view of the current page of the document (the page where the insertion point is). The easiest way to move page by page through your document while in Print Preview is to use the Pg Up or Pg Dn keys as needed. (Pg Up moves to the previous page, Pg Dn to the next page.)

FIGURE 2-8

The Print dialog box

Print
Printer: Epson EPL-7000 on LPT1:
Print What: Document
Copies: 1
Page Range
All
Current Page
Selection
Pages:
Enter page numbers and/or page ranges separated by commas. For example, 1,3,5-12
Print: All Pages in Range
OK
Cancel
Options...
Printer...
Help
Print to File
Collate Copies

To leave Print Preview:

- Choose Print Preview from the File menu again or just press Esc. (See Chapter 9 for more on Print Preview.)

Finally, we have been working up to now in *Normal view.* This is the normal (default) way of looking at your documents because it is the best all-around way to display your document when you are entering and formatting text. Normal view gives you the fastest response; in this view Word doesn't spend a lot of time calculating the exact location of all the elements of a page. However, Word has one other way of viewing your documents that is often useful—it gives you almost as good a feel for how your documents will look as Print Preview but, on many faster computers, you can still edit the document almost as fast as you can in Normal view. This is called *Page Layout view.* In Page Layout view, you can see the margins of your document, how pages break, graphics, and many other elements almost exactly as they will appear in the printed document.

To switch to Page Layout view:

- Choose Page Layout from the View menu (Alt P, V) or click on the Page Layout View button on the horizontal scroll bar.

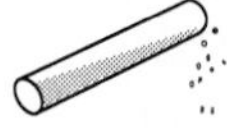

NOTE *Depending on the speed of your machine, you may find Page Layout view too slow to work with comfortably for any length of time.*

To change back to Normal view:

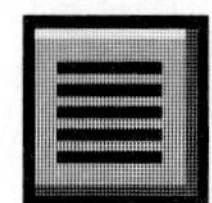

- Choose Normal from the View menu (Alt V, N) or click on the Normal View button on the horizontal scroll bar.

EXERCISES

1. Create a new document and enter some text. Click on the Print Preview button. Use the ToolTip to explore the toolbar buttons on the Print Preview screen. Close the Print Preview screen.
2. Select Print from the File menu and review the various options in the Print dialog box. Cancel the print operation.

3. Press Ctrl+P and note that this shortcut is the same as choosing the Print command on the File menu. Cancel the print operation.
4. Click on the Print button on the standard toolbar. Notice how it's different from Ctrl+P and the Print option on the File menu.

2.6 HELP

When you install Word, an extensive on-line help system is automatically installed. (*On-line* means "always available while you work on your computer.") The on-line help system contains the equivalent of many thousands of pages of documentation, so it can be overwhelming. But the system is also quite friendly. For example, you have already seen one very friendly aspect of the help system: the ToolTips that show up below toolbar buttons when you place the mouse pointer over them.

TIP *You may want to put off reading this section until you feel the need to use Word's help system.*

The help system is also easier to use because it includes *context-sensitive help*. This means that you can press F1 at the appropriate time and bypass the help menus to go directly to the needed information. For example, whenever you're in a dialog box or have highlighted a menu option, press F1 to get information about that particular dialog box or menu option.

A third way to invoke help is via the Help button on the standard toolbar. Double-clicking on this button brings up the help system's Search dialog box. A single click changes the mouse pointer to a help pointer. Clicking this pointer over various elements on the screen causes the help system to display context-sensitive help text on the element in question.

TIP *If you're using Help frequently and have a machine with enough memory, don't close the Help window between uses; just shrink it to an icon or press Alt+Tab. You will switch back to Word and the next time you call for Help it will load much faster.*

EXAMPLES

1. Press F1 from within the Save As dialog box. You will see a screen much like the one shown in Figure 2-9.

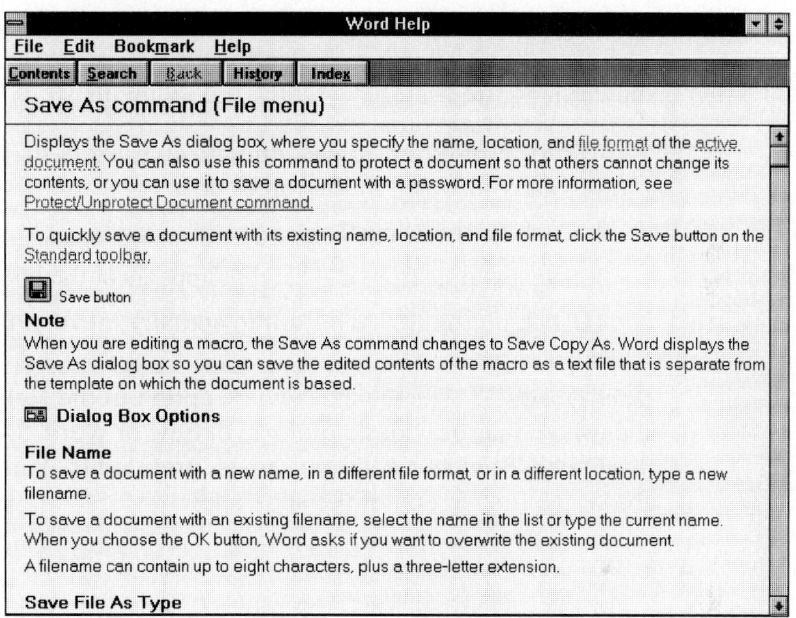

FIGURE 2-9 *The help screen for the Save As dialog box*

THE HELP MENU

To orient yourself if you want to go further with the help system, here are short descriptions of the most important of the items on the Help menu, which is shown here:

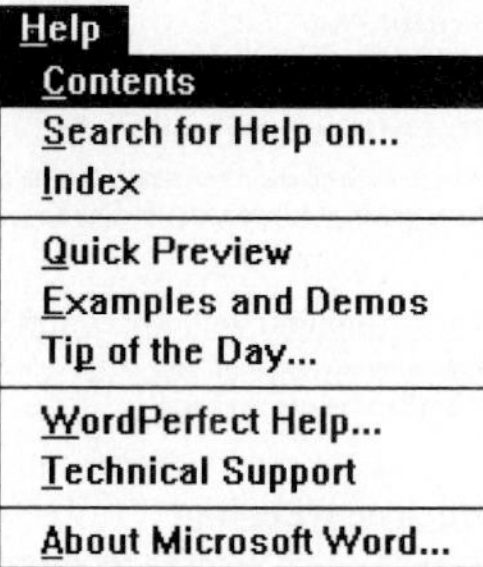

Contents The Contents option—activated by pressing Alt H, C (or C alone if the Help menu is open)—tells you how the Word help system is organized. The contents page is shown in Figure 2-10.

Search for Help On The Search option—activated by pressing Alt H, S (or S alone if the Help menu is open)—lets you search for help on a specific topic. Selecting this option opens a screen like the one shown in Figure 2-11. Now follow the following steps:

1. Type a topic (or at least enough characters so Word can identify what you want) in the topics box.
2. Click on the Show Topics button.
3. Select a topic from the list that appears at the bottom of dialog box.
4. Click on the Go To button to actually move to the topic you want.

Quick Preview The Quick Preview option in the Help menu starts a slide show that provides a quick overview of Word. Some people find this Quick Preview a good way to get oriented to Word. Figure 2-12 shows the first screen of the slide show.

FIGURE 2-10

The Help Contents screen

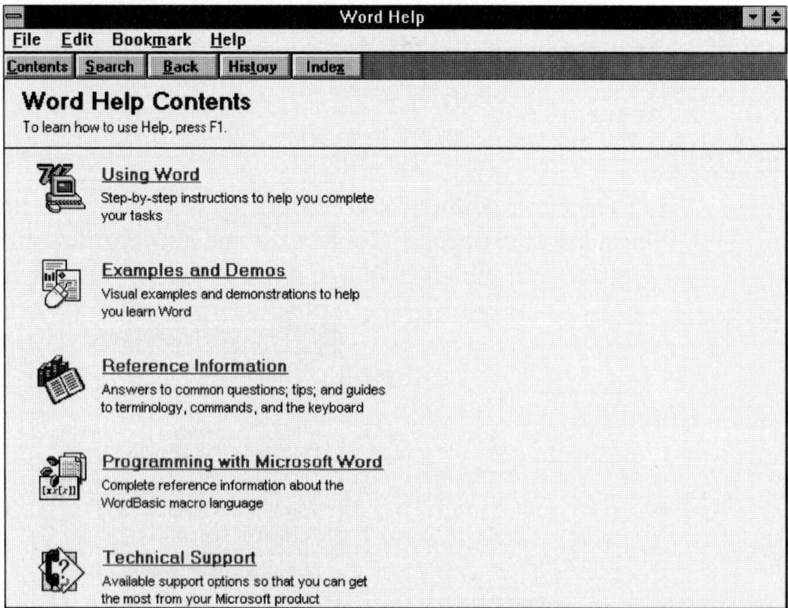

FIGURE 2-11

The Search dialog box in the help system

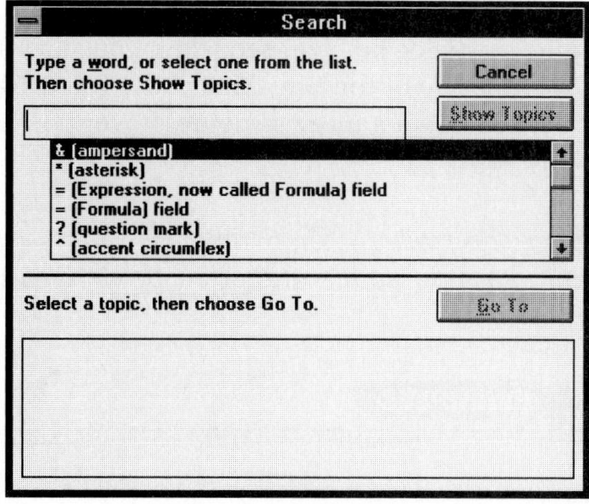

NOTE *These previews can be incredibly slow if you don't have a fast computer.*

Examples and Demos The Examples and Demos option on the Help menu gives you examples of how to work with various kinds of documents. You can open a sample document and see how it was formatted. Then you can print it to see how it looks.

FIGURE 2-12

Initial Quick Preview screen

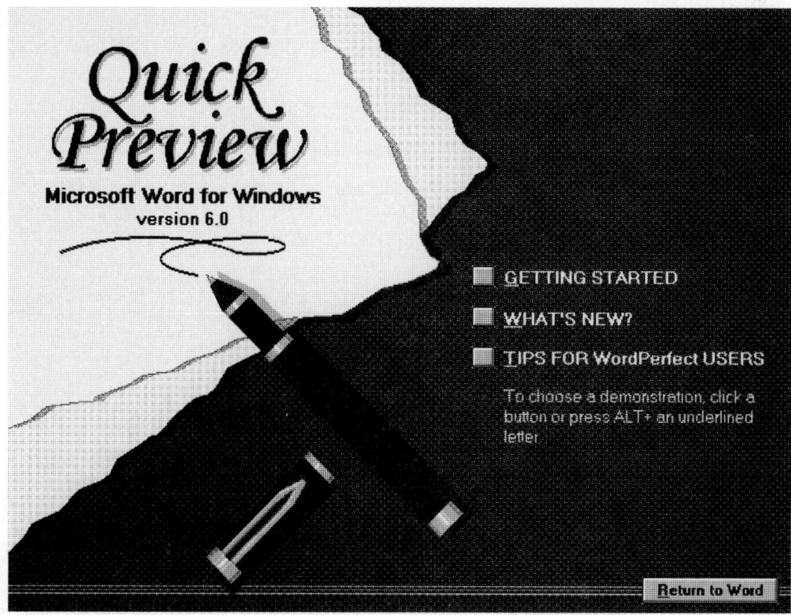

Tip of the Day The Tip of the Day option in the Help menu opens the same tip dialog box you see when you start Word (see Chapter 1). From the Tip of the Day dialog box, you can go through the tips using Next Tip or get a more structured overview of the tips by selecting More Tips.

WordPerfect Help The WordPerfect Help option is designed to make the transition from WordPerfect to Word easier.

EXAMPLES

1. The opening screen of the Getting Started Quick Preview is shown in Figure 2-13. Click on the box marked Next to begin moving through this show. Click on cancel to end the preview.
2. Choose the Tip of the Day option from the Help menu. If the box marked Show Tips at Startup on the bottom right isn't checked, you miss this amusing (and useful) feature when you start Word in the morning.
3. Figure 2-14 shows an example of what the screen looks like if you choose to search for information on opening a document. To get to the screen shown in Figure 2-14,

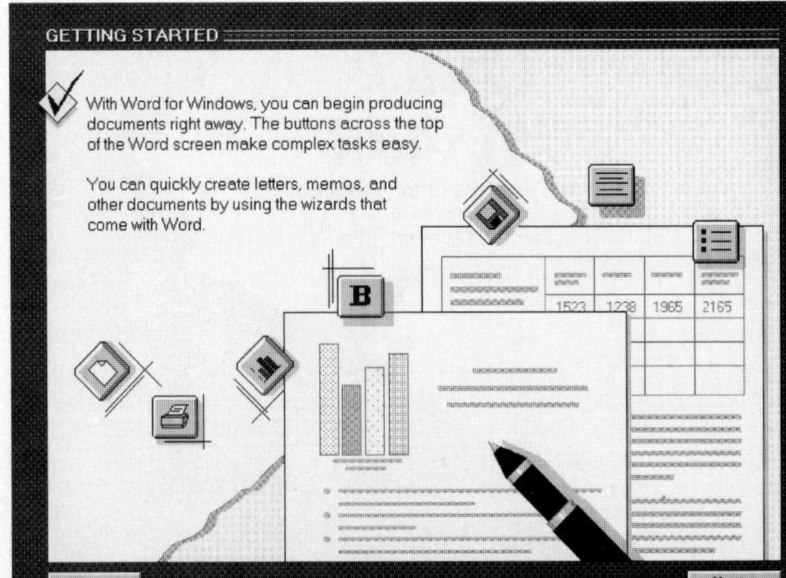

FIGURE 2-13 *Getting Started demo opening screen*

FIGURE 2-14

The Search dialog box with opening files highlighted

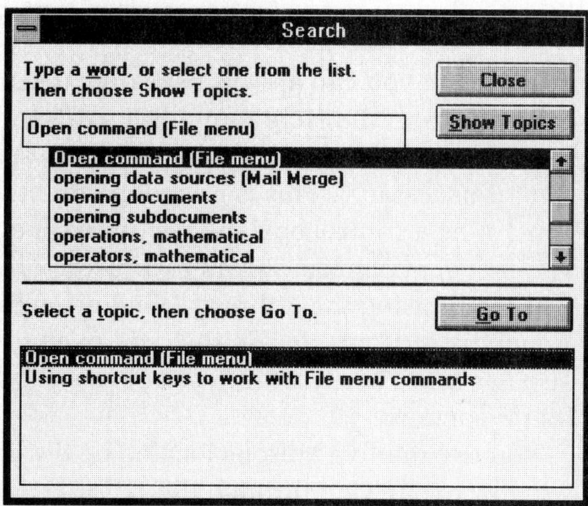

a. Choose Search from the Help menu.

b. Type **Open** in the search text box and then click on the Show Topics button.

4. Figure 2-15 is an example of what the screen looks like if you choose the second topic listed in Figure 2-14. This item on using shortcut keys speeds things up as you become more familiar with Word. (See the inside cover for a convenient list of shortcuts.)

FIGURE 2-15

Using shortcut keys to work with File menu commands

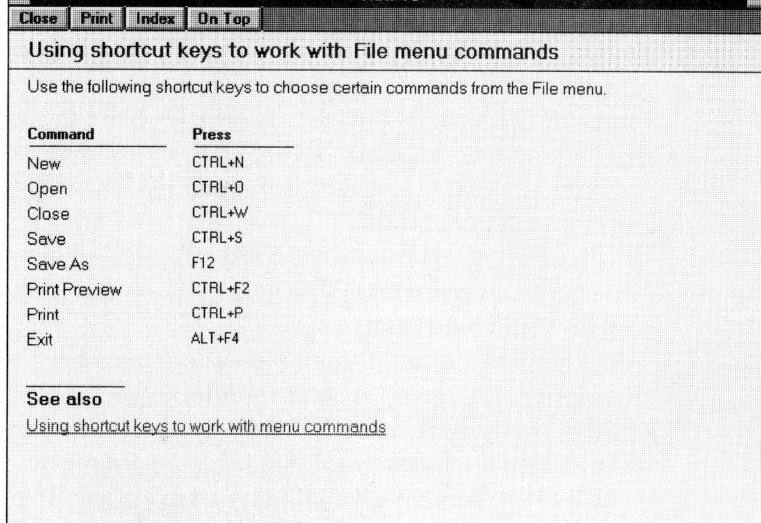

WORKING WITH THE HELP SYSTEM

Although you can always use context-sensitive help, selecting Contents from the Help menu is also a good way to get into the help system. This leads you to the initial help screen (refer back to Figure 2-10, if necessary). This is an independent window with a title bar containing a control box and minimize and maximize buttons. This lets you move, maximize, shrink to an icon, or close the Help window as you see fit using the ordinary Window techniques that you can find in Appendix A (if you decide that you need to do this). The help window also has scroll bars that let you move easily through the information that it contains.

You use the five buttons located below the menu bar in the help window to navigate through the help system. If an option makes no sense in the current context—for example, you can't move backward from the initial screen—its button is grayed. The most important of these buttons (Contents, Search, and Index) correspond to items on the Help menu.

HOW THE HELP SYSTEM IS TIED TOGETHER

The help system is tied together by links that are indicated by an underline. (They also are highlighted in green on color monitors.) These underlined terms or phrases, called *jumps*, are used as gateways to new information. If you move the mouse pointer to a jump, the pointer changes into a little hand. At this point, if you click the left mouse button, you are immediately taken to a help screen on the indicated topic. You can also use the Tab key to move forward between jumps and press Shift+Tab to move back. If you use the Tab key, the jump you moved to is highlighted. Press Enter to choose the highlighted topic.

When you jump around via these links, Word keeps track of where you were. You can press Alt+B or click on the Back button to move back to a previous help screen.

If a word or phrase in the help system is marked with a dotted underline (also green on color monitors), you can get a short definition of the term by clicking on it. The help system displays a short definition in a window until you click to remove it.

Many help screens give you just an overview. If you need specific directions on how to accomplish a specific task you can often get Word to open a "How To" window telling you how to accomplish a specific

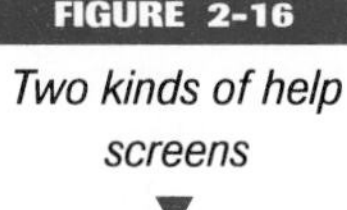

FIGURE 2-16

Two kinds of help screens

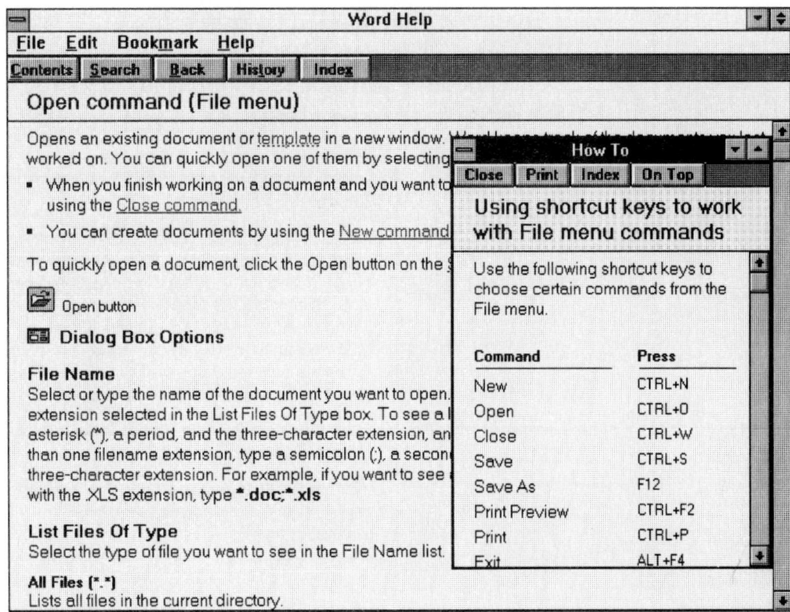

task. Examples of these two types of windows are shown side by side in Figure 2-16.

EXAMPLES

1. Choose Search from the Help menu and then search for the item called "Word Workplace." Choose the topic marked "The Word Workplace" from the topics box and click on the Go To button. If you move the mouse pointer around you can see the mouse pointer assume the hand shape each time it's positioned over a jump. Here's an example of this:

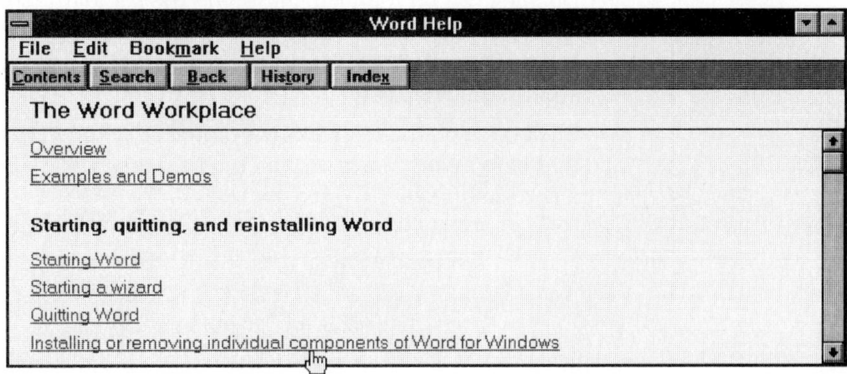

2. Choose the item marked Overview from the "Word Workplace Topic". Click on it to be sent to this jump. The next screen has many items underlined indicating a definition is just a mouse click away. Here's the definition of a Word *toolbar* that you would see if you clicked on this item.

Toolbar

A bar with buttons that perform some of the most common tasks in Word, such as opening, copying, and printing files. Some toolbars are available throughout Word, including the Standard and Formatting toolbars. Other toolbars, such as the Outlining toolbar, are available only when you perform a specific task. You can also create custom toolbars.

To display a list of toolbars available in Word, choose Toolbars from the View menu.

You may need to enlarge the Word window to the full width of the screen to see the entire toolbar.

EXERCISES

1. Select Contents from the Help menu. From the menu on this screen, select How to Use Help from the Help menu. This gives you general help on using the help system. Choose Exit from the File menu to exit from the help system.
2. Double-click on the Help button on the standard toolbar. Type **tooltip** in the text box in the Search dialog box. Press Enter twice to get information on ToolTips. Click on a part of the Word screen showing around the Help screen to get back into Word.
3. Click once on the Help toolbar button. Use the help mouse pointer to find help on any screen element. Try using the help mouse pointer on a portion of text.

1. Close any existing documents and then open a new document and type the following text, complete with errors, noting that Word corrects "teh" automatically. [2.1]

   "If you know how to spend less than you get, you have teh philospers stone." – Franlin

2. Correct the spelling of "philosopher's" and "Franklin." [2.1, 2.2]
3. Overtype "Franklin" with "FRANKLIN" using the Caps Lock key and overtype feature. [2.1, 2.2]
4. Undo and then redo the correction to "philosopher's." [2.1]
5. Save the document and name it MASTER1, and then close it. [2.3]
6. Open MASTER1.DOC. [2.4]
7. Get help on the Print Preview feature. [2.6]
8. Display a Print Preview of MASTER1.DOC. [2.5]
9. Exit Word. [1.3]

1. Start Word. [1.2]
2. Open any existing DOC file; MASTER1 from the above skills check will do. [2.4]

3. At the end of the document, enter a blank line and the following text, complete with errors, noting that Word corrects "teh" automatically. [2.1, 2.2]

   "Mokery is teh fume of little hearts."
   Tennyson, Idyll's of teh King.

4. Correct "Idyll's" to "Idylls." [2.1, 2.2]
5. Undo and then redo the correction. [2.1]
6. Save the file as an MS-DOS Text file called MASTER2.TXT. [2.3]
7. Close the document, noting that Word does not prompt you to save changes because you haven't changed the text since you last saved it. [1.5]
8. Exit Word. [1.3]

3

Working Within a Word Document

chapter objectives

After completing this chapter, you will know how to

3.1 Move through a document

3.2 Select text

3.3 Delete and rearrange your document by cutting, copying, pasting, or dragging and dropping text

3.4 Search for text within your document

3.5 Replace text within your document

THIS chapter builds on the methods for working with text that you have already seen. When you finish this chapter, you will have mastered most of the basic techniques for working with text.

First, you'll learn how to move through a document rapidly. Then, you'll discover some of the more sophisticated methods for working with text within a document. Most of these methods follow the fundamental rule for Windows applications:

> First you must select the object (text, a graphic, and so on); only then can you ask the program to do something to it.

NOTE *The phrase in the jargon for this is simply:* ***Select, then do****.*

This means you'll first need to know how to select text. Once you know how to select text, you'll see how easy it is to cut and paste or drag and drop text within your documents. The last technique covered in this chapter is how to search for or replace text within your document.

review skills check

During this chapter's Review Skills Check, you will be asked to create, save, and then reload a document into Word. You can use this document throughout the chapter to try out the topics you learn.

1. Start Word and enter your favorite text of 1000 words or more into a new document. [2.1]
2. Save the document with the name BIGDOC.DOC in the C:\WINWORD directory. [2.3]
3. Close BIGDOC.DOC. [1.6]
4. Reload the file BIGDOC.DOC into Word. [1.2, 2.4]
5. Search the help system for the topic "insertion point." [2.6]
6. Practice moving the insertion point around in the text using all the cursor movement keys, including Pg Up and Pg Dn. [1.4]

7. Backup the BIGDOC.DOC on a floppy instead of saving it again in the WINWORD directory. [2.3]

3.1 MORE ON MOVING THROUGH A DOCUMENT

The magic of word processing lies in how easy it is to revise your work. Few people are satisfied with their first draft of a document. When each revision meant ret 12yping the entire document from scratch, you probably made fewer changes. With Word, you can revise your work almost effortlessly. Since the process is so easy, you have more time to spend perfecting your documents.

You have already seen a few methods for moving the insertion point around (see Chapter 1, section 1.4), but moving the insertion point around your documents is so important, it pays to master a few more ways. The goal is always to get to the place you want to work on in your document as quickly as possible. This makes the inevitable revising and rewriting as efficient as possible. So now it's time to master more powerful techniques for moving the insertion point around!

If you can see on the screen the place you want to be, then:

1. Move the mouse pointer (it looks like an I-beam) until it's in the desired spot.
2. Click the left mouse button.

If the place you need to get to is not visible on your screen but you know roughly where it is within your document, you can use the mouse or keyboard to sail from one place to another within your document. Making different parts of your document roll across the screen is called *scrolling* through your document. (Think of scrolling as one of those old-fashioned penny arcade movies: the window stays fixed while the view moves.)

It's worth keeping the distinction between scrolling and moving the insertion point inside your document clear: moving the insertion point in your document lets you change where you will enter text. Scrolling through your document lets you see different parts of the document more easily without moving the insertion point. If, after scrolling through the document you find where you want to be, you must still make sure the insertion point is at the new location (by a mouse click for example) in order to start editing.

USING THE MOUSE TO NAVIGATE THROUGH A DOCUMENT

You use the mouse to march through your documents with small steps or giant steps. In either case, you need to use the *vertical scroll bar*. (The *horizontal scroll bar* is used to move within the left and right margins of the page. Use this scroll bar when the document is too wide to fit on the screen.) As you can see in Figure 3-1, each scroll bar has two arrows at the end of a channel that also contains a little box (usually called the *thumb* or *scroll box*). The scroll box is the key to moving rapidly through a document; use the arrows in the vertical scroll bar to move through the document line by line. Dragging the scroll box enables you to quickly move long distances to an approximate location in your document. For example, if you drag the scroll box in the vertical scroll bar to the middle of the channel, you'll scroll to approximately the middle of your document.

Table 3-1 summarizes how to move through a document using the mouse inside the vertical scroll bar.

Dragging the scroll box is the fastest way to scroll, but you will usually need to fine-tune your location using one of the first four methods to get to exactly where you want.

FIGURE 3-1

Vertical and horizontal scroll bars

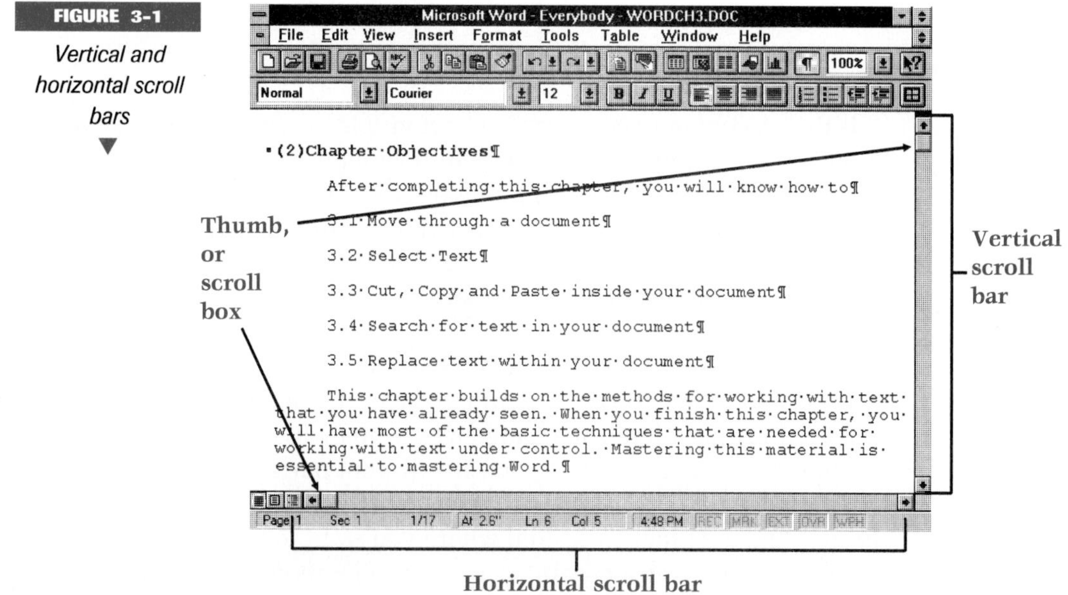

To Move	Do This
Up one line	Click on up arrow in the vertical scroll bar
Down one line	Click on down arrow in the vertical scroll bar
Up a screen	Click anywhere above the scroll box
Down a screen	Click anywhere below the scroll box
A certain proportion of the document	Drag the scroll box up or down inside the channel that proportion

TABLE 3-1 *Moving Through a Document with the Mouse in the Vertical Scroll Bar*

REMEMBER *These methods do not move the insertion point. Once you have scrolled to the desired spot in your document, make sure the I-beam mouse pointer is where you want and click the left mouse button to actually move the insertion point.*

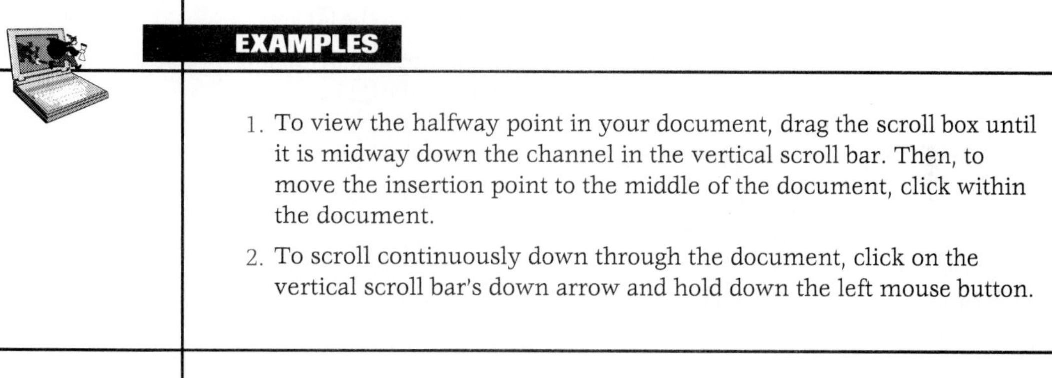

EXAMPLES

1. To view the halfway point in your document, drag the scroll box until it is midway down the channel in the vertical scroll bar. Then, to move the insertion point to the middle of the document, click within the document.
2. To scroll continuously down through the document, click on the vertical scroll bar's down arrow and hold down the left mouse button.

USING THE KEYBOARD TO MOVE THROUGH A DOCUMENT

Chapter 1 explained how the ← and → keys can move you through a line. There are additional keystrokes for most of the other common movements within a document. Touch typists, for example, tend to use keystrokes more and the mouse less. Scrolling with the mouse is usually reserved for document scanning rather than document revising.

REMEMBER *Unlike scrolling with the mouse, using the keyboard to move through a document will change the location of the insertion point.*

Table 3-2 lists the keystrokes that let you move the insertion point within a document. (If you are using the numeric keypad on your keyboard for the arrow keys, remember to turn off the Num Lock key.) The screen doesn't start scrolling until the insertion point reaches the top or bottom of the screen.

It may seem strange that the Pg Up and Pg Dn keys move only a screen. There is a way to move a whole (printed) page, but Word users usually think about page numbering at the final stage—when they are getting ready to print the document. Word shows a dotted line at page breaks. It moves the page breaks when necessary as you enter more text. For more on pages in Word, please see Chapter 8. (If you're interested, the keystrokes for moving up or down one whole page are Alt Ctrl+Pg Up or Alt Ctrl+Pg Dn, respectively.)

EXAMPLES

1. To move the insertion point continuously down line by line through the document, press and hold down the ↓ key.
2. To move the insertion point continuously up line by line through the document, press and hold down the ↑ key.

To Move	Press
Up one line	↑
Down one line	↓
To beginning of line	Home
To end of line	End
To word to the left	Ctrl+←
To word to the right	Ctrl+→
Up a paragraph	Ctrl+↑
Down a paragraph	Ctrl+↓
Down a screen	Pg Dn (leaves insertion point in same location relative to the screen)
Up a screen	Pg Up (leaves insertion point in same location relative to the screen)
To bottom of screen	Press Ctrl+Pg Dn
To top of screen	Press Ctrl+Pg Up
To beginning of document	Ctrl+Home
To end of document	Ctrl+End

TABLE 3-2 *Moving Through a Document with the Keyboard*

GO BACK AND GO TO

Sometimes, you want to bounce back and forth between different parts of your document. It's easy to do this because Word remembers the last three places you entered or edited text. Each time you use Shift+F5, Word returns to the previous location. Press the Shift+F5 combination four times and you return to your starting place.

On the other hand, sometimes you want to move directly to a page within your document. You can do this by pressing F5 or double-clicking on the page number located in the status bar to bring up the Go To dialog box shown here.

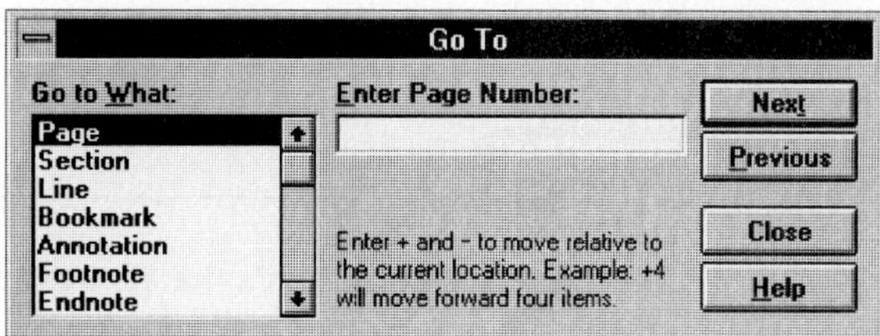

If you know what page you want to go to, type the page number in the Enter Page Number text box and then click on OK. Press Esc or click on the Close button to close this dialog box. (The Go To box can also be used to go to specific lines, footnotes, and so on. This feature is very convenient when you start adding these elements to your documents. See Chapters 6, 7, 8, and 12 for more on adding these elements.)

EXAMPLE

1. Suppose the status bar says your document has 10 pages, as shown here:

Page 5 then is roughly the middle of the document. To go to page 5 you would fill in the Go To dialog box as follows and then click on the Go To button to move to the middle of the document.

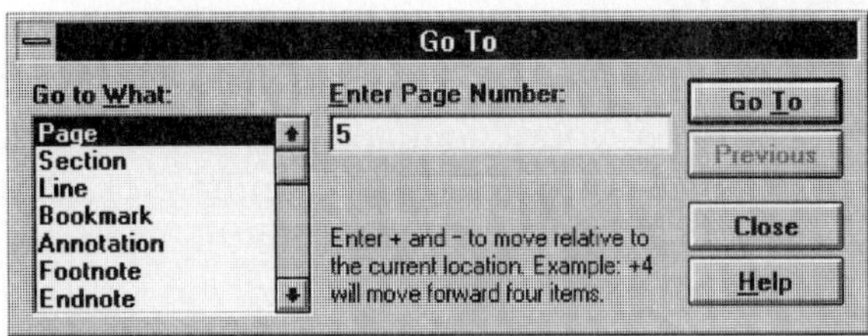

EXERCISES

1. Load BIGDOC.DOC if it's not already loaded (see Skills Check at the beginning of the chapter).
2. Double-click on the page number in the status bar and go to page 2. Close the Go To dialog box using Esc.
3. Press Shift+F5 to return to the location you were in before you went to page 2. Then press Shift+F5 until you return to page 2.
4. Note where the scroll box is on the vertical scroll bar. Move the scroll box to the bottom of the scroll bar and then release it. Then move the scroll box to the top of the scroll bar and release it. Press Shift+F5 several times and note that using the scroll bar didn't move the insertion point.
5. Press Ctrl+Home before—and undo any typing after—each of the following exercises. Note where the insertion point is each time you start to type.
   a. Use Go To to move to page 2 and type **Hello**.
   b. Use the vertical scroll bar to move to the middle of the document and type **Hello**.
   c. Use the down arrow on the vertical scroll bar and type **Hello**.
   d. Use the ↓ on the keyboard and type **Hello**.

e. Press Pg Dn and type **Hello**.

6. Use the keyboard arrow keys, Home, End, Pg Up and Pg Dn with and without the Ctrl key, to move around the document. Note the location of the insertion point with each move.

3.2 SELECTING TEXT

Selecting text is probably the most common prelude to revising your documents. Remember, the rule for editing text in Word is

Select, then do.

You always select the text to be affected, and then make changes to it. An example of what selected text looks like on screen is shown here:

Unprovided·with·original·learning,·unformed·in·the·habits·of·thinking,·unskilled·in·the arts of composition, I resolved--to write a book.¶
¶
Edward·Gibbon¶

Selected text always appears highlighted. You can select text with either the mouse or the keyboard; as you work more with Word, you will discover which method works better for you. Before starting to work with selecting text you have to be aware of one of Word's default features: Anything you type will replace the selected text.

Although this is a standard feature of Windows products, some people find that this feature drives them batty. Word (unlike many Windows products) does let you change the default so that if you type something with text selected, Word just enters the text at the insertion point. With the Typing Replaces Selection option off, any keystroke also cancels the selection.

To turn off the Typing Replaces Selection feature:

1. Choose Options from the Tools menu (Alt T, O).
2. Click on the Edit tab, as shown in Figure 3-2, if it is not showing in front.

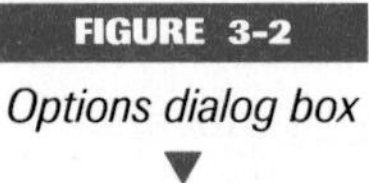

FIGURE 3-2

Options dialog box

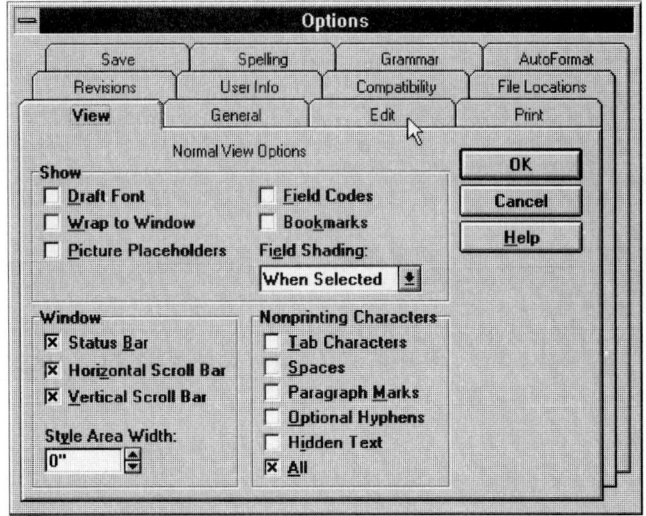

3. Make sure the Typing Replaces Selection check box is not selected (doesn't contain an "x"), as shown in Figure 3-3.

TIP *You can change the case of text by first selecting it and then pressing* Shift+F3*. This cycles through the various possible capitalization styles. (You can also choose Change Case from the Format menu [*Alt O, E*] and work with the dialog box that pops up.)*

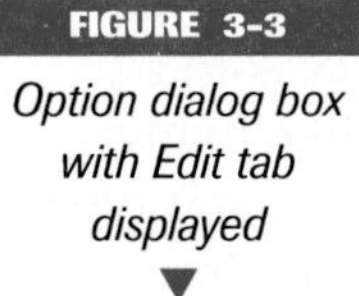

FIGURE 3-3

Option dialog box with Edit tab displayed

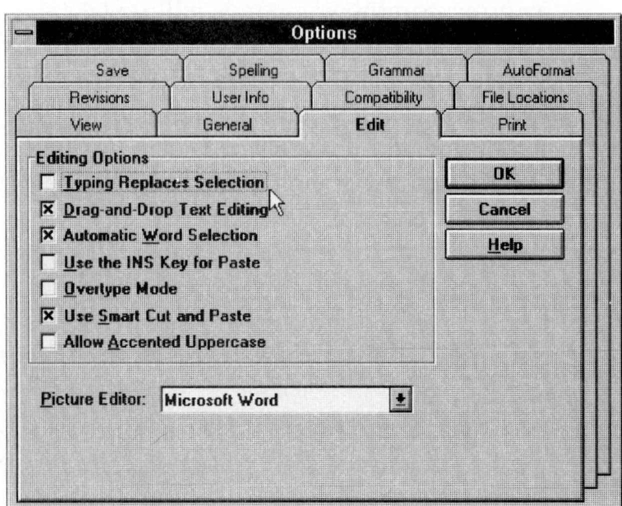

SELECTING TEXT WITH THE KEYBOARD

When selecting text with the keyboard, you use the same techniques you use when moving through the document, but you also hold down one of the Shift keys. Once you hold down the Shift key, using any method for moving through the document selects the region you moved through.

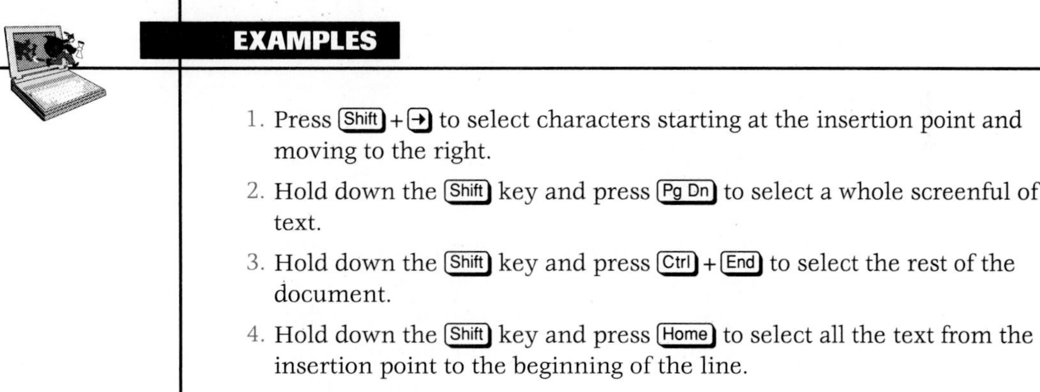

EXAMPLES

1. Press Shift + → to select characters starting at the insertion point and moving to the right.
2. Hold down the Shift key and press Pg Dn to select a whole screenful of text.
3. Hold down the Shift key and press Ctrl + End to select the rest of the document.
4. Hold down the Shift key and press Home to select all the text from the insertion point to the beginning of the line.

CANCELLING A SELECTION

Before you get further into how or what to do with selected text, you should know how to cancel a selection. You can do this in two ways. Either

- Click anywhere outside the selected area

or

- Press any arrow or direction key.

SELECTING TEXT WITH THE MOUSE

Because selecting text with the mouse requires you to take you hands off the keyboard, many touch typists prefer the keyboard techniques you just learned. However, the mouse is the only way to select a vertical block—a block of text that doesn't extend to the margins—like the one shown here.

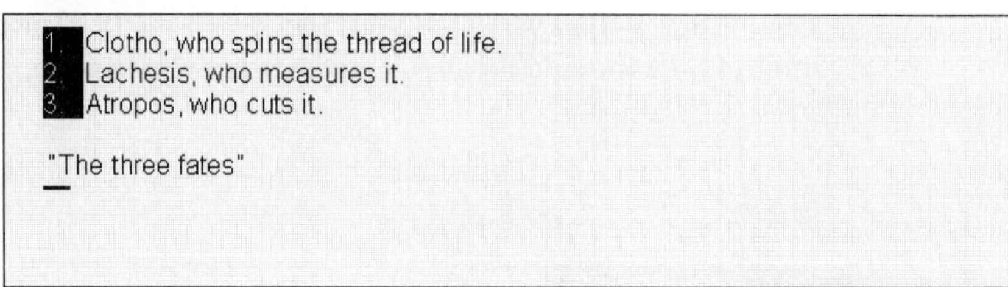

To select text using the mouse,

1. Click the left mouse button and drag until the text you wanted to select is highlighted.

It requires good "mouse technique" to select exactly the amount of text you want. By default, Word automatically selects whole words when you select more than a single word by dragging with the mouse. To turn this feature off, go to the Edit tab on the Options menu that you just saw and make sure that the Automatic Word Selection check box is not selected.

You can also select text starting at the insertion point by:

1. Holding down the Shift key.
2. Moving the mouse pointer to the end of the text you want to select.
3. Clicking the left mouse button.

The following table summarizes some other methods for selecting text with the mouse.

To Select	Do This
A word	Double-click the word
A sentence	Hold down the Ctrl key and click in the sentence
A paragraph	Triple-click inside the paragraph

The remaining methods for selecting text with a mouse make use of the *selection bar.* This area is not marked in any way on your screen, but is the thin blank area directly to the left of the text in your document, as shown here:

1. Clotho, who spins the thread of life.
2. Lachesis, who measures it.
3. Atropos, who cuts it.

"The three fates"

TIP *The way to tell that you're in the selection bar is that the mouse pointer changes into a rightward-pointing arrow (it usually points to the left).*

This table summarizes how to select text by using the selection bar.

To Select	Do This
A line of text	Click in the selection bar directly to the left of the line
Multiple lines	Drag up or down through the selection bar directly to the left of the lines
A paragraph	Double-click in the selection bar to the left of the paragraph you want to select
The whole document	Triple-click in the selection bar

SELECTING VERTICAL BLOCKS OF TEXT

Word's ability to select a vertical block of text that cuts across multiple lines is a nifty feature that can save you a lot of work. (This is especially true when working with lists; see Chapter 10.) To select a vertical block of text.

1. Hold down the Alt key and then click the left mouse button.
2. Drag to select the region you want.

EXAMPLE

1. Type the following list of great writers—all of which have the same number of letters in their last name:

   Asimov, Isaac
   Austin, Jane
   Bierce, Ambrose
   Gibbon, Edward

Now suppose you need to change all the last names to uppercase. Hold down the Alt key when you are at the A in "Asimov" and drag until you are at the "n" in Gibbon. Press Shift+F3 twice.

SELECTING THE ENTIRE DOCUMENT

Occasionally you will need to select the whole document. One way to do this is to triple-click in the selection bar. Another is to choose Select All from the Edit menu (Alt E, A), but probably the easiest method is to use the Ctrl+A shortcut. Selecting the whole document is especially common when you need to change how the individual characters in the document look. See Chapter 5 for more on this.

EXERCISES

1. Hold down Shift and use the keyboard arrow keys, Home, End, Pg Up, and Pg Dn with and without the Ctrl key to move around the document. Note the extent of the text selection with each move. Cancel each selection by moving the insertion point.
2. Drag with the mouse to select some text. Cancel the selection by moving the insertion point.
3. Double-click on a word to select it, press Ctrl while clicking on a word to select a sentence, and triple-click on a word to select a paragraph. Cancel your selection between tries by clicking outside the selected text. (Note the shape of the cursor when it is and isn't over selected text. This topic is covered in more detail in the next section.)

4. Move the mouse pointer in front of a line of text; it should change into an arrow. Click once, click and drag down the selection bar, and then triple-click in the selection bar.
5. Challenge Yourself! Get Help on Extended Text and use the cursor movement keys with Shift to extend already selected text.

EXTENDING A SELECTION

Often you will need to extend a selection you have already made (for example, if you cut off the selection one word too early). To extend an existing selection (the jargon says: move to *extended selection mode*):

Press F8

Notice, as shown here, that the EXT marker on the status bar is not greyed anymore.

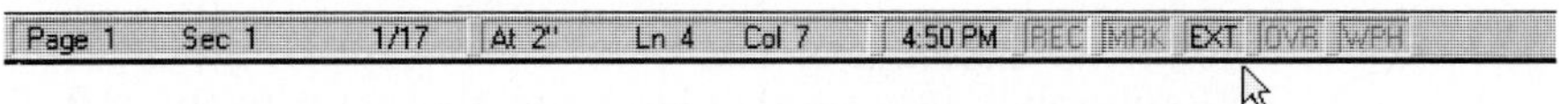

(You can also move in and out of extended selection mode by double-clicking on the EXT button on the status bar.)

Each time you press F8 again Word increases the selection by the next unit of text. For example, if you stopped the selection inside a word, the next press of F8 increases the selection to include the rest of the word. Press F8 one more time and the selection increases to include the next sentence. Press F8 one more time and Word increases the selection to include the next paragraph, and so on. Use Shift+F8 to reduce the selection by the next unit of text.

As long as you are in extended selection mode, you no longer need to hold down the Shift key to extend the selection using one of the navigation keys (like the arrow keys).

To leave extended selection mode, press Esc (or click on the EXT button on the status bar).

TIP *If you are in extended selection mode, then you can press a character to extend the selection to the next occurrence of that character.*

EXAMPLE

1. Enter the following quote of Edward Gibbon in a new document:

   Blind and absolute dependence may be necessary, but it can never be delightful. Freedom is the first wish of our heart; freedom is the first blessing of our nature; and unless we bind ourselves with voluntary chains of interest or passion, we advance in freedom as we advance in years.

2. Select the word Blind. Hit F8 to move to extended selection mode; hit F8 again to select the first sentence.
3. Still in extended mode, press the "b"; notice how the selection moves to the "b" in "blessing".

3.3 DELETING AND REARRANGING TEXT

When you are revising text, moving the insertion point and then pressing Backspace or Del is the easiest way to erase a single character. (Remember, Backspace deletes the character to the left of the insertion point, while Del eliminates the one to the right.) Be careful not to unintentionally delete paragraph marks: If you delete the paragraph mark (¶) between two paragraphs, Word combines the two paragraphs into one larger unit.

There are also quick methods for deleting the words on either side of the insertion point. If the insertion point is between two words:

- To delete the word before the insertion point, press Ctrl+Backspace.
- To delete the word after the insertion point, press Ctrl+Del.

If the insertion point is inside a word, Ctrl+Backspace deletes all the characters from the insertion point to the beginning of the word; Ctrl+Del deletes all the characters from the insertion point to the end of the word.

If you need to delete a larger area of text:

1. Select the text to be deleted.
2. Press Backspace or Del.

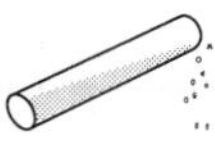

NOTE *If you delete something that you really didn't want to, use Word's Undo feature to get it back (Alt E, U or Ctrl+Z) or use the Undo button on the Standard toolbar.*

EXAMPLES

1. Suppose you enter the following Benjamin Franklin quotation:

   He that teaches himself hath a fool for a master.

   If you decide to change "hath" to the more modern "has," follow these steps:

   a. Place the insertion point between the "a" and the "t" in "hath."
   b. Press Ctrl + Del.
   c. Type **s**.

2. Now suppose you want to change a Franklin quotation that you may agree with even less. The original quotation goes like this:

   God works wonders now and then; behold a lawyer, an honest man.

   You want to change it into the simpler phrase:

   God works wonders now and then.

   a. Select the text from the semicolon to the end of the sentence.
   b. If you have left the Typing Replaces Selection feature on, simply type a period. If not, press the Del key and then type a period.

SMART CUTTING AND PASTING

Often when you cut text around a punctuation mark, you leave the extra space around the punctuation mark by mistake. As a convenience, Word by default removes any spaces between the remaining word and the remaining punctuation mark if you delete the word before a punctuation mark. This feature is called *Smart Cut and Paste.*

EXAMPLES

1. Suppose a pedantic teacher rewrote the beginning of Lincoln's Gettysburg address as follows:

   Four score and seven years ago our fathers brought forth on this continent (87 years ago i.e. in 1776),

   You can use Word's Smart Cut and Paste feature, to make it read correctly:

   Four score and seven years ago our fathers brought forth on this continent,

   a. Select the text from the open parenthesis to right before the comma.
   b. Delete the text by pressing the Del key.

   Notice that Word removed the extra space automatically.

2. To turn off the Smart Cut and Paste feature:

   a. Choose the Options item on the Tools menu (Alt T, O).
   b. Choose the Edit tab.
   c. Make sure the Use Smart Cut and Paste check box is not selected.

MOVING TEXT VIA DRAGGING AND DROPPING

Once you select text, you can easily move it from one portion of the document to another. If you can see the place you want to move the text to, using the mouse to *drag and drop* is often the easiest way to move text.

To move text with drag and drop:

1. Select the text you want to move.

2. With the mouse pointer over the selection, hold down the left mouse button. The mouse pointer changes so that it has a little box at its end.
3. With the mouse button still held down, drag until you are where you want the text to be moved. (Look for the vertical dashed line that marks the place where the text would go.)
4. Release the mouse button to move the text.

Notice how the status bar indicates that you have started to move text, as shown here.

Move to where?

EXAMPLES

1. Enter the following two lines from Bierce's *Devil's Dictionary*:

   Acquaintance: a person whom we know well enough to borrow from, but not well enough to lend to.

   Acquaintance: a degree of friendship called slight when its object is pure or obscure, and intimate when he is rich or famous.

   Because of the strict rules of alphabetization, the second sentence should go before the first. To do this:

   a. Select the second sentence by holding down the Ctrl key while clicking anywhere inside the sentence.
   b. Make sure the mouse pointer is inside the selected text and hold down the left mouse button.
   c. Still keeping the mouse button down, move the pointer until it is where you want the new text to be. (Again look for the dashed vertical line which marks where text ends up.)
   d. Release the mouse button.

MOVING TEXT WITH THE KEYBOARD SHORTCUTS

Dragging and dropping is very useful if you're moving text a short distance and you don't mind taking your fingers off the keyboard. To move text over longer distances or if you prefer keeping your hands on the keyboard most of the time, here's how you move text.

1. Select the text you want to move.
2. Choose Cut from the Edit menu (Alt E, T or Ctrl+X).

3. Move the insertion point to the place you want the text to be.
4. Choose Paste from the Edit menu (Alt E, P or Ctrl+V).

TIP *A good memory aid for these operations works like this:*

Ctrl+V	*X out (for Cut)*
Ctrl+C	*C for Copy*
Ctrl+V	*V is the editors mark to "insert text here" (for Paste)*

Also, if you click the right mouse button when the I-beam mouse pointer is in selected text, a mini-menu pops up that includes the Cut, Copy, and Paste items. You can see the same shortcut menu by moving the insertion point into the selected text and pressing Shift+F10.

COPYING TEXT

Copying text is very similar to moving text. For example, to use a version of "drag and drop" to copy text instead of moving it:

1. Select the text you want to move.

2. Hold down Ctrl and press the left mouse button. The mouse pointer acquires a little box at its end (like for ordinary dragging and dropping) only this time it has a little + sign with it.
3. Still holding down the mouse button, move the pointer until it is where you want to move the text. (Again look for the dashed vertical line that marks the spot where the text will end up.)
4. Release the mouse button.

Again notice how the status bar changes as shown here.

Copy to where?

To copy text with the keyboard, on the other hand:

1. Select the text you want to move.

2. Choose Copy from the Edit menu (Alt E, C or Ctrl+C).
3. Move the insertion point to where you want the text to be.

4. Choose Paste from the Edit menu (Alt E, P or Ctrl+V).

When you use the Cut and Copy commands on the Edit menu (or their keyboard shortcuts), Word always keeps a copy of whatever you last cut or copy in its Clipboard. (*The Clipboard* is a temporary storage location used to hold information to be copied or moved.) You can have only one piece of text in the Clipboard at any one time. However, the same item remains in the Clipboard until you put something new there. This means you can paste the same item many times to many different parts of your document: Just move to the next place and choose the Paste command again (and again and again if you like).

NOTE *The drag and drop technique for moving or copying text does not use the Clipboard. This gives you one way to copy or move text while keeping the contents of the Clipboard intact for further use.*

USING THE SPIKE TO MOVE TEXT

Unfortunately, the Clipboard can only hold one item at a time. You can't use the Clipboard to assemble lots of pieces of your document and then move them all to the same place in one fell swoop. Word does lets you do this with a device called the *Spike.* (Think of the Spike as one of those pointy devices people stick their messages on.)

To add selected text to the Spike:

1. Select the text you want to add to the Spike.
2. Press Ctrl+F3. (Word will cut the text out of your document.)

Now repeat steps 1 and 2 for each item you want to add to the Spike. When you insert the items from the Spike into your document, you can either empty the Spike or not. If you don't empty the Spike, you can paste its contents repeatedly.

- To empty the Spike while inserting its contents into the text, move the insertion point to where you want the text to appear and press Ctrl+Shift+F3.
- To insert the Spike's contents into the text without clearing out the Spike, move the insertion point to where you want the text to appear, type **spike** as a separate word, and press F3.

If you still have information in the Spike when you finish a Word session, Word can save this information for another session. In particular, you may see a dialog box that looks like the following when you try to exit Word. At this point, it is safest to click on the No button. (NORMAL.DOT is where Word keeps information on "normal" documents—please see Chapter 7 for more on what happens if you click on the Yes button.)

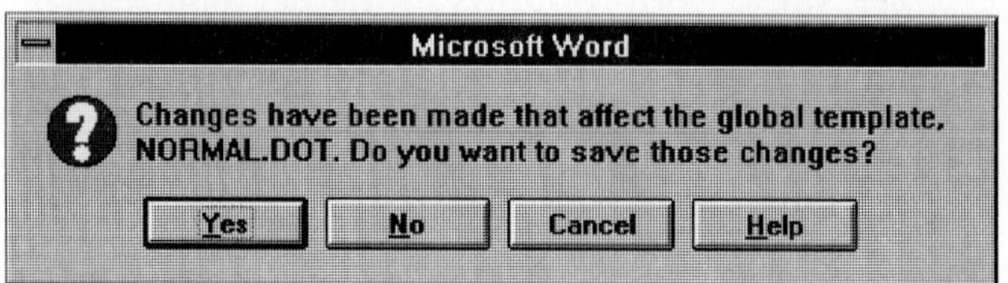

EXERCISES

1. Create a new document and type

   The quick brown fox jumped over the lazy dog's back.

2. Press Ctrl+Backspace a few times, press Home, and press Ctrl+Del a few times.
3. Press Ctrl+V to paste text from the Clipboard. Note that the words removed from the preceding sentence were not on the Clipboard.
4. Click on the Undo button on the standard toolbar until the sentence is reconstructed.
5. Using only drag and drop, change the sentence to:

   The quick brown dog jumped over the lazy fox's back.

6. With one click, select the sentence. Then use drag and drop to make a copy of it. (Add a blank line after the sentence before starting. Having the Show/Hide button depressed may make things easier.)
7. Enter **The quick brown fox jumped over the lazy dog's back** again. Using only the keyboard movement and selection keys, and the shortcut keys for Cut and Paste (Ctrl+X and Ctrl+V), rearrange the text as in Exercise 5.

8. Challenge Yourself! Reverse the changes from Exercise 5 using only the keyboard movement and selection keys, and the Cut and Paste shortcut keys (Ctrl+X and Ctrl+V).

3.4 SEARCHING FOR TEXT IN YOUR DOCUMENT

It is very useful to be able to search for certain text in your document. Word has a very powerful search facility. For example, you can

- Search for words that do or do not exactly match the case of what you are looking for.
- Search for words that sound like (but are not necessarily spelled like) the ones you are looking for.
- Search for words using *wildcards* (or *pattern matching*). For example, you could search for three-letter words that start with "ca" by entering **ca?**.

To start the searching process, you need to bring up the Find dialog box shown here. You can do his by pressing Alt E, F or Ctrl+F.

The basic method of finding text is simple:

1. Type what you want to find in the Find What text box.
2. Click on the Find Next button.

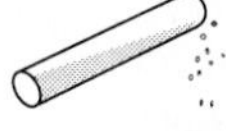

NOTE *You can continue to click on the Find Next repeatedly to find further instances of what you are searching for. If you want to change the search area to up (or down) from where the insertion point is, pull down the Search box and choose Up (or Down).*

You can edit your document while the Find dialog box is open; this is a very useful feature since often you will be searching for something in order to edit the surrounding text. To do this, move the mouse pointer until the insertion point is at the place inside your document where you want to edit. Make your editing changes and then click inside the Find dialog box to reactivate it.

TIP *You can move the Find dialog box to relocate it if it is covering the text you want to edit. This is done with one of the standard Windows techniques for dragging a dialog box (see Appendix A): make sure the mouse pointer is in the title bar of the Find dialog box. Hold down the left mouse button. Now drag the Find dialog box to where you want it.*

If you change the choice in the Search drop-down list box from All to Down, Word finds the last instance of the word you're searching for and it pops up this dialog box:

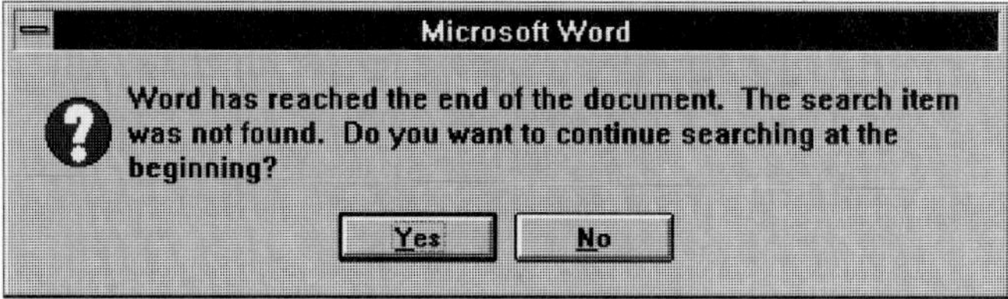

If you click on the Yes button, Word returns to the beginning of the document and continues the search.

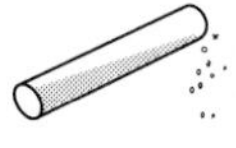

NOTE *You can also close the Find dialog box before finding the last instance of the text you're searching for; to do this, just press* Esc.

EXAMPLE

1. Type the following quote from Edward Gibbon about his school days (This quote precedes the one you saw earlier in this chapter in his autobiography.):

   A school is a cavern of fear and sorrow. The mobility of the captive youths is chained to a book and a desk; an inflexible master commands their attention, which every moment is impatient to escape. They labor like the soldiers of Persia, under the scourge, and their education is nearly finished before they can apprehend the sense or utility of the hard lessons they are forced to repeat.

Search for the word "scourge." The Find dialog box will look like this:

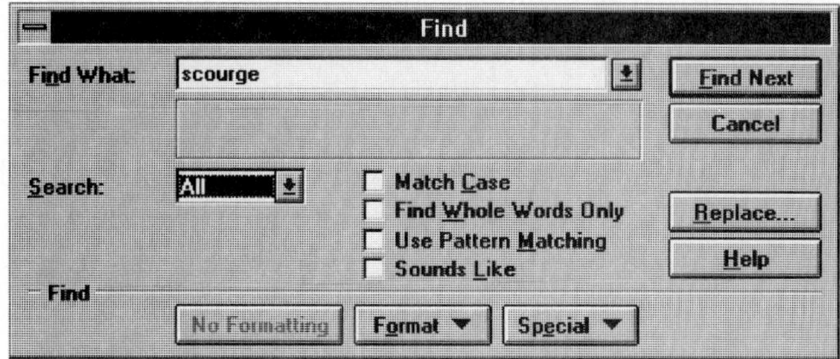

You might want to save the Gibbon quote for future reference—you might even want to save it as a Word document with the name GIBBON.DOC for use later on in the chapter.

OPTIONS IN THE FIND DIALOG BOX

Let's go over some of the options in this dialog box. (We won't cover them all here—see Chapter 5 for more on these options.)

The Find What Text Box This is where you type what you want to find. You can even insert text into this box using Word's Paste facility. Finally, clicking on the down arrow to the right of this box lets you look for the last few items you have previously searched for.

The Search Text Box Do you want to search downwards or upwards from the insertion point? Do you want to search the whole document? Click on the down arrow to the right of the Search box and choose the desired item from the list that drops down. If you choose the All option, Word searches the whole document even if you have previously selected text.

TIP *If you have selected text and don't choose the All option, Word only searches through the selected text. This feature can be a real time saver.*

(When finished searching through a section, Word politely asks you via a dialog box whether you want to continue searching through the rest of the document.)

Match Case Do you need to search for a specific combination of uppercase and lowercase letters? (Word's default is that it ignores case for searches.) Specify the exact combination in the Find What box and choose this option.

Find Whole Words Only If you are looking for the word "be" you probably don't want to find the words "become," "bet," and so forth. If you choose the Find Whole Words Only option, Word will find only matches that are not part of a larger word.

Use Pattern Matching Pattern matching can be very useful once you learn Word's wildcards. For example, the * means that Word will match any number of characters (including none). If you select Use Pattern Matching and type **be*n** in the Find What text box, Word will find "ben," "between," "bean," "begin," and so on. The ? means that Word will match a single character. So type **be?n** and you will find only words like "bean" and "been."

Sounds Like If you select the Sounds Like option, Word tries to find words that sound similar to what you are looking for even if they are spelled differently. This facility isn't perfect. For example, it doesn't seem to find the variants on "two" yet. But it does work with things like "Kathy" and "Cathy" and "colour" and "color."

Format and No Formatting The Format button provides access to an advanced Search capability that allows you to search for specific paragraph formatting, fonts, foreign language entries, and paragraph styles. The No Formatting button resets advanced format search selections. This feature will make more sense after we go over character and paragraph formatting later in the book. (See Chapters 6 and 7, respectively.)

Special The selections under Special insert search strings for special characters such as paragraph marks, tabs, and others. For example if you type **it.** in the Find What box, click Special, and select Paragraph

Marks, a "^p" (that Word uses to identify paragraph marks) will be added to make the search string "it.^p". This Find command will find all paragraphs that end with "it."

Replace Often you decide to move from searching for a specific text, to replacing it with something else. Clicking on the Replace button in the Find dialog box opens the Replace dialog box (which is covered next). A good time saver is that if you click on this button, any information you typed in the Find What text box is retained so that you don't have to retype it in the Replace dialog box.

EXAMPLES

1. Issue the Find command (Alt E, F or Ctrl+F) and search for occurrences of the word "Kathy" using Sounds Like by entering "cathy" in the Find dialog box and checking the Sounds Like box. Here is what the Find dialog box might look like:

2. Sounds Like is especially useful when you aren't sure how to spell the word but do know how to pronounce the word. Enter the following quote from Henry Adams:

   Philosophy: unintelligible answers to insoluble problems.

   Now suppose you can't remember how to spell the word "philosophy" but remember how it is pronounced (filosofy). If you enter "filosofy" into the Find What dialog box and check off the Sounds Like feature, Word will find the word "philosophy."

3. Issue the Find command (Alt E, F or Ctrl+F) and search for all words that begin with "be" and end with "n" (including "bean," "between," and so on). Here's what your Find dialog box would look like.

EXERCISES

1. Close the current document you are working in and open the Gibbon quotation and use the Find command to find the word "the." Use Find Next until you reach the end of the quotation.
2. Select the Find Whole Word Only and the Match Case check boxes and repeat the find operation.
3. Enter **th*** in the Find What text box and check Use Pattern Matching, making sure the match case box is still checked.

3.5 SEARCHING FOR AND REPLACING TEXT IN YOUR DOCUMENTS

Word's replace facility nicely complements the search (find) facility; that's why the designers put the Replace button in the Find dialog box. Use Find when you want to move to a specific area in your document;

use Replace when you want to make changes. Most of the possible ways you have seen to search through your document are also available for "search and replace" operations.

To start the replacing process, you need to bring up the Replace dialog box shown here. You can do this by choosing Replace from the Edit menu (Alt E, E) or by pressing Ctrl+H.

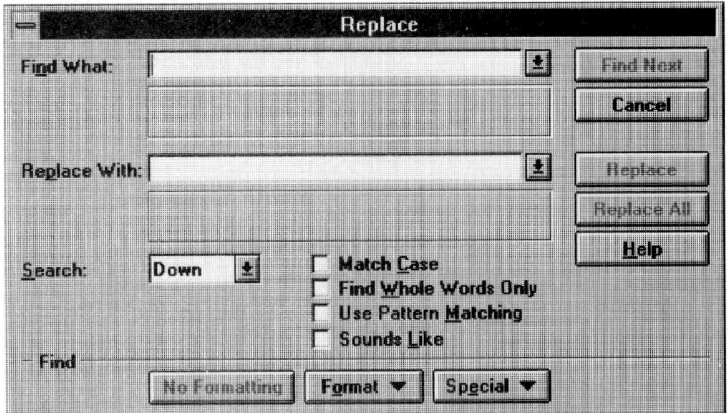

The basic method of replacing text is simple and is much like the process for finding text.

1. Type the text you want to find in the Find What text box.
2. Type what you want to replace it with in the Replace With text box.

Now you have to choose: do you want to think about each change or do you want to make multiple changes at once?

If you click on Replace All, Word will look for and change *every* occurrence of the text listed under Find What. Luckily, if you inadvertently choose this option, you can undo it by choosing Undo from the Edit menu if you change your mind soon enough.

On the other hand, if you click on the Find Next button, Word looks for the next occurrence of the text. If it finds one, click on the Replace button to change that text. If you click on Find Next, Word searches for the next occurrence of the text. Click on Cancel to close the Replace dialog box.

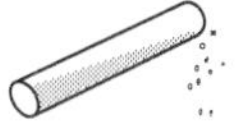

NOTE *As with the Find dialog box, you can also edit your document while the Replace dialog box is open. Drag the title bar as discussed with the Find box.*

Finally, the options like Match Case and Find Whole Words Only work as they do in the Find dialog box, as discussed earlier.

EXAMPLES

1. Suppose you wanted to replace all occurrences of "Abe Lincoln" with "Honest Abe." Here's what the Replace dialog box would look like. Now click where the mouse pointer is.

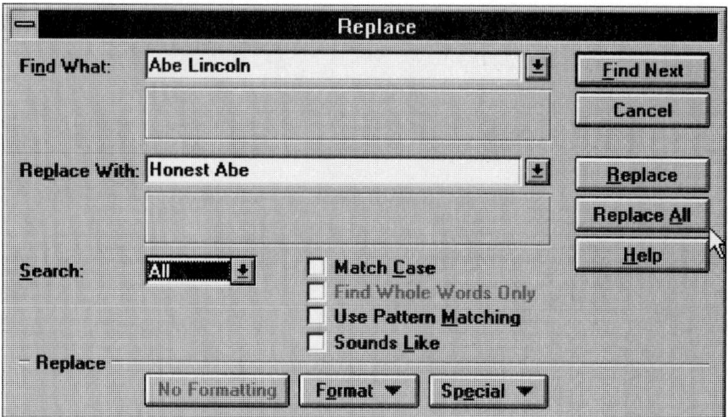

2. Here's what the Replace dialog box would look like if you wanted to replace all occurrences of words that sound like "Cathy" with "Kathy."

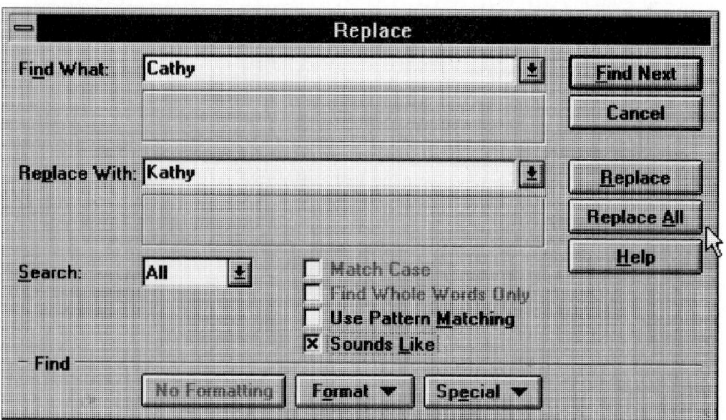

EXERCISES

1. The desktop publishing folks just called and they can only accept paragraphs with sentences that end in a period followed by one space (or a period followed by two spaces—whichever one you didn't do)! Make the corrections to your Gibbon quote.
2. Count the number of "the's" by using the Replace feature. Uncheck Use Pattern Matching, check Find Whole Words Only, and enter **the** in the Find What text box. Enter **the** in the Replace With text box, and select Replace All. How many words were "replaced"? Make the replace case sensitive and count the number of "the's" again.
3. Challenge Yourself! Make each sentence its own paragraph (i.e., add a "hard return" after each period). If some of your sentences begin with spaces or don't end with periods, undo the changes and try again.

mastery skills check

1. Using the keyboard only, move to the end, beginning, and middle of BIGDOC.DOC. [3.1]
2. Using only the mouse, move to the end, beginning, and middle of BIGDOC.DOC. [3.1]
3. Move to the middle of the document and enter the following text exactly as is (complete with typos). [3.1]

   Laugh and the world laughs with you; Weep, and you weep alone; For the sad old earth must borrow it's mirth; But has trouble enough of it's own.
   Ella W. Willcox, "Solitude"

4. Using the keyboard and the Clipboard, move a copy of the Wilcox quote to the beginning of BIGDOC. [3.2, 3.3]
5. Using drag and drop, make another copy of the Wilcox quote at the beginning of the document. [3.3]

6. Change all occurrences of "Willcox" to "Wilcox" using the Replace feature [3.5].
7. Move the Wilcox quote from the middle of BIGDOC.DOC to the Spike. [3.3]
8. Exit Word, discarding all changes to BIGDOC.DOC. [1.3]
9. Challenge Yourself! Use the Replace feature on the Wilcox quotation and add a paragraph mark after each semicolon. (If some of the lines begin with a space, undo the changes and try again.) [3.5]

cumulative skills check

1. Clear out the Spike if necessary and then add the Wilcox quote to the Spike. Close the document. [3.3, 1.3]
2. Start up a new document, enter the following: **Isn't the Spike a time saver?** [1.6, 2.1]
3. Add this to the Spike. [3.3]
4. Move to the top of the document and add the following [3.1, 2.1]:

   Gary–I thought you might like this quote:

5. Add a few blank lines after the quote and empty the Spike now. You should now have another copy of the Wilcox quote followed by a note to Gary, followed by a comment on the Spike. [3.1, 2.1, 3.3]
6. Using the Replace feature change "this quote:" to "the above quote." in the appropriate copy of the note. [3.5]
7. Undo the just completed change and then use drag and drop to move the note before the quote. [3.3]
8. Undo the just completed change and then use the Clipboard to move the note before the quote. [3.3]
9. Select the word "Gary" and replace it with "Vicki". [3.2]
10. Save the document as WILCOX1 and exit Word. [2.3, 1.3]

4

Wizards

chapter objectives

After completing this chapter, you will know how to

4.1 Define what a Wizard is

4.2 Use the Award Wizard

4.3 Use the Agenda Wizard

4.4 Use the Calendar Wizard

4.5 Use the Letter Wizard

4.6 Use the Resume Wizard

4.7 Use the Memo Wizard

4.8 Use the Fax Cover Sheet Wizard

After completing this chapter, you will be able to use some of Microsoft's most advanced wizardry—called, naturally enough *Wizards*—to create common documents easily and efficiently. A Wizard guides you through the process of creating a document. When using a Wizard you'll find it easy to produce awards, agendas, calendars, resumes, and memos by a sort of "paint-by-numbers" approach to document construction.

NOTE *Once you are comfortable with one or two of the Wizards, you'll find they all work similarly. For this reason, we only cover a few of them in any depth here.*

1. Start Word and open an existing document. [1.2, 2.4]
2. Select Print Preview from the File menu (Alt F, V) to see what the document will look like when printed. [2.5]
3. Using the Print option on the File menu, print the first two pages of BIGDOC.DOC. [2.5]

4. Click on the Print button on the standard toolbar to start printing BIGDOC. Be sure to cancel the print job unless you really want the whole document printed. [2.5]
5. Using the Find command, search BIGDOC.DOC for the word "printer." [3.4]
6. Open PRINTERS.WRI from your \WINDOWS directory. Search for the name of your printer. Close PRINTERS.WRI. [2.4, 3.4]
7. Close BIGDOC.DOC. [1.6]

4.1 WHAT IS A WIZARD?

As software gets more powerful, it often seems harder to get it to do what *you* want. The manuals get longer, the available features grow and grow until the program seems to be almost impossible to master. (There's even a buzzword for this disease; it's called *creeping feature-itus.*) Now, some users just throw up their hands and say loudly, "Get us a Volkswagen, there are just too many bells and whistles in this car." However, a far better solution than forgoing powerful programs is to use a powerful program whose designers made that program's features easy to use.

Microsoft took a great leap forward in making their ever more powerful products easier to use when they introduced Wizards. *Wizards* guide you through the process of document creation by asking you questions using a series of dialog boxes. After you have answered the questions by filling in the dialog boxes, all the complex formatting needed to produce a professional-looking document is done automatically.

Word comes with ten Wizards for everything from making an agenda for a meeting to creating a resume. You'll see seven of the Wizards in this chapter; two others (for tables and newsletters) are covered in Chapters 10 and 13. (The tenth is for use in preparing certain legal documents.)

To start a Wizard:

1. Choose New from the File menu. (Close any documents that you are no longer working on to save memory. Also you cannot use the New button on the Standard toolbar or the Ctrl+N keyboard shortcut to initiate a Wizard.)

   You'll see this dialog box:

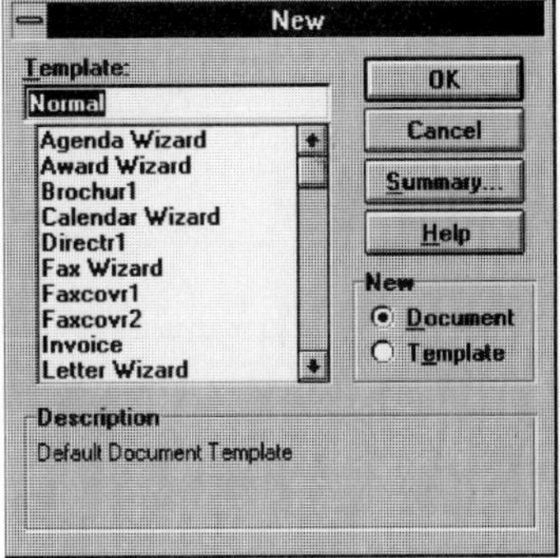

2. Scroll through this box until you get to the Wizard you want.
3. Make sure the Document button under new is selected and click on OK.

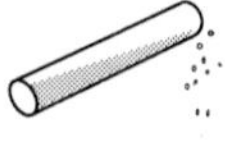

NOTE *If, after you create a Wizard, your screen looks a little unfamiliar, don't worry. What has happened is that Word has changed to Page Layout view, a more realistic way to view your document. As mentioned in Chapter 2, Page Layout view is no different than Normal view (the default) as far as editing goes.*

EXAMPLE

1. Choose New from the File menu and highlight the Award Wizard. Your screen will look like this:

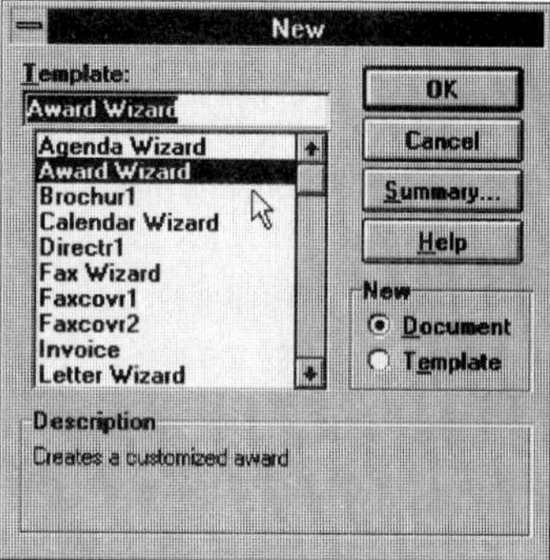

EXERCISES

1. Use Alt F, N to invoke the New dialog box.
2. Click once on the list of items in this box. Use the arrow keys to scan the list, watching the comments in the Description box. Note that some of the items on the list are identified as Wizards and others are

not. (The ones that are not are *templates*—templates are covered in Chapter 7.)

3. Close the New dialog box.
4. Use Ctrl+N to open a new document. Notice how you bypass the New dialog box displayed when you choose New from the File menu; so you cannot start a Wizard this way.
5. Close the newly created document without saving it.

4.2 USING THE AWARD WIZARD

The Award Wizard makes it easy to prepare professional-looking certificates.

TIP *Many professional print shops can handle Word files. This lets you print the award certificate on the kind of heavy paper that your own printer probably can't handle.*

After you choose the Award Wizard from the New dialog box and click on OK, you may need to wait a few seconds while Word retrieves the information it needs from your disk. Soon, however, you see the first screen of the Award Wizard. It looks like this:

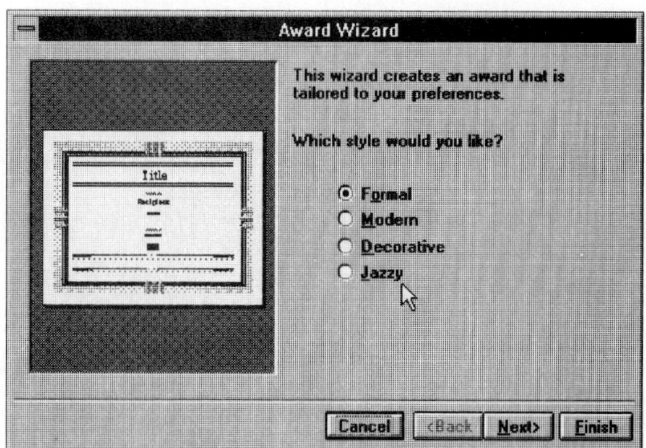

Notice the four style options: Formal, Modern, Decorative, and Jazzy. Each time you click on one of these options, the left side of the dialog box displays a capsule version of what an award certificate will look like in this style. Now:

1. Choose the style of certificate you want.
2. Click on the Next button (Alt+N is the shortcut).

This takes you to the screen shown here, which asks two questions. Again, as you make selections by clicking on one of the buttons, the capsule version of the certificate changes to reflect your new choices.

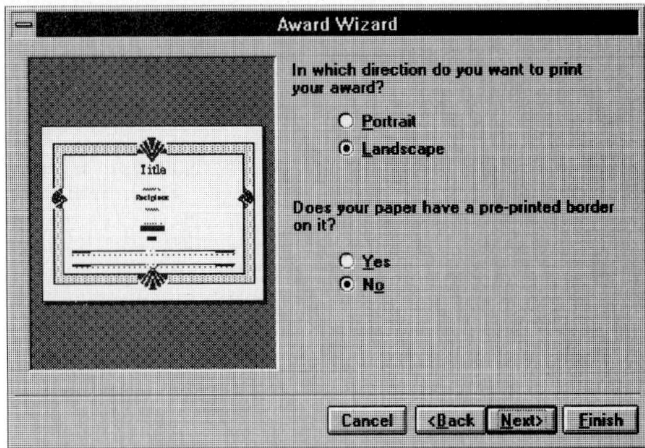

Once you've made your choices,

3. Click on the Next button. This moves you forward to the next screen, which looks like this. (When you use a Wizard, you can always click on the Back button if you need to backtrack through the dialog boxes. Click the Back button enough and you can start over from the first screen.)

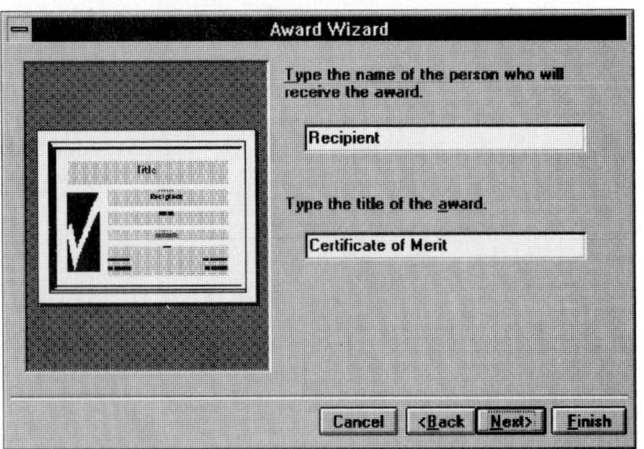

4. Fill in the name of the award recipient and the reason for the award. You can use all the Word editing techniques you have learned to fill in data when you use a Wizard. Here's an example of what your screen might look like.

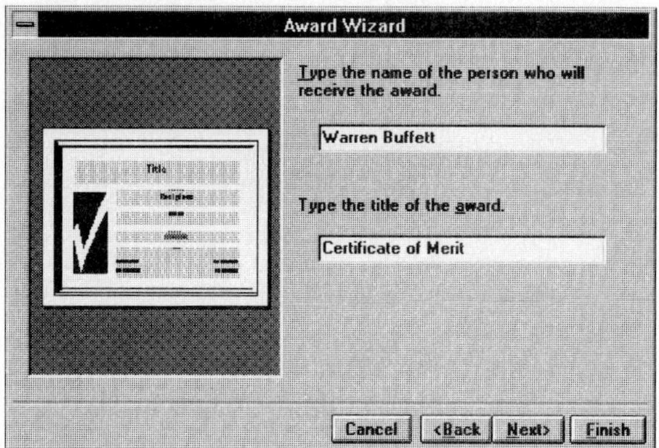

When you have completed your responses,

5. Click on the Next button (Alt+N) to move forward. This takes you to a screen for the names of the people who will sign the award. The one shown here is already filled in with a name. When you are satisfied,
6. Click on the Next button (Alt+N) to move forward.

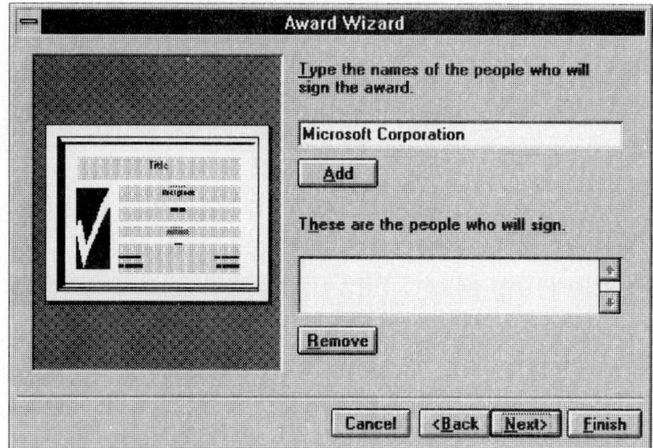

7. Fill in the name of the group presenting the award, see the following example.

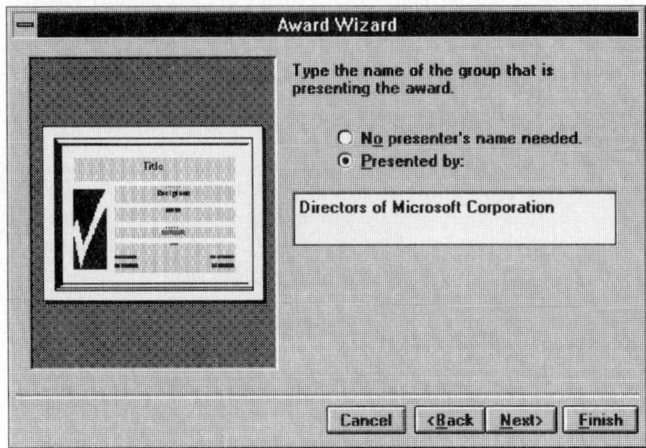

8. Click on the Next button and you are taken to a screen where you have to fill in the date and any additional information needed. Sample information is shown here.

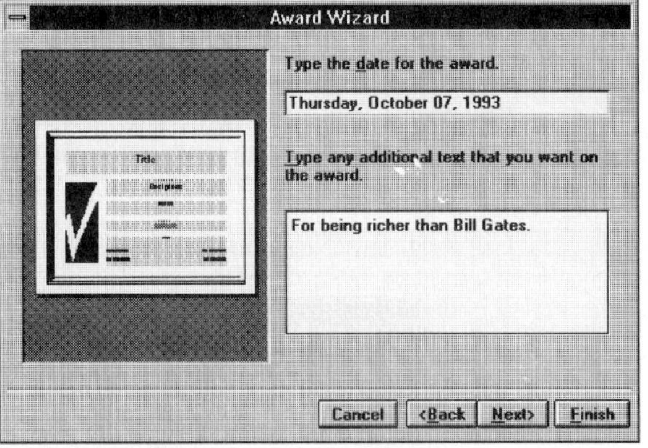

That's it. If you click on the Next button you are taken to the "finish line" screen shown in Figure 4-1. Since you will rarely want to look at the Help files when using a Wizard, why not click on the No button and then click on the Finish button. Word then works for a little while and pops up the award as a finished document. The certificate for our example is shown in Figure 4-2.

FIGURE 4-1

Typical Wizard finish line

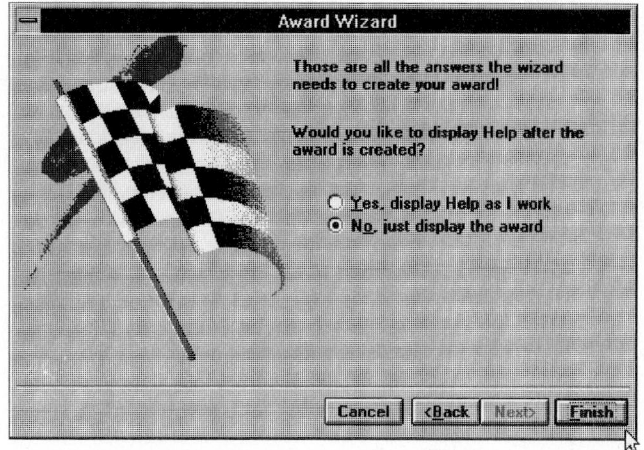

FIGURE 4-2

Completed award certificate created by the Award Wizard

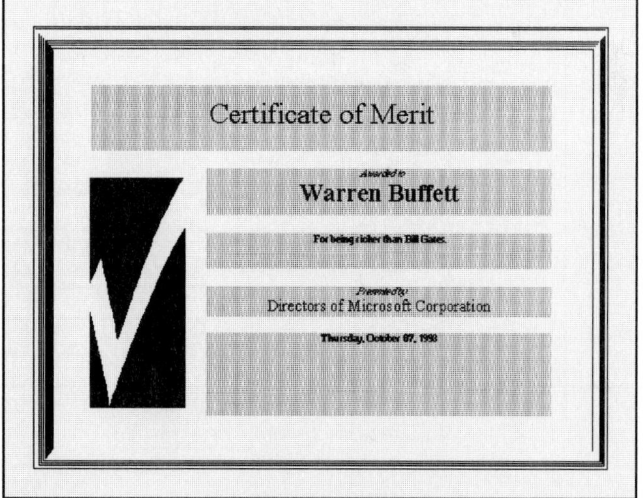

Once the award document is displayed on your screen, you can save it, modify it, print it, and use Word's editing techniques to change it in any way. It's just an ordinary Word document at this point. Except for the fact that this document was easier to create using the Wizard, it is no different than a document you created yourself!

EXAMPLE

1. Figure 4-3 is an example of a finished award certificate in the Jazzy style.

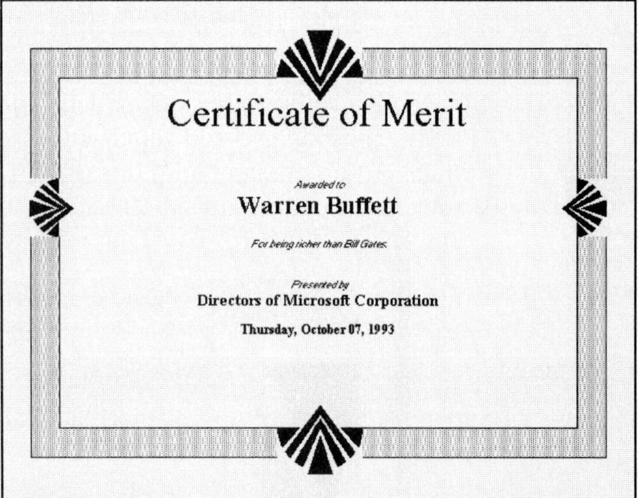

FIGURE 4-3 Completed award certificate in the Jazzy style

EXERCISES

1. Choose New from the File menu and select the Award Wizard.
2. Preview the various award styles by clicking on the buttons for Formal, Modern, Decorative, and Jazzy.
3. Create an award for a deserving person you know using something other than the Jazzy style.
4. Edit the award by changing the person's name.
5. Use the Print Preview option on the File menu to preview the award, and then print a copy of it.
6. Close the document without saving your changes.

4.3 USING THE AGENDA WIZARD

The Agenda Wizard lets you create organized agendas for your meetings. To fill out the necessary information for the Agenda Wizard, you need to know the following information:

- Which style of agenda looks best for your organization (a boxed, modern, or more traditional "standard" style)?
- When is the meeting?
- What is the main topic (title) of the meeting?
- What headings are needed to specify the type of meeting? Is it a board meeting, an ad-hoc committee meeting, and so on?
- Who is at the meeting, who is in charge, and who is taking notes?
- What additional topics are to be covered?

After you use the Agenda Wizard to fill in these questions the Wizard leaves space for the meeting notes. You can save the document prepared by the Agenda Wizard, and can then add the notes at a later date.

To start the Agenda Wizard:

1. Choose New from the File menu. (Remember to close any open documents that you are no longer working on to save memory.)
2. Choose the Agenda Wizard from New dialog box. This takes you to the screen shown here.

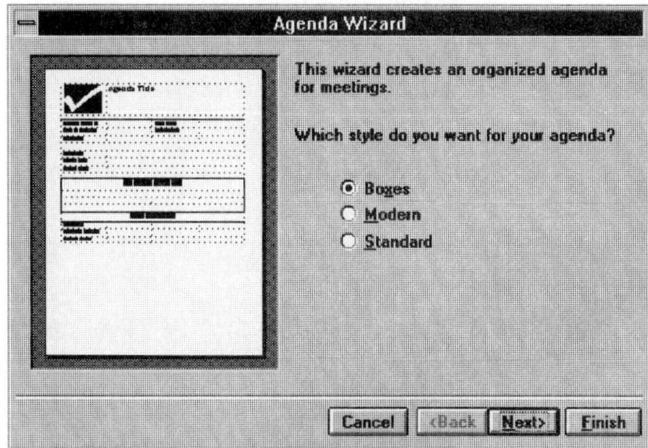

3. Choose how you want the agenda to look by clicking on one of the three style buttons shown above.
4. When you are satisfied, click on the Next button (Alt+N) in order to move on. Now, as you can see here, you need fill in the date and time for the meeting.

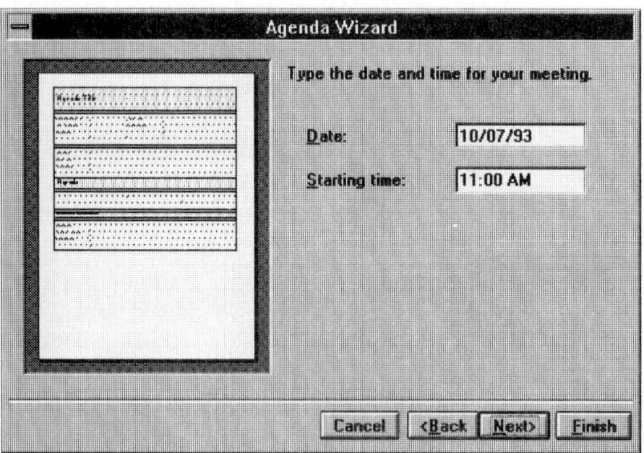

5. Click on the Next button again. This takes you to the screen shown here; provide the title and location of the meeting.

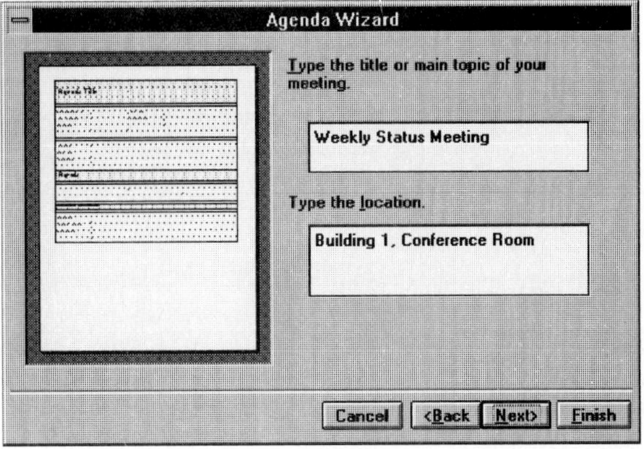

6. Click on the Next button again to move on to a screen like the one shown here. Now you have to decide what headings to include. Word gives you four choices, but you can easily customize the document after Word finishes to take into account other possibilities. Since these are check boxes (see Appendix A) rather than buttons, you can select all, some, or none of them.

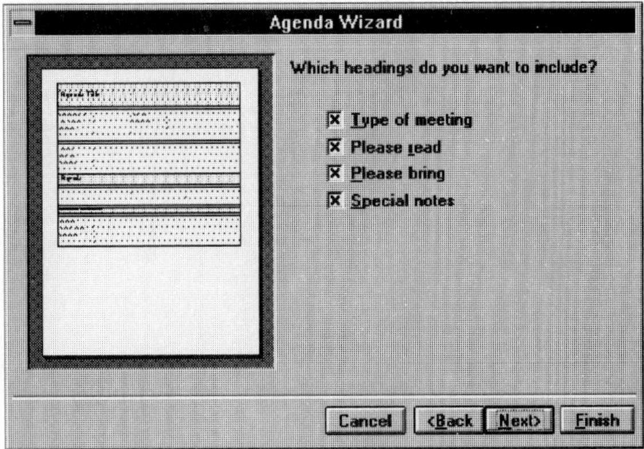

7. Click on the Next button yet again to go to a screen like this one. This screen lets you decide what names should be on the agenda.

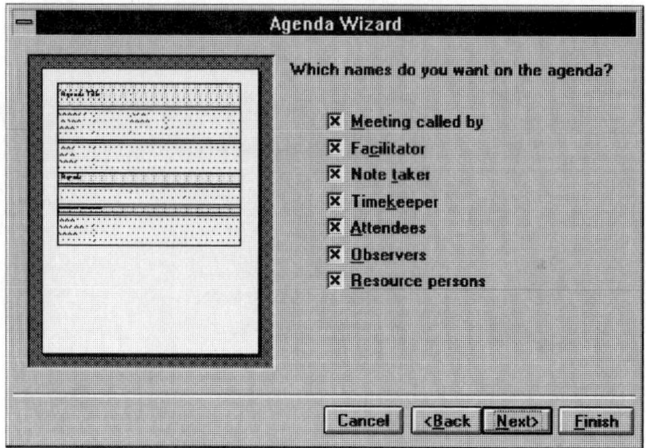

8. Again click on the Next button. This brings up a fairly complicated dialog box, an example of which is shown here, for including the agenda topics. As the Tip in the dialog box says, you move from box to box using the Tab key, or you can move the mouse pointer to a specific box and click in order to edit the contents of one of these text boxes. Clicking on the More Agenda Topics button displays an identical screen that provides room for five more topics.

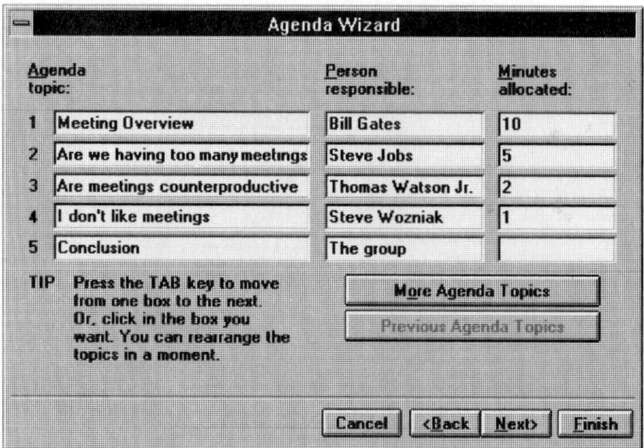

9. When you are satisfied that you have filled in the boxes correctly, click on the Next button. This displays a screen that lets you rearrange the order of topics, as shown here. To rearrange the order of topics, click on the item to be moved and then press the Move Up or Move Down button to rearrange the order as needed.

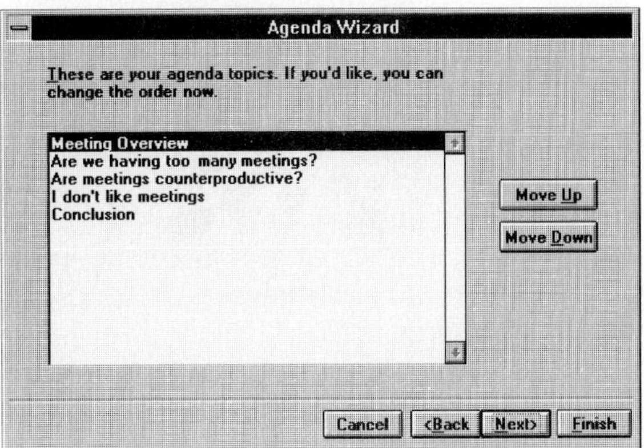

10. When you are satisfied with the order of the agenda items, click on the Next button to go to a screen like this one. This dialog box lets you add room to the agenda for note taking. Choose the Yes or No button, depending on what you want to do.

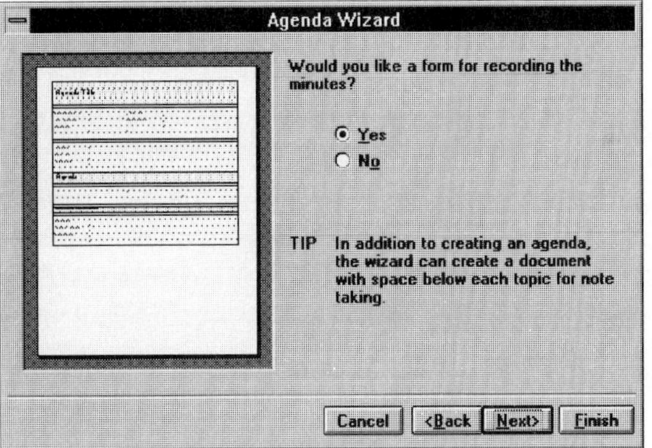

That's it. The next screen, as shown here, is the standard Wizard "finish line" screen. If you don't want to see the Help files, make sure the No button is selected and click on Finish. Word will display the finished agenda ready for editing or printing.

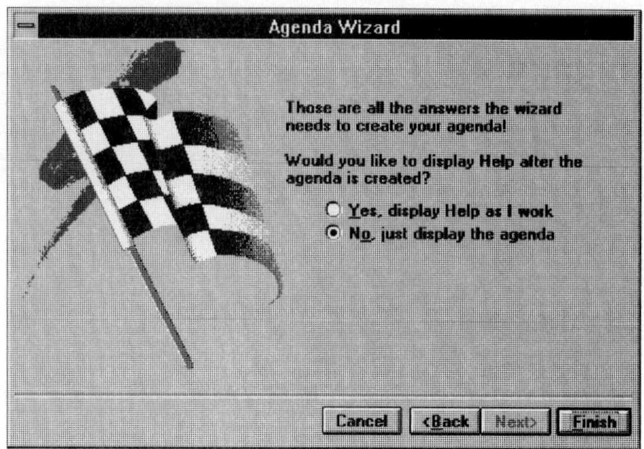

EXAMPLE

1. Figure 4-4 shows a finished agenda in the Standard style.

FIGURE 4-4

Completed agenda in the Standard style

Ad-Hoc Meeting

1/1/94
9:00 AM to 9:28 AM
Building 1, Conference Room

Meeting called by:		Note taker:	
Type of meeting:		Timekeeper:	
Facilitator:			

Attendees:	
Please read:	
Please bring:	

Agenda

1. Meeting Overview	Bill Gates	9:00-9:10 AM
2. Are we having too many meetings?	Steve Jobs	9:10-9:15 AM
3. Are meetings counterproductive?	Thomas Watson Jr.	9:15-9:17 AM
4. I don't like meetings	Steve Wozniak	9:17-9:18 AM
5. Conclusion	The group	9:18-9:28 AM

Additional Information

EXERCISES

1. Choose the New option from the File menu and select the Agenda Wizard.
2. Preview the various agenda styles by clicking on Boxes, Modern, and Standard.
3. Create an agenda for an upcoming meeting. At the end of the process, select Yes when asked if you want to see the help files.
4. Edit the agenda, changing the date and time.
5. Use the Print Preview option on the File menu to preview the agenda, and then print a copy of it.
6. Challenge Yourself! Choose Print Preview from the File menu to

preview the agenda. Experiment with the Zoom Control button shown here. (For more on Zooming see Chapter 9.)
7. Close the document without saving your changes.

4.4 USING THE CALENDAR WIZARD

The Calendar Wizard is a lot of fun because Word actually figures out which days occur on what days of the week before it makes the calendar for the month. To fill out the needed information for the Calendar Wizard, you need to know the following:

- Which style of calendar do you want? You have three choices: one with boxes and borders, one with the month in a banner on the side, and a more unrestrained Jazzy style.
- Do you want the calendar printed normally (in *portrait orientation*) or across the length of the paper (this is called *landscape orientation*)? Figure 4-5 shows a calendar in both portrait and landscape orientation.
- What are the starting and ending dates for the calendar?

Word leaves room for a picture so you can add a logo or some other decoration to the calendar if you want.

Using the Calendar Wizard is similar to using the other two Wizards you have already seen, so the discussion that follows isn't quite as detailed. To use the Calendar Wizard:

FIGURE 4-5

Calendars in portrait and landscape orientation

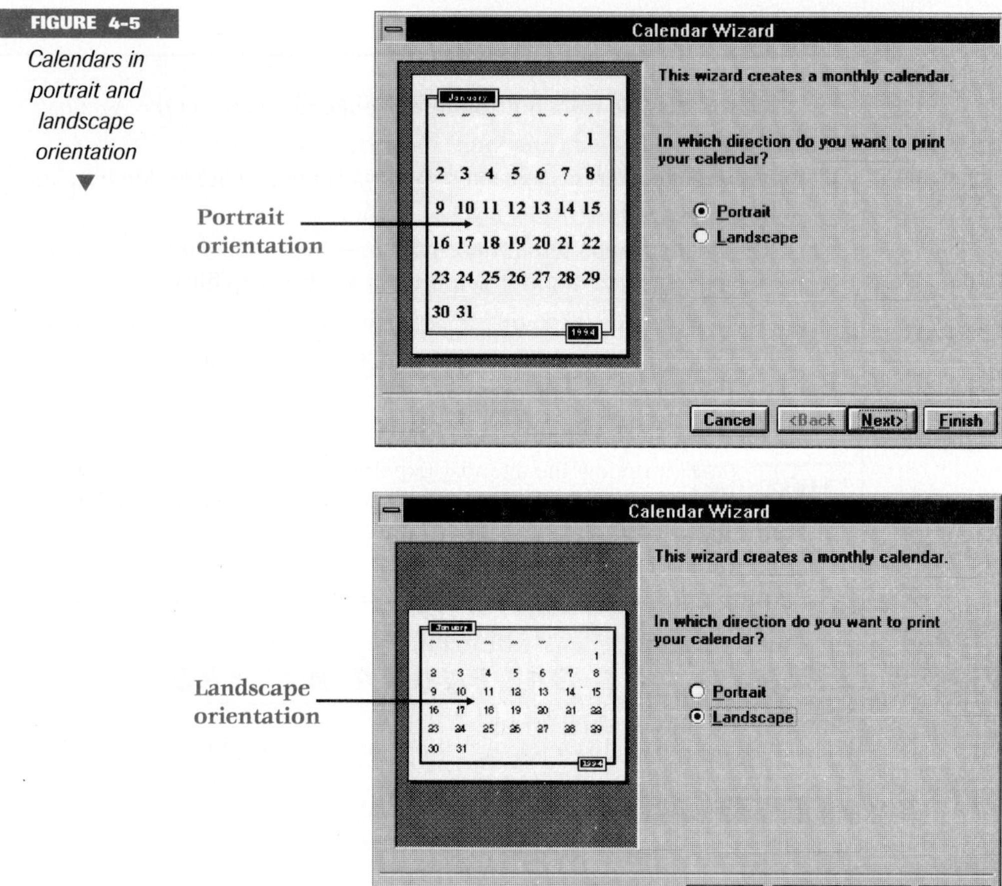

1. Choose New from the File menu. (Again, remember to close any open documents that you are no longer working on to save memory.)
2. Choose the Calendar Wizard from the list in the dialog box.

   This takes you to the first screen for the Calendar Wizard—the one that controls the orientation. It looks like Figure 4-5.
3. Choose the orientation you want by clicking one of the buttons. (As with all Wizards, the capsule version changes to reflect your choice.)

4. Now click on the Next button. Word takes you to a screen like this one that lets you choose what type of calendar you want. Make your choice among the three styles.
5. Click on the Next button when you're done. This brings up a screen which lets you leave room for a picture. (Chapter 13 describes how to add pictures to your Word documents.)

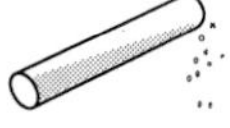

NOTE *The Jazzy style doesn't list the months by name–which some people don't like, even though they like the style of the calendar. The solution is to use the style but be prepared to go in and replace the numbered month by an abbreviation for its name when the Wizard finishes its calculations.*

6. Clicking on the Next button here displays a screen like this one, which lets you choose the calendar's starting and ending month. Click on the downward arrows to display a list of months; you may need to enter the year directly (as was done for this illustration) in order to change the 1994 default value.

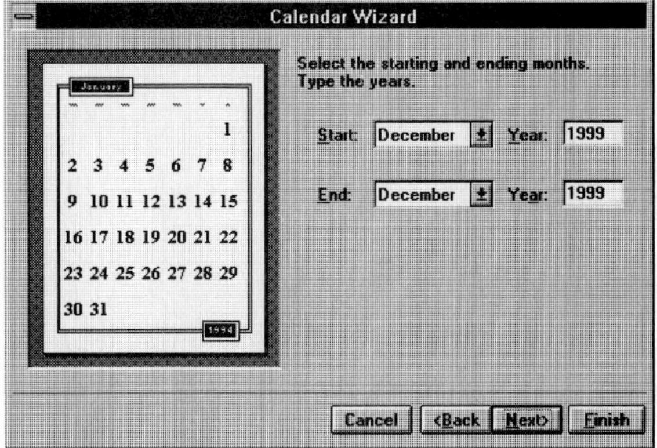

That's it. You can either click on the Finish button now or click on the Next button to see the typical Wizard "finish line" screen. In any case, after you click on the Finish button, Word takes a little time to do the necessary calculations, and then the calendar shows up in Word's document window ready for editing.

EXAMPLES

1. Figure 4-6 shows what a calendar for January 2000 will look like in the Jazzy style.

FIGURE 4-6

Jazzy calendar for January 2000

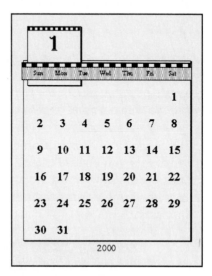

1

Sun	Mon	Tue	Wed	Thu	Fri	Sat
						1
2	3	4	5	6	7	8
9	10	11	12	13	14	15
16	17	18	19	20	21	22
23	24	25	26	27	28	29
30	31					

2000

2. Figure 4-7 shows what part of the Jazzy calendar looks like with the month abbreviated instead of numbered. This modification was done by working with the calendar in the document window.

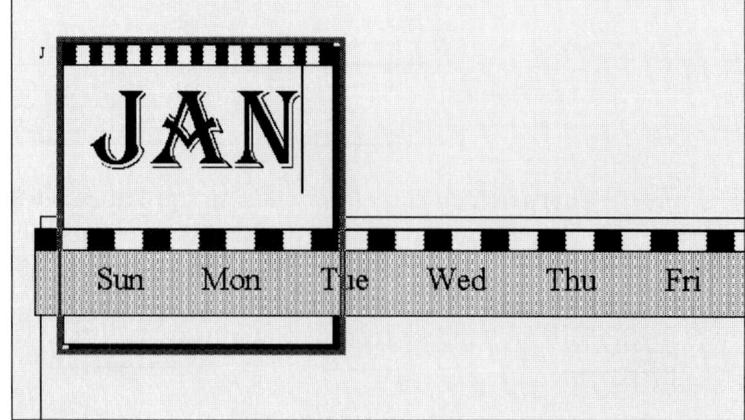

FIGURE 4-7

Jazzy calendar for January 2000 modified by hand to include month name

EXERCISES

1. Choose New from the File menu and select the Calendar Wizard.
2. Preview the various calendar styles by clicking on Boxes and border, Banner, and Jazzy.
3. Create a monthly calendar in the Jazzy style.
4. Edit the calendar and add the name of the month to it instead of the number of the month.
5. Use the Print Preview option on the File menu to preview the calendar, and then print a copy of it.
6. Save the calendar document and then close it.

4.5 USING THE LETTER WIZARD

The Letter Wizard provides dozens of possibilities. It includes over a dozen letters, written by professionals, for standard business situations. You can modify these letters for your own needs, and can print them in three ways. The letters categories include resume cover letters, collection letters, letters for cancelling an order, and lots more (including a letter to Mom!).

If you don't want to use one of the standard business letters supplied with Word, the Letter Wizard can guide you through the process of preparing a standard business letter or a personal letter. (You have to supply the text of course.) In addition to the text itself and the name and address of the recipient, you need to know the following information:

- What style do you want? Do you want a classic (block) business letter, a more contemporary look, or a typewritten look?
- Are you going to have the page number, attachments, enclosures, and so on?
- Are you using plain paper or letterhead? (Once you tell it which type of paper you're using, Word automatically adjusts the top margin accordingly.)

When you are done, Word can also prepare the envelope and the mailing label; see Chapter 14 for additional details. Otherwise, using the Letter Wizard is much like using the Wizards you have seen before.

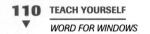

EXAMPLES

1. Figure 4-8 shows an example of what a letter to Mom looks like prepared with the Letter Wizard.

FIGURE 4-8
Letter to Mom

William Henry Gates
1 Microsoft Way
Redmond, Washington 98052

June 7, 1993

Mary Gates
1 Microsoft Way
Redmond, Washinton 98052

Dear Mom,

How are you doing? Everything is fine with me!

I'm sorry that I haven't written for a while, but I've been really busy! As you know, I really like computers, and I'm spending long hours in front of a screen both at work and at home.

In fact, I just bought a great program. It's really neat — a collection of business letters that I can customize any way I want. For example, there's a letter to people who are late paying their bills and another one that complains about a defective product.

I'm sure it'll save me a lot of time and energy — you know how hard it is for me to write letters! Now I'll be able to think about business instead of worrying about what to say in letters.

Too bad they don't have one for writing to you! Ha ha ha. They should also have one for thanking Aunt Patty for the cookies! Nah — form letters could never replace the personal touch!

Gotta run now, Mom! All my love!

2. Figure 4-9 shows what a professional-looking letter might look like.

FIGURE 4-9
A standard business letter

Microsoft Corporation
William Henry Gates
1 Microsoft Way
Redmond, Washington 98052

June 7, 1993

Mary Gates
1 Microsoft Way
Redmond, Washington 98052

Dear Mom,

Thank you for your past purchases and continuing support of Microsoft Corporation. The enclosed price list shows the prices that apply to all purchases effective Jan 1, 1994. As you can see, there have been some price increases.

Because of the current business climate, our costs have increased. We can no longer maintain all of our prices at their past levels and still continue to provide the superior quality and service that you have come to expect from us.

We value you as a customer and hope that these increases will not affect our good relationship with you.

Sincerely,

William Henry Gates

4.6 USING THE RESUME WIZARD

If you need to prepare a resume, the Resume Wizard is extremely useful. This is especially true because most businesses expect standardized resumes and, although the form may seem like a straitjacket, you escape from it at your own risk. Word can prepare four different kinds of resumes in three different styles: classic, contemporary, and elegant (classic and contemporary are the safest for most situations).

NOTE *Word may also list a CV Wizard—this is just another name for the Resume Wizard.*

Entry Level Resume An entry level resume looks like the one shown in Figure 4-10. Some job counselors suggest this as the best type of resume at the beginning of your career.

Chronological Resume The chronological resume explains what you did, and when you did it. A sample is shown in Figure 4-11. This is the standard model of resume for someone with a lot of experience.

FIGURE 4-10

Entry level resume

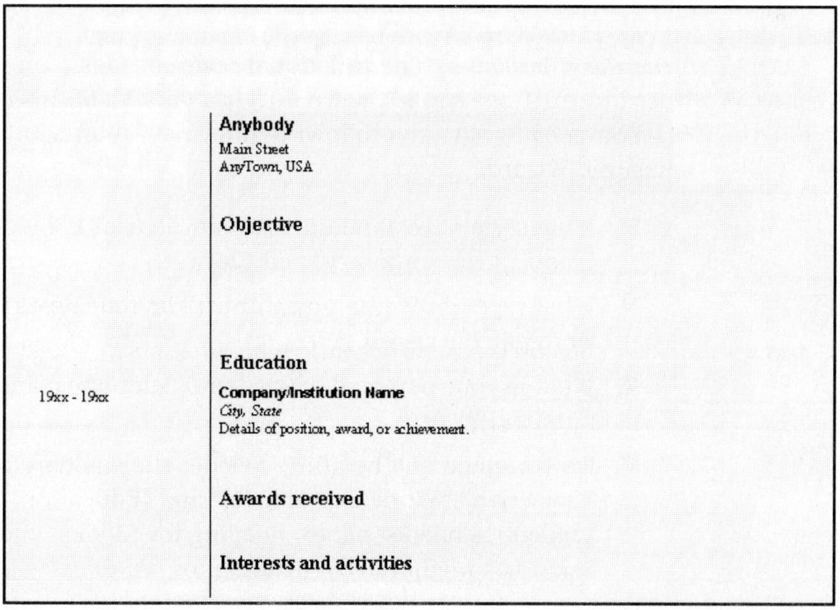

Anybody
Main Street
AnyTown, USA

Objective

Education

19xx - 19xx | **Company/Institution Name**
City, State
Details of position, award, or achievement.

Awards received

Interests and activities

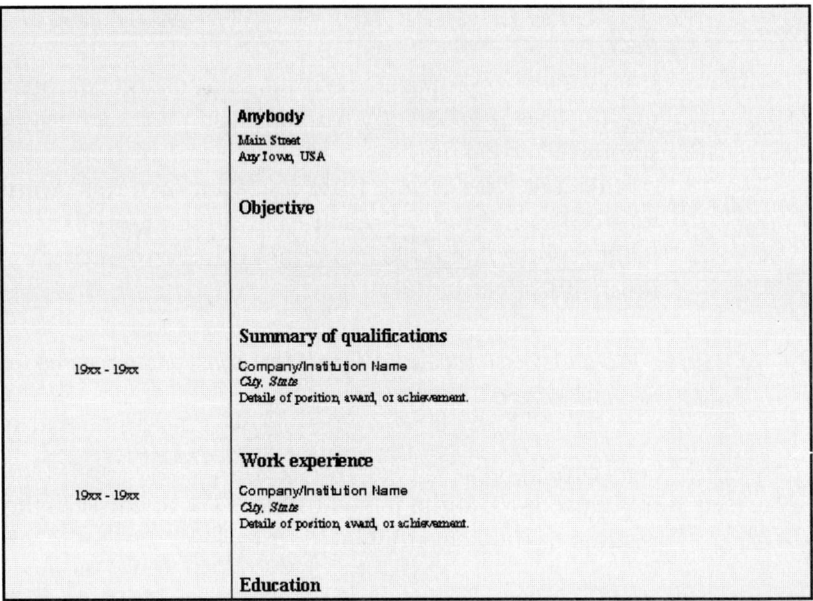

FIGURE 4-11 Chronological resume

Professional Resume Use a professional resume when degrees, books, and papers are what matters—for example, if you're a scientist or academic applying for a position. Figure 4-12 shows a sample professional resume.

Functional Resume The functional resume is less common, and is used mostly in schools. Figure 4-13 is a version of this resume.

You need to have the following information on hand to use the Resume Wizard:

- What style of resume do you want to use? (The options are Classic, Contemporary, and Elegant.)
- What type of resume you want? (The four types of resumes were just discussed.)
- What is your personal data (name, addresses, and phone numbers)?
- Do you need any headings besides the standard ones "Objective," "Work Experience," and "Education"? For example, academics need separate heading for "Books" and "Papers." Scientists might have a heading for "Patents."

FIGURE 4-12

Professional resume

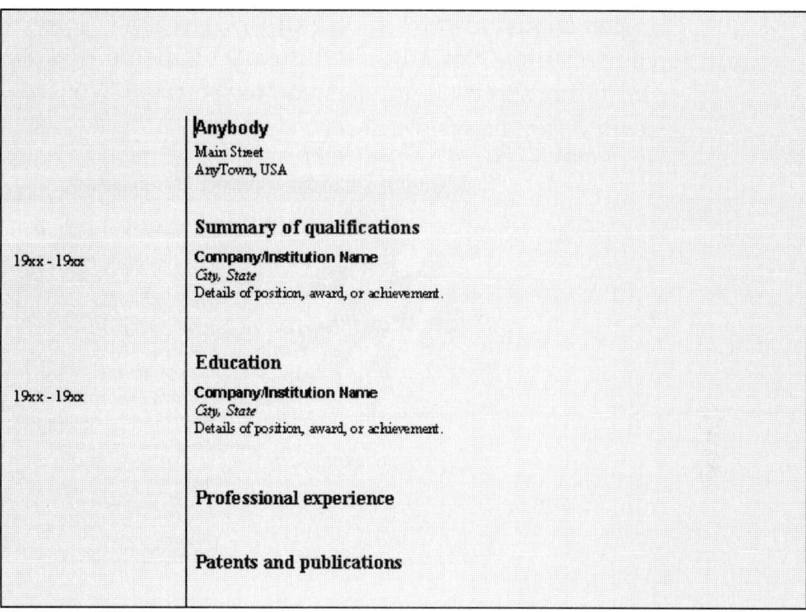

FIGURE 4-13

Functional resume

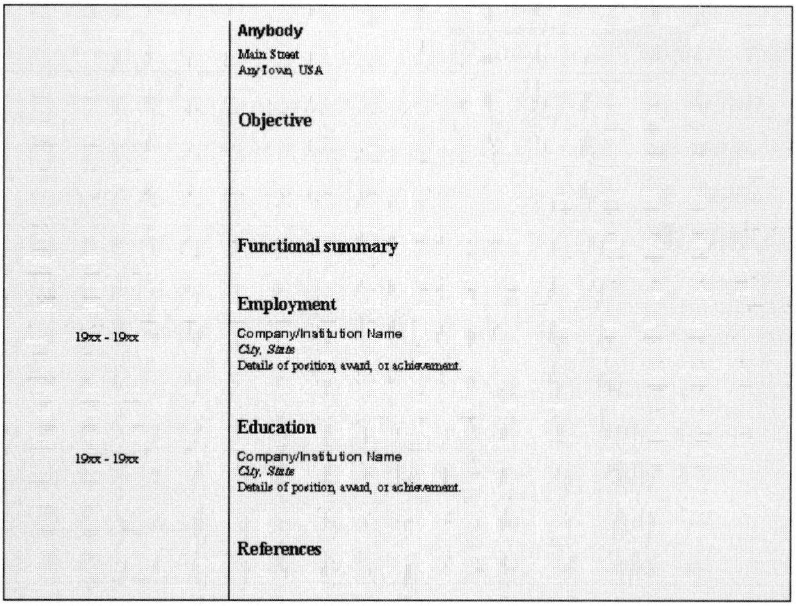

Anybody
Main Street
AnyTown, USA

Objective

Functional summary

Employment

19xx - 19xx
Company/Institution Name
City, State
Details of position, award, or achievement.

Education

19xx - 19xx
Company/Institution Name
City, State
Details of position, award, or achievement.

References

You should also work carefully on the cover letter to accompany your resume. Word makes this easy by including an option on the finish line screen that takes you to the Letter Wizard to prepare your cover letter, as shown here.

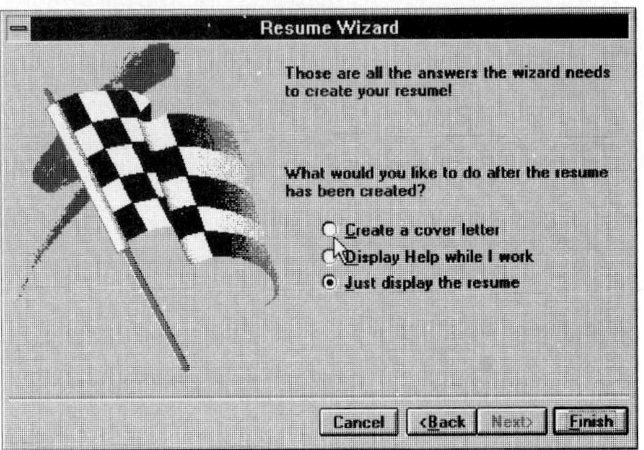

Otherwise, filling out the Resume Wizard is much like using the Wizards you have seen before.

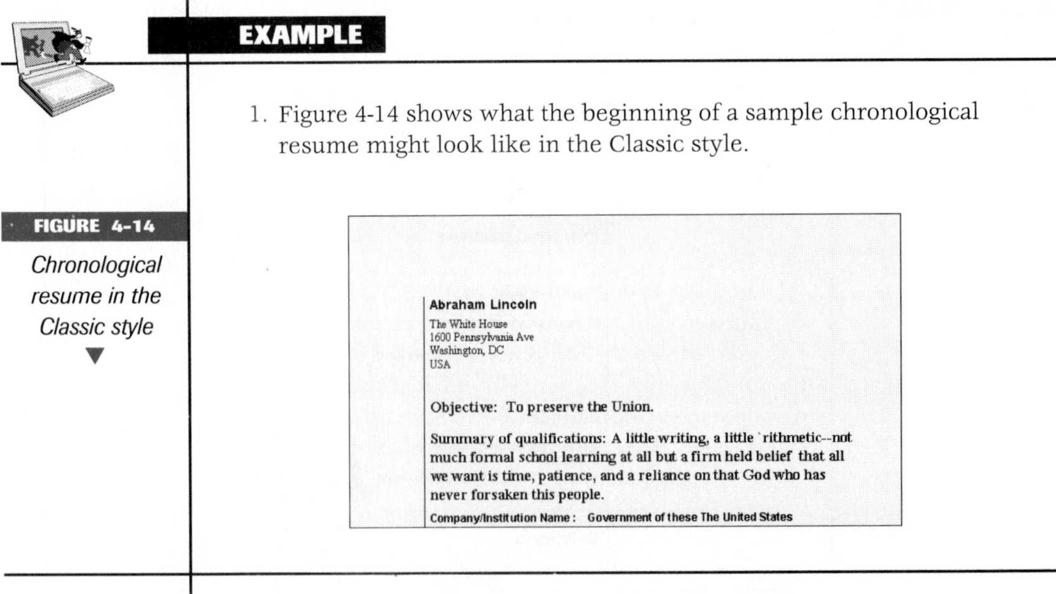

EXAMPLE

1. Figure 4-14 shows what the beginning of a sample chronological resume might look like in the Classic style.

FIGURE 4-14 *Chronological resume in the Classic style*

Abraham Lincoln
The White House
1600 Pennsylvania Ave
Washington, DC
USA

Objective: To preserve the Union.

Summary of qualifications: A little writing, a little `rithmetic--not much formal school learning at all but a firm held belief that all we want is time, patience, and a reliance on that God who has never forsaken this people.

Company/Institution Name : Government of these The United States

EXERCISES

1. Choose New from the File menu and select the Resume Wizard.
2. Preview the various resume styles by clicking on the buttons Classic, Contemporary, and Elegant.
3. Write your resume.
4. Use the Print Preview option on the File menu to preview your resume, and then print a copy of it.
5. Save a copy of your resume for later updating and close its document window.

4.7 USING THE MEMO WIZARD

Sometimes it seems that businesses float on a sea of memos. The Memo Wizard can make the task of generating memos at least somewhat less tedious. To use the Memo Wizard, you'll need to know the following information:

- What style of memo is acceptable in you company? (The available styles are Classic, Contemporary, and Typewriter.)
- What will the heading for the memo will be?
- Who is writing the memo and to whom is the memo going (this is called the *distribution list*)?
- Is the memo confidential or not?
- Will there be other items such as enclosures or attachments?

EXAMPLE

1. Figure 4-15 shows what a completed confidential memo in the classic style might look like.

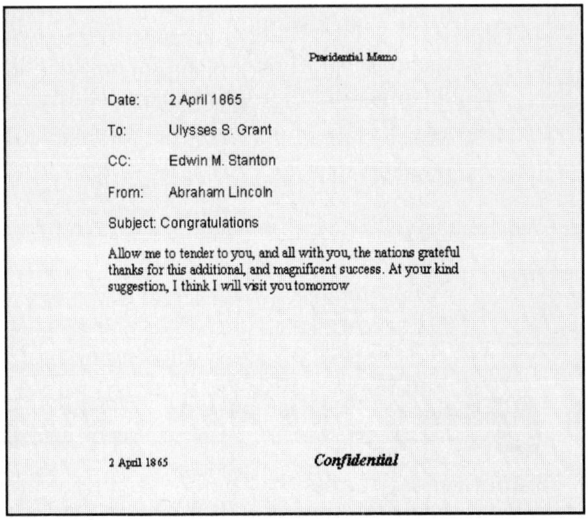

FIGURE 4-15

A confidential memo

Presidential Memo

Date: 2 April 1865

To: Ulysses S. Grant

CC: Edwin M. Stanton

From: Abraham Lincoln

Subject: Congratulations

Allow me to tender to you, and all with you, the nations grateful thanks for this additional, and magnificent success. At your kind suggestion, I think I will visit you tomorrow

2 April 1865 *Confidential*

EXERCISES

1. Choose New from the File menu and select the Memo Wizard.
2. Preview the various memo styles by clicking on the Classic, Contemporary, and Typewriter buttons.
3. Write a memo justifying 4MB more memory and a bigger hard disk for your computer.
4. Use the Print Preview option on the File menu to preview your memo, and then print a copy of it.
5. Close the memo document and save your work.

4.8 USING THE FAX WIZARD

The Fax Wizard lets you prepare a cover sheet for your fax machine or fax modem. The resulting document is one you will want to save, since it's easier to retrieve the cover sheet and enter the name of the person to whom the fax is going than to reuse the Wizard.

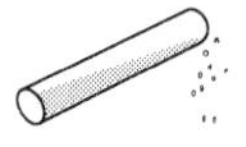

NOTE *Although Word doesn't have built-in fax capabilities, many fax programs can actually add an item to the File menu so that you can fax a document without having to leave Word.*

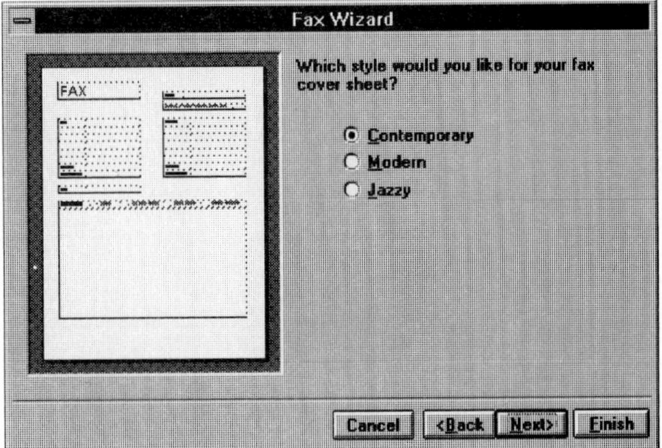

Finally, you have to decide if you want your name and address to be included. (If not, just choose Finish in the first Fax Wizard screen.)

NOTE *Fax cover sheets are almost certainly worth saving as files. In addition, if you need to print hundreds of copies of the blank cover sheet for use by a stand-alone fax machine, it is usually cheaper to photocopy them rather than use a laser printer.*

EXAMPLE

1. Figure 4-16 shows what a Jazzy cover sheet might look like.

FIGURE 4-16

A Jazzy fax cover sheet

FAX

Date 10/14/93

Number of pages including cover sheet

TO:

Phone
Fax Phone

FROM: William Henry Gates
Microsoft Corporation
1 Microsoft Way
Redmond, WA 98052

Phone 206-882-8080
Fax Phone 206-936-7329

CC:

REMARKS: ☐ Urgent ☐ For your review ☐ Reply ASAP ☐ Please Comment

EXERCISES

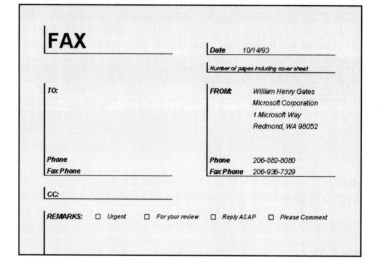

1. Choose New from the File menu and select the Fax Wizard.
2. Preview the various fax cover sheet styles by clicking on the Contemporary, Modern, and Jazzy buttons.
3. Write a fax cover sheet for your resume.
4. Use the Print Preview option on the File menu to preview your fax cover sheet, and then print a copy of it.

mastery skills check

1. Use the Letter Wizard to write a business letter to Osborne/McGraw-Hill and ask for their latest book catalog. Here's the address: [4.5]

   Osborne/McGraw-Hill
   2600 Tenth Street
   Berkeley, CA 94710

cumulative skills check

1. Create a new document. [1.6]
2. Enter text to remind yourself to update your resume once a quarter and to rewrite the resume cover letter once a month. Close the document, saving it as TICKLER.DOC. [2.1, 2.3]
3. Open your resume and update it with an entry saying that you know how to use Wizards in Word for Windows. Save your work. [2.4, 2.3]
4. Use the Fax Wizard and create a one page fax requesting the latest catalog from your favorite publishing house. [4.8]

Teach
Yourself

5

Using Word to Help Your Writing

chapter objectives

After completing this chapter you will be able to

5.1 Check the spelling in a document

5.2 Use Word's built-in Thesaurus to look up alternative words

5.3 Use Word's grammar checker

5.4 Use Word's AutoText facility

SOME people can spell; others can't. Some people have a broad vocabulary; others need help looking up alternative words. Some people's mastery of grammar is more than adequate; others need all the help they can get in writing a coherent sentence. Word's powerful writing tools—including a spell checker, a thesaurus, and a grammar checker—help to level the playing field. These tools help you concentrate on what you want to say and worry less about typos, grammatical errors, and overuse of cliches.

Finally, if you constantly reuse large blocks of text, you will see how Word's AutoText feature lets you add such *boilerplate* text easily and efficiently. AutoText complements the AutoCorrect feature you already know.

1. Enter the following text into a blank document. [2.1]

   Mickey Mouse
   c/o DisneyLand
   1 Mousehouse Way
   Anaheim, CA 99999

2. Select the previous four lines of text and copy them to the Clipboard. [3.2, 3.3]
3. Close the document containing Mickey's address, saving your work in a file named ADDR1.DOC. [2.3]
4. Use the Letter Wizard and write a business letter. Paste Mickey's address from the Clipboard when asked for the recipient's address. Enter your own address in the Sender's field. [4.5, 3.3]
5. Enter the following text into the body of the letter, mistakes and all. [2.1]

   How are you and Minnie, Goofy, and the rest oof the gang?
   I'm fine fine. I hope everything's AOK with you two to.
   See'ya soon!

6. Save your letter as MICKEY1.DOC. [2.3]

5.1 SPELL CHECKING

Word's spelling checker can do far more than catch misspellings. It will

- Report double words
- Report improper capitalization
- Memorize the first occurrence of correctly spelled words for future reference.

(As you will soon see, it can even be an incredible aid for doing crossword puzzles!)

You can check the spelling of a single word, the whole document, or any portion of the document that you have previously selected. The dialog boxes Word uses are essentially the same, so let's start with a single word.

To have Word check a single word,

1. Select the word you want to check. (For example, double-click on the word.)

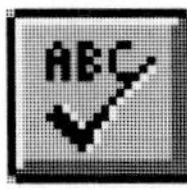

2. Choose Spelling from the Tools menu (Alt T, S, or use the shortcut key, F7). If the word is incorrectly spelled, Word pops up a dialog box like this.

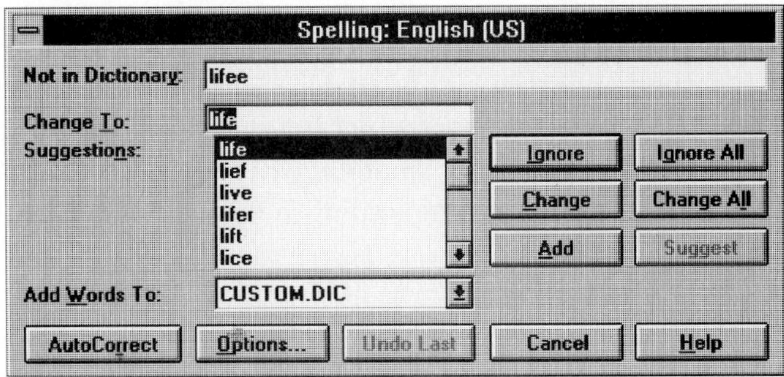

3. As you can see, the spell checker makes a suggestion as to how to spell the word. At this point, you can take one of several courses of action:

   a. If you agree with the suggestion, click on the Change button.

   b. If one of the other entries in the Suggestions box is the correct one, highlight (or click) on that one. Then click on the Change button.
   c. If none of the suggestions are right but you know the correct spelling, type it into the Change To text box and then click on the Change button.
   d. Click on Ignore if the spelling is correct.
4. Finally, click on Cancel or press Esc to close the spell checker.

When Word finishes spell checking a single word, it pops up this dialog box:

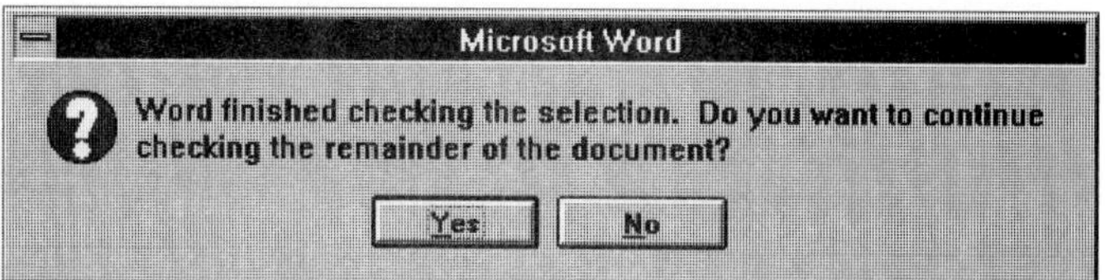

This is the same dialog box you will see when Word finishes checking any selected text. Click on Yes to continue checking the whole document.

Spell checking a larger selection of text is similar to spell checking a single word. Word will stop on each word in the selection that it doesn't recognize, displaying the Spelling dialog box you saw when checking a single word. And when Word finishes with the selection, it also asks whether you want to continue checking the rest of the document.

Many people prefer to start at the beginning of a document when spell checking an entire document. (Remember, you can just press Ctrl+Home to move quickly to the top of the document.) Otherwise, you can start spell checking anywhere in the document; in this case, when it reaches the end of the document, Word starts spell checking at the top.

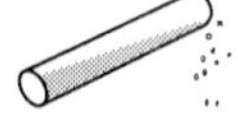

NOTE *You can always return to your document to edit it while the Spelling dialog box remains on the screen. Go to the place you want to edit, and click there. After you have finished editing, click on the Start button inside the Spelling dialog box to continue spell checking. (You can drag the Spelling dialog box around the screen if you need to–see Appendix A if you need to recall how to use this technique.)*

EXAMPLES

1. Type the following (deliberately mangled) quote from the original edition of Strunk and White's *The Elements of Style*, including spelling mistakes and duplicated words so you have something to spell check. Then use Ctrl+Home to move to the beginning of the text.

   The splling of english words is not not fixed and invariable, nor does it depend on any other authority than general greenmint.

   The first dialog box you see is this one, which picks up the mistake in "spelling" and suggests the correct spelling.

   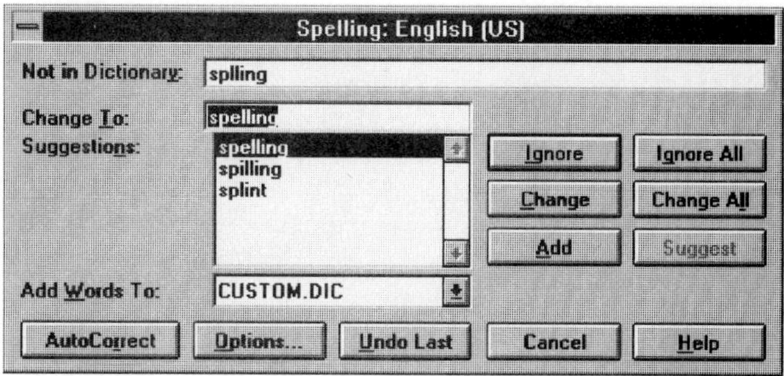

   Click on Change or use Alt+C to make the change.

2. The next dialog box you see is this one, which picks up that English (being a proper adjective as the grammarians put it) should be capitalized.

   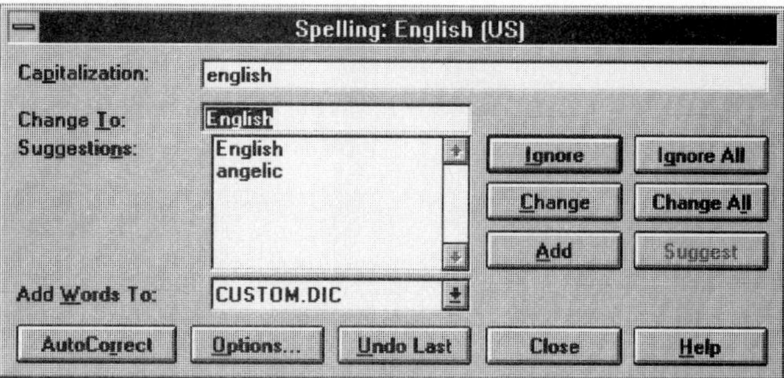

   Make the change by selecting Change and move on.

3. The next dialog box you see, shown here, is slightly different than the ordinary spell checking box. It appears whenever the spell checker detects a repeated word.

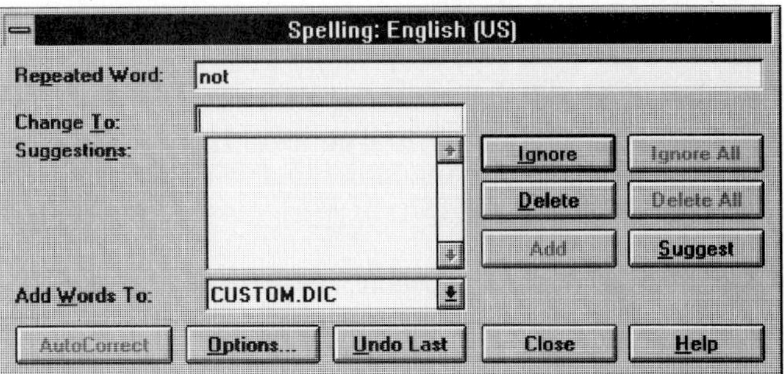

To delete the double word, click on the Delete button. Click on Ignore to retain both copies of the word.

4. Next the spell checker moves on to the word *greenmint* and pops up this dialog box.

Unfortunately, there are no suggestions. At this point, let's suppose you know how to spell the word "agreement" but actually make a typo when you enter the correct spelling in the Change To dialog box by typing **agreemnt**.

Word automatically checks whatever you enter into the Change To dialog box and pops up the following dialog box if need be.

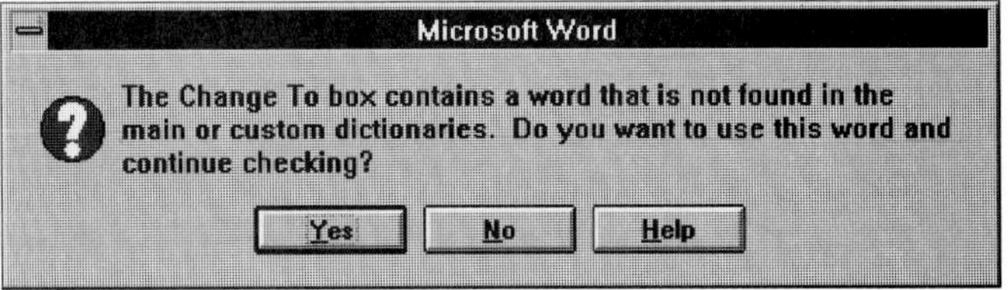

In this case, there was a mistake, so we would click on the No button to go back to the Spelling dialog box and add the "e" to agreement.

IF THE SPELL CHECKER FAILS YOU

If Word doesn't give you the correct suggestion and you don't know how to spell the word, all is not lost. You could, of course, turn to your favorite dictionary, but Word's spell checker has a nifty feature that can often solve your problems. This feature can also be a crossword puzzle solver's salvation. What you can do is have the spell checker search through Word's dictionaries using pattern matching. This means you only have to know a few letters in the word and be able to recognize it from a list. Pattern matching is done with a * when you need to match one or more characters and a ? when you want to match a single character. (These are usually called *wildcards*.)

To use this feature you must be working with a single word. So, if you are working with a larger selection or the whole document, stop the spell checker by pressing Esc or clicking on Cancel. Now:

1. Enter the portion of the word that you know how to spell correctly.
2. Insert an * inside the word each time you know you are skipping many characters; enter a **?** each time you know you are missing a single character.
3. Select the "word" you just entered, including all the wildcards, and activate the spell checker (F7).
4. Word now looks through its dictionary, finding all words that match.

EXAMPLES

1. Enter ***gr*ment**, select it, and invoke the spell checker by pressing F7. Here is what your screen will look like:

Spelling: English (US)

Not in Dictionary:	*gr*ment
Change To:	aggrandizement
Suggestions:	aggrandizement agreement disagreement disgruntlement engrossment self-aggrandizement
Add Words To:	CUSTOM.DIC

Ignore | Ignore All | Change | Change All | Add | Suggest | AutoCorrect | Options... | Undo Last | Cancel | Help

Notice that Word gives you the correct spelling of "agreement" as the second possibility. Select this and click on Change to actually correct the spelling.

2. Now you'll use both the ? and the * wildcards. Enter **c?l*y**, select it, and press F7. Here's what your screen will look like:

3. To use Word to help you with your crossword puzzles, suppose that you need to find a six-letter word with the clue:

Roll on, type on.

and what you know so far is that the first two letters are "pl" and the last two are "en." Enter **pl??en**, select it, and activate the spell checker. Your screen will look like this:

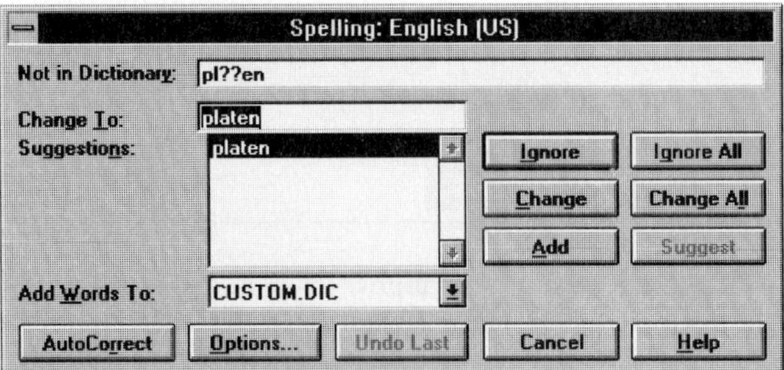

(A *platen* is the name of the roller on an old-fashioned typewriter against which the keys strike.)

OTHER OPTIONS IN THE SPELLING DIALOG BOX

You have now learned how to use the basic features of the spell checker: the Not in Dictionary text box, the Change To text box, the

Suggestions list box, and the Ignore and Change/Delete buttons. (The Delete button appears if you have a double word or if the Change To box is empty.) Here are short descriptions of the other spell checking features that you may want to take advantage of.

The Add Words To Drop-Down List Box Word can use special dictionaries, called *custom dictionaries*, that contain specialized words common to specific fields such as medicine, law, and so on. As you use Word, you will start building up your own custom dictionaries of words—such as people's names and product names—that are not in Word's standard vocabulary. See the next section for more information on custom dictionaries.

The Ignore All Button and the Add Button If you click on the Ignore All button when the spell checker has stopped on a word, Word will no longer question that word for the rest of the current Word session. Once you exit Word, these words are forgotten. If you add words to the CUSTOM.DIC file by clicking on the Add button, however, Word will remember them for future sessions as well. (Custom dictionaries are discussed later in this chapter.)

The Start Button The Start button only appears when you deactivate the Spelling dialog box to make a change in the document. Click on Start to resume the spell check.

The Change All and Delete All Buttons Use the Change All and Delete All buttons when you know that the mistake may occur again in the selection or in the document. When you click on the Change All button, Word changes every instance of the word in the Not In Dictionary box to the word in the Change To box. If the Change To box is empty, the name of the button changes to Delete All. Clicking on this button deletes all instances of the selected word in the document or selection. You can use the Undo Last button if you click on one of these buttons by mistake.

The AutoCorrect Button Clicking on the AutoCorrect button adds the selected word to the AutoCorrect list, which you learned about in Chapter 2. This is a good way to build up your own AutoCorrect list to reflect your own spelling patterns.

The Options Button Clicking on the Options button displays a dialog box in which you can specify the rules that Word uses to check spelling. This is the Spelling tab in the Options dialog box, which is covered in the next section.

The Undo Last Button The Undo Last button is the equivalent, during spell checking, of clicking on the Undo button on the standard toolbar. You can reverse the last five actions made during the current spell check.

The Cancel and Close Buttons The Cancel or Close button either cancels or closes the Spelling dialog box. The button's name changes to Close from Cancel after you make a change in the document.

THE SPELLING TAB IN THE OPTIONS DIALOG BOX

The Spelling tab in the Options dialog box shown in Figure 5-1 pops up when you click on Options while spell checking a document. You can also open this dialog box by choosing Options from the Tools menu (Alt T, O) and then clicking on the Spelling tab. Making changes to items in this dialog box lets you affect how the spell checker works or what dictionaries it uses.

FIGURE 5-1

The Spelling tab in the Options dialog box

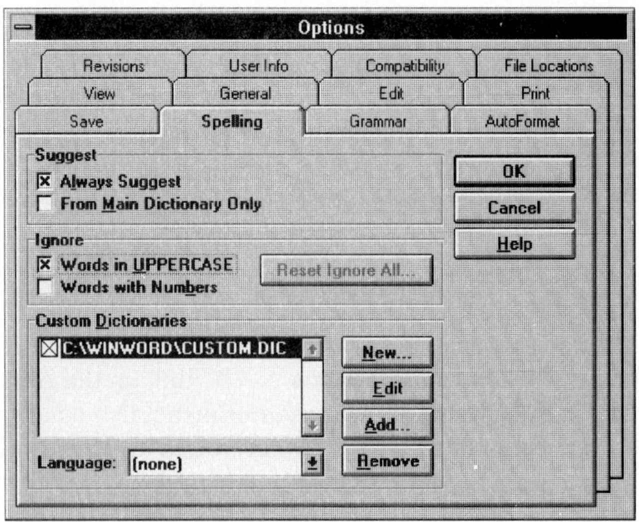

Here are short descriptions of the options available on the Spelling tab of the Options dialog box.

The Suggest Options You will almost always want the Always Suggest check box to be selected. If it is not, Word will flag misspelled words but won't make any suggestions as to how to fix them. If you are using a custom dictionary (see the next section), make sure that the From Main Dictionary Only check box is *not* selected; otherwise Word will not use the information contained in your custom dictionaries.

The Ignore Options Use the check boxes under Ignore to tell Word to ignore uppercase words (often technical terms anyway) or words that include numbers. If you have used the Ignore All button to have Word bypass specific words, you can use the Reset Ignore All button to start flagging those words again.

The Custom Dictionaries List Box You can select up to ten custom dictionaries to be used during spell checks. See the next section for more information about custom dictionaries.

EXAMPLE

1. Suppose you want to ignore words in uppercase, but check words with numbers in them. Go to the Spelling tab in the Options dialog box and make sure that the check box next to Words in UPPERCASE is not checked, but that the box for Words with Numbers is.

WORKING WITH CUSTOM DICTIONARIES

Word comes with an extensive general dictionary. However, many words that you use frequently may not be in that dictionary. For example, you can hardly expect Word's general dictionary to know many names or technical terms. By using a custom dictionary you prevent Word from stopping repeatedly on correctly spelled names and technical terms (besides finding them and making suggestions *if* they are misspelled). This increases not only the accuracy but the speed of the spelling check.

You have two choices: You can create your own custom dictionary, or you can buy more specialized ones. You'll probably want to purchase a specialized dictionary if you are in medicine, law, or some other field with a specific vocabulary. The standard custom dictionary supplied with Word is called CUSTOM.DIC. Word can use up to ten custom dictionaries at any one time.

It's easy to add a word to CUSTOM.DIC. In the standard Spelling dialog box shown here, make sure CUSTOM.DIC is selected under Add Words To, and then just click on Add every time you want to add a word to CUSTOM.DIC.

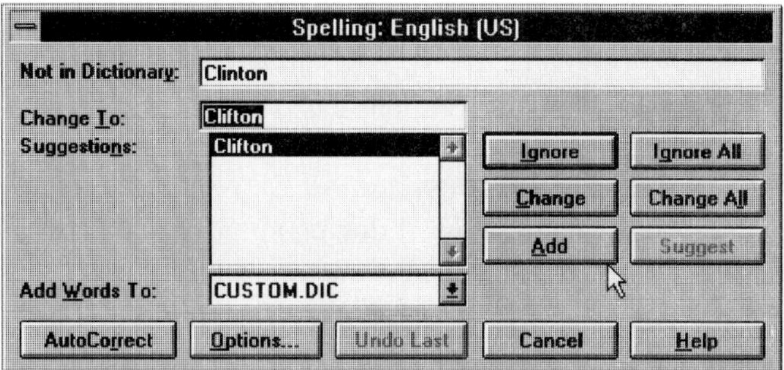

However, adding words to custom dictionaries is not enough: You also have to tell Word what dictionaries to use while spell checking your documents. (Although Word knows about the CUSTOM.DIC dictionary by default, you still must tell Word to actually use it for spelling checking.) To have Word use a custom dictionary, follow these steps:

TIP *Unless you have a very fast machine with lots of memory, don't go overboard on custom dictionaries. Using too many on most machines will slow spell checking down to a crawl.*

1. Choose Options from the Tools menu and click on the Spelling tab.
2. Make sure the From Main Dictionary Only check box is *not* selected.

3. Under Custom Dictionaries, make sure that the check boxes representing any custom dictionaries you want to use are selected and the ones you don't want to use are not selected.
4. Click on OK.

EXAMPLES

1. Suppose you have four custom dictionaries available: one for chemistry (CHEM.DIC), one for law (LAW.DIC), one for physics (PHYSICS.DIC), and the standard custom dictionary (CUSTOM.DIC). You want to tell Word to use the ordinary custom dictionary and the ones for Physics and Chemistry. You need to make the Spelling tab in the Options dialog box look like Figure 5-2.

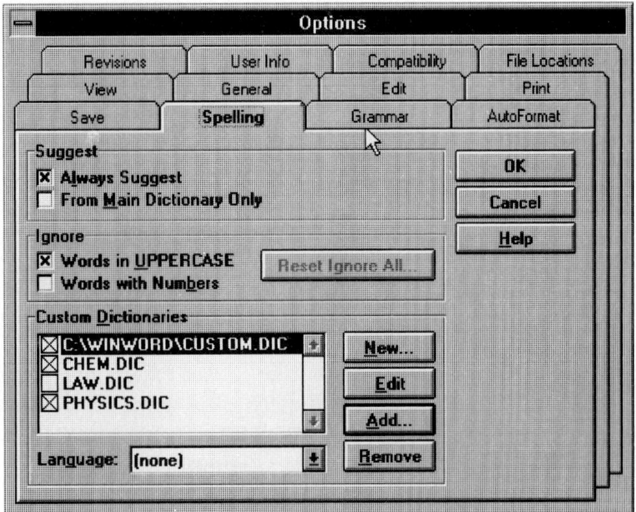

FIGURE 5-2
Adding custom dictionaries

2. Suppose you want to add a custom dictionary. Click on the Add button under Custom Dictionaries. This opens the following dialog box:

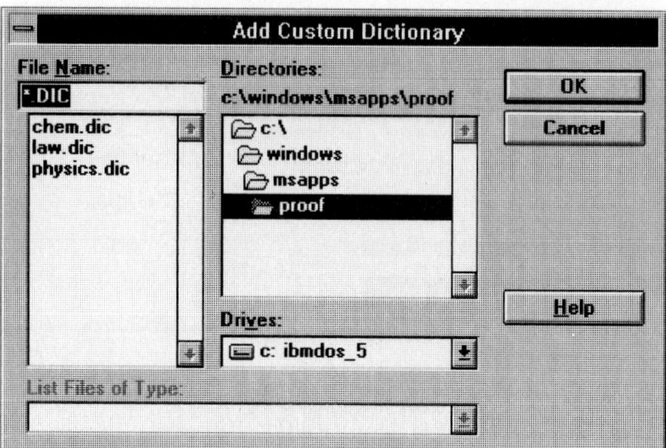

Notice the default location for custom dictionaries is the PROOF subdirectory two levels below the WINDOWS directory. Tell Word where your custom dictionary is located by making selections from the Drives and Directories list boxes, and then click on OK.

3. Click on the New button to create a custom dictionary from scratch. You'll see this dialog box:

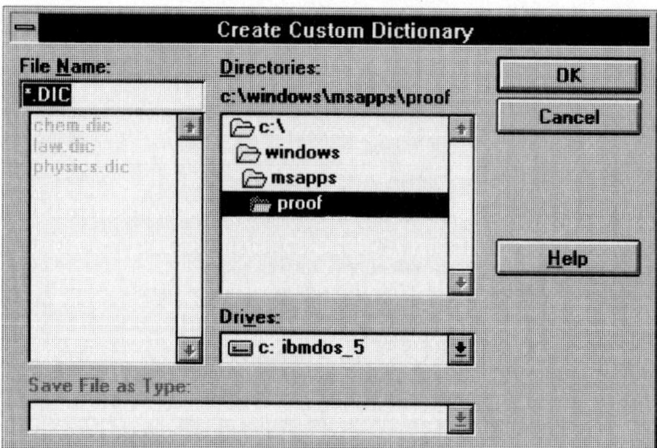

Don't bother giving an extension to name your custom dictionary. Word automatically gives these files the extension .DIC—like LAW.DIC or MED.DIC. Clicking on OK adds the custom dictionary to the list box under Custom Dictionaries on the Spelling tab in the Options dialog box.

EXERCISES

1. Load MICKEY1.DOC, which you created in the Review Skills Check at the beginning of this chapter.
2. Start spell checking the document.
3. Use Add to add to CUSTOM.DIC any words from your name and address that the speller complains about.
4. Correct the capitalization of "DisneyLand."
5. Continue the spell check by adding "Mousehouse" and "Minnie" to CUSTOM.DIC and accepting the corrections, even if they are wrong, for the balance of the text. Then exit from the spell checker.
6. Use the undo feature to remove the change of "See'ya" to "Seedy" and "AOK" to "OAK."
7. Save your work as MICKEY2.DOC

5.2 USING WORD'S THESAURUS

Using the same word over and over can make your writing seem boring and repetitive. Word's thesaurus lets you look up alternative words with similar meanings (synonyms) while you are writing. Word will usually allow you to look up opposites (antonyms) as well. To use the thesaurus, follow these steps:

1. Make sure the insertion point is within the word or simply highlight the word or phrase you want to check. (Word's thesaurus can help with some but not all phrases.)
2. Choose Thesaurus from the Tools menu (Alt T, T) or use the shortcut, Shift+F7.

This opens a dialog box like the one shown here. Let's go over the important items in this dialog box one by one.

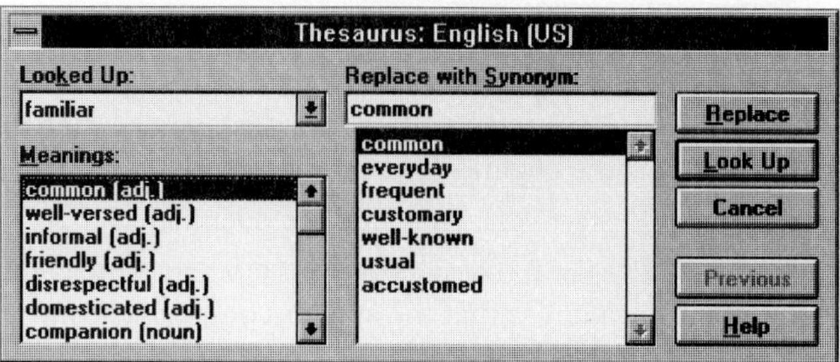

The Looked Up Drop-Down List Box The Looked Up drop-down list box contains the word or phrase you are looking up.

The Meanings List Box The Meanings list box contains many possible meanings for the word you're looking up. Since a word can have more than one meaning, you need to tell Word which possible meaning to use for its search through the thesaurus. Click on the correct meaning to display its synonyms in the list box to the right. For example, as you can see, a word like "familiar" has many possible meanings.

The Replace with Synonym Text Box In the Replace with Synonym text box, click on the word you want to replace the original text with.

The Replace Button Click on the Replace button to replace the original word or phrase with the new word or phrase.

The Look Up Button You can use the Look Up button to look up further related words. Click on this button and Word will look up the words related to the suggestion you highlighted in the Replace with Synonym list box.

EXAMPLES

1. Enter **stately** and press Shift+F7 to display the Thesaurus dialog box, which should look like this:

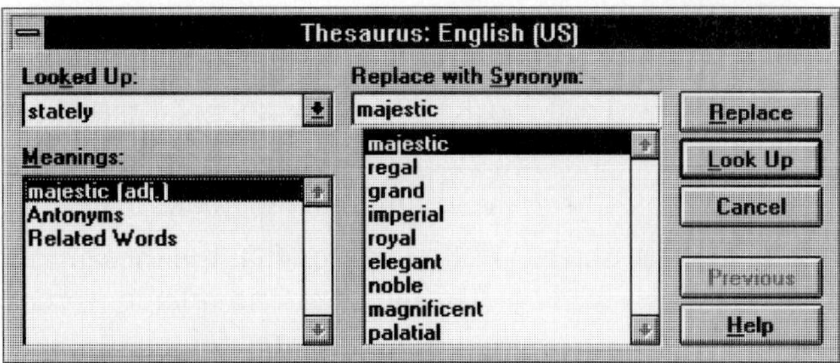

2. Click on Antonyms in the Meanings list box. The Replace with Synonym list box becomes a Replace with Antonym list box, as shown here:

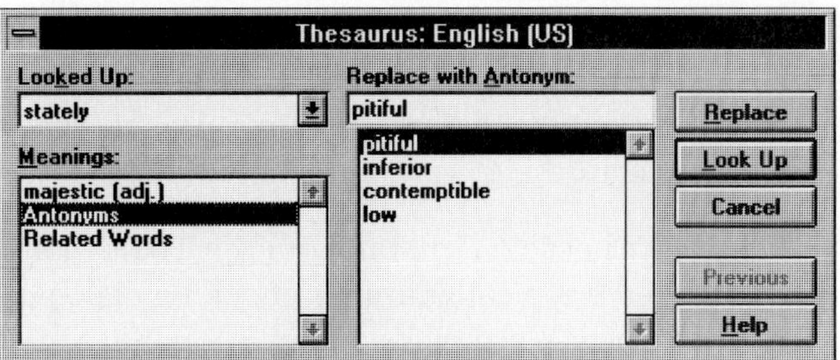

3. Finally, click on Related Words in the Meanings list box. The Replace with Antonym list box becomes a Replace with Related Word list box, as shown here:

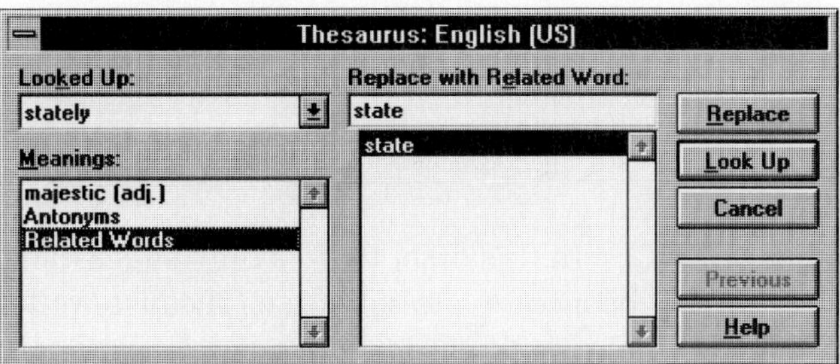

EXERCISES

1. Load MICKEY2.DOC if it's not already loaded.
2. Select the word "fine" and check the thesaurus for an alternative. Check the antonyms also. Make a substitution of your choosing.
3. Select "AOK" and see what the thesaurus proposes as alternatives. Use the Look Up button to find related words. Don't make any changes.
4. Save MICKEY2.DOC.

5.3 GRAMMAR CHECKING

Word's grammar checker is far from a cure-all. Many people prefer not to use it at all. Some people find it a useful adjunct but far from a replacement for careful proofreading. You can check part of your document or the entire document using the grammar checker.

To start the grammar checker, follow these steps:

1. Choose Grammar from the Tools menu (Alt T, G). This opens the typical grammar checking dialog box shown here. Notice how Word picks out an offending sentence.

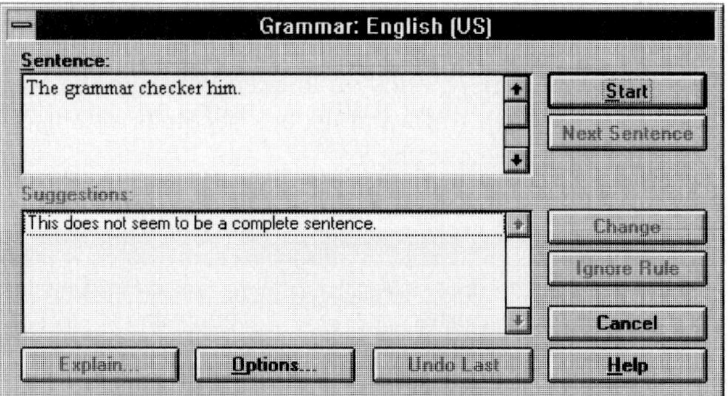

   In this case, Word's only suggestion is that this appears not to be a complete sentence (because we left out the verb "helps").

2. At this point, you click on the Ignore button to disregard Word's suggestions or on the Change button that Word activates when it has a suggestion to make.

FIGURE 5-3

The Readability Statistics message box

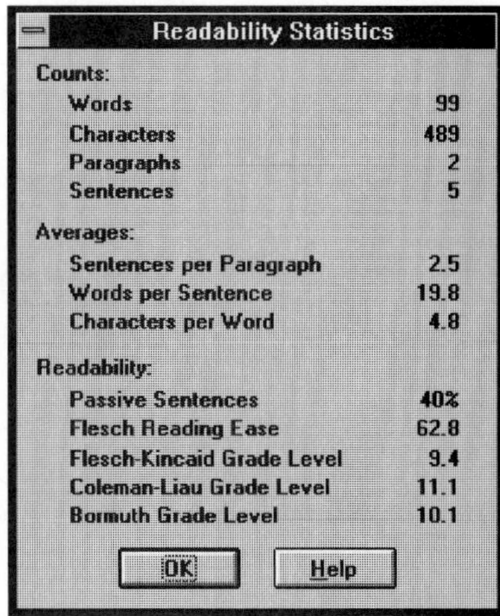

Readability Statistics
Counts:
Words 99
Characters 489
Paragraphs 2
Sentences 5
Averages:
Sentences per Paragraph 2.5
Words per Sentence 19.8
Characters per Word 4.8
Readability:
Passive Sentences 40%
Flesch Reading Ease 62.8
Flesch-Kincaid Grade Level 9.4
Coleman-Liau Grade Level 11.1
Bormuth Grade Level 10.1
OK
Help

TIP *Do not take the grammar checker's suggestions blindly. It is frequently wrong because of the complexity and many variations on the rules for English grammar. That words can have many meanings also complicates the task of a grammar checker.*

3. When Word finishes grammar checking your document, it pops up a box of "Readability Statistics," as shown in Figure 5-3. Unless you want to write like Bill Buckley, keep your grade level down to 7-10. Long sentences with obscure words make it harder to get your message across! When you're done reviewing the Readability statistics, click on OK to return to your document.

EXAMPLES

1. Here's an example of Word making a reasonable suggestion.

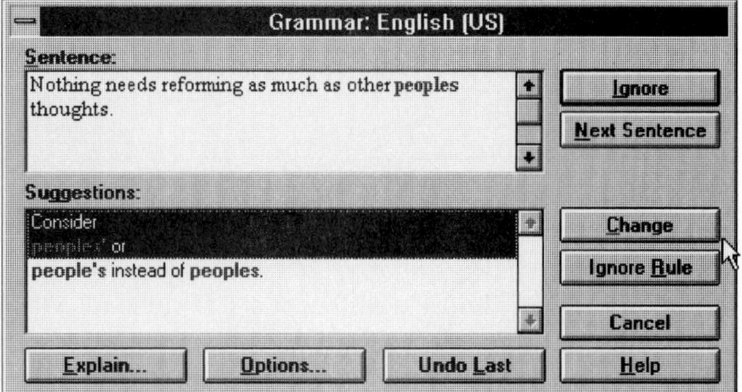

Click on change to accept this.

2. Word will also pick up on the overuse of the passive tense. (If you write "The ball was thrown by Bill." instead of "Bill threw the ball." you're using the passive tense.) Here's an example of the Grammar dialog box you'll see in this situation.

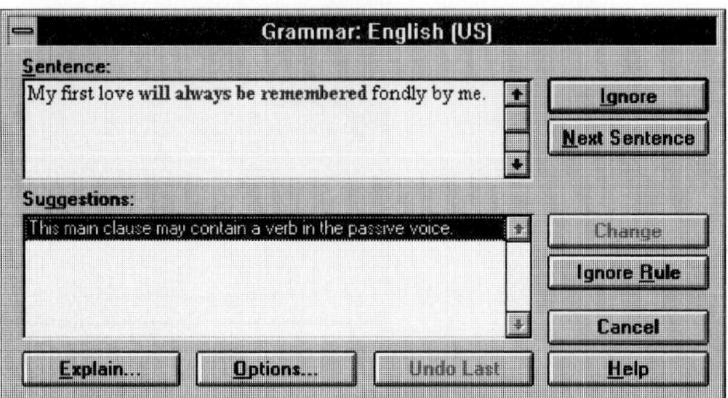

Word will also check your spelling while doing a grammar check unless you change an option on the Grammar Tab in the Options dialog box available on the Tools menu as shown here.

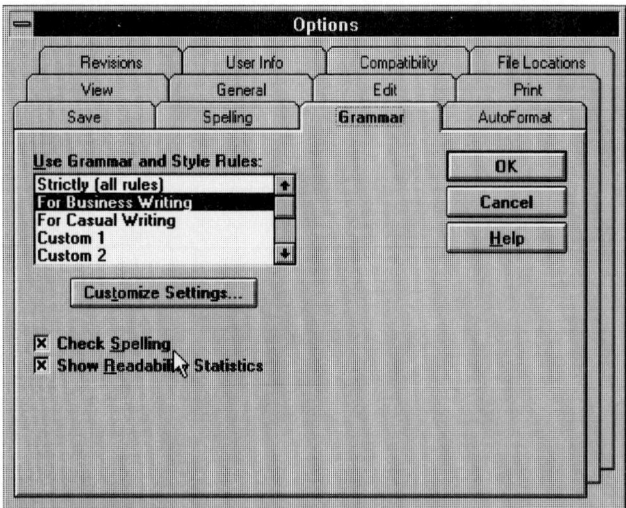

You can choose a different set of rules for Word to follow by making a different selection in the Use Grammar and Style Rules list box in this tab.

EXERCISES

1. Open MICKEY2.DOC.
2. Run the grammar checker against MICKEY2.DOC.
3. Accept the change of "I'm" to "I am."
4. Change "to" to "too" by editing the document and click on Start to restart the grammar checker.
5. Save your work in MICKEY3.DOC.
6. Undo the changes made by the grammar checker.
7. Close MICKEY3.DOC without saving your changes.
8. Challenge Yourself! Select Options from the Tools menu, choose the Grammar tab if necessary, and explore Customize Settings.

5.4 USE WORD'S AUTOTEXT FACILITY

Word's AutoText feature (called the Glossary in earlier versions of Word) is an extension of the AutoCorrect feature you have already seen. AutoText, like AutoCorrect saves you time when you need to enter text repeatedly. Use AutoText when you don't want Word to make the change automatically. Another difference between AutoText and AutoCorrect is that you can use ordinary words (which are easier to remember) for AutoText entries but you shouldn't use them for AutoCorrect entries. For example, if you created an AutoCorrect entry called **home** that inserts your address, your address will be inserted anytime you type **home**, even if you're just saying "I won't be home that night."

AutoText is extremely useful when you need to prepare different form letters for different situations or just get tired of doing something like typing your home address all the time. (This text is often called *boilerplate* text.)

To create an AutoText entry, follow these steps:

1. Type the text you want to be your boilerplate and select it.
2. Choose AutoText from the Edit menu (Alt E, X). You'll see the following dialog box:

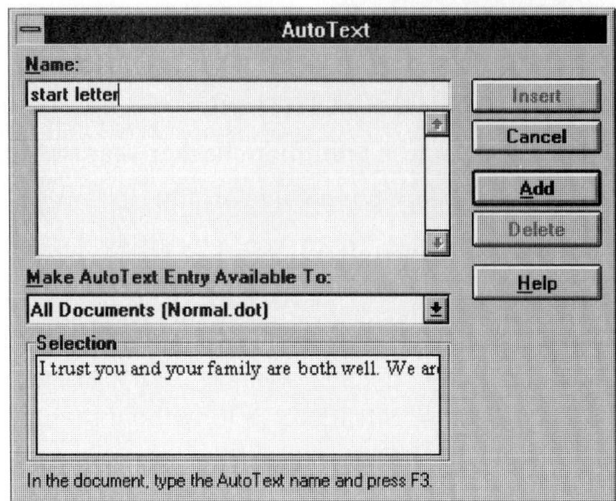

Notice how Word inserts the highlighted text in the Selection box.

3. In the Name text box, type a name for the AutoText entry or accept what Word proposes. AutoText names can be up to 32 characters long and unlike AutoCorrect entries can include spaces. The case is irrelevant. (The example above uses "start letter.")
4. Click on Add.

To insert an AutoText entry into your document, follow these steps:

1. Type the text that identifies the AutoText entry in your document. Make sure to leave spaces on either side of the AutoText name. If the AutoText name is more than a single word, make sure it is highlighted; if not, make sure the insertion point is in the text or in the space after the AutoText text.
2. Click on the AutoText button on the standard toolbar (F3 is the keyboard shortcut).

If you can't remember the AutoText entry name or what boilerplate Word has associated with the AutoText name, you will need to review your AutoText list before inserting the boilerplate. To review the AutoText entry before inserting it:

1. Choose AutoText from the Edit menu to display the AutoText dialog box. Highlight the item from the list of AutoText entries under Name and make sure that the item is what you want in the Preview box before clicking on the Insert button.

EXAMPLES

1. Since you may use the words *Home address* in your letters, you decide to create an AutoText entry for this rather than using the AutoCorrect feature. Here is what your screen might look like:

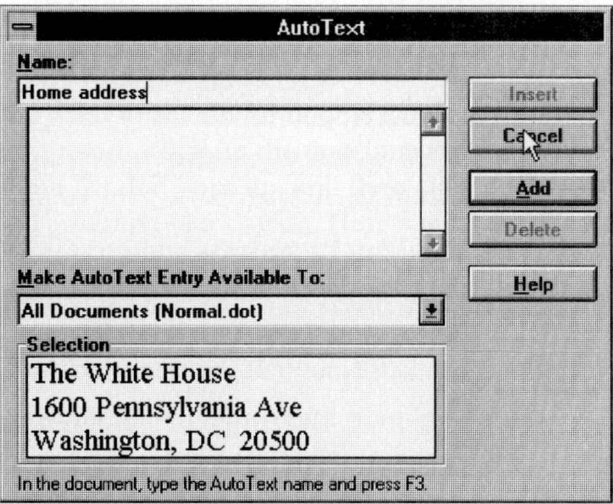

2. To change an AutoText entry, highlight the new text (a new address perhaps) and choose AutoText from the Edit menu. Then choose the item you want to change and click on Add. Word pops up this dialog box:

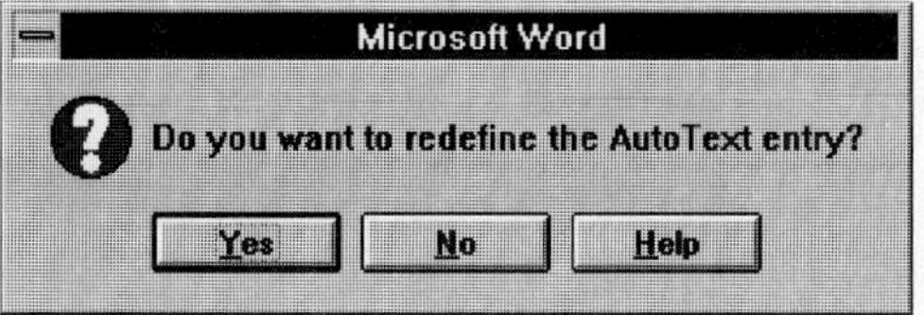

Choose Yes to replace the old AutoText entry with the new text you've selected.

EXERCISES

1. Open MICKEY3.DOC.
2. Highlight your name and address and choose AutoText from the Edit menu.
3. Add your address as an AutoText entry with the name **MyAddress**.
4. Highlight Mickey's address and select AutoText from the Edit menu.
5. Add Mickey's address as **Micks Address**.
6. Close MICKEY3.DOC and create a new blank document.
7. Type **myaddress** (with the spaces around it) and press F3. (Notice that capitalization for AutoText entries is irrelevant.)
8. Type **micks address** and press F3. (Note that this won't work because this AutoText entry is not a single word.)
9. Select AutoText from the Edit menu and select Micks Address from the list. Note that the text "mickey's address" was not replaced.
10. Highlight the words "micks address" and press F3.
11. Challenge Yourself! Select Mickey's address, add it as the AutoText entry MMAddress, and try using F3 to insert his address.

1. Open MICKEY1.DOC.
2. Run the spell checker and notice that "Mousehouse" and "Minnie" passed the spell check. (Remember, you added them to CUSTOM.DIC.) [5.1]
3. Undo any changes the spell checker made. [5.1]

4. Select Options from the Tools menu. Select the Grammar tab, change the setting in the Use Grammar and Style Rules list to Strictly (all rules), and make sure the Check Spelling box is checked. [5.3]
5. Run the grammar checker against MICKEY1.DOC, noting that the grammar check does a spell check at the same time if requested. Make corrections as indicated. [5.3, 5.1]
6. Add **Yours** after "Sincerely." Then use the thesaurus and find a substitute for "Sincerely." [5.2]
7. Highlight your replacement for "Sincerely Yours" and add it as an AutoText entry **syour**. [5.4]

cumulative skills check

1. Create a new blank document. [1.6]
2. Use the AutoText feature to insert your address. [5.4]
3. Use the AutoText feature to insert Mickey's address. [5.4]
4. Write Mickey a letter. [2.1]
5. Add "all okay" as an AutoCorrect entry called AOK. [2.1]
6. Add a sentence using "AOK" in your letter to Mickey. [2.1]
7. Check the grammar in your document. [5.3, 5.1]
8. Use the Print Preview option on the File menu (Alt F, V) to preview your letter to Mickey. [2.5]
9. Save your work as MICKEY4.DOC. [2.3]

Teach
Yourself

part two

Mastering Word

6

Changing How Text Looks

chapter objectives

After completing this chapter, you will be able to

6.1 Make text bold, italic, smaller, larger, and so on

6.2 Know what fonts are and how to change them

6.3 Insert special characters such as © or ™

6.4 Copy, search for, or replace special characters, fonts, and formatting

At this point, you are probably quite comfortable with the mechanics of entering, correcting, and even polishing text in Word. However, with a word processor as powerful as Word, restricting yourself to plain vanilla text would be like going to the flavor lab at Ben and Jerry's Ice Cream and not trying anything *but* vanilla.

We all know that when you make new flavors of ice cream, there are two things you can do: start with vanilla and add (think Chocolate Chip Cookie Dough) or start with a whole new flavor and, if necessary, add good stuff to it (think Wavy Gravy). In Word, you change what is called the *character formatting* (or *character attributes*) if you keep the "base flavor" the same but make the characters bold, italic, smaller, larger, and so on. Here are examples of some possible changes in character formatting:

This has no special formatting.
This is in italics.
This is in bold.
This is 18 point.

If you actually change the "base flavor" (the shape of the characters), you are changing the *font* (or *typeface* in printer jargon).

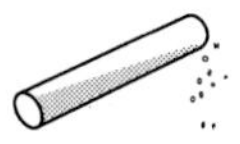

NOTE *Computer jargon (are you surprised?) differs from ordinary English once again in that, in English, a font is a typeface plus a specific size of type; in computer jargon, font is used for the name of the typeface as well.*

Here are some examples of words written in different fonts; notice how different the same letter looks in each font.

This is Helvetica.
This is Palatino.
This is Bookman.
This is Courier.
This is AvantGarde.

The purpose of this chapter is to supply you with the tools needed to jazz up your text. Here's a warning, however: There is a tendency at first to become infatuated with fonts, and to include too many typefaces—in too many styles and sizes—in your documents. But making your documents too elaborate puts your readers in the position of having to eat a melange of strawberry-chocolate-peanut butter-Tropical Rain Forest Crunch with a few cherries mixed in—they might gag.

review
skills check

1. Create a new document and enter the following text. [1.6, 2.1]

   Not snow, nor rain, nor heat, nor gloom of night stays these couriers from the swifte completion of their appointed rounds. -- U.S. Postal Services: Motto

2. Select just the word "swifte" and request a spell check. [3.2, 5.1]
3. Select just the first sentence and request a grammar check. [3.2, 5.3]
4. Save the document for use later in the chapter. [2.3]

6.1 CHANGING HOW CHARACTERS LOOK

You can change character formatting as you type or after you type. This is purely a matter of taste. It seems that most Word users prefer to enter text first and worry about changing how it looks later because this works out faster for most people. You can concentrate first on what the text *is* and then turn to how the text will *look*.

The rule for changing existing text follows the rule that you know so well:

Select, then do.

You first select the text that you want to affect, and then make any changes to it.

You can use the keyboard or the mouse to actually pick the new format for the character. Let's start with the easiest changes: making text bold, italic, or underlined.

- To make selected text bold, press Ctrl+B or use the Bold button on the Formatting toolbar.

- To make selected text italic, press Ctrl+I or use the Italic button on the Formatting toolbar.

- To underline selected text (including any spaces between words), press Ctrl+U or use the Underline button on the Formatting toolbar.

If you only need to change a single word, just make sure the insertion point is within the word. Then use the keyboard shortcut or click on the appropriate toolbar button. You can also combine character formats by applying these techniques repeatedly to the same text. For instance, you can create text that is both bold and italic.

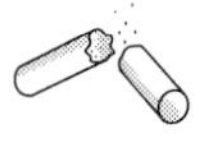

CAUTION *There's one "gotcha" that you need to be aware of when you change a character's format: If you type text inside or immediately after text you have changed, the text you enter takes on the new format as well.*

If you need to enter plain text inside or immediately to the right of text that you have changed, it's easiest to enter the text first and then change it back to plain vanilla.

To strip out all character formatting and return to the default format:

- Select the text and press Ctrl+Spacebar.

If you prefer to format your text as you type, just tell Word to start using the new formatting before you begin to type. To do this:

- Click on one (or more) of the toolbar buttons before typing the text or use the appropriate keyboard shortcut (Ctrl+B, Ctrl+I, or Ctrl+U).

When you change character formatting in this way, the formatting remains in effect until you cancel it. To cancel any formatting that is currently in effect:

- Choose the same toolbar buttons or use the same keyboard shortcuts again.

In other words, these techniques are just like a bank of light switches (also called toggles). Click once to turn them on; click again to turn them off. (Remember, toolbar buttons that are toggles look pressed in when they're on and not pressed in when they're off.)

EXAMPLES

1. Abraham Lincoln was quite fond of using emphasis in his writing. The editors of his papers choose to use italics for this emphasis. Enter the following from a famous passage on government that he wrote in 1854:

   The legitimate object of government, is to do for a community of people, whatever they need to have done, but cannot do, at all, or cannot, so well do, for themselves.

   The actual text in his collected papers has the *at all* and *so well do* in italics. To make these changes:

   a. Highlight the words "at all" and press Ctrl+I.
   b. Highlight the words "so well do" and press Ctrl+I.

2. Suppose you know that you want to type a sentence like this, including boldfacing:

   We will meet at **9:30 AM** in **Conference Room 5**.

   In this case, it's easiest to boldface the text as you type. To do this:

   a. Type **We will meet at**.
   b. Press Ctrl+B.
   c. Type **9:30 AM**.
   d. Press Ctrl+B once more to turn off boldfacing.
   e. Type **in**.
   f. Press Ctrl+B again.
   g. Type **Conference Room 5**.
   h. Press Ctrl+B again to turn off boldfacing.
   i. Type the period.

REMEMBER *If you forget to turn off boldfacing, not only will the period be boldfaced, but all subsequent text will be as well.*

3. Type the following text,

   This text is bold.

   This text is in italic.

   This is clearly overkill.

4. Change the text as you see it below, adding bold, italic, and finally a combination of bold, italic, and underline. The last line combines all attributes, which is probably going overboard! (On the other hand, it's quite common to both boldface and italicize text for emphasis.)

   This text is in bold.

   This text is in italic.

   <u>This is clearly overkill.</u>

REMEMBER *The convention used in this book to indicate user input is boldface type; don't confuse that with how to apply the boldfacing attribute described here.*

CHARACTER SIZE

With most printers and screens Word can print and display many fonts in almost any size. The size of a character is measured in *points,* with each point being roughly 1/72 of an inch. (A 72-point font is about one inch high.) Since screen size and the zoom control can affect how large the on-screen text appears, *points* refers to how large the text will be *when it is printed.* How good a character looks when printed larger than usual depends on the printer you are using and the kind of font you are using. Most of the default Word fonts print quite well in all sizes on most laser printers.

This is 8 point.

This is 12 point.

This is 16 point.

This is 24 point.

This is 36 point.

To change the size of a font, you can, as usual, either change the size of selected text or change the size of text as you type. If you do not select text, the size change goes into effect for everything you type after the insertion point. To change the size of selected text:

1. Select the text.
2. Type the new size in the Size text box or click as shown here to pull down the list box.

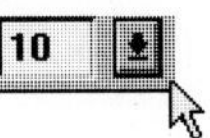

3. Choose the size you want from the list that appears, as shown here:

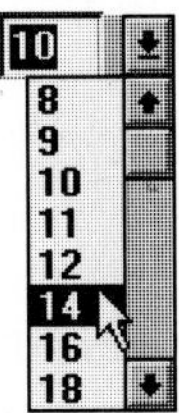

Notice that this box doesn't list all possible font sizes. You can enter a size (like 13 point type) that is not listed. However, increasing the size by one point is hardly noticeable except in the smallest sizes.

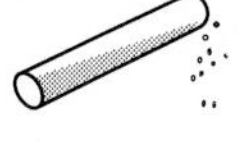

NOTE *If you use a size much smaller than the ones listed in the Size box (8 point in this case), your text may be too small to read when printed, or, for that matter, to see on the screen .*

To change the size of text as you type,

1. Change the font size by typing a new size in the Font Size text box or by dropping down the Font Size list box and choosing a new font size.
2. Start typing.

REMEMBER *When you use this method to change the size of text, you have to change the font size again if you want to go back to the original size.*

EXAMPLES

1a. Suppose you enter the text shown below. Here's what your screen will look like before you change the selected text.

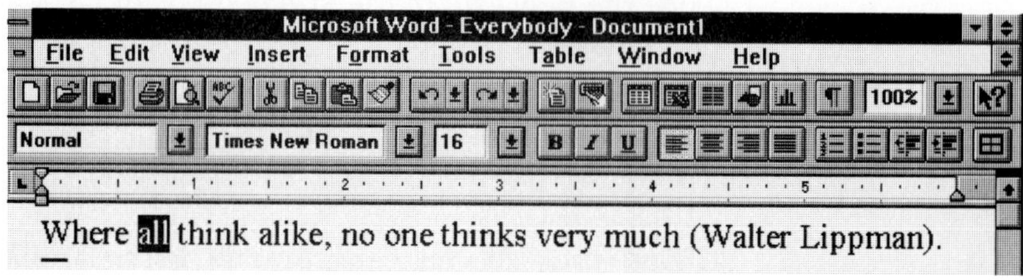

1b. Now change the font size to 18 point.

THE FONT DIALOG BOX

If you want to alter text using techniques other than those available on the Formatting toolbar, you will most often use the Font dialog box, an example of which is shown in Figure 6-1 (Alt O, F). Besides letting you change text, this dialog box gives you (in the lower-right corner) a preview of what the changes look like. Here are short descriptions of the elements of this dialog box that you need to know about now. (You'll learn more about some of the other items, like the Font list box located in the upper-left corner, in later sections of this chapter.)

FIGURE 6-1

The Font dialog box

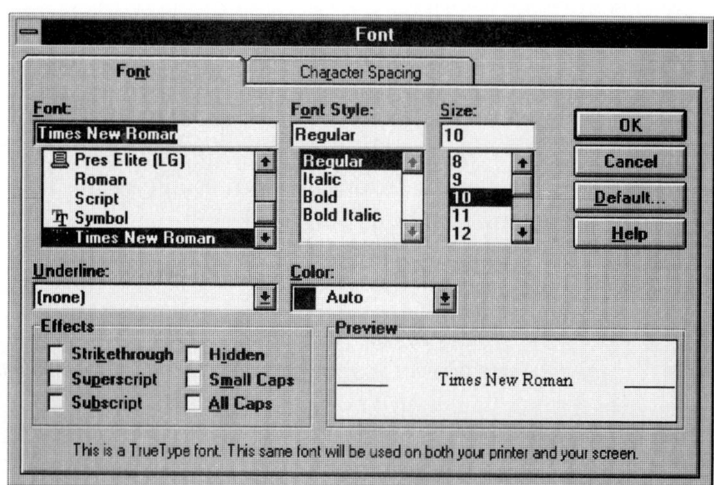

The Preview Box The Preview box (shown here) lets you see the effects of your changes before you actually put them into place. This is extremely useful feedback. The Preview text shown here is boldfaced, underlined, and in small caps.

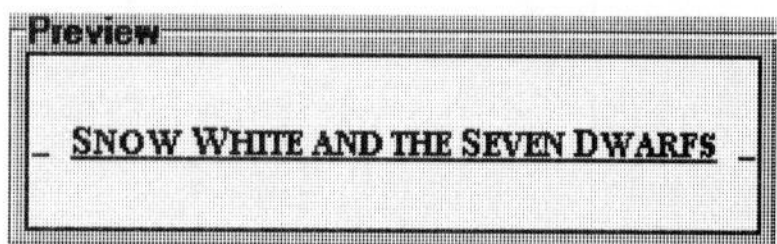

The Font Style Box As shown here, the Font Style list box lets you select a style—such as bold or italic—for your text if it is available. To revert to the default type style, choose Regular.

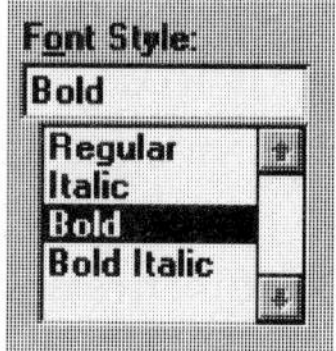

The Size Options Type a size in the Size text box or select a size from the Size list box by clicking on it (use the scroll bars if necessary to find the desired size). The available sizes depend on the printer and the font you are working with. If the size you type in the Size text box is not available on the current printer, Word chooses the closest available size.

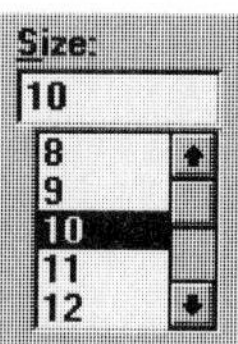

The Underline Drop-Down List Box As shown here, there are four possible options for underlining text:

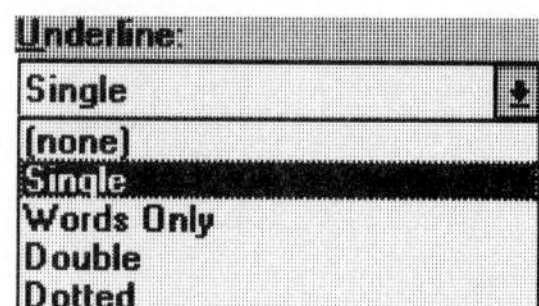

- (none) This option removes underlining.
- Single This option places a single line under all words and characters, including the spaces between them.
- Words Only This option places a single line under all words and characters, but not the spaces between them.
- Double This option places a double line under all words and characters, including the spaces between them.
- Dotted This option places a dotted line under all words and characters, including the spaces between them.

The Color Box You can make selections from the Color drop-down list box to change the color of your text. Word allows you to both display *and print* text in color. Any color monitor running Windows will enable you to display text in color. To actually print text in color, however, you need the appropriate kind of printer (and possibly a printer *driver* supplied by the maker of your color printer). If you don't see the desired color, scroll through the list—in all, 16 colors are available.

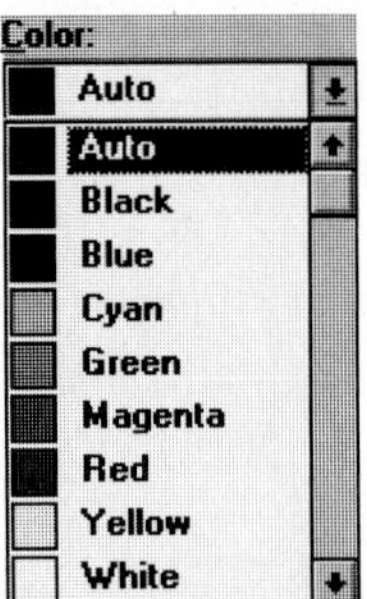

Effects Options The six check boxes listed under Effects let you select various text formatting options, as shown here:

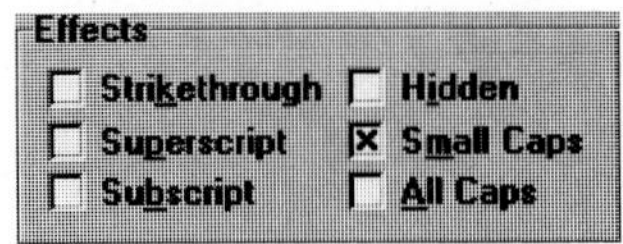

You can combine any or all of the effects (except where they don't make any sense; you can't have a superscript also be a subscript, for example). The six possible effects are as follows:

- Strikethrough This option draws a line through text, as shown here.

  ~~Snow White and the Seven Dwarfs~~

- Superscript and Subscript These options make characters smaller and then raise or lower them, as shown here for a subscript.

  H_2O

  You can actually customize how high superscripts will be (or how low subscripts will be) by working with the Character Spacing tab on the Font dialog box. For example, the Position option on this tab lets you control how far up (or down) superscripts (subscripts) appear.

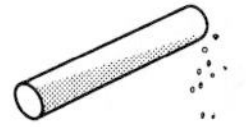

NOTE *Superscripts and subscripts may not show up in the Preview box. They do, of course, always show up on screen.*

- Hidden This option enables you to optionally hide text on screen and also to prevent it from printing. Hidden text is most often used for personal notes or internal comments. If you have clicked on the Show/Hide toolbar button—for example, to make paragraph marks visible—you can see hidden text on your screen. (It is shown with a dotted underlining.) Normally, hidden text is not printed. See Chapter 9 for details on how to print hidden text.

  Snow·White·and·the·Seven·Dwarfs¶
  Well·they·used·to·call·her·Snow·White--but·she·drifted¶

- Small Caps This option displays lowercase characters in uppercase but reduces their size. This is occasionally a nice effect in headings. The Small Caps option does not affect numbers, punctuation, nonalphabetic characters, or text you typed originally in uppercase. Of course, whether you can actually print small uppercase letters depends on whether your printer can handle the smaller size needed.
- All Caps This option provides another way to change lowercase characters to uppercase. It is more direct then cycling using Shift + F3.

NOTE *The Effects check boxes work a little differently than ordinary check boxes. Two possibilities are standard: If the box is clear the text is not changed, and if the box is selected the text is changed. A third possibility is that a box can be grayed. In this case, some of the selected text has the indicated effect but some of it does not. These three possibilities are shown in the following illustration:*

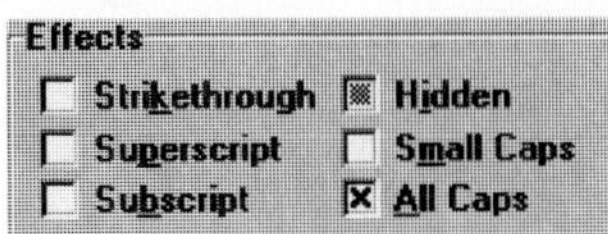

EXAMPLES

1. Here is text that combines many attributes.

H_2O·is·the·formula·for·*ordinary·water*.¶

Enter the text. To make the text appear as above. Select each part of the text and change the effect as shown above. (Notice here how the Preview box does not show the subscript.)

Effects
Strikethrough
Superscript
Subscript
Hidden
Small Caps
All Caps

Preview
H2O is the formula for or

THE KEYBOARD SHORTCUTS

You already know the keyboard shortcuts for boldfacing, underlining, or italicizing text. It turns out there are keyboard shortcuts for almost everything you can do via the Font dialog box. While you would hardly like to memorize the following table, most people do like to learn the keyboard shortcuts for their favorite text format so they don't need to take their hands off the keyboard *too* often.

REMEMBER *You can use these shortcuts on selected text or you can use them to change text as you type it. Most are toggles; use the shortcut once to turn them on and again to switch them off.*

To Do This	Use This Shortcut
Boldface text	Ctrl+B (toggle)
Underline text	Ctrl+U (toggle)
Underline single words	Ctrl+Shift+W (toggle)
Double underline text	Ctrl+Shift+D (toggle)
Italicize text	Ctrl+I (toggle)
Create small capital letters	Ctrl+Shift+K (toggle)
Make subscripts (auto spacing)	Ctrl+= (toggle)
Make superscripts (auto spacing)	Ctrl+Shift+= (toggle)
Return to default formatting	Ctrl+Spacebar
Remove formatting applied using shortcut keys or menu commands	Ctrl+Shift+Z
Change the case of letters	Shift+F3
Create capital letters	Ctrl+Shift+A (toggle)
Create small caps	Ctrl+Shift+K (toggle)

The following table shows the keyboard shortcuts for changing the size of text:

To Do This	Use This Shortcut
Increase the font size to the next available size	Ctrl+Shift+>
Decrease the size to the previous available size	Ctrl+Shift+<
Increase the font size by 1 point	Ctrl+]
Decrease the font size by 1 point	Ctrl+[

EXAMPLES

1. To change text to all capital letters, select it and press Ctrl+Shift+A.
2. If the font and available font sizes are as shown here, press Ctrl+Shift+> to switch text from 10 to 12 point.

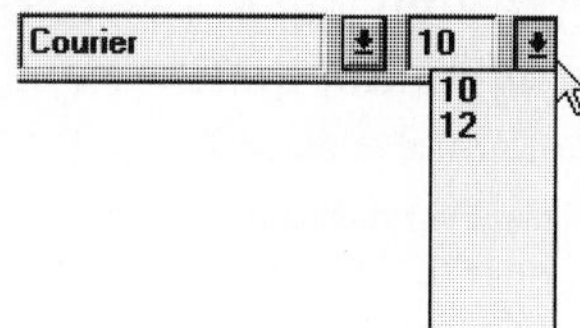

EXERCISES

1. Open the Postal Services motto created in the Review Skills Check.
2. Select the line "U.S. Postal Services: Motto" and make it italic.
3. Select "snow" and make it bold.
4. Underline "rain."
5. Double underline "gloom of night."
6. Move the insertion point around within the text you just modified and watch the buttons on the Formatting toolbar (notice how they looked "pressed in").
7. Select the words "nor rain" and watch the buttons on the Formatting toolbar.
8. Place a dotted line under "couriers" and watch the buttons on the Formatting toolbar.
9. Select the first sentence and remove the formatting from it.

6.2 FONTS

A *font* is nothing more than a group of characters that share the same style, design, and size. (The actual design is usually called the *typeface,* although as mentioned earlier in computer jargon, "font" is often used as a synonym for typeface.) Font design has a long and distinguished history: Many of the greatest printers, including Gutenberg himself, designed fonts for their printing presses. The idea is to make a font that is both beautiful and readable. (Too ornate a font may be beautiful but will usually be difficult to read.)

Here are both a standard font and a very ornate font:

This is the alphabet in Palatino:
abcdefghijklmnopqrstuvwxyz
This is the alphabet in Marriage:
abcdefghijklmnopqrstuvwxyz

Fonts are further divided into *serif* and *sans serif* fonts. A *serif* font means the characters have little strokes at the end, as shown here.

Sans serif font characters do *not* include embellishments at the end. Sans serif fonts give a more stark and unadorned look.

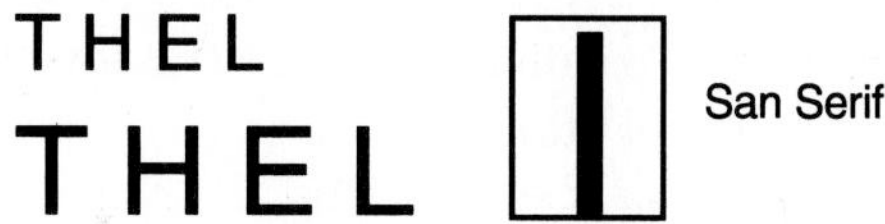

Fonts are also distinguished by whether or not they are proportionally spaced. (Nonproportional fonts are sometimes called *monospaced.* In Word for Windows, Courier is the standard nonproportional font.) When fonts are proportionally spaced, letters like "i" take up less room than letters like "m." Here are two fonts, one proportionally spaced and the other not:

This is a proportional font.

`This is a monospaced font.`

FONTS IN WORD

It's easy to change fonts. To change existing text, first select it. (You can also change the font of text as you type.) Then follow these steps:

1. Choose Font from the Format menu (Alt O, F).
2. Choose the font you want from the Font list box, an example of which is shown here:

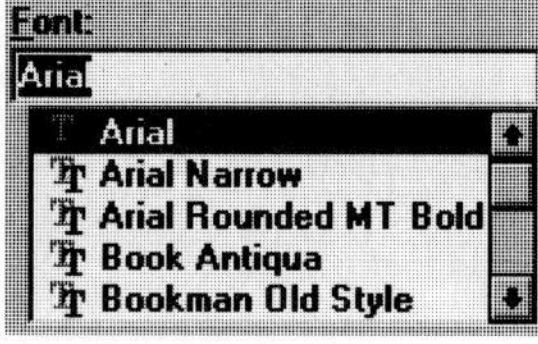

REMEMBER: *What you will see will depend on which fonts you have installed on your system.*

When you change the highlighted item in the Font list box, notice how the Preview box changes to reflect your choices.

3. Click on OK to put your selection into place.

There is one other way to change the font. This method is a little faster than using the Font dialog box, but does not let you preview the changes. To quickly change the font using the Formatting toolbar, follow these steps:

1. Click on the Font drop-down list box on the Formatting toolbar, as shown here:

You'll see the version of the drop-down list box with the fonts you have, as shown here:

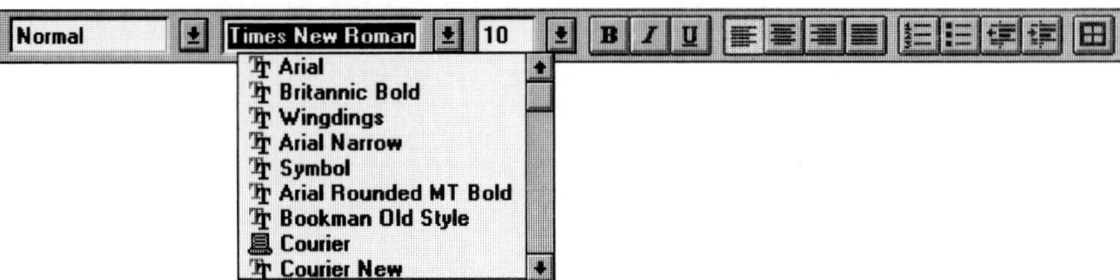

Notice that the first few items are not in alphabetical order. Word keeps track of the last few fonts you have used and names them at the top of this list.

2. Click on a font to select it and close the drop-down list box (or use the arrow keys and press Enter).

The default font for Word is *Times New Roman.* Many people, such as the author, don't like it very much. (You will soon see how to change Word's default font to reflect your own aesthetic sense.) The author's favorite of the standard fonts supplied with Windows is called

Arial, which is based on the Helvetica font. Here are examples of the same 12 point text in Times New Roman and in Arial.

A quote from Disraeli displayed in Times New Roman:

"It is much easier to be critical than correct."

A quote from Disraeli displayed in Arial:

"It is much easier to be critical than correct."

Finally, you need to be aware that times have changed: originally, after the designer drew the typeface, someone had to laboriously cast the characters in molds using molten metal. This obviously meant that typefaces were scarce and expensive. Now there are software tools that make font design much cheaper. Moreover, the designs can be stored in digitalized form on a hard disk, floppy disk, or CD-ROM. (Because of how much storage a font can use, many font packages are distributed only on CD-ROMs.)

Anyway modern technology means that you can buy hundreds if not thousands of different fonts for very little money per font. Many fonts are actually available free or as shareware. (If you buy another font for Windows, that font may come with directions on how to install it; if not, consult a standard Windows reference like Tom Sheldon's *Windows 3.1 The Complete Reference*, Osborne/McGraw-Hill, 1992.)

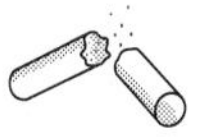

CAUTION *If you try to install hundreds of fonts into Windows at the same time, you run two risks (aside from how much room they take up). The first is that Windows will slow down and behave erratically. The second is that you will drown in a sea of choices and not be able to get a real sense of what each font looks like.*

In any case, no matter how many fonts you have stored on your hard disk, Word knows (and can therefore display for you) only the fonts that Windows tells it are available. Finally, how (and which) fonts you can print will depend on your printer. Even if you can print a given font on your printer, how it ultimately looks depends very much on the printer.

EXAMPLES

1. The following are the 12 standard Windows text fonts. To display each font name in its own font enter the text as shown here, select each one successively, and then change the font to the one indicated.

   Arial — Courier New — Times New Roman
   Arial Italic — Courier New Italic — Times New Roman Italic
   Arial Bold — Courier New Bold — Times New Roman Bold
   Arial Bold Italic — Courier New Bold Italic — Times New Roman Bold Italic

2. Word also has two fonts with symbols called Wingdings and Symbol. Here are all characters available in the Wingdings font. To see this illustration on your screen, choose Symbol from the Insert menu and choose Wingdings from the Font drop-down list box on the Symbol tab.

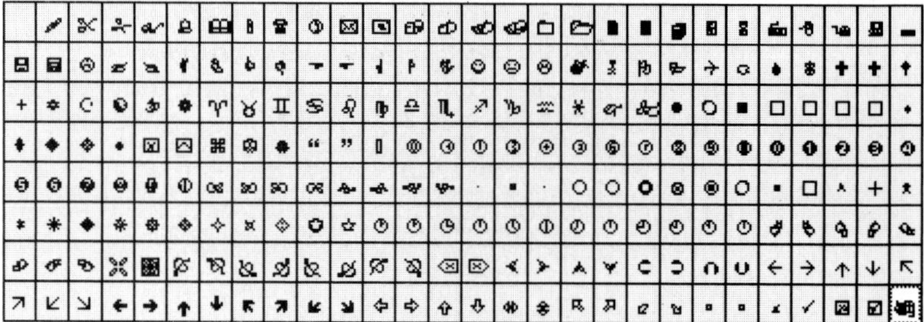

3. Here are the characters available in the Symbol font. To see this illustration on your screen, choose Symbol from the Insert menu and choose Symbol from the Font drop-down list box on the Symbol tab.

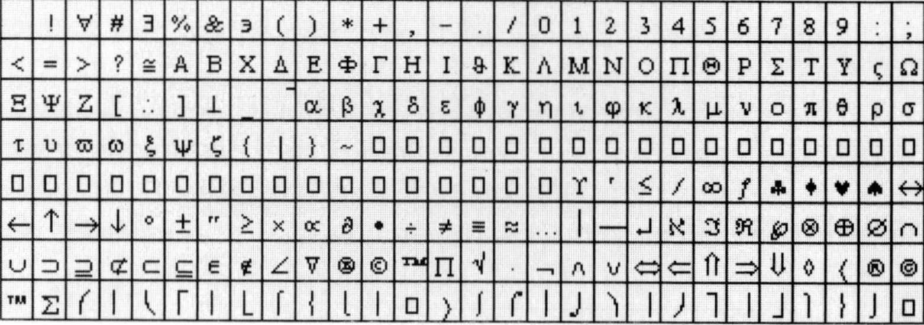

USING BIGGER OR SMALLER CHARACTERS FROM A FONT

In the old days, when each different size font required new castings from hot metal, you obviously had only a restricted choice of sizes available within each font family. The modern day equivalent of each size font in the same family being stored separately is usually called a *bitmapped font* or a *nonscalable font.* Such fonts are stored in your printer's hardware in certain fixed sizes. This means that any attempt to print text using a bitmapped font in a size different from those supplied with your printer will either be impossible or look ragged and not at all pleasing to the eye. (It will also be slower.)

Microsoft included a new technology called *TrueType* in Windows 3.1. TrueType fonts can easily expand or contract with little, if any, loss of quality. (Truetype fonts are therefore called *scalable* fonts.) You may have scalable fonts from a company called Adobe; Adobe scalable fonts work the same as Microsoft's and Word will handle them as effortlessly as it handles TrueType fonts. Although scalable fonts look much better than nonscalable fonts in nonstandard sizes, they do require more time to print. This is because Windows needs to do the necessary calculation to scale the font up or down.

To tell whether a font is a TrueType (scalable) or a printer font (generally nonscalable), look at the Font drop-down list box, an example of which is shown here:

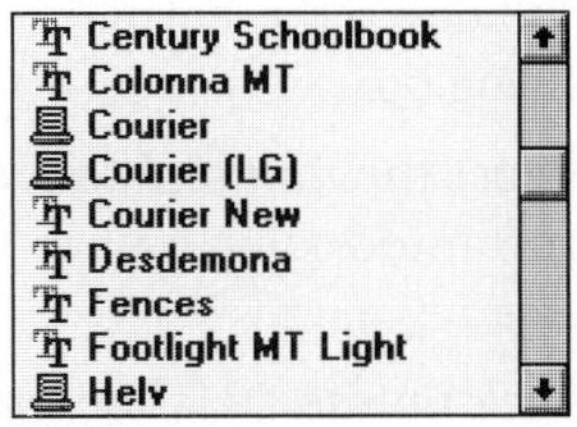

Fonts with a symbol next to their names are TrueType fonts and fonts with a symbol next to their name are printer fonts.

TIP *If you use TrueType (or Adobe Type Manager) fonts, your screen will more closely resemble what your document will look like when printed.*

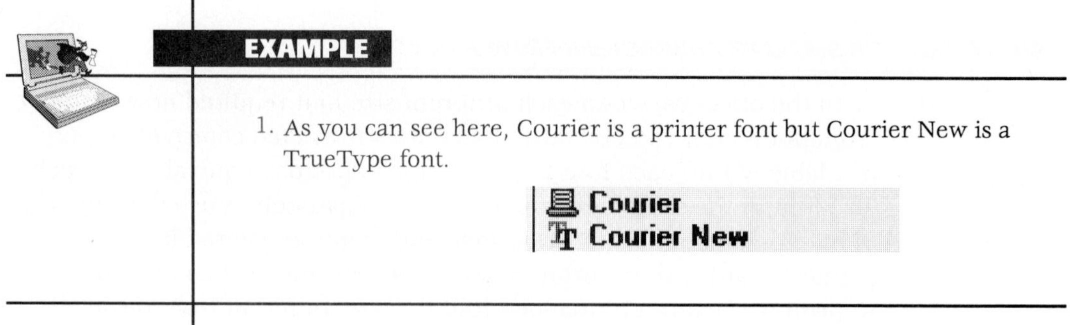

1. As you can see here, Courier is a printer font but Courier New is a TrueType font.

CHANGING THE DEFAULT FONT AND FORMATTING

As you become more familiar with fonts, you may want to change the default font that Word uses to match your own sense of aesthetics (or because your job has certain style guidelines!). This way you can start a document assured that it will look the way *you* want rather than the way someone else wanted.

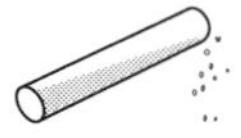

NOTE *Changing the default font changes which font is in effect when you open new documents in the future. This does not affect fonts in documents you have already created.*

To change the default font or formatting:

1. Pull down the Format menu and choose Font to open the Font dialog box.
2. Select the font and font size you want. Make sure there are no unwanted selections in this dialog box or the Character Spacing tabs.
3. Click on the Default button.
   You see this message box:

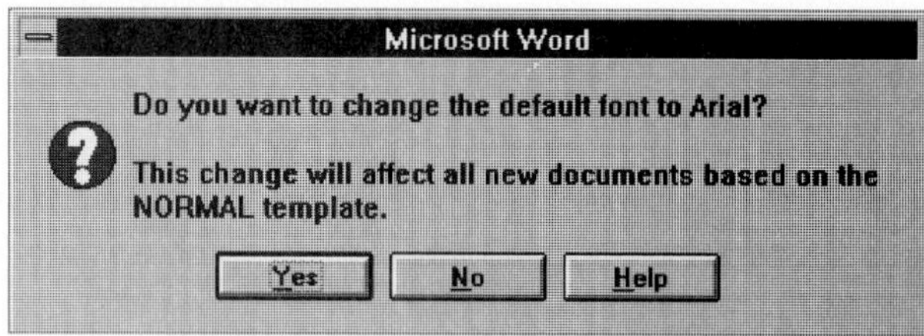

4. Click on OK to have this font go into effect for all ordinary documents—documents you open with the New button on the

standard toolbars or by choosing New from the File menu and clicking on OK to accept the default settings.

EXAMPLE

1. Start the process of changing the default font to 12 point Arial by making the changes on the Font tab on the Font dialog box and clicking on the Default button. Here is the message box you will see if you try to change the default font to 12 point Arial. (Click on Yes if you want to change the default or on No to stay with the current setting.)

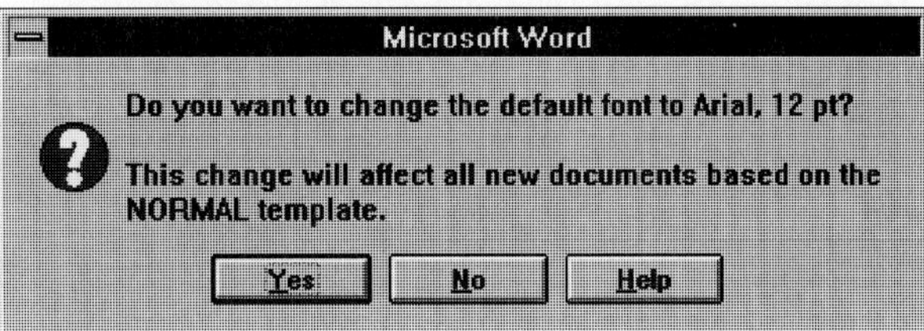

EXERCISES

1. Using the Postal Services Motto, change the font of the first sentence to Arial.
2. Change the font size of the first sentence to 14.
3. Select "completion" and make it bold.
4. Select "completion" again if needed and reset its formatting by using Ctrl + Spacebar.
5. Undo the last change. Select "completion" again if needed and reset its formatting by using the Bold button on the Formatting toolbar.
6. Change the font of the first sentence to Courier New.
7. Determine whether Courier New a fixed or proportionally spaced font. Determine whether it is a serif or sans serif font.
8. Determine whether Arial is a fixed or proportionally spaced font. Determine whether it is a serif or sans serif font.

6.3 INSERTING SPECIAL CHARACTERS

The number of symbol fonts that you have available depends on which fonts you have installed. As you just learned, Windows comes with the Symbol and Wingdings fonts, which include loads of useful symbols. To insert a special symbol:

1. Choose Symbol from the Insert menu. This opens the Symbol dialog box, which is shown in Figure 6-2.
2. Click on a symbol and then click on the Insert button to insert the selected symbol into the document at the insertion point. (Now you can insert as many symbols as you want while this dialog box is open. This was not true in earlier versions of Word.)
3. Click on the Close button to close the Symbol dialog box when you are done. (The Cancel button from Figure 6-2 changes to close once you have inserted a symbol.)

If you looked closely at Figure 6-2, you may have noticed the Special Characters tab lurking in the background. Clicking on this tab enables you to insert such special characters as copyright and trademark symbols, as you can see in Figure 6-3. As on the Symbols tab, you insert characters from this tab into your document by highlighting the character and then clicking on the Insert button.

Word also comes with a full-fledged Equation Editor for entering sophisticated science and mathematical symbols and equations. However, covering the equation editor would carry us too far afield.

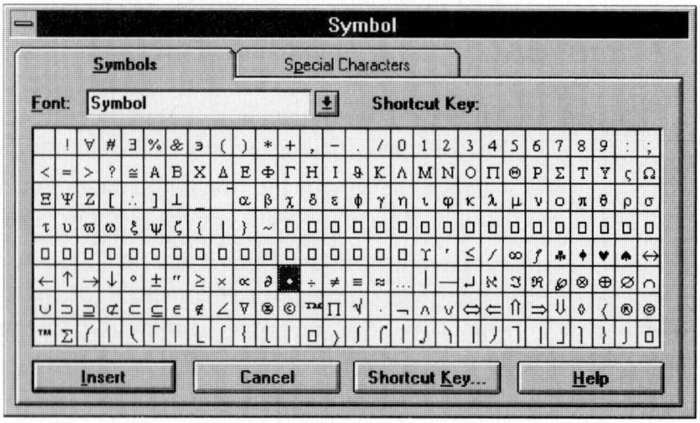

FIGURE 6-2

The Symbols tab on the Symbol dialog box

The Special Characters tab on the Symbol dialog box

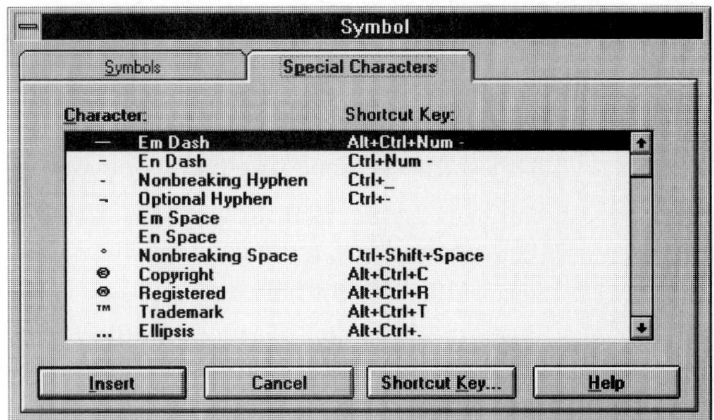

You might want to consult Mary Campbell's *Microsoft Word for Windows: The Complete Reference* (Osborne/McGraw-Hill, 1993) for more on the Equation Editor.

EXAMPLES

1. Switch to the Wingdings font and type **ABCDEFG**. Here's what you see:

2. Type the same **ABCDEFG** in the Symbol font, here's what you see:

DEVISING SHORTCUT KEYS FOR SPECIAL CHARACTERS

If you constantly use a special character, you might want to consider giving it a shortcut key if Word doesn't already supply one. That way you will be able to insert the symbol without removing your fingers from the keyboard.

To create a shortcut key for a symbol, follow these steps:

1. Pull down the Insert menu and choose Symbol (Alt I, S) to open the Symbol dialog box.
2. Choose the symbol for which you want to create a shortcut key.
3. Click on the Shortcut Key button shown earlier in Figure 6-3. This opens the Customize dialog box shown in Figure 6-4. Now carry out these steps:
4. Place the insertion point within the Press New Shortcut Key box and hold down any combination of the Shift, Alt, Ctrl keys and a keyboard key.

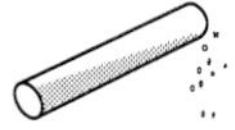

NOTE *Word warns you if the keyboard shortcut you choose is already in use. An example of what you'll see in the bottom left of the Keyboard tab is shown here:*

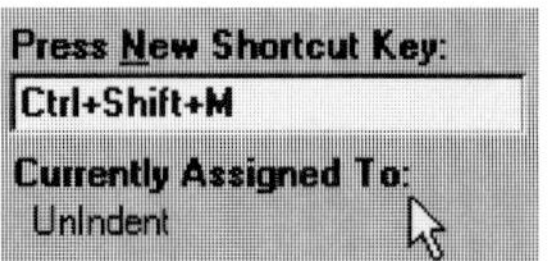

To have this shortcut available for all your documents, make sure the Save Changes In box says Normal.dot, as shown in Figure 6-4.

FIGURE 6-4

The Customize dialog box for keyboard shortcuts

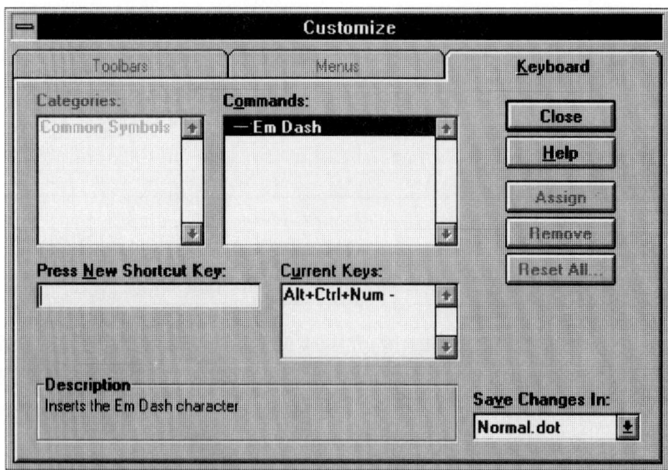

EXAMPLES

1. The copyright symbol © is already assigned the Alt+Ctrl+C combination. So to enter the copyright symbol, move the insertion point to where you want it to appear and hold down the Alt, Ctrl, and C keys simultaneously.
2. The Special Characters tab on the Symbol dialog box gives a long list of symbols and their shortcuts. To see this box choose the Special characters tab from the Symbol dialog box available from the Insert menu.
3. Suppose you want to assign Ctrl+Alt+M to the Greek lowercase mu (μ). Fill in the keyboard tab as shown here:

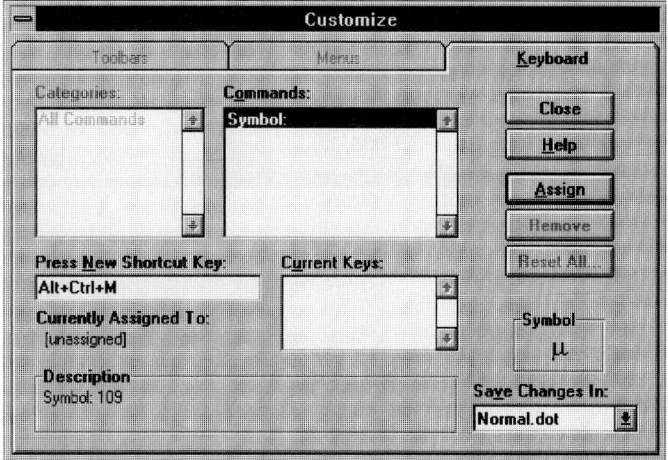

EXERCISES

1. Place a copyright symbol at the end of the Postal Service Motto by pulling down the Insert menu, choosing Symbol, and selecting the Special Characters tab.
2. Add a line below the motto containing a copyright symbol (use the Alt+Ctrl+C shortcut key) and the words **1970 U.S. Postal Service**.
3. Add a trademark symbol after "U.S. Postal Service."
4. Change the double dash to an em dash using the Special Characters tab in the Symbol dialog box. Note the shortcut key.

6.4 ADVANCED SEARCH, REPLACE AND COPYING: SPECIAL CHARACTERS, FORMATTING, OR FONTS

You have already seen how to use Word's search, replace, and copy features in Chapter 3. Word also allows you to search for (or replace) certain special characters such as tabs or paragraphs, as well as text in a specific font or format. You can also copy specific formatting or fonts from one part of a Word document to another.

ADVANCED SEARCH AND REPLACE

Let's start with more sophisticated searches—searches for special characters. Here's the Find dialog box available by choosing Find from the Edit menu (Alt E, F) that you have been using all along:

First, suppose that you need to search for tabs, multiple hard returns (the ¶ symbol that shows up when you press the Enter key), or most other nontext characters. Clicking on the Special button in the Find dialog box opens a long list of special characters that you can search for, as shown here:

Paragraph Mark	Field
Tab Character	Footnote Mark
Annotation Mark	Graphic
Any Character	Line Break
Any Digit	Manual Page Break
Any Letter	Nonbreaking Hyphen
Caret Character	Nonbreaking Space
Column Break	Optional Hyphen
Em Dash	Section Break
En Dash	White Space
Endnote Mark	

If the character you want to search for is on this list, just click on it to initiate the search. (Don't worry if some strange codes appear in the

Find box; that's how Word identifies certain characters. For example, it uses ^p to represent the Enter key.)

Using Word's Replace command (Alt E, E—see Chapter 3 for basic information on Word's replace feature) to change special characters works the same way, except, of course, you have to fill in both the Find What and Replace With text boxes.

EXAMPLES

1. Suppose you want to search for double carriage returns. Choose Find from the Edit menu, click on the Special button and choose Paragraph Mark from the list that pops up, and then click on the Special button and choose Paragraph Mark again. Here's what the Find dialog box looks like.

Find
Find What: ^p^p
Find Next
Cancel
Search: All
Match Case
Find Whole Words Only
Use Pattern Matching
Sounds Like
Replace...
Help
Find
No Formatting
Format
Special

2. Suppose you want to replace all double carriage returns with single carriage returns. Choose Replace from the Edit menu, move to the Find What box and click on the Special button. Choose Paragraph Mark once and then repeat the process. Then move to the Replace With box, click on Special and choose Paragraph Mark once. Here's what the completed Replace dialog box looks like.

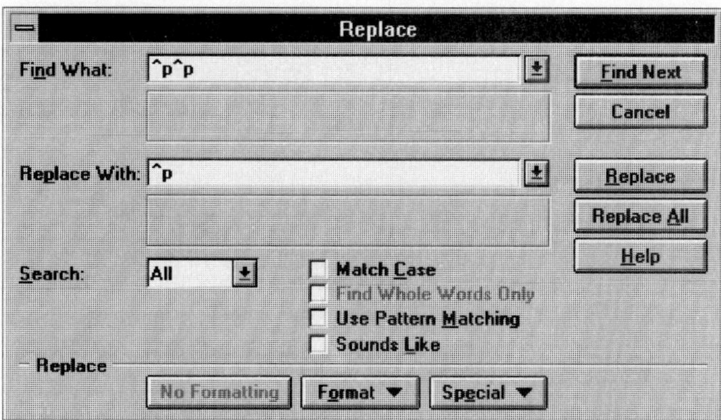

SEARCHING FOR AND REPLACING FORMATTED TEXT

The techniques for working with formatting in the Find or Replace dialog box are essentially the same. We will illustrate them first with the Find dialog box. Let's suppose you click on the Format button on the Find dialog box, as shown here.

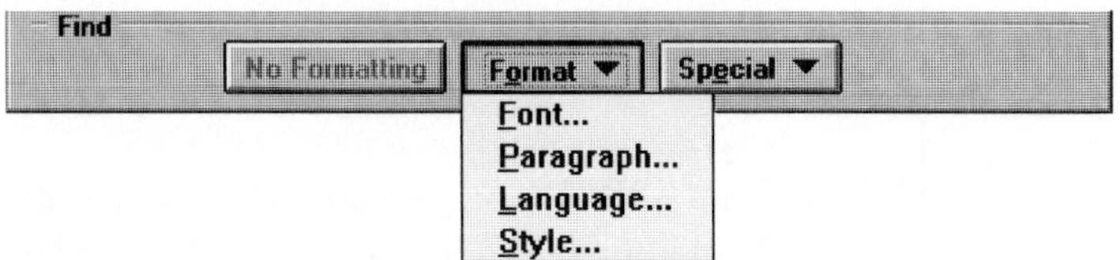

Notice that you can choose to search for a font, paragraph formatting (Chapter 6), a language, or a style (Chapter 7). For instance, if people's names in your document were always in 12 point bold Arial, you could make these selections and easily find all the names that occurred in your document.

At this point let's concentrate on searching for fonts. Choosing the Font option takes you to the dialog box, an example of which is shown in Figure 6-5. This variation on the Font dialog box is called the Find Font dialog box. As you check off options in this dialog box, Word adds them to the search criteria. When you're done making choices, click on OK to return to the Find dialog box.

When you have finished making your choices, the Find dialog box looks something like this. Notice how the Format box describes the choices you made in the Find Font dialog box and that we are requiring that the case be matched.

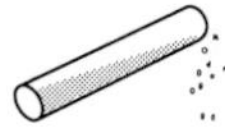

NOTE *Once you make a choice of font or special characteristics, Word will skip over any occurrences of the text that do not satisfy these more stringent conditions.*

FIGURE 6-5

The Find Font dialog box

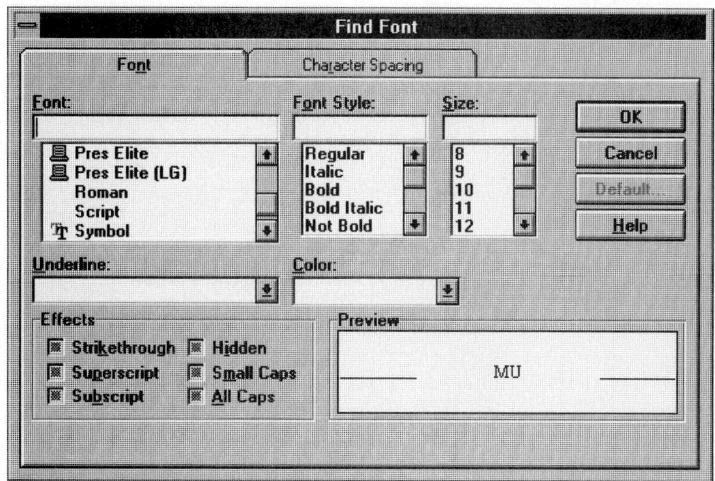

For example, if you search for "Peace" in bold, Word will not find any non-bolded occurrences of the word "Peace".

Finally, remember all these techniques work exactly the same in the Replace dialog box—except now you must also fill in the Replace With text box with the text and or the formatting you want.

TIP *If you want to replace (or find) attributes (such as bold or italic) rather than specific text strings with those attributes, leave the Find What and Replace With (if applicable) text boxes blank and just choose the appropriate formatting.*

EXAMPLES

1. Suppose you want to search for all occurrences of the word "Peace" in boldface. Enter the word **Peace** in the Find dialog box and make sure that the Match Case box is checked. Click on the Format button, choose Font and select Bold from the Font Style list. The Find dialog box you create would look like this:

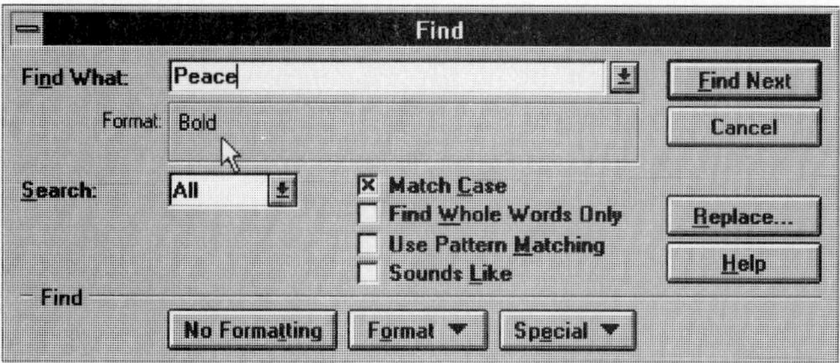

2. Suppose you wanted to search for all occurrences of the word "Peace" in boldface and in 14-point type. Follow the previous steps if need be (since Word remembers the previous state of the Find dialog box you may not have to re-enter this data.) This time also choose 14 point from the Size list box in the Font dialog box. Your Find box would look like this:

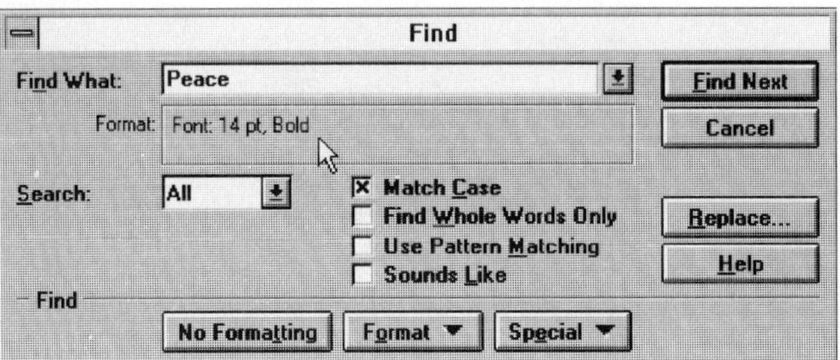

3. If you wanted to search for all occurrences of the word "Peace" in boldface, in 14 point type, and in the Arial typeface, follow the previous steps if needed and now choose Arial from the Font list box. The Find dialog box would look like this:

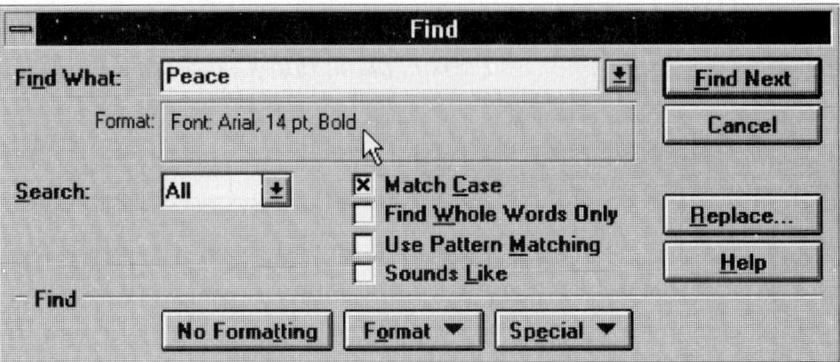

4. Suppose you wanted to replace all occurrences of the word "Peace" with the words "Peace Now." Moreover, you wanted all the occurrences to be in 24 point bold italic in the font called Brittanic Bold. (You may not have this font, of course.) Here's what your Replace dialog box would look like:

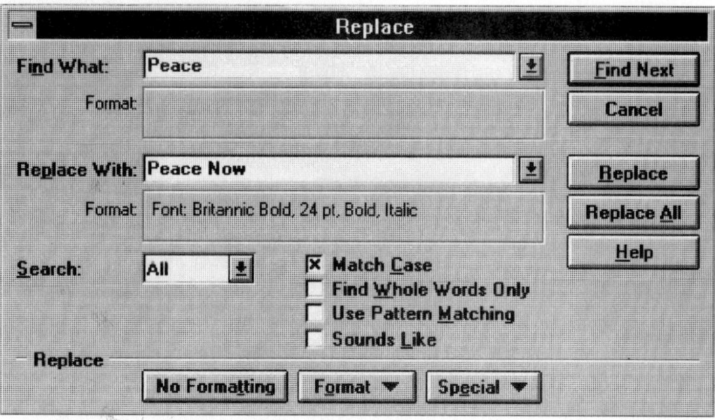

5. Suppose you wanted to replace all bold text with italic text. Leave the Find What box blank but click on the Format button and choose Font. Now choose Bold. Similarly, leave the Replace With box blank, click on the Format button and choose Font. Now choose Italic. The Replace dialog box would look like this:

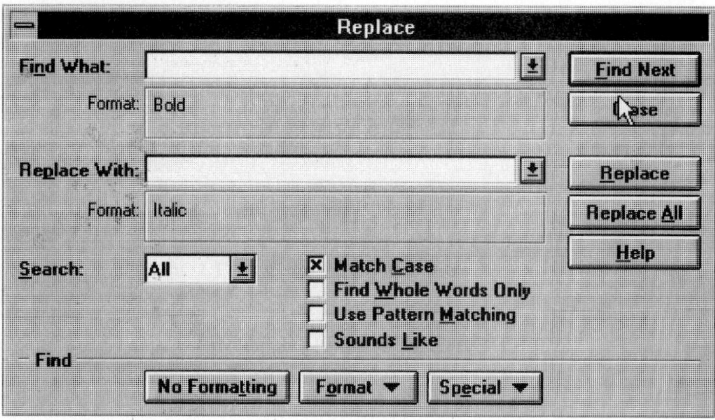

6. Here's the Replace dialog box needed to replace an MU by a (μ) everywhere it occurs:

To get to this box is a little tricky. You need to know that the µ is the "m" in the Symbol font. So what you need to do is type a lowercase m in the Replace With box, click on the Format button, choose Font from the list that pops up and then choose the Symbol font.

COPYING CHARACTER FORMATTING

Suppose you are happy with how a passage of text looks and you want to apply the same combination of text characteristics to another part of a document. What you obviously need is a quick way of copying, not text, but formatting information. If instead of applying boldfacing, italic, underlining, and a new typeface and point size, for example, you can accomplish this all in a single operation, you can save a lot of time.

To copy formatting information with the keyboard, follow these steps:

1. Select any text that includes the formatting you want to copy.

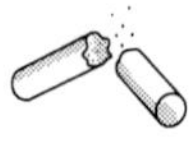

CAUTION *If you don't want to also copy the shape of the paragraph (see Chapter 7), do not select the paragraph mark at the end of the text.*

2. Press Ctrl+Shift+C.
3. Select the text to which you want to apply the formatting from the text you selected initially, and press Ctrl+Shift+V.

You can also use the mouse to copy formatting:

1. Select any text that includes the formatting you want to copy. (Again be careful not to include the paragraph mark unless you want to copy the shape of the paragraph as well).

2. Click on the Format Painter tool on the Standard toolbar.

   Notice how the pointer has changed into a little paintbrush attached to the usual I-beam pointer.

3. Now drag the mouse across the portion of text that you want to format. When you release the mouse button, Word applies the new format to the passage you dragged across.

REMEMBER *These methods copy every font characteristic set via the Font dialog box; using this method, you can easily change the form, size, and shape of any text to follow any model that satisfies you.*

Sometimes you need to copy the way a paragraph works. If you click once on the Painter Format tool, you can copy formatting to a single text selection. If you double-click on the Format Painter button, you can copy formatting to multiple text selections. The mouse pointer stays in the shape of a paintbrush until you once again click on the Format Painter button.

EXERCISES

1. Type the following quotes from Shaw in a normal font:

   If all economists were laid end to end, they would not reach a conclusion.
   You must not suppose, because I am a man of letters, that I have never tried to earn an honest living.
   Censorship ends in logical completeness when nobody is allowed to read any books except the books nobody can read.

   Change the first text to 12 point bold italics in the Arial font and use the format painter to change the next two quotes to the same shape. Try the same exercise with the keyboard shortcuts.

2. Using Replace, remove the italics from the quotes, leaving them just in bold.
3. Using the Postal Service motto, search for the em dash.

mastery skills check

1. Enter the following quotation, using only the keyboard (including the shortcut keys) for underlining and returning to the default format. [6.1]

   When dealing with people, let us remember we are not dealing with creatures of logic. We are dealing with creatures of emotion, creatures bustling with prejudices and motivated by pride and vanity.
   – Dale Carnegie, How to Win Friends and Influence People

2. Underline "pride" and "vanity" by using the Format Painter button on the Standard toolbar or by copying and pasting formats only. [6.4]
3. Format "Dale Carnegie" as small caps. [6.1]
4. Italicize "How to Win Friends and Influence People." [6.1]
5. Change the quotation to a sans serif, proportionally spaced font. [6.2]
6. Change the quotation's font size to a pleasing one. Use Page Layout view and the Ctrl+] or Ctrl+[shortcuts. [6.1, 6.2]
7. Removing the underlining from all words at one time. [6.1]

cumulative skills check

1. Re-create the following screen on your computer using the Arial 12 point font. [6.1]

Normal Text
Bold Text
Italic Text
Bold Italic Text
Underlined Normal Text
Underlined Words
Double Underlined Text
Dotted Underlined Text
SMALL CAPS TEXT
ALL CAPS TEXT
~~Strikethrough Text~~
superscript
subscript

2. Check the spelling of your new document. [5.1]
3. Preview and then print your document. [2.5]
4. Save your document as SAMPLES.DOC. [2.3]
5. Change the font in the sample from Arial to Times New Roman. [6.2]
6. Print your document. [2.5]
7. Exit from Word without saving SAMPLES.DOC again. [1.3]

Teach
Yourself

7

Lines, Paragraphs, and Styles

chapter objectives

After completing this chapter, you will know how to

7.1 Change the shape of a paragraph including its indents, spacing between lines, and alignment

7.2 Jazz up a paragraph with features like borders and shadings

7.3 Use Word's styles

7.4 Use Word's templates

7.5 Use Word's automatic formatting feature

A Word document is like a tripod—its strength is based on three legs: characters, paragraphs, and pages. The last chapter explained how to control the way characters look; this chapter shows you how to control the way paragraphs look. (The next chapter explains how to control how a page looks.) You'll see how to center text, make text double spaced, align it, center it, and even add shading and borders around text.

The last three sections in this chapter introduce you to three of Word's most powerful features: styles, templates, and automatic formatting. *Styles* are what Word calls a group of formats that you can apply to a paragraph or to text. They save you the trouble of having to repeatedly reformat paragraphs and text manually. *Templates* are the framework in which you construct your document. Think of a template as a document design; this includes specifications for margins, fonts, any standard text, and so on. The Wizards that you saw in Chapter 4 are based on some of Word's built-in templates. Templates make it easy to give documents the same look and feel. This is important both in the business and educational worlds, where consistency of presentation is important. Finally, *automatic formatting* is a Word feature that analyzes and then reformats your document according to how Word thinks you are using each element. Lists might be numbered, paragraphs might change to reflect that Word thinks you mean them to be headings, and so on. Automatic formatting can sometimes improve (but not replace) manual formatting.

1. Create a new document and enter the following standard text that should appear in a memo. [1.6, 2.1]

   To:
   From:
   CC:
   Subject:
   Date:
   ++

2. Enter the following quotation into the memo. [2.1]

   There is no beautifier of complexion, or form, or behavior, like the wish to scatter joy and not pain around us.

   – Ralph Waldo Emerson, *Conduct of Life*

3. Fill in the To, From, CC, Subject, and Date fields in your memo and add some text to introduce the quotation. [2.1]
4. Increase the point size of the font used for the quotation. [6.2]
5. Italicize the quotation source. [6.1]
6. Save the document as MYMEMO1.DOC. [2.3]

7.1 SHAPING HOW A PARAGRAPH LOOKS

Word does not use paragraphs as they are used in ordinary English. You probably think of a paragraph as a group of sentences that deals with a single topic. In Word, by contrast, a paragraph is *any* amount of text (or even special characters or graphics) that ends with a press of the Enter key (a *hard return*, in the jargon). For example, a chapter title on a line of its own is considered a paragraph in Word, even though it may not qualify as a paragraph in the eyes of your high school English teacher.

As you learned in Chapter 1, clicking on the Show/Hide tool lets you see the paragraph symbol that marks the end of a paragraph.

If you need to start a new line within a single Word paragraph, use Shift+Enter instead of Enter. The Shift+Enter key combination shows up as a (↵) when you have displayed hidden characters using the Show/Hide button on the Standard toolbar. One of the most common reasons to use the Shift+Enter combination to add a new line within a paragraph is that it keeps separate lines as a common unit so you don't have to format each line separately. For example, you might use this technique for an address.

Two terms come up repeatedly with reference to paragraphs: margins and indents. *Margins* mark the boundary of the ordinary page—the usual distance from the edge of the paper where printing will begin. In Word, the default top and bottom margins are 1 inch and the default left and right margins are 1 1/4 inches. On an ordinary 8 1/2 × 11-inch piece of paper this gives you a 6 × 9 inch area to work with. (You'll see how to adjust margins in the next chapter.) *Indents,* on other the hand, are specific to a paragraph; they measure how far from the margin the paragraph should begin. You can even create negative indents, in which the text sticks out into the margin, as shown here:

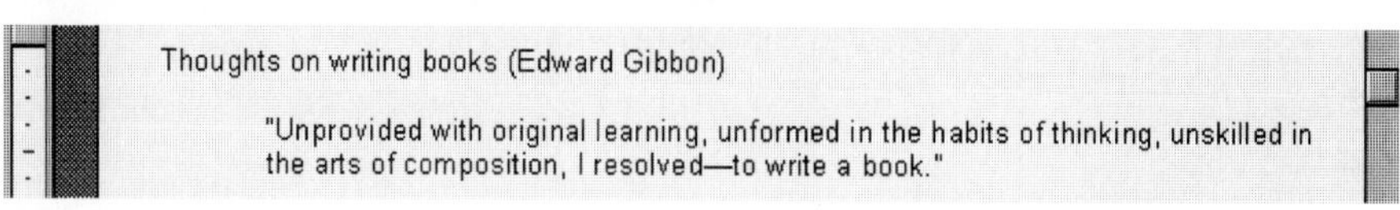

Thoughts on writing books (Edward Gibbon)
"Unprovided with original learning, unformed in the habits of thinking, unskilled in the arts of composition, I resolved—to write a book."

Many people like to indent the first line in each paragraph. Your first instinct may be to press the Spacebar a few times. *This is a terrible idea in Word* because the amount of room a "space" occupies depends on the font you have chosen. If you use the Spacebar, your paragraphs could have wildly different indentation patterns depending on the font.

A better option is to use the Tab key. This is fine if you just use this technique to indent the first line of your paragraph. (It is not optimal because Word gives you a more precise way to set the indent for the first line of a paragraph. See the section, "Indents via the Paragraph Dialog Box," a little later in this chapter.)

On the other hand, if you try to line up words within a paragraph by using the Tab key, the word wrap feature will almost inevitably cause you problems. You may end up with tabs in all the wrong places. (For the best ways to make lists and tables in Word, please see Chapter 10.)

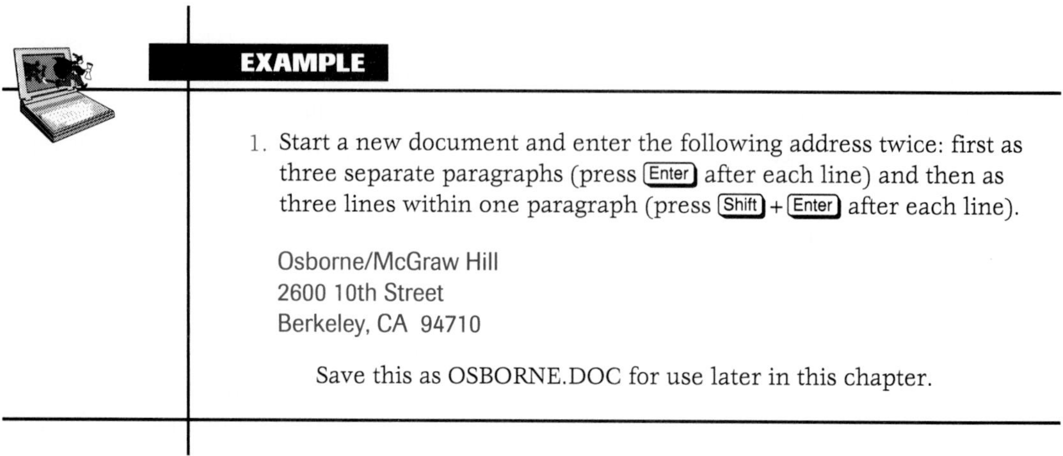

EXAMPLE

1. Start a new document and enter the following address twice: first as three separate paragraphs (press Enter after each line) and then as three lines within one paragraph (press Shift+Enter after each line).

   Osborne/McGraw Hill
   2600 10th Street
   Berkeley, CA 94710

   Save this as OSBORNE.DOC for use later in this chapter.

TABS VIA THE RULER

One of the easiest ways to control how paragraphs look is with Word's ruler. The ruler gives you a visual clue as to where tab stops and indents are set. Here's a picture of the ruler:

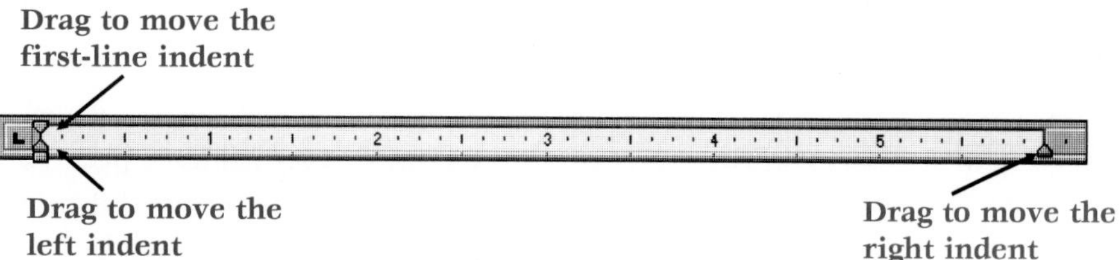

NOTE *If the ruler isn't showing, then choose Ruler from the View menu (Alt V, R).*

Word comes with tab stops set at every half inch. (You'll see how to change the defaults in the section, "Setting Tabs and Leaders via the Tab Dialog Box," a little later on in this chapter.) However, occasionally you will need to set your own tab stops or change how Word treats text at the tab stops. (These are usually called custom tab stops.) If you set a custom tab stop, this temporarily turns off all default tabs stops to the left of it.

There are four different kinds of tabs in Word.

- Left aligned   Text starts at the tab stop, so the start of the text is flush left with the tab stop. The symbol on the ruler is a (└).
- Centered   Text is centered around the tab stop. The symbol on the ruler is a (⊥).
- Right aligned   Text ends at the tab stop. The symbol is a (┘).
- Decimal   Text or numbers are aligned at the decimal point. (This type of tab stop is very useful for making numbers align neatly.) Text or numbers without a decimal point extend to the left of the tab stop. The symbol is a (⊥·).

Setting tabs with the ruler is a two-step process:

1. Click on the box at the left end of the ruler until the symbol representing the desired kind of tab stop appears (left aligned, centered, right aligned, or decimal):

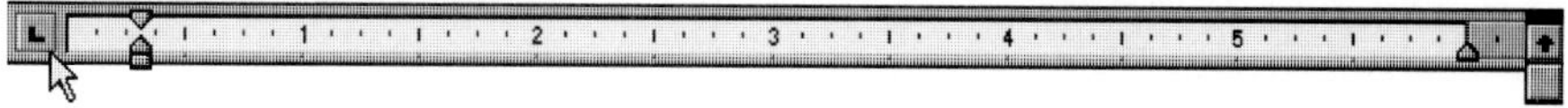

2. Click inside the ruler where you want the tab stop to be. You can repeat this process to set as many tab stops as you want. Each tab stop is shown by one of the four tab symbols.

To get rid of a custom tab stop that you have set using the ruler, simply:

▼ Drag it off the edge of the ruler.

The ruler gives you reasonable control over how your paragraphs look and how tabs are set. For most purposes, the ruler works fine. Occasionally, where accuracy is needed (or just because you prefer filling in dialog boxes to dragging with the mouse), you will turn to two of Word's dialog boxes: the Paragraph dialog box and the Tab dialog box. The Paragraph dialog box also controls how your paragraphs are spaced, and the Tab dialog box controls advanced tab features such as inserting vertical lines through your paragraph at a tab stop.

TIP *Do not use tabs to align complex tables; use Word's table feature instead (see Chapter 10).*

EXAMPLE

1. Suppose you wanted to line up the following items at their decimal points.

Seltzer	.02
Egg cream	.05
Steak	1.10

   Make the second tab stop into a decimal tab stop by clicking on the Tab box on the far left edge of the ruler until the decimal tab symbol shows. Then, on the ruler, click where you want the numbers to line up. Enter the data and Word will automatically align the numbers at the decimal point.

INDENTS VIA THE RULER

You can also set a paragraph using a ruler. Drag the upward pointing triangle on the far left side of the ruler until it is at the place on the ruler you want the left paragraph indent to be. Notice that a dotted vertical line moves across the document as you drag the indent marker to give you a visual clue as to where the indent will be. For the right paragraph indent do the same for the upward pointing triangle on the far right. (Depending on the point size you use, you may have to use the horizontal scroll bars to see the ends of the ruler.)

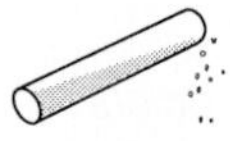

NOTE *Many people prefer to set paragraph indents via a dialog box. We cover this next.*

EXAMPLE

1. Suppose you wanted to indent the following Lincoln quotation roughly one half inch on both sides using the ruler:

   If we would first know *where* we are, and *whither* we are tending, we could then better judge *what* to do and *how* to do it.

   Drag the upward pointing triangle on the far left side of the ruler until it is at the one half inch mark on the ruler. Notice that a dotted vertical line moves across the document as you drag the indent marker to give you a visual clue as to where the indent will be. Do the same for the upward pointing triangle on the far right.

INDENTS VIA THE PARAGRAPH DIALOG BOX

To use the Paragraph dialog box to apply formatting to one or more paragraphs:

1. Make sure the insertion point is inside the paragraph if you just want to affect a single paragraph; or, select the paragraphs to be affected.
2. Choose Paragraph from the Format menu (Alt O, P). (You can also choose Paragraph from the shortcut menu that pops up when you click on the right mouse button.)

This opens the dialog box shown in Figure 7-1. (If the Indents and Spacing tab isn't showing as in Figure 7-1, click on the appropriate tab.)

3. Now you can adjust the indent settings as you wish by entering measurements in the Left and Right text boxes (use the spin buttons to increase or decrease the measurements).

4. Click on OK to have them go into effect. If you want the text to extend into the margin (sometimes called an *outdent*), put a negative number in the appropriate box.

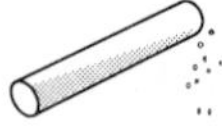

NOTE *The default unit of measurement Word uses is inches. This means if you leave out the units, Word will assume you mean inches. By placing the correct abbreviation after the measurement, you can also use centimeters (cm), points (pt), or picas (pi-one pica is 1/6 of an inch or 12 points). You can control what units Word uses for its default measurement type by going to the General tab on the Options dialog box and resetting the current setting in the Measurement Units drop-down list box. In this book we always assume the default measurement is inches.*

If you only want to have the indent apply to the first line of the paragraph, pull down the Special drop-down list box by clicking on its downward pointing arrow, as shown here:

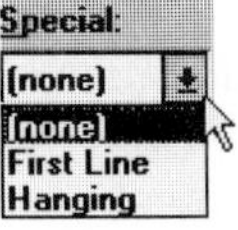

Now you can decide how to treat the first line of the paragraph. Choosing First Line indents the first line of the paragraph to the right by the amount specifies in the By box. Choosing Hanging shifts the first line of the paragraph to the left by the amount specified in the By

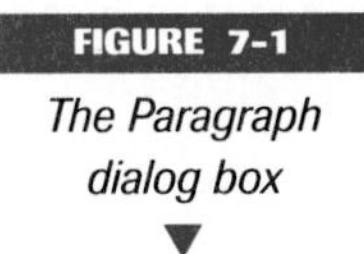

FIGURE 7-1

The Paragraph dialog box

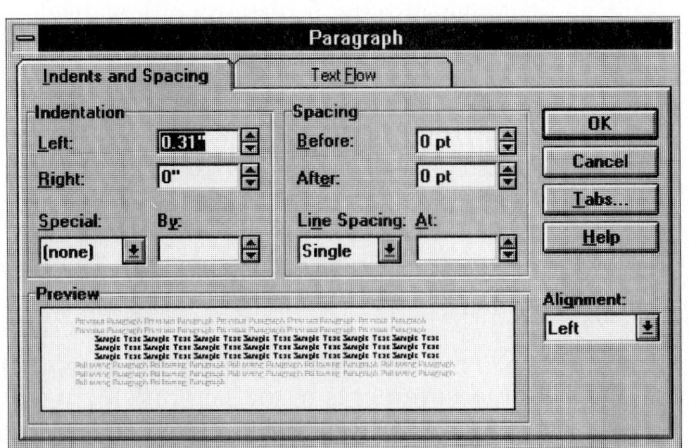

text box, so that it "hangs" out in the left margin. All subsequent lines in the paragraph will appear using the settings you choose for Left and Right. Here's an example of how a hanging indent looks in the Preview box:

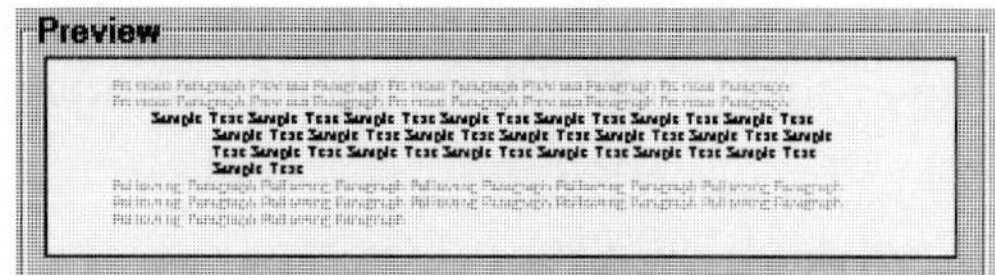

EXAMPLES

1. Suppose you want the first word in the first line of a paragraph to stick out one half inch in the left margin. Using the Paragraph dialog box, make sure the Special list box says First Line and enter **–.5** in the By text box.
2. A common style for quotations is that both left and right margins should be indented the same amount after the lead-in text. Suppose you enter the following quote, which might be in a political science paper.

   Lincoln was very concerned about the proper role of government–he was very aware that government has a vital role to play. He wrote the following in 1854:

   > The legitimate object of government is to do
   > for the people what needs to be done, but which they
   > cannot, by individual effort, do at all, or do so
   > well, for themselves.

   Enter this text. To indent the second paragraph three quarters of an inch on each side, place the insertion point inside the quotation, open the Paragraph dialog box (Alt O, P), make sure the Indents and Spacing tab is showing and then enter **.75** in both the Left and Right text boxes. Click on OK to have these changes go into effect.
3. Suppose you wanted to have a paragraph indented one centimeter. Make sure the insertion point is inside the paragraph, open the Paragraph dialog box (Alt O, P), make sure the Indents and Spacing tab is showing and then enter **1cm** in the Left text boxes. Click on OK to have this change go into effect.

SETTING SPACING AND ALIGNMENT VIA THE PARAGRAPH DIALOG BOX

There are lots of other features in the Paragraph dialog box (shown in Figure 7-1) that you may find useful. You've already seen the Special list box, which lets you indent only the first line of a paragraph. Let's go over some of the most important remaining features of this dialog box.

Paragraph Spacing The Spacing area determines the amount of space between lines inside a paragraph as well as the space between paragraphs. For example, the Before text box determines the amount of space above the first line of the current (selected) paragraph. The amount is measured in the points (the abbreviation is pt) that you learned about in the last chapter. (There are 72 points in an inch.) Similarly, the After text box determines the amount of space below the last line of the paragraph. These values are cumulative: a before value of 1 and an after value of 2 amounts to 3 points between paragraphs.

Line Spacing The Line Spacing At drop down list box looks like this when dropped down:

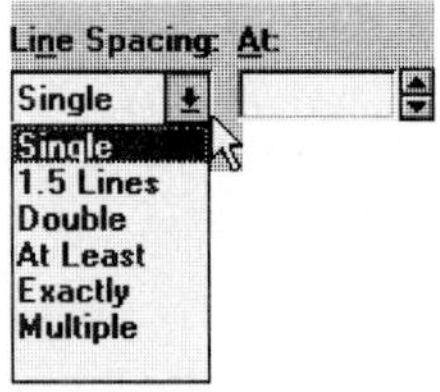

As you can see, you can choose whether you want single spacing, double spacing, one and a half spacing, and more. Word uses just a bit more than the height of the characters in the paragraph for each line. If you use a 12-point font, Single spacing is just a bit more than 12 points, 1.5 Lines is a bit more than 18 points, and so on.

The At Least option sets a minimum spacing for each line. This means that Word might add space for something like superscripts, but will never make the spacing less than the amount you enter in the At box. On the other hand, if you choose the Exactly option, Word will not adjust the line spacing; it will use the exact value you enter in the At box. Choosing this option may produce characters that are clipped.

The Multiple option on the Line Spacing drop-down list box allows you to go to triple spacing, quadruple spacing, or more. The default is 3, for triple spacing.

The Alignment Drop Down List Box Want to center a title? You can use the paragraph alignment feature in the Paragraph dialog box. However, an easy shortcut is to click on the toolbar buttons shown next to each method described below. Here's what the Alignment drop down list box looks like when you drop it down:

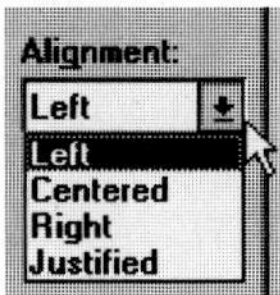

Aligning text means changing its position relative to the left and right margins. You can do a lot more than simply center text. For example, you can have Word *justify* text, which means that Word inserts extra spaces where needed so the text lines up perfectly at each margin—much as many books do.

Button	Alignment	Effect
	Left	Aligns the selected paragraph(s) at the left indent for the paragraph. (Keyboard shortcut is Ctrl+L.)
	Centered	Centers selected paragraph(s) between the left and right indents. (Keyboard shortcut is Ctrl+E.)
	Right	Aligns selected paragraph(s) at the right indent. (Keyboard shortcut is Ctrl+R.)
	Justified	Adds spaces between words in the paragraphs to position text exactly at the left and right indents. (Keyboard shortcut is Ctrl+J.)

TIP *For the best possible look for a centered paragraph, make sure the left and right indents are the same (most commonly 0).*

EXAMPLES

1. Titles are commonly centered. Suppose you want to center the following title:

   The Non-Idiot Yet Complete Beginner's Guide to Word

   Enter the text, make sure the insertion point is in the paragraph, and use the Ctrl+E shortcut to center the text.

2. Justified text appeals to many people. Enter the following quotation from Edward Gibbon and switch between justified (Ctrl+J) and left-aligned text (Ctrl+L) to see which you like better.

   I relinquished forever the pursuit of mathematics, nor can I lament that I desisted before my mind was hardened by the habit of rigid demonstration, so destructive of the finer feelings.

SETTING TABS AND LEADERS VIA THE TAB DIALOG BOX

Here's a picture of the Tabs dialog box which is available by opening the Format menu and choosing Tabs (Alt O, T):

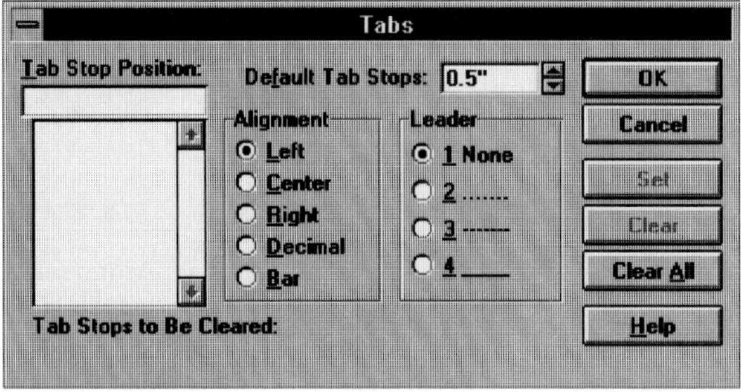

As you can see, the default tab stops are set to half an inch (.5").

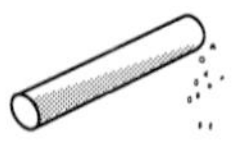

NOTE *Default tabs can only be set at intervals, and only in this dialog box. Custom tab can be set from either this dialog box or the ruler. If you set a custom tab stop, this temporarily turns off all default tabs stops to the left of it.*

To create a new default tab stop:

- Type the measurement in the Tab Stop Position text box using a decimal number.

You can also change or delete an existing custom tab stop. For example, to change a custom tab stop:

- Select the tab you want to change in the Tab Stop Position text box and then type the new measurement.

To delete a custom tab stop:

- Select the tab you want to delete in the Tab Stop Position list box and click on the Clear button.

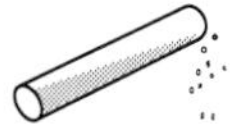

NOTE *When you press Enter at the end of a paragraph that includes paragraph formatting such as custom tabs, Word copies your settings into the next paragraph. To avoid carrying your special settings forward, move the insertion point out of the paragraph.*

Here are short descriptions of the important features of the Tabs dialog box:

Default Tab Stops The Default Tab Stops box gives the spacing for the default tab stops. Although this box starts out at one half an inch (.5"), you can enter a new measurement in the box to change the default.

Tab Stops to Be Cleared When you ask Word to clear a custom tab stop, Word removes the item from the Tab Stop position list box but nothing happens until you click on the OK button. Word keeps a list (as shown here) of the tab stops that will be cleared from the selected paragraphs when you click on OK.

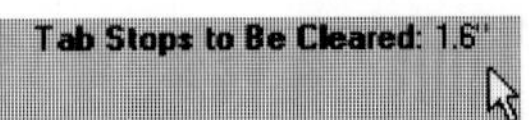

Alignment As discussed earlier, Word can align text at a tab in any of four ways. Click on the appropriate button in the Alignment box to make your choice. The Bar choice tells Word to insert a vertical line through the selected paragraph at the ruler position you specify.

Leader *Leader* ("lead the eye") is printer jargon for the type of character you use to fill the empty space to the left of a tab stop. You can create leaders that are dotted, dashed, or solid lines. (You can also turn off leaders by choosing None.)

The Set Button The Set button starts the process of setting a tab stop for the (selected) paragraphs at the position you type in the Tab Stop Position box. Word also adds this position to the Tab Stop Position list box. The new tab stop uses the current setting for Alignment and Leader. Word actually sets all tab stops selected in the Tab Stop Position list box only when you choose the OK button. If you choose Cancel, none of the changes will go into effect.

The Clear Button After you select a tab stop in the Tab Stop Position list box, clicking on the Clear button tells Word to clear this tab stop. Word lists these tabs under Tab Stops to Be Cleared at the bottom of the Tab dialog box. Word actually clears these tab stops only when you choose the OK button.

REMEMBER *Clear and Clear All apply to custom tabs stops only; they do not apply to default tab stops.*

The Clear All Button The Clear All button clears all the tab stops you have set in the selected paragraphs. The changes only go into effect after you click on OK, so you can click on Cancel if you decide not to clear all the tabs after all.

EXAMPLE

1. Suppose you wanted to have a table of contents that looked like this:

   Introduction 1
   Last year's Expenditures 5
   Last year's Revenues 9
   Projected Expenditures 12
   Projected Revenues 15

This requires using a right-aligned tab with a leader.

a. Before you enter any information in the paragraph, open the Tab dialog box and set up a right-aligned tab stop at a distance larger than the length of the text above (3.5" works well). Make sure that the dotted leader box is on (the second one).

b. Enter the first line. Press the Tab key, type the page number, and press Enter. Continue this process until you finish the table.

EXERCISES

1. Open or switch to MYMEMO1.DOC and, using the Paragraph dialog box, add a .75" hanging indent to the CC line.
2. Add more than one CC recipient by using Shift+Enter rather than using separate paragraphs.

   CC: Fred
   Sally
   Tom

3. Using the ruler, adjust the indents of the To, From, Subject, and Date lines to match the CC: line.
4. Add 6 points of space before the To, From, CC, Subject, and Date lines using the Before text box in the Indents and Spacing tab on the Paragraph dialog box.
5. At the top of the memo, add a centered paragraph containing the one word "MEMO."
6. Add 6 points of space after the paragraph containing the word "MEMO" using the Before text box in the Indents and Spacing tab on the Paragraph dialog box.
7. Give the Emerson quotation, including the quotation source, a left and right indent of .75."
8. Justify the text in the paragraph containing the quotation.
9. Add a right-aligned tab at .5" in the quotation source and use it to align the paragraph.
10. Save MYMEMO1.DOC.

7.2 JAZZING UP A PARAGRAPH

Have you ever needed to box a paragraph or give it some shading for emphasis? Then this section is for you; it contains information that is both fun and useful. Since this section can only cover some of the basics, consult Mary Campbell's *Microsoft Word for Windows: The Complete Reference* (Osborne/McGraw-Hill, 1994) if you want to learn more about Word's artistic features.

First, you'll learn about a special toolbar called the Borders toolbar, which provides some easy ways to control the borders and shading of paragraphs. Then, the next few sections explain how to use the Paragraph Borders and Shading dialog box to control the borders around paragraphs. This dialog box gives you access to a few features not available from the Borders toolbar.

The easiest way to bring up the Borders toolbar is to click on the Borders button on the Formatting toolbar. This adds a third toolbar to the basic two that you usually see. (The Borders button is a *toggle.* Click on it again to make the Borders toolbar go away.) The Borders toolbar looks like this:

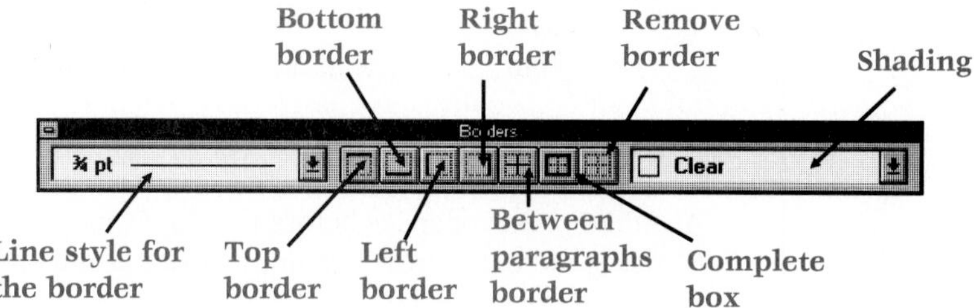

TIP *As you use more toolbars you may not want them all stacked at the top of the document window. You can move a toolbar anywhere on the Word screen by dragging its title bar.*

BORDERING A PARAGRAPH USING THE BORDERS TOOLBAR

Once you've displayed the Borders toolbar, you can introduce borders around your paragraphs by following these steps:

1. Make sure the insertion point is in the paragraph you want to put a border around. (If you want to work with several paragraphs, make sure they are all selected.)

2. Choose the type of border from the Borders toolbar by clicking on the desired button. The available buttons are described below.

Button	Effect
	Puts a line above the paragraph (or above the top paragraph)
	Puts a line below the paragraph (or below the last paragraph)
	Puts a line on the left side of the paragraph (or the left side of all selected paragraphs)
	Puts a line on the right side of the paragraph (or the right side of all selected paragraphs)
	Puts lines between all the selected paragraphs
	Puts a box around the paragraph (or puts a single large box around all the selected paragraphs)
	Removes the border from the paragraph with the insertion point or the selected paragraphs

SHADING A PARAGRAPH USING THE BORDERS TOOLBAR

To shade a paragraph using the Borders toolbar, first make sure it is visible. Then place the insertion point inside the paragraph you want to shade (or select the paragraphs). Now pull down the Shading drop-down list box from the Borders toolbar, as shown here:

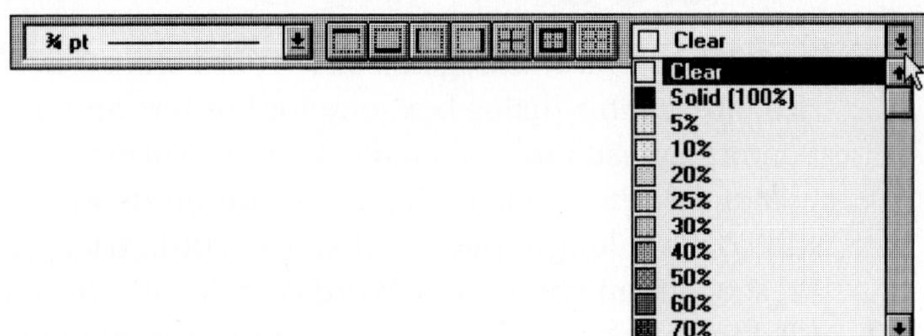

Now choose the shading you want for the paragraph.

EXAMPLES

1. Suppose you wanted to make a sign of the following fundamental Word principle, and you wanted to make it centered, boxed, and in a very large font:

   Select, then do.

   a. Choose a very large pretty font. Switch to this font and enter the text in a new document.
   b. Center the text (Ctrl+E).
   c. Display the Borders toolbar if necessary and click on the Box button on the toolbar.
2. Now lets suppose you want to shade this boxed text 20%. Pull down the Shading drop-down list box in the Borders toolbar and choose 20%.

BORDERS VIA THE BORDERS AND SHADING DIALOG BOX

If you are happy with the effects that the Borders toolbar gives you, you might want to skip this section. To work with the Paragraph Borders and Shading dialog box:

1. Place the insertion point in the paragraph to be affected or select the paragraphs to be affected, if you want to work with multiple paragraphs.
2. Choose the Borders and Shading option on the Format menu (Alt O, B).

This opens the dialog box shown in Figure 7-2. Notice that there are two tabs on this dialog box: one for borders and one for shading. If the Borders tab isn't displayed, click on it to bring it to the front.

Many of the items in Figure 7-2 are pretty easy to use. Shortly, we will cover at length the few that are a little tricky. For example, the Presets option shows how Word comes with three preset borders. Clicking on one of the Presets options lets you choose the overall

FIGURE 7-2

The Borders tab on the Paragraph Borders and Shading dialog box

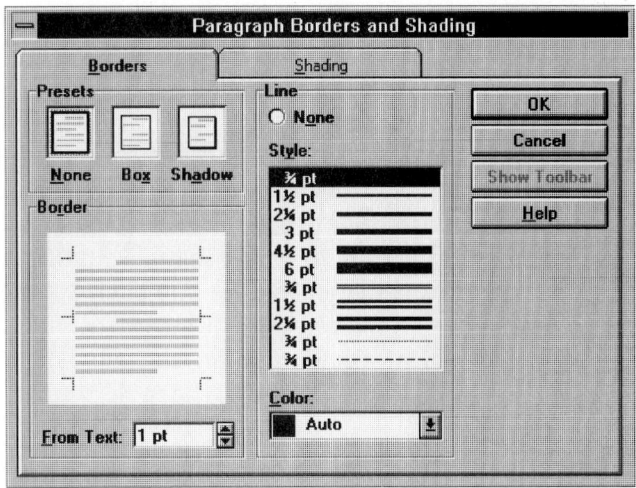

border style. If you click on the Box item under Presets, Word puts a box around the selected paragraphs. If you select the Shadow option, Word creates a shadowed border, much like a frame on a painting. The default is, of course, no border around a paragraph. You then use the rest of the options in this dialog box to modify the look of the border by making the sides thicker or thinner, changing their color, or even removing one or more of them completely. For example, to remove the border around a paragraph, select the paragraph and click on the None box under Presets.

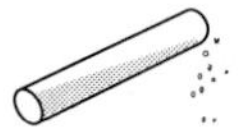

NOTE *A shadowed border is not available from the Borders toolbar. It's only available in the Paragraph Borders and Shading dialog box.*

Once you have decided what type of border you like, the Style list box lets you select the kind of lines you want in the border. You can drop down the Color drop-down list box to select a new color for the lines. Obviously, you must have a color monitor to see a colored border, and you must have a color printer in order to print a colored border. The Auto (default) option in this box uses the default color for the text on your screen—usually black.

The From Text text box lets you determine the amount of space you want between the text and the border. As you might expect by now, this is measures in *points*. The default is 1 point, or roughly 1/72 of an inch.

The Border Box The Border box located in the lower-left corner of Figure 7-2 would seem to be just another version of the preview box that you've seen in many Word dialog boxes.

The Border box certainly does provide a preview of the border options you choose. However, it also works like the boxes on the Borders toolbar. By clicking at certain spots inside this box, you can add or remove pieces of the border, and even put a border between paragraphs if your selection includes multiple paragraphs.

The trick is that each time you click on one of the boundaries of the Border box, Word removes or inserts that side. (The little triangles mark the side.) Click again on that side and Word restores its border using the current settings in the Style list.

TIP *If you have multiple paragraphs in the selection, click inside the Border box to add or remove a border between the paragraphs in the selection.*

EXAMPLE

1. A shadowed border can give a rather nice three-dimensional effect. Suppose you wanted to make a shadowed box around the following Mark Twain quotation:

   When in doubt, tell the truth.

   Make sure the insertion point is inside the paragraph. Choose Borders and Shading from the Format menu. Click on the Shadow box, and change the Style to 1 1/2 pt. Then try a 3 pt border and a 1 1/2 pt double border. Which one do you like best?

SETTING SHADING VIA THE PARAGRAPH BORDERS AND SHADING DIALOG BOX

The Shading tab of the Paragraph Borders and Shading dialog box (shown in Figure 7-3) provides many of the features available on the Borders toolbar. In addition, it lets you introduce color shading into the printed text if you are lucky enough to have a printer that can handle

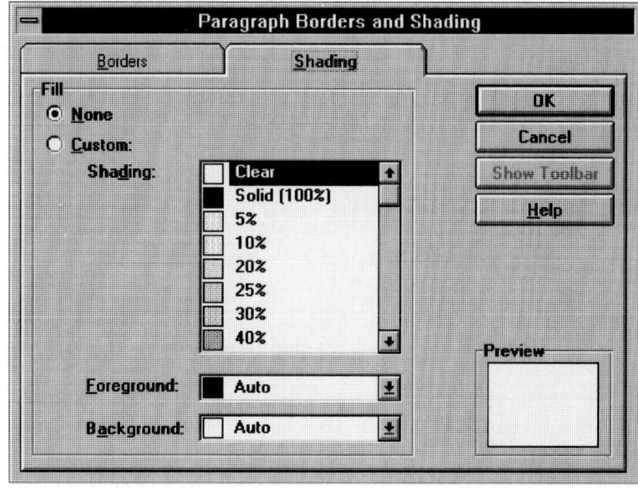

FIGURE 7-3
The Shading tab on the Paragraph Borders and Shading dialog box

this. (If you don't have a color printer, Word will convert colors to shades of grey—the exact shades will depend on your printer.)

Most of the options in this dialog box should be familiar to you. For example, the Fill buttons lets you decide whether or not to shade the paragraph. The Shading boxes let you apply gray shading in densities from 5 percent to 90 percent—as in the Borders toolbar. The Shading list box also offers both dark and light fill patterns (like grids and diagonal lines), and you can use these with colors too.

The new feature is that the Clear check box under Shading tells Word to apply the background color you select, and the Solid check box under Shading tells Word to apply the selected foreground color. Pull down the Foreground or Background drop-down list boxes to see a list of colors you can choose from. (The default Auto is black for foreground and white for background.) On a color monitor, the Preview box will show you the result of the color options you choose.

DROP CAPS

Drop caps are one of this author's favorite features. The idea is that Word can format a letter, word, or selected text as a large capital letter that *drops* down two or more lines of text. Drop caps go back to the days of illuminated manuscripts and were very popular in the early days of printing (each chapter in this book begins with a drop cap).

You can only create drop caps at the beginning of a paragraph, but otherwise the way to create drop caps in Word is simplicity itself:

1. Select the character, word, or words at the start of the paragraph that you want to drop.
2. Choose Drop Caps from the Format menu (Alt O, D). This pops up a dialog box that looks like this:

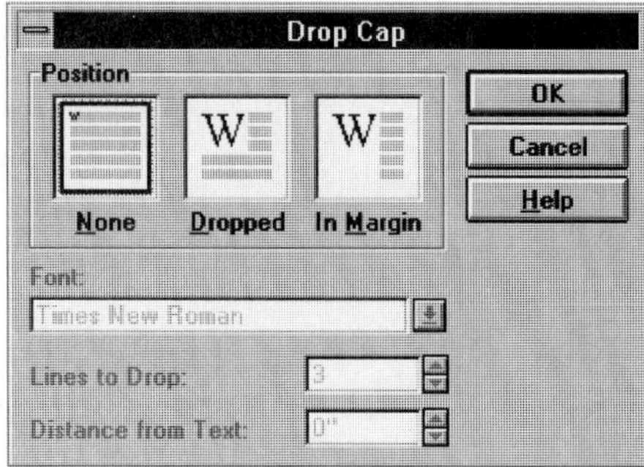

Now click on the box that gives the position you want; you can choose either Dropped or In Margin. A click on the None button removes the drop caps from the selected paragraph. The Dropped box makes the dropped capital letter flush with the left margin, placing the drop cap inside the main text area. Choose the In Margin button to put the drop cap in the left margin, beginning at the first line of the paragraph.

You can choose from any of the fonts Word knows about (it's customary to use a fairly ornate font for a drop cap). The Lines to Drop box lets you enter the number of lines in the paragraph you want the dropped cap to extend downward. Finally, the Distance from Text box lets you select the amount of space you want between a dropped capital letter and the text in the paragraph.

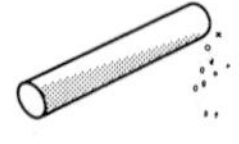

NOTE *You will need to be in Page Layout view to see the drop caps on the screen. (Page Layout view was introduced in Chapter 2 and you saw it at work in Chapter 4. Page Layout view becomes more useful the more elaborate your Word documents become.)*

In fact, if you add a drop cap to text while you are in Normal view, Word presents you with a dialog box that looks like this:

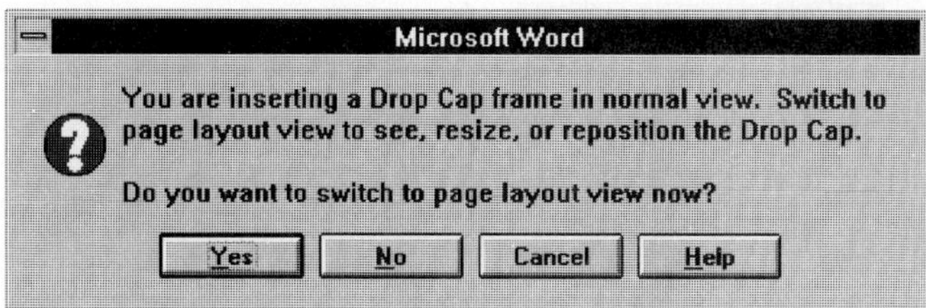

Choose Yes if you want to see the drop cap on the screen.

After you are happy with your results you can choose Normal from the View menu (Alt V, N) or use the Normal button on the status bar to go back to Normal view but it is probably better to stay in Page Layout view as long as you are using Word features like drop caps that require seeing precisely where objects are on the screen.

EXAMPLE

1. Suppose you wanted to print for a child the following story told by Lincoln at the end of a speech he gave in 1859.

   It is said an Eastern monarch once charged his wise man to invent for him a sentence, to be ever in view, and which should be true and appropriate in all times and situations. They presented him with these words: "*And this, too, shall pass away.*"

   You decide to change the initial I to a drop cap. Enter the story in a new document using a large font suitable for a child (16 point for example). Choose Drop Cap from the Format menu and click on the Dropped box. Then click on OK. If you print the document, it will look something like this:

   It is said an Eastern monarch once charged his wise man to invent for him a sentence, to be ever in view, and which should be true and appropriate in all times and situations. They presented him with these words: "*And this, too, shall pass away.*"

EXERCISES

1. Open or switch to MYMEMO1.DOC.
2. Add a 20% shading to the "MEMO" header.
3. Add a bottom border to the separator line containing the plus signs. Delete the plus signs.
4. Add a double line border around the quotation and the quotation source.
5. Try a single 3 point line shadowed border around the quotation.
6. Save MYMEMO1.DOC.

7.3 USING STYLES

Styles may seem mysterious, but if you think of them as a bunch of rules for formatting your text or paragraphs that you can name and then apply in one fell swoop, you won't ever go too far wrong. There are two actually two types of styles:

- Paragraph styles, which work on the paragraph as a whole by controlling such features as indents.
- Character styles, which work on the characters inside the paragraph.

Paragraph styles apply to the entire paragraph that contains the insertion point, or that have any part selected (or to multiple paragraphs if they are selected), while character styles affect only the selected characters.

Styles can save you time: if you find yourself repeatedly indenting a quotation one inch from both margins and changing it into a smaller point size, it's probably time to think about setting up a style to automate the process.

Unless you changed the default font (as described in the previous chapter), every paragraph you type starts out as flush left in the 10-point Times New Roman font. This is the default for Word's *Normal* style. Normal style is what Word uses automatically when you start a new document (when you click on the New button or choose Normal from the New dialog box that pops up after choosing New from the File menu). A useful shorthand is to refer to documents started this way as *normal documents*. If you have changed the default font to 10 point Arial, then *your* Normal style is now flush left in 10 point *Arial.*

Word comes with around 75 styles—far more than most people will ever need. There are styles for different kinds of headings, styles for lists, styles for envelope addresses. And, if one of Word's built-in styles doesn't fill your needs, it's easy to create your own styles. Probably the easiest way to get used to styles is to start with Word's heading styles. Heading styles are very useful for making text stand out (and also for using Word's outlining feature—see Chapter 11). The first heading style (called Heading 1) is used for things like Chapter titles—text that is at the highest organizational level in your document.

APPLYING STYLES VIA THE FORMATTING TOOLBAR

First make sure the insertion point is inside the paragraph you want to make into the highest level heading. Click on the arrow in the Style box on the Formatting toolbar, as shown here:

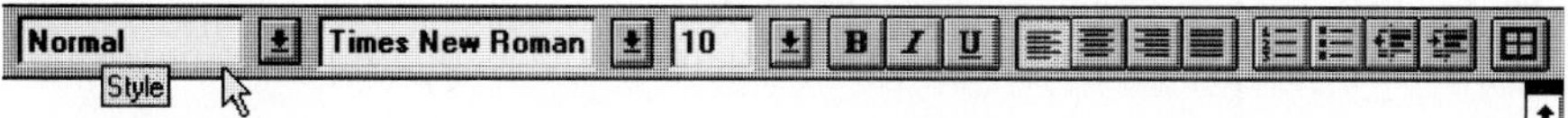

Word drops a list with the styles it currently expects you to be using, as shown here:

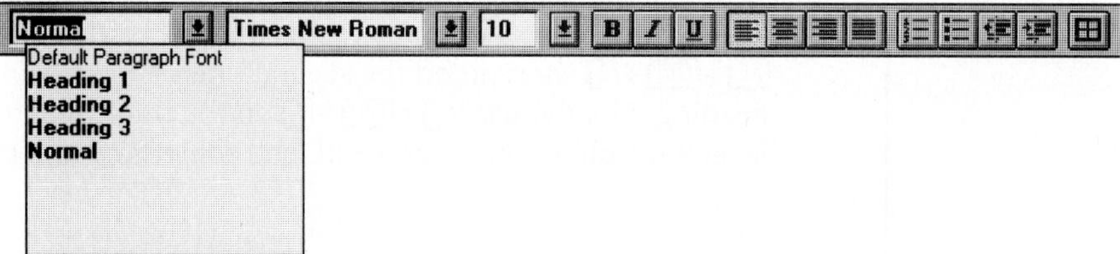

Now choose Heading 1. Word automatically reformats the paragraph according to the rules for a level 1 heading.

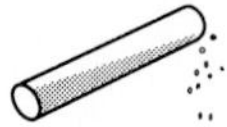

NOTE *To see all the styles Word currently has to offer, hold down the* Shift *key before you click on the arrow to drop down the list of styles.*

Word comes with a few built-in shortcuts for applying styles and you can make up your own as well. (See the section on the Modify Style dialog box later in this chapter.)

Style	Shortcut
Normal	Ctrl+Shift+N
Heading 1	Alt+Ctrl+1
Heading 2	Alt+Ctrl+2
Heading 3	Alt+Ctrl+3

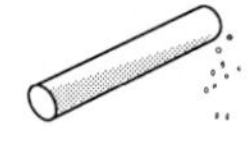

NOTE Ctrl+Spacebar *removes styles that you've applied.*

EXAMPLE

1. Type the following in a new document, pressing Enter between each line.

   This is an example of heading 1
   This is an example of heading 2
   This is an example of heading 3

   Move the insertion point into the first line and use the Alt+Ctrl+1 shortcut to make this into a level 1 heading. Use the Alt+Ctrl+2 shortcut on the second line to make it into a level 2 heading. Finally, use Alt+Ctrl+3 on the third line to make it into a level 3 heading. The screen will look something like this:

   This is an example of heading 1

   This is an example of heading 2

   This is an example of heading 3

THE STYLE DIALOG BOX

To do additional work with styles, you need to go beyond the list presented in the style box, to the full power of the Style dialog box. To open this dialog box, which is shown in Figure 7-4, choose Style from the Format menu (Alt O, S). Choosing All Styles from the List drop-down box gives you another way to see the full list of styles available to Word (besides holding down Shift while clicking on the arrow in the Style drop-down list box). You can also use this dialog box to preview, modify, or create a new style.

To apply a style using this dialog box:

1. Select the desired text or paragraphs.
2. Open the Style dialog box.
3. Choose the desired style. (If the style you want is not showing in the Styles list box on the left side of the Style dialog box, open the List drop-down list box on the bottom left of Figure 7-4 and choose All Styles.)
4. Click on the Apply button.

As you experiment with different settings in this dialog box, keep in mind that the Paragraph Preview box in the center of Figure 7-4 shows you how the paragraph would appear if you clicked on the Apply button. Similarly, the Character Preview box shows you how the fonts in the selected text in a document would appear if you applied the style you are experimenting with. (If no text in your document is selected, Word displays the name of the font and how it would look.)

FIGURE 7-4

The Style dialog box

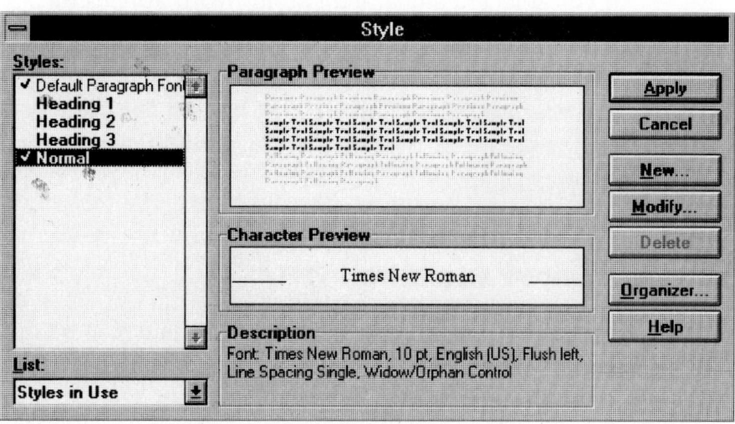

Let's go over the remaining options in the Style dialog box more carefully:

The List Drop-Down List Box The List drop-down list box gives you three options. You can choose Styles in Use to see the styles you are currently using. (This is the same as what you usually see in the Style box on the toolbar unless you hold down the Shift key before clicking on the arrow.). As mentioned earlier, you can choose All Styles to see which styles are available to the document. The third option, User-Defined Styles, shows you only the styles you have created for the active document (see the section on creating a style later in this chapter).

The Styles List Box The Styles list box checks the current setting in the List drop-down list box and then lists the appropriate styles here. Select the name of the style you want to apply or change. Paragraph styles are shown in bold; character styles are shown in plain text. First choose All Styles in the List drop-down box, then, by scrolling through the Styles list box, you can select the style you want.

Description The Description area provides a (rather terse) description of the formatting options in the style currently highlighted in the Styles list box.

The Apply Button Click on the Apply button to have Word apply the style highlighted in the Style box to the selected text or paragraphs. Keep in mind that if you select a paragraph style, Word applies the style to the paragraph containing the insertion point. If you have selected multiple paragraphs, Word applies the style to all the paragraphs. Finally, if you selected a character style, Word applies the style to any selected text or the word that contains the insertion point.

The New and Modify Buttons Click on the New or Modify button to either create or modify a style. You'll learn more about these options in later sections.

SIMPLE WAYS TO MODIFY OR CREATE A STYLE

Modifying an existing Word style is not to be done casually because many Word styles build on other Word styles. This means that when you change one style, you may find yourself affecting a style that you meant to leave alone. For example, almost every Word style builds on the style called Default Paragraph Font. When you change the default font to, say, Arial, you have modified almost every other Word style to use Arial in place of Times New Roman. And if you change the Normal style to be indented, you will probably have made lots of unwanted changes, since almost every Word style is also built upon the Normal style.

You can tell if a style depends on another style by looking at the Description area in the Style dialog box. For example, as shown here, you can see that the description for the Heading 1 style starts with the words "Normal + Font." This means that the Heading 1 style depends on the Normal style and the Font style (which is an abbreviation for the Default Paragraph Font style).

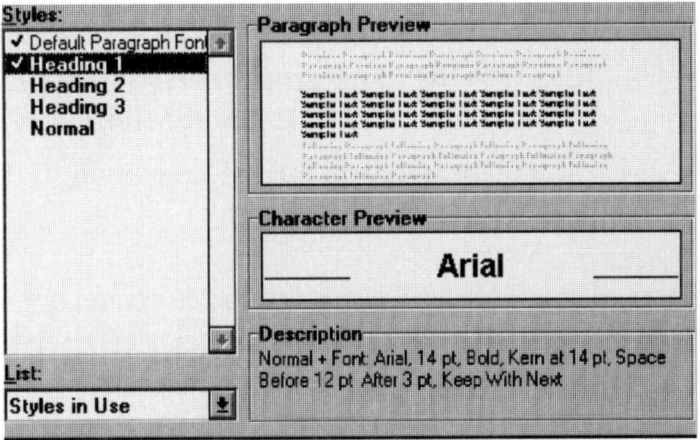

There are two ways to modify a style. The easiest method is only available if there is a paragraph or text in your document formatted in the style you want to modify. (You'll see the more sophisticated and more powerful method in the next section.)

If there is a paragraph or text formatted using the style you want to change, just follow these steps:

1. Modify the paragraph (or text) that is currently in the style you want to change. (Indent it, make the font larger or smaller, and so on.)
2. Select the whole paragraph (or text).
3. Move the mouse pointer (the I-beam) to the Style drop-down list box on the Formatting toolbar and click, then press Enter.

Word pops up a dialog box that looks like this:

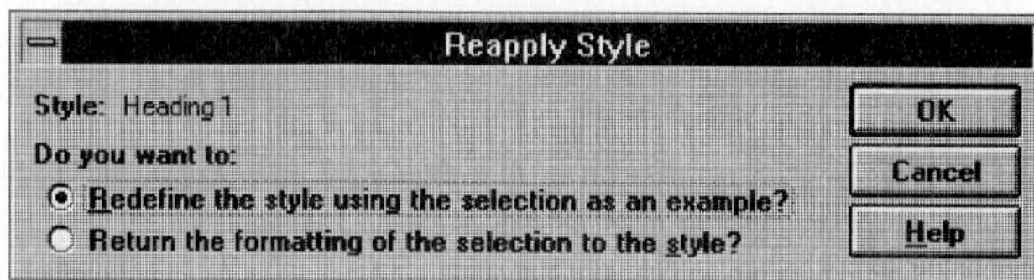

4. Make sure the first option button is selected, as shown in this illustration. Then click on OK.

There are also two ways to create a style. The easiest way is to first apply the desired formatting to a paragraph or selected text in your document. Then follow these steps:

1. Select the whole paragraph (or text).
2. Go to the Style drop-down list box on the Formatting toolbar by moving the mouse pointer there and then clicking.
3. Type the name for the new style in the Style box, and press Enter.

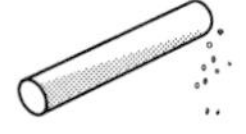

NOTE *A style name can contain up to 253 characters, including spaces. The only characters you can't use are a backslash (\), semicolon (;), or curly braces ({ and }). Also Style names are case sensitive. For example, heading 1 and Heading 1 are considered two different styles.*

Finally, you need to have Word save any styles you create or modify in its *Normal template* if you want to be able to reuse them for all your normal documents—those started with the New button or by choosing Normal in the New dialog box. When you try to exit Word, you'll see a dialog box that looks like this:

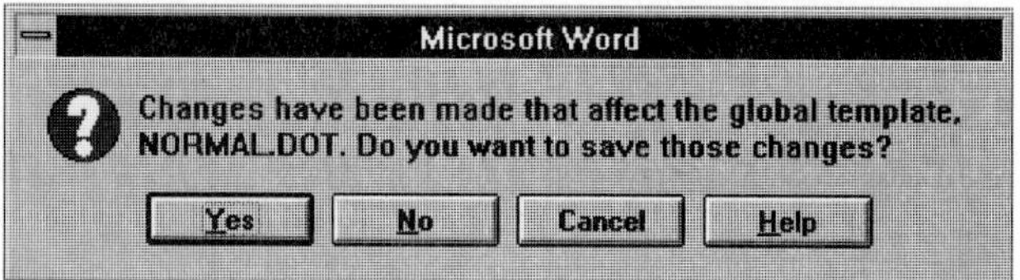

If you want to be able to use the style for all normal documents, click on Yes. (See Section 7.4 for more on Templates and more on what this dialog box is really doing.)

EXAMPLE

1. Suppose you want to create a Quotation style that is indented three quarters of an inch on each side.
   a. Enter the following in a separate paragraph:

      This will be indented three quarters of an inch on each side.

   b. Make sure the insertion point is inside the paragraph. Open the Paragraph dialog box by choosing Paragraph from the Format menu and set the indents to .75" in both the Left and Right box. Click on OK to put these changes into effect.
   c. Move the mouse pointer to the Style list box on the Formatting toolbar, type **quote**, and press Enter.
2. Type the following quotation from Edmond Burke:

   The use of force is but *temporary*. It may subdue for a moment; but it does not remove the necessity of subduing again; and a nation is not governed, which is perpetually to be conquered.

   Apply the new quote style to this paragraph by making sure the insertion point is in the paragraph, opening the Style list box on the Formatting toolbar, and choosing quote.

CHANGING STYLES VIA THE MODIFY STYLE DIALOG BOX

This dialog box gives you the most control over how a modified style will look. It also is the only way to assign a shortcut key to a style. First make sure that the style you want to modify is highlighted in the Styles list box in the Style dialog box.

Now, if you click on the Modify button in the Style dialog box, you are taken to the Modify dialog box, shown in Figure 7-5. Many of the options in this dialog box are clear. For example, the Name list box lists the name of the style and the Style Type list box shows whether it is a character or paragraphs style. (This box is always dimmed because you cannot change the type of an existing style, but you can still see whether the style you are modifying is a paragraph or character style). As usual, the Preview box shows you how the modified style will look. The Description box gives you the usual terse description of the formatting options included in the modified style.

FIGURE 7-5

The Modify Style dialog box

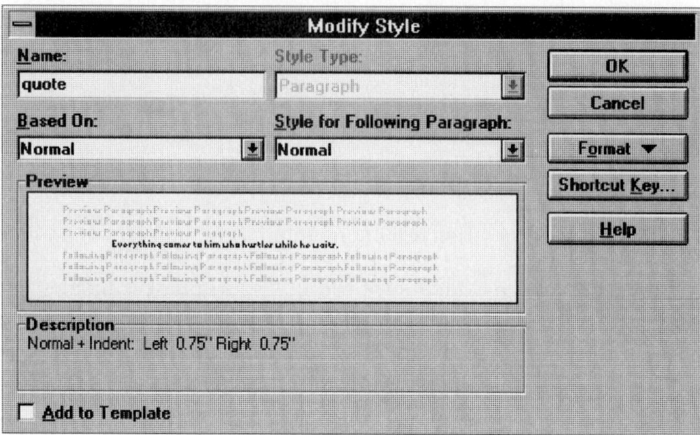

Here are brief discussions on some of the remaining items in the Modify Style dialog box. Assigning your own shortcut keys to styles is covered in the next section.

The Style for Following Paragraph Drop-Down List Box The Style for Following Paragraph drop-down list box lets you choose which (existing) style will automatically be applied to the next new paragraph you enter after any paragraph formatted with the modified style. The idea is that certain styles almost automatically follow other styles. After a heading style, you would almost certainly want a Normal (or Body Text) style.

The Add to Template Check Box The Add to Template check box is an important option. However, to really understand how it works you need to understand more about templates, which are covered in Section 7.4.

The Format Button A click on the Format button drops down a list that looks like this:

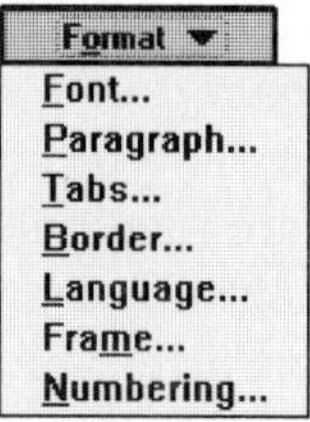

Clicking on one of these items takes you to a dialog box for adjusting that characteristic. For example, choosing Font takes you to the Font dialog box you saw in the last chapter and clicking on Paragraph takes you to the Paragraph dialog box you saw earlier in this chapter.

ASSIGNING SHORTCUT KEYS

Assigning shortcut keys is so useful for styles that it's worth spending a little extra time making sure you are comfortable with the method. If you click on the Shortcut Key button in the Modify Style dialog box, you are taken to the Customize dialog box shown in Figure 7-6. Make sure the Keyboard tab is in front. (The other two tabs on this dialog box are used for customizing menus and toolbars; these advanced topics are beyond the scope of this book.)

Here's how you assign a shortcut key to the style that you are already working with:

1. First decide what keyboard combination you want to use. Most style shortcuts use either two or three keys held down simultaneously.
2. Make sure the insertion point is inside the Press New Shortcut Key textbox.
3. Press the key combination you want, *making sure to hold down the keys simultaneously.*

If the Key combination is in use, Word warns you by telling you the current use of that key combination in the bottom left of the dialog box, as shown here.

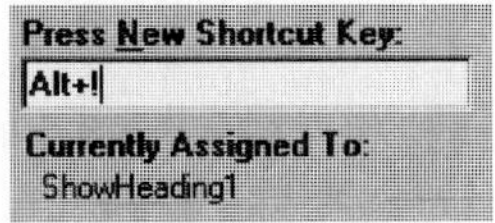

Notice the Save Changes In drop-down list box in the right corner of the dialog box. To have this shortcut available for all normal documents, make sure you choose Normal.dot in this list box.

Once you click on the Assign button and click on Close, Word memorizes the shortcut. If you chose Normal.dot as the place to save it, you can use this shortcut in all your normal documents.

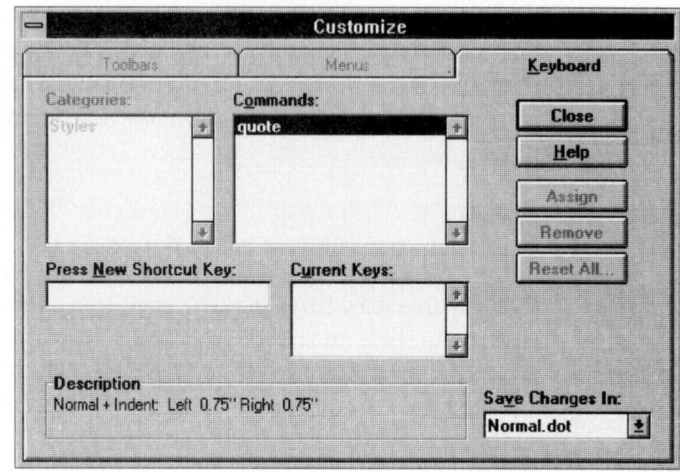

FIGURE 7-6 *Assigning shortcut keys via the Customize dialog box*

To remove an existing shortcut:

1. Highlight the item in the Current Keys list box, which is shown in Figure 7-6.
2. Click on the Remove button.

EXAMPLE

1. Suppose you wanted to continue the standard style shortcuts by applying Alt+Ctrl+4 to the Heading 4 style.
   a. Open the Format menu and choose Style drop. Make sure the All Styles item is selected in the List drop-down list box. Then highlight the Heading 4 style.
   b. Click on the Modify button and then click on the Shortcut Key button.
   c. In the Customize dialog box, make sure the insertion point is in the Press New Shortcut Key box. Then press Alt+Ctrl+4, *making sure to hold down all the keys simultaneously.*

SHORTCUTS FOR COPYING AND WORKING WITH STYLES

Although you have already seen how to set your own shortcuts for styles, there are a couple of shortcuts for applying or removing styles built into Word that are worth keeping in mind:

- To apply a style to a paragraph after you have just applied it to another paragraph, move the insertion point to the new paragraph and press Ctrl+Y. (This is Word's usual Repeat feature applied to styles.)

- To quickly see what styles have been applied to text or a paragraph, click on the Help button (the mouse pointer changes to an arrow plus a question mark). Then click at the text or inside the paragraph.

Many people actually prefer to see the styles that they are applying to the text in the left margin at all times. You can do this only in Normal view. To add a *style area* to your documents:

1. Open the Tools menu and choose Options.
2. Select the View Tab and set the Style Area Width text box to be wide enough to show the styles you are using (.5" is fine).

(Set this text box back to 0 to eliminate the style area.)

Finally, if you select text in a certain character style, the Format Painter button that you saw in Chapter 6 on the Standard toolbar gives you a quick method to copy the style. Similarly, if you select the paragraph mark at the end of a paragraph in the style you want to copy, and then click on the Format painter tool, all you need to do to copy the paragraph style to the new paragraph is click inside the paragraph you want to restyle.

CREATING A NEW STYLE USING THE STYLE DIALOG BOX

The dialog box you see when you choose the New button on the Style dialog box is shown in Figure 7-7. It is essentially the same as the one used for modifying a style (Figure 7-6). However, it is usually easier to create a new style by making the paragraph or text assume the shape and form that you want the style to have (as described earlier), so that you may not need to ever work with this dialog box.

FIGURE 7-7

The New Style dialog box

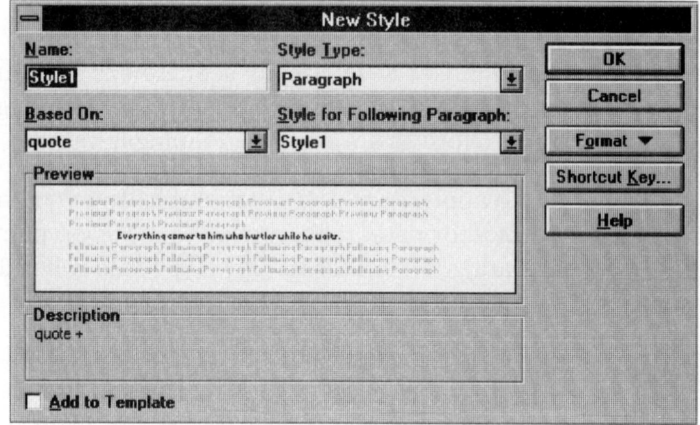

To create a style using this dialog box, click on the Format button and choose the item you want to adjust from the list that drops down. For example, if you choose Font, you would go to the standard Font dialog box that you saw in Chapter 6. If you choose Paragraph, you would go to the Paragraph dialog box you saw at the beginning of the chapter. Make the changes you want using these dialog boxes and click on OK when you are satisfied. (The Shortcut key button leads to the same dialog box that you saw when you wanted to add a shortcut to an existing style.)

EXERCISES

1. Open or switch to MYMEMO1.DOC.
2. Switch to Normal view, select Options from the Tool menu, and choose the View tab. Set your Style Area Width to 1 inch.
3. Make the MEMO header a Heading 1 paragraph, center it, and add 25% shading.
4. Move the insertion point into the From line and define a new style called "My Memo Header."
5. Modify the My Memo Header style to use a 12-point Arial font.
6. Define a style for the separator line.
7. Save MYMEMO1.DOC.

7.4 USING TEMPLATES

A template is a blueprint for the text, graphics, and formatting of a document. Templates contain all the styles used in that document, all the margins, and almost everything that determines the ultimate look of a document. There may be some specific text, but there are lots of "holes" left for the content.

For example, a letter template has a certain standard shape (block, semi-block, and so on). This leads to certain styles for paragraphs such as indented paragraphs for informal writing, for example. However, a letter also uses a certain amount of standard text, words like "Dear," so the template includes this text in the correct position. What is left for the user of the template is to fill in the obvious "holes" later on (Dear *Who?*).

Now you can see the main difference between a Wizard and a template: a Wizard asks you questions and uses the answers to fill in the "holes" in a template. When you use a template, you need to fill in this information by working directly within the document.

The real reason templates can save so much time is that most of your documents fall into just a few categories. Businesses write memos, business letters, proposals, and so on. Students write reports, manuscripts, theses, and so on.

When you choose New from the File menu, Word pops up the New dialog box that you have seen so often.

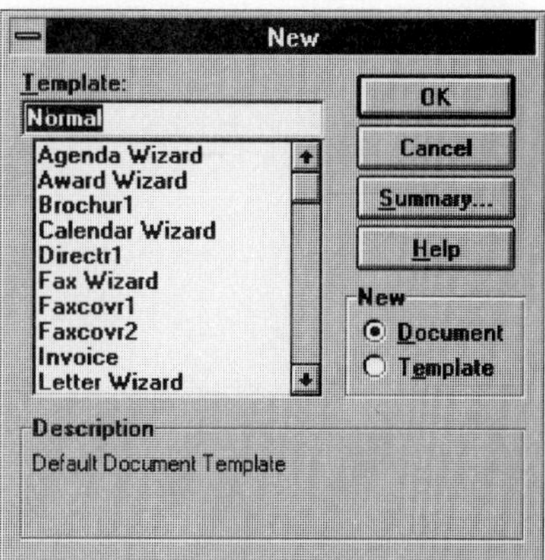

So far you have always chosen Normal (or a Wizard) from this list. (Clicking on the New button on the Toolbar gives the same result as choosing Normal.) Thus, building your document on the framework provided by the *Normal template* is the default for any Word document. However, all the items not marked as a Wizard on this list are actually templates. When you choose a different template from this list and click on OK, Word creates documents based on that template. The template you choose determines the margins, the indents, the styles available, and so on.

REMEMBER *Word documents are all based upon templates.*

CHANGING THE TEMPLATE CURRENTLY IN USE

Templates are like clothes for documents: often you will want to try them on before you buy one for your document. The Style Gallery command on the Format menu (Alt O, G) leads to the Style Gallery dialog box, shown in Figure 7-8, which is like Word's dressing room. This dialog box shows you how a document will look if it is formatted with the styles from a different template, and then lets you change the template attached to your document. Notice the Template list box, which lists each template Word knows about.

The Preview box in the lower-left corner of Figure 7-8 has three buttons. When Document is on, Word show you how changing the

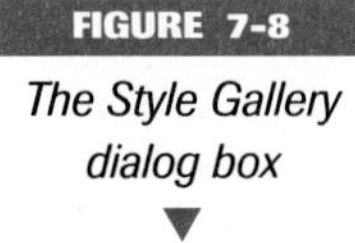

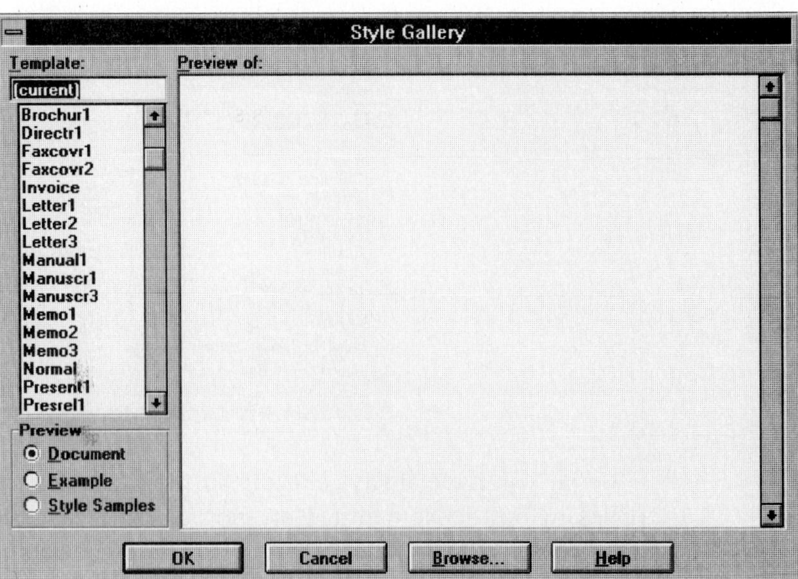

FIGURE 7-8

The Style Gallery dialog box

template would affect the current document. (Normally, you'll have a document on the screen which will show up here if the Document button is selected under Preview.)

If you want to see how a new template choice would affect your document, make sure that the Document button is on, then select the Template in the Template list box on the left-hand side of the Style Gallery. If you double-click on a template name, Word attaches the template into the document and closes the Style Gallery dialog box. This means all the styles in your document will now reflect the characteristics they have in the new template. Finally, selecting the [current] item in the Template list shows you how the current document looks before Word reformats it using another template choice.

If you select the Example option button, you'll see a sample document already formatted using the highlighted template name—scroll through the Template list box to see samples of the other templates. If you select Style Samples option button, Word shows you a list of all of the styles in the selected template and samples of the style formats. (The trouble is that the preview box is too small to make this easy to see on many monitors.)

A click on the Browse button brings up a dialog box that selects templates from any drive or directory using techniques like the ones for navigating through disks or directories to Open or Save a file. (Having templates stored in a directory other than C:\WINWORD \TEMPLATE is most common if you are working with Word on a network.)

Finally, templates are always stored with file names ending in .DOT. The Normal template is actually a file called NORMAL.DOT stored in the \TEMPLATE subdirectory of the directory in which Word is stored. When you see a message box like this:

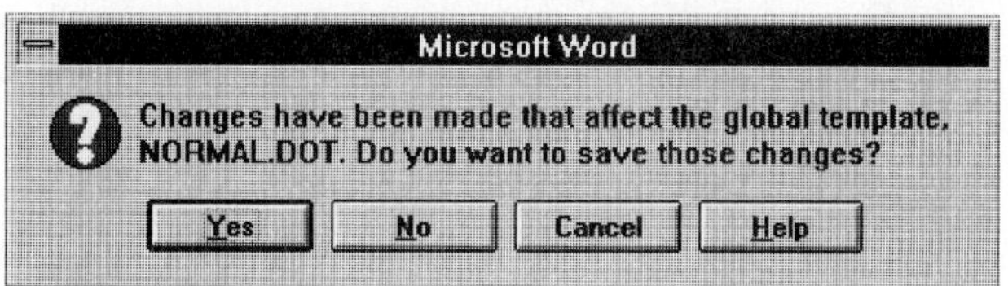

Word is really telling you that you are changing the NORMAL.DOT file—and therefore changing the Normal template.

EXAMPLES

1. Suppose you write a letter and want to try the various letter templates to see which one looks best. Choose Style Gallery from the Format menu and click, in turn, on the Letter 1, Letter 2, and Letter 3 styles, each time keeping your eye on the Preview box.
2. Suppose you want to see what the three different memo templates look like. Go to the Style Gallery and make sure that the Example option button is selected under Preview. Click successively on Memo 1, Memo 2, and Memo 3, each time keeping your eye on the Preview box.

EXERCISES

1. Open or switch to MYMEMO1.DOC.
2. Switch to Normal view and open the Tools menu and choose Options. Next, choose the View tab, and set your Style Area Width to .5 inch (if it's not already set).
3. Create a new document based on MEMO1.DOT. Fill in the blanks in your new memo.
4. See how the styles in the new document based on the MEMO1.DOT template are defined by using the Style dialog box on the Format menu.
5. Change the template to MEMO2.DOT using the Style Gallery and return to the main document. Study the styles in the memo (which is now based on MEMO2.DOT). View the styles used in this document by dropping down the Style drop-down list box on the Formatting toolbar.
6. Study the styles in the new document based on MEMO2.DOT by using the Help button and clicking in the various paragraphs.
7. Select Format, Style Gallery and preview how your new memo would look using MEMO3.DOT.
8. While in the Style Gallery, highlight one of the memo templates and select Style Samples to preview all the styles available.

7.5 AUTOMATIC FORMATTING

Automatic formatting is a way to have Word reformat your document automatically. Word will analyze the document, trying to decide which styles apply where, and which make your document look best. You then have the option of reviewing each automatic change or accepting them *en masse*.

Automatic formatting is one of the highly-touted new features in Word 6.0, but choosing styles yourself gives you a lot more control over the appearance of your document, even though it takes a bit more work. In any case, few people would suggest letting Word make changes to your document without reviewing them after the fact.

Here's some of what Automatic Formatting can do to your documents:

- Remove extra hard returns. (These are marked on your screen with paragraph marks.)
- Replace indents inserted with the Spacebar and Tab keys with paragraph indents.
- Use bullets instead of asterisks, hyphens, or other similar characters that you may have used for bulleted lists.
- Replace (C), (R), and (TM) with copyright (©), registered trademark (®), and trademark symbols (™).

The delicate issue is that the automatic formatting feature also can choose which style to apply to a paragraph—and you may not agree with its choices.

You can format either the whole document or a selection within the document. In both cases,

1. Choose AutoFormat from the Format menu (Alt F, A). This pops open a dialog box that looks like this:

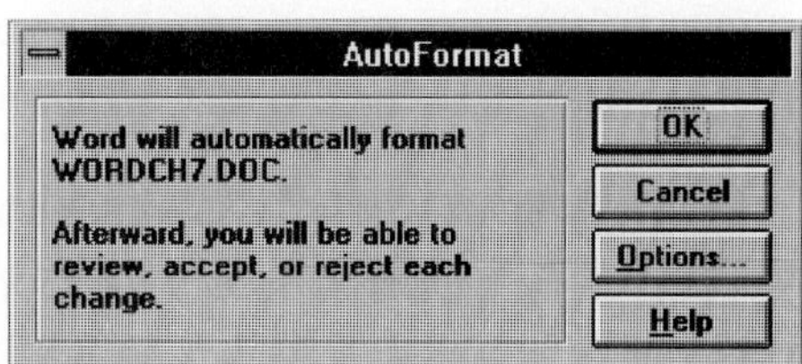

2. Click on OK to start the process. (It will take some time on most machines.) When Word is done, it pops up a dialog box that looks like this:

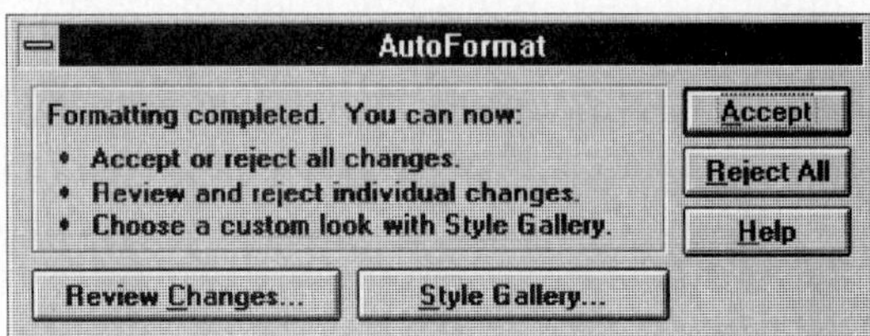

3. Click on the Review Changes button to see what Word did. (If you click on the Style Gallery button, Word takes you to the Style Gallery dialog box that you have already seen.) Word pops up a dialog box that looks like this:

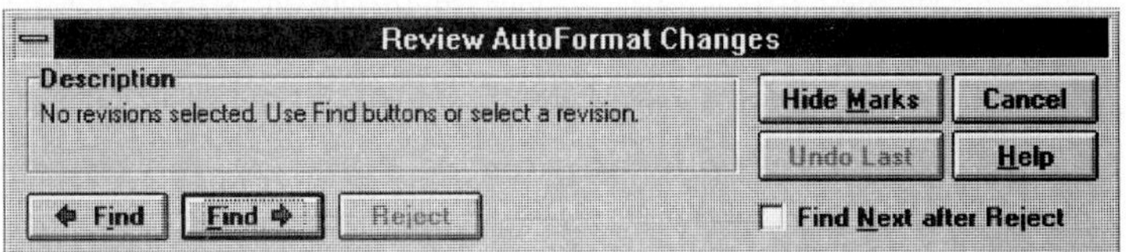

The best thing to do is to work through the changes one by one using one of the Find buttons to move forward or backward through the newly formatted document. Word uses temporary revision marks to indicate what it wants to do. The following table summarizes these marks (you'll need a color monitor to take best advantage of them):

Revision Mark	Indicates that Word Did the Following
Blue paragraph marks	Applied a style to the paragraph
Red paragraph marks	Deleted the paragraph mark
Strikethrough character	Deleted text or spaces
Underline	Added the underlined characters

You can move the Review Changes dialog box by dragging its title bar if it is blocking your view of the document. To review, reject, or revise changes, make sure the revision marks are displayed. (Pay particular attention to the blue colored paragraph symbols since they tell you whether Word has applied a style to the paragraph!) To see the document as it would look if you accepted all of the changes, choose the Hide Marks button.

If you click on the Reject button, Word undoes that specific change. Each time you click on one of the Find buttons rather than the Reject button, the change remains in your document. (The Undo Last button lets you restore the last automatic formatting change you rejected.)

When you click on the Cancel button to end the reviewing process, Word pops up the AutoFormat dialog box.

Now you have to decide: if you click on Accept, *all the changes you didn't reject previously go into effect.*

Note that the Undo button on the Standard toolbar lets you change your mind if you accepted the changes and then changed your mind.

CAUTION *Word has an AutoFormat button available on the Standard toolbar. The problem with using this button is that it does not give you the opportunity to review the changes. If you use this button, you must either accept the changes en masse or reject them en masse.*

EXAMPLES

1. Enter the following:

   Using AutoFormat to replace the copyright (c) and trademark (TM) symbols is a *small* timesaver.

   Choose AutoFormat from the Format menu. Your screen will look like this after Word finishes. Notice the struck through text:

   Using AutoFormat to replace the copyright symbol ©~~(c)~~ and the trademark symbol ™~~(TM)~~ is a *small* timesaver¶

   Review AutoFormat Changes
   Description
   No revisions selected. Use Find buttons or select a revision.
   Hide Marks | Cancel | Undo Last | Help
   ← Find | Find → | Reject
   Find Next after Reject

   Now you can click on the accept button in the AutoFormat dialog box to accept these changes or follow the procedure discussed earlier to review the changes one by one.

2. Suppose you enter the following into a new document, in the format given here:

   We were on a dig in Stratford, England and we found a very old piece of paper that was really strange. It said:

   "Eye of newt, and toe of frog
   Wool of bat, and tongue of dog."

   This recipe is copyright (c) 1597 W. Shakespeare.

   Choose AutoFormat from the Format menu. When the AutoFormat dialog box pops up, click on the Review Changes button and then click on the Find button with the right arrow to review the changes. Notice that, except for removing some extra paragraph marks and changing the copyright symbol, Word has mostly made rather silly suggestions.

THE AUTOFORMAT OPTIONS BOX

To control how Word autoformats your documents, choose Options from the Tools menu (Alt T, O) to display the Options dialog box. If you click on the AutoFormat tab in the Options dialog box, you'll see the AutoFormat tab shown in Figure 7-9. This lets you set the rules that Word follows when it automatically formats text.

FIGURE 7-9

The AutoFormat tab on the Options dialog box

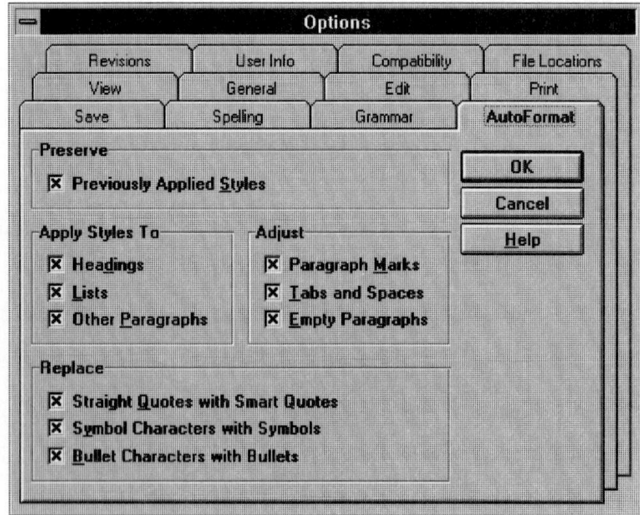

The options on the AutoFormat tab are a little obscure at first. Here are short descriptions of them.

Previously Applied Styles A check here tells Word to keep the styles *you* applied to the document.

Apply Styles To Area These three check boxes control where you want Word to do autoformatting. For example, if you check Headings, Word automatically applies Heading 1 through Heading 9 styles to what it thinks are the headings in your document. Check Lists and Word automatically applies list and bullet styles to numbered, bulleted, and multilevel lists. By default, Word removes any manually inserted numbers or bullets before fixing a list. The Other Paragraphs check box tells Word to automatically apply paragraph styles other than the styles for headings and lists—this is the most delicate one—the one, where if you leave this option on, you will probably need to review before accepting Word's choices!

The Adjust Area These check boxes let you select which of these elements you want Word to try to adjust when it automatically formats the document. For example, checking Paragraph Marks means that if you inserted a paragraph mark at the end of a line instead of using word wrap, Word removes the paragraph mark.

TIP *This is a very nice feature if you import a document and discover that it has carriage returns at the end of every line.*

The other checkboxes are also occasionally useful to allow Word to modify automatically. For example, if you check Tabs and Spaces, Word replaces spaces with tab characters and removes unnecessary tab characters and spaces. If Empty Paragraphs is checked, Word removes blank lines between paragraphs with certain styles—such as between two Normal or Body Text paragraphs. (This is useful if you press Enter twice by mistake.)

The Replace Area Allowing Word to have its way with these options is mostly harmless and actually fairly useful. For example, checking Straight Quotes With Smart Quotes changes straight quotation marks (" and ") to "smart" (curly) quotation marks (“ and ”). The Symbol

Characters With Symbols check box lets you replace characters used in place of symbols with symbols that may not be on your keyboard but that your printer can print. For example, you can replace (C) with the copyright symbol (although you *could* have just used the symbol font).

EXERCISES

1. Load or switch to MYMEMO1.DOC. Highlight the whole document and assign the Normal style to all paragraphs.
2. Autoformat the document.
3. Undo the autoformat operation and experiment with autoformat by:
   a. Adding spaces or tabs to indent the quotation.
   b. Splitting the quotation over more than one paragraph.
4. Close MYMEMO1.DOC without saving your changes.
5. Create a new document and add the following text, using only Normal style paragraphs, and then use Format, AutoFormat to format the document.

   Centered Title

   Introduction

   This is the introduction. Each paragraph in this sample document has a blank line between paragraphs.

   The following is a list:

   *   Copyright (C)
   *   Trademark (TM)
   *   Registered Trademark (R)

   Section Header

   This is the summary and is the last paragraph in the document.

   View the document in Page Layout view. How did AutoFormat do in selecting styles for this document?

6. Use the Review Changes feature to review the changes AutoFormat made. (Remember, this is only available if you used the Format, AutoFormat command).
7. Use the Style Gallery and view your document based on a few different templates.
8. Undo all the changes AutoFormat made; change the asterisks to the numbers 1, 2, 3; and try AutoFormat again.
9. Close the document without saving your changes.

mastery skills check

1. Write a business letter using only the Normal paragraph style and then use Format, AutoFormat. [7.3, 7.5]
2. Review the changes AutoFormat suggested and complete the AutoFormat process. [7.5]
3. Switch to Normal view and, using Tools, Options, set your Style Area Width to one inch. [7.3]
4. Review the styles applied to your letter and view the available styles listed in the Style drop-down list box located on the Formatting toolbar. [7.3]
5. Use the Format, Style Gallery and preview your document based on the Letter1, Letter2, and Letter3 templates. Apply one of these templates to your document. [7.3, 7.4]
6. View the available styles provided by the template listed in the Style drop-down list box located on the Formatting toolbar. [7.3, 7.4]
7. Add some text in three paragraphs and use the Block Quotation, Block Quotation First, and Block Quotation last styles. [7.3]
8. Determine what different spacing settings the three types of block quotation styles use. [7.1]

9. Add a 3/4-point double line border around the quotation. [7.2]
10. Add a shadow around the quotation border and add 3 points of space between the text and the border. [7.2]

cumulative skills check

1. Create a new document and enter the following table of contents [2.1]:

   INTRODUCTION 1
   LAST YEAR:
   Expenditures 5
   Revenues 9
   PROJECTED:
   Expenditures 12
   Revenues 15

2. Format the table of contents as follows:
   a. Make the chapter heading bold text and the font size 16 points. [6.1]
   b. Change the fonts for the section heads to Arial. [6.2]
   c. Set a tab stop at 2" and make them right-aligned tabs. [7.1]
   d. Add dot leaders for the tab stops. [7.1]
   e. Place a border around the whole table of contents. [7.2]
   f. Add 20% grey shading to the table of contents. [7.2]

8

Laying Out a Page

chapter objectives

After completing this chapter, you will know how to

8.1 Switch between Page Layout view, Normal view, and Full Screen mode, and zoom into your documents

8.2 Set up a page by adjusting the margins and size or source of the paper

8.3 Work with page numbers, headers, and footers

8.4 Create footnotes and endnotes

THE last chapter explained how to work with your documents one paragraph at a time. This chapter examines the techniques for determining how each page of your document looks. For example, in the last chapter you saw how to indent individual paragraphs. In this chapter you will learn how to change the margins and how to add headers and footers at the top or bottom of every page in your document.

The first section reviews and extends the ways of looking at your document that you saw in Chapter 2. These are important when you need to better understand how objects are positioned on a page. The second section describes methods for changing the size and shape of the printed area of the page. The third section explains how to add page numbers and footers, features that are particularly important for longer documents. The final section covers footnotes and endnotes.

1. Use the Memo Wizard to write a simple memo. Accept the Wizard's default settings. [4.7]
2. Use your document editing skills to alter the To and Subject fields and add some body text. [2.2]
3. Run a spell check on your memo. [5.1]
4. Open the Style Gallery and see how your memo would look in the other memo styles. [7.4]
5. Use the Print Preview feature to preview your memo. [2.5]
6. Print your memo and notice the header at the top of the page and the footer at the bottom of the page. [2.5]
7. Close your memo, saving it as MYMEMO2.DOC. [1.6, 2.3]

8.1 NEW WAYS TO VIEW YOUR DOCUMENT

So far we have mostly been working in *Normal view*. This is the default view because it is the best all-around way to display your document when you are entering and formatting text. Normal view gives you the fastest response; in this view Word doesn't spend a lot of time calculating the exact location of all the elements of your page. However, when you want to see a more accurate rendition of your page—but still need to edit the document almost as fast as you can in Normal view—switch to *Page Layout view*. In Page Layout view, you can see the margins of your document, graphics, and many other elements almost exactly as they will appear in the printed document.

Page preview, which you were introduced to in Chapter 2 (and which you will see more about in Chapter 9), gives you the best rendition of what your document will look like when printed, but it is more difficult to edit your document in this view.

To switch to Page Layout view:

- Choose Page Layout from the View menu (Alt P, V) or click on the Page Layout button on the horizontal scroll bar.

Word displays your document in a slightly different way. Figure 8-1 shows a document in both Normal view and Page Layout view. Notice that you can see a page break as well as where the top and bottom of the margins are in Page Layout view but not in Normal view. (In Page Layout view you can also move through your document one page at a time by clicking on the double headed arrows at the bottom of the vertical scroll bar.)

NOTE *Depending on the speed of your machine, you may find Page Layout view too slow to work with comfortably for any length of time.*

In Page Layout view, you can edit your document using all the ordinary editing techniques that by this point you know quite well.

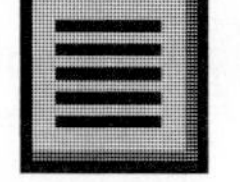

To change back to Normal view:

- Choose Normal from the View menu (Alt V, N) or click on the Normal button on the horizontal scroll bar.

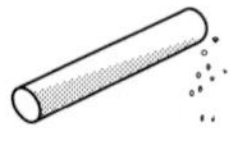

NOTE *You may want to stay in Page Layout view for the rest of this chapter.*

FIGURE 8-1

Normal view versus Page Layout view

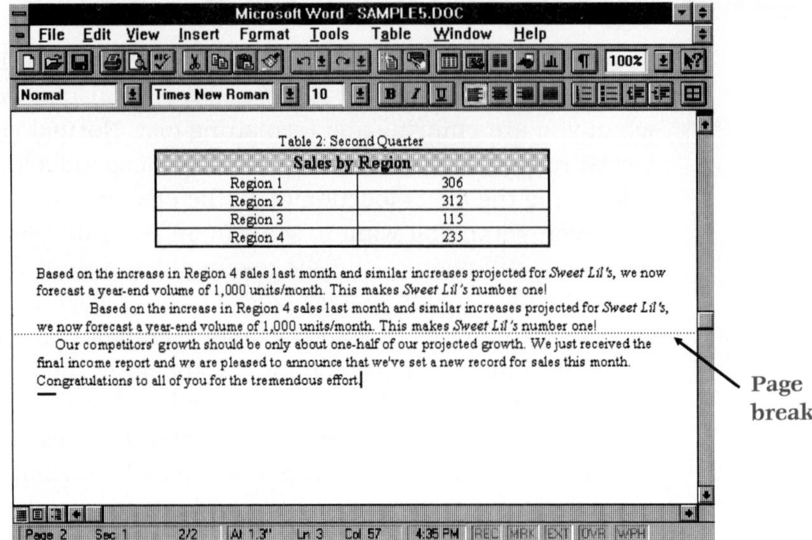

Normal view

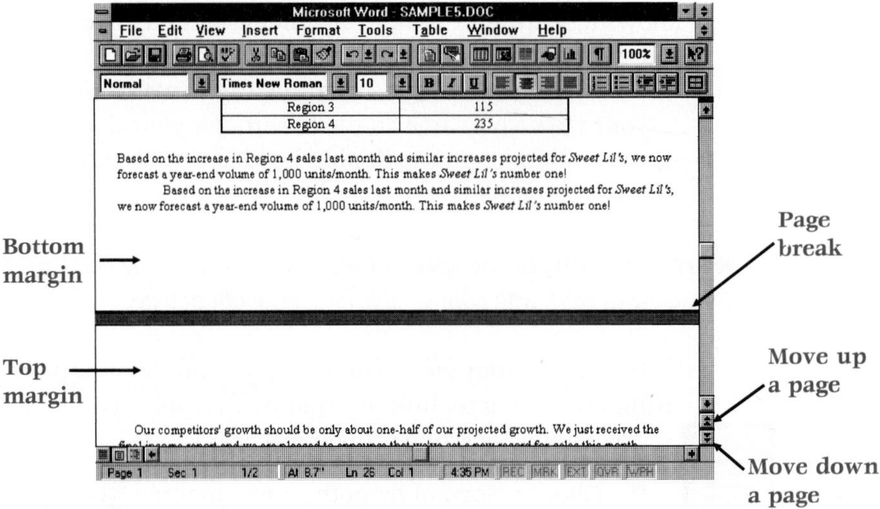

Page Layout view

EXAMPLE

1. Start up the Award Wizard and construct a simple award. When you are done, open the View menu and notice that you are already in Page Layout view. Switch to Normal view and notice that you see nothing! (This is because Normal view does not show the highly ornate graphics elements involved in an award certificate.)

FULL SCREEN MODE

In some cases, you may prefer not to see all the toolbars and other gadgets that are normally displayed on the screen in Word. If so, Word's *Full Screen mode* is for you. Switching to Full Screen mode enables you to see more of your document at a time on the screen. (Toolbars, menu bar, title bar, status bar, and so on are all hidden.) Note that you can use Full Screen mode in both Normal view and Page Layout view.

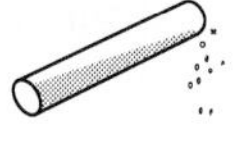

NOTE *When you choose Full Screen mode, you remain in the view you happen to be in at the time (Page Layout view or Normal view). You are simply giving yourself more room to see your text.*

To switch to Full Screen mode:

- Choose Full Screen from the View menu (Alt V, U).

Figure 8-2 shows an example of a blank Word screen in Full Screen mode—pretty barren isn't it? Notice the Full Screen button pointed to in this screen. Click on this button or press Esc to return to the ordinary Word screen. Although Figure 8-2 doesn't show it, Word does allow you to keep the ruler displayed in Full Screen mode; simply select View, Ruler (Alt V, R) once you are in Full Screen mode.

When you are in Full Screen mode, you can use all the usual editing techniques. You can also use keyboard shortcuts (such as Ctrl+P for print) and even menu commands. Somewhat surprisingly, all the ordinary Word menus are still available in Full Screen mode—if you can remember the appropriate Alt key combination.

FIGURE 8-2
Word in Full Screen mode

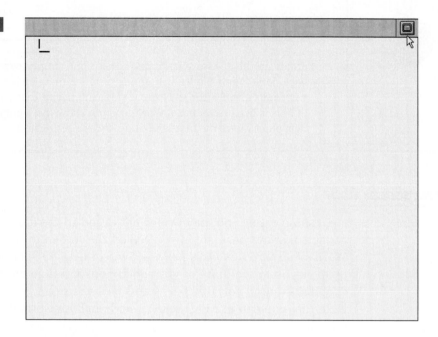

REMEMBER *The inside front cover has short tables listing the most common shortcuts.*

EXAMPLES

1. Open a new blank document, switch to Full Screen mode, and press Alt and then an E. Notice that the ordinary Edit menu opens, as shown here:

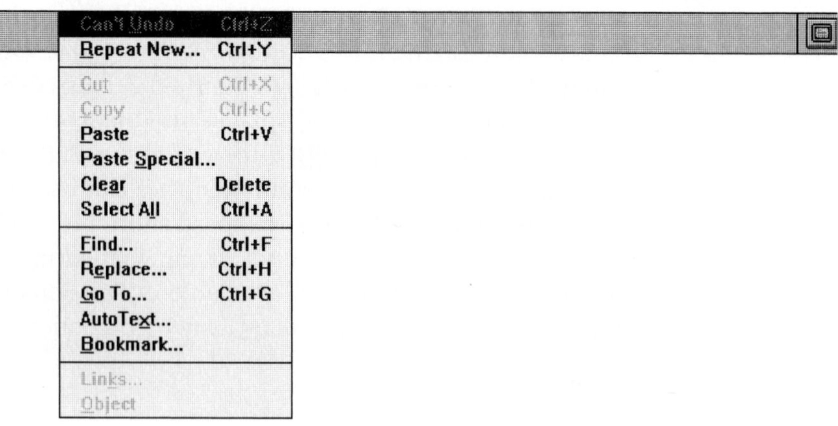

2. Still in Full Screen mode, enter some text into your document. Select the text and press Ctrl+C to copy it to the Clipboard. Move the insertion point somewhere else in the same document (still in Full Screen mode), and then use the Ctrl+V shortcut to paste the text that you had placed on the Clipboard.

MAGNIFYING YOUR DOCUMENT WITH THE ZOOM FEATURE

Word lets you put your document under a magnifying glass or a telescope with its zoom feature. Zooming in is especially useful if you are working with a laptop or have trouble seeing, say, 10 point Times New Roman on your screen. Of course, you can always change the font size (see Chapter 6), but this will affect the printed document. The disadvantage of magnifying your document, of course, is that unless you have a very large monitor you will no longer be able to see a whole line on the screen. The more you magnify your document, the less of it you can see at any one time. (Zooming out of your document gives you a better sense of how a page will look. However, unless you have a very big monitor, this is most often done in Print Preview mode right before printing.)

To use the zoom feature, follow these steps:

1. Click on the Zoom Control box on the Standard toolbar. You'll see a list box that looks like this:

2. Now choose the magnification level you want.

You can also choose Zoom from the View menu (Alt V, Z), which displays this dialog box:

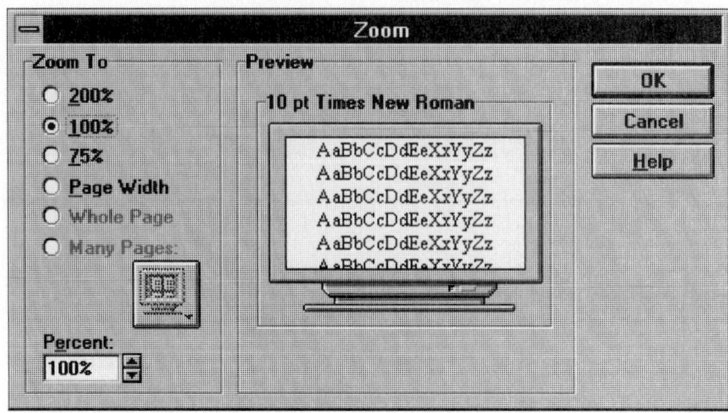

This gives you another way to choose the magnification you want.

TIP *If you use a larger-than-life (greater than 100%) magnification, use the horizontal scroll bars to see the whole line.*

EXAMPLES

1. Create a new document, and make sure you're in Page Layout view. Enter the following Blaise Pascal quotation, which should fit on one line of your screen.

   I have made this a rather long letter because I haven't had time to make it shorter.

   Zoom the screen to 200%. The line will no longer fit on the screen; you will need to use the horizontal scroll bars to see it all.
2. Close the previous document and create a new one. Enter the following Oscar Wilde quotation in 20 point type:

   A gentleman is one who never hurts anyone's feelings—unintentionally.

   Notice that although the letters are the same size as in the previous example, the text is wrapped to the next line instead of continued off screen, as when you used the zoom feature at 200%.

EXERCISES

1. Open MYMEMO2.DOC.
2. View your memo in Page Layout view.
3. Adjust the zoom level to 200%.
4. Adjust the zoom level to view a full page.
5. Adjust the zoom level so you can view the entire width of the page.
6. Choose Full Screen mode and repeat steps 2 through 5.
7. Press Esc to exit from Full Screen mode.
8. Return to Full Screen mode.
9. Press Alt V and select Normal view while remaining in Full Screen mode.
10. Leave Full Screen mode.
11. Switch to Page Layout view.
12. Close MYMEMO2.DOC.
13. Highlight a word in your memo.
    a. While the mouse pointer is an arrow over your highlighted word, click the right mouse button (use Shift+F10 if you don't have a mouse).
    b. Use the shortcut menu and make your highlighted word bold.

8.2 PAGE SETUP

Word gives you complete control over the size and shape of each page, but whether you can take advantage of all of Word's powers depends on your printer. To start the process of controlling the shape of each page:

▼ Choose Page Setup from the File menu (Alt F, U).

This opens up the dialog box shown in Figure 8-3. Notice that there are four tabs in this dialog box. As usual, clicking on one of these tabs moves a different "page" of the dialog box to the forefront. The other tabs on this dialog box let you control the paper size, the paper source, and the layout of a page. You will learn only a bit about the Layout tab in this section; later sections of this chapter will demonstrate how to take advantage of more of its features. Let's start with the Margins tab shown in Figure 8-3.

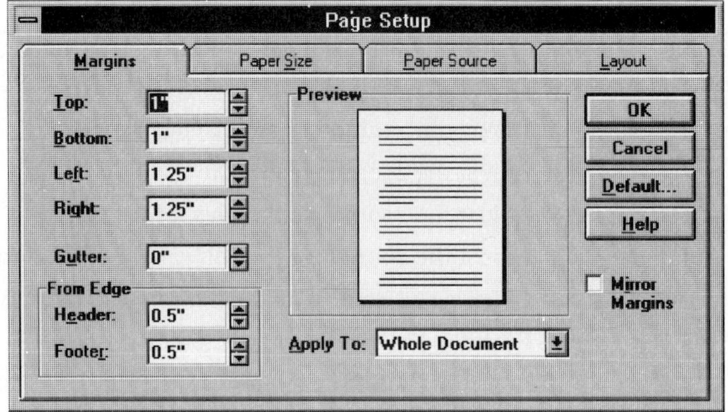

FIGURE 8-3

The Margins tab on the Page Setup dialog box

THE MARGINS TAB

Margins are the areas on the four sides of a piece of paper that are usually left blank. (As you saw in the last chapter, you can move into the margin using a negative paragraph indent.) When changing the margins, keep in mind that paragraph indents (see Chapter 6) are always calculated relative to the margins. If you set a left paragraph indent to half an inch and change the left margin to one inch, Word will tell your printer to start the paragraph one and a half inches from the edge of the paper. Word will warn you if you try to set a margin that your printer can't handle, as shown here:

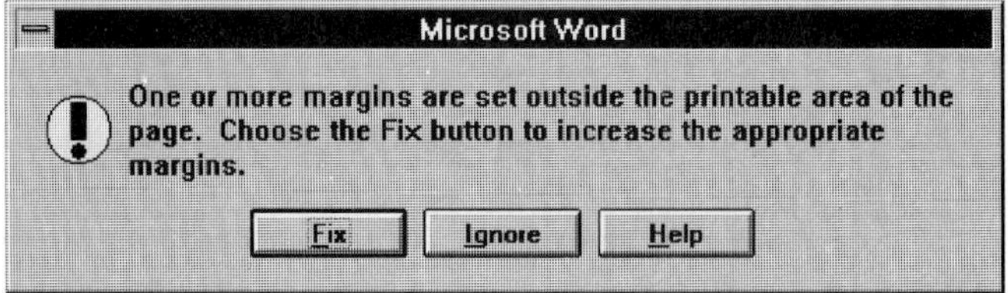

Click on the Fix button to have Word calculate the closest your printer can do to your original, impossible choice.

To set a margin, you just need to enter a number (which Word will assume is in inches) or click on the spin buttons in the appropriate box, as shown in Figure 8-3. (You can use Word's other units of measurement such as centimeters (cm) or points (pt) in these boxes.) For example, to adjust the distance between the top of the page and the *top* of the first line on the page, change the value in the Top box. Similarly, change the value in the Bottom box to set the bottom margin; this adjusts the distance between the bottom of the page and the *bottom* of the last line on the page. The left margin box sets the distance between the left edge of the page and the left end of each line that has the left indent set to zero; similarly, the right margin box sets the distance between the right edge of the page and the right end of each line that has the right indent set to zero. Notice how the Preview box shows you the result of the margin settings you specify.

You're probably not familiar with the Mirror Margins check box in the lower-right corner of Figure 8-3. This option makes the margins on facing pages the same or, in other words, *mirror images* of each other. For example, if odd pages have left margins of 1 inch and right margins of 2 inches, having the Mirror Margins check box on would produce even pages with left margins of 2 inches and right margins of 1 inch. Use this option if you are lucky enough to have a printer that can print on both sides of a page or want to copy the document using a two-sided copier. (Unfortunately, most laser printers recommend against feeding paper through a laser printer twice in order to print on the other side.) When you select Mirror Margins, the Left and Right margin boxes change to Inside and Outside, as shown here:

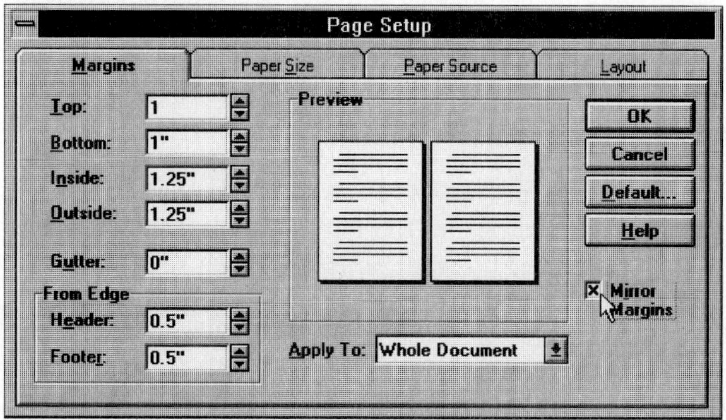

The Gutter Option *Gutter* is jargon for the amount of extra space you want to add to a margin to allow for binding. For example, binding the book you are reading now took about a half inch of extra space. If you prepare a memo that will be spiral bound, you should probably leave a gutter of about three-quarters of an inch. Gutter space is added to the left margin of all pages when the Mirror Margins check box is off, or to the inside margin (which is different on odd and even pages) when it is not.

The From Edge Options This option is used when you have a header or footer in your document. *Headers* and *footers* are text that is repeated at either the top or bottom of each page. You'll learn more about headers and footers later in this chapter. The important point is this option controls how much room you leave for them. In the From Edge boxes you will need to type or select the distance from the top or bottom edge of the page you want to leave blank for this information.

The Apply To List Box The Apply To drop-down list box shown here tells Word which part of the document you want to apply the settings to. To take full advantage of any option other than Whole Document, you need to know something about *sections*, which are covered in Chapter 11.

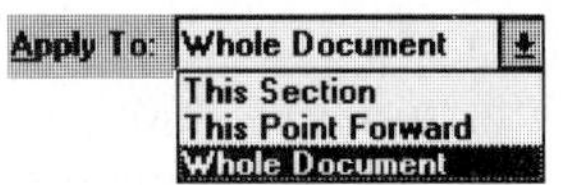

The Default Button Clicking on the Default button changes your new margin settings as defaults. Word saves the new settings in the attached template. Whenever you base a document on that template in the future, Word uses the new margin settings.

THE PAPER SIZE TAB

Let's now move on to the Paper Size tab. To get there, again choose Page Setup from the File menu and then click on the Paper Size tab in the dialog box that pops up. You'll see this dialog box:

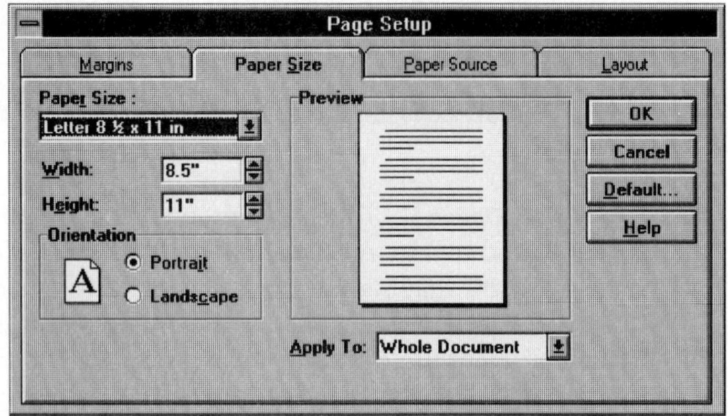

Most of these options are fairly self-explanatory. The items you will see on the Paper Size tabs depend on the current default printer. However, clicking on the downward-pointing arrow on the Paper Size drop-down list box displays a list similar to this:

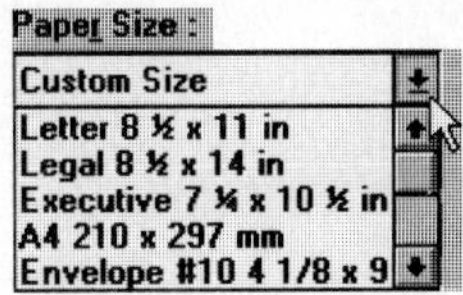

If the paper size you want is on this list (scroll through it if need be) *and* your printer can handle it, you're home free. If not, select Custom Size (the last item on the list) and then fill in the Width and Height boxes, an example of which is shown here:

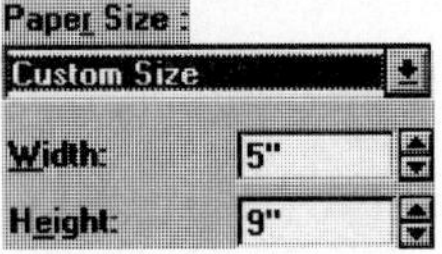

The Orientation buttons let you switch between printing a page in Portrait (vertical-taller than the page is wide) or Landscape orientation (horizontal-wider than the paper is tall). When you change the orientation of a page, Word switches the Top and Bottom margin measurements to the Left and Right margin measurements, and vice versa.

The Apply To list box lets you indicate the area of the document to be affected. (To take full advantage of this you'll need to know something about sections. See Chapter 11.)

As usual, clicking on the Default button changes the default paper size and page orientation settings. Word saves the new settings in the current template and overwrites the old settings. Then whenever you base a document on this template, Word uses the new settings.

THE PAPER SOURCE TAB

Use the Paper Source tab if you have the luxury of using a printer with multiple trays. What you will see may depend on your printer. Here's a picture of a typical version of this dialog box:

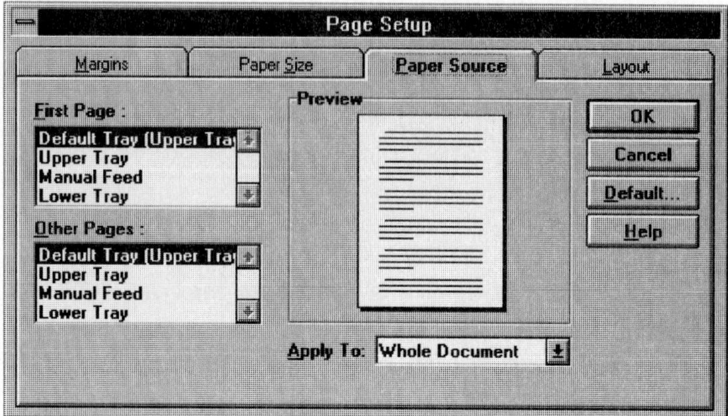

If you have a printer with two trays, you can put letterhead (for the first page) in one tray and plain paper (for the other pages) in another. Then you can tell Word to print the first page using letterhead and every other page using plain paper. You can also use the first page option if you have added an envelope to the first page of the document or need to feed in the first page manually.

As before, use the Apply To list box to affect different portions of your document (see Chapter 11 for details), and click on the Default button to change the default paper source settings for use by the current template.

THE LAYOUT TAB

Here's a picture of the Layout tab:

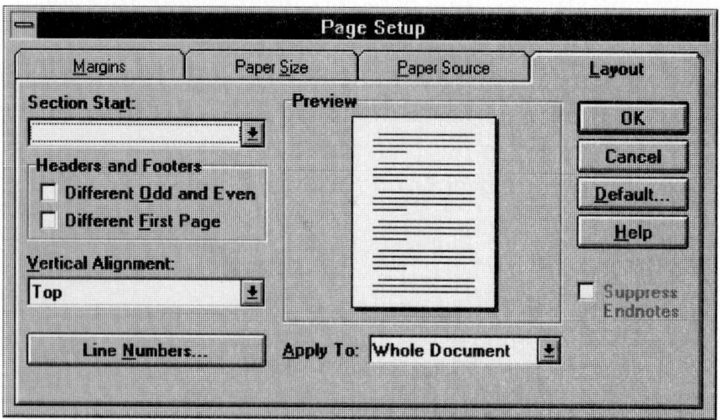

You'll need to tap the power of this dialog box when you add headers and footers to your own documents; this topic is covered a little later on in this chapter. For now though let's concentrate on two other options in this dialog box.

Vertical Alignment The Vertical Alignment drop-down list box shown here determines how Word aligns your text vertically on the page. The default setting is Top, which means that Word aligns the top line with the top margin. If you choose Center, Word centers the text between the top and bottom margins. If you choose Justified, Word expands the space between the paragraphs on the page to align the top line with the top margin and the bottom line with the bottom margin.

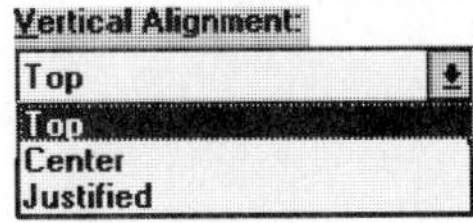

Line Numbers Certain people (lawyers for example) need to number the lines on each page of their documents. If this applies to you, click on the Line Numbers button to pop up this dialog box:

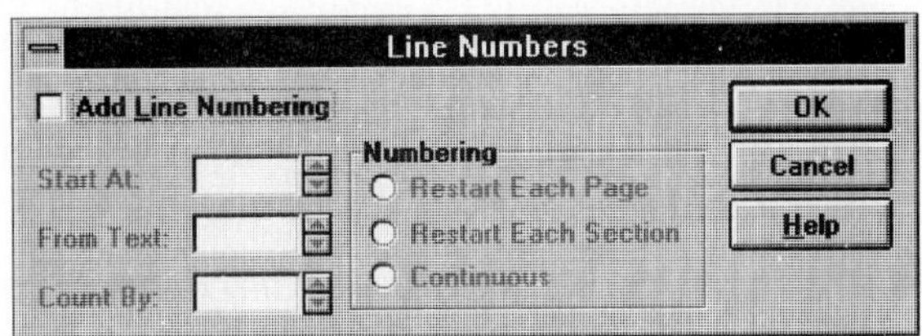

Now click on the Add Line Numbering check box and set the options you want.

EXAMPLE

1. To center the current document on the page:
    a. Choose the Layout tab from the Page Setup dialog box.
    b. Pull down the Vertical Alignment drop-down list box.
    c. Choose Center from the list box.

EXERCISES

1. Open MYMEMO2.DOC.
2. Issue Page Setup from the File menu and then choose the Size tab, and set the page orientation of your memo to Landscape.
3. Zoom to Whole Page.
4. Challenge Yourself! Choose Options from the Tools menu and then select the View tab. Select Text Boundaries under Show (you have to be in Page Layout view).
   a. View the effects on your screens.
   b. Turn off Text Boundaries if you'd like.
5. Close MYMEMO2.DOC without saving your changes.

8.3 PAGE BREAKS, PAGE NUMBERS, AND GENERAL HEADERS AND FOOTERS

Before you learn how to add page numbers or any other information to the bottom (footer) or top (header) of each page, you need to know a little bit about how Word paginates your document—that is, how it decides to go on to another page when one page is filled with text. By default, Word recalculates page boundaries as you enter text. This *background repagination* is automatic.

TIP *If you have a slow computer, you may want to turn off background repagination. You can do this from the General tab on the Options dialog box available from the Tools menu, as shown here:*

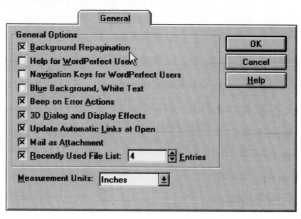

General
General Options
[X] Background Repagination
[ ] Help for WordPerfect Users
[ ] Navigation Keys for WordPerfect Users
[ ] Blue Background, White Text
[X] Beep on Error Actions
[X] 3D Dialog and Display Effects
[X] Update Automatic Links at Open
[X] Mail as Attachment
[X] Recently Used File List: 4 Entries
Measurement Units: Inches
OK
Cancel
Help

Word indicates page breaks with a dotted line in Normal view. (Page breaks that Word calculates are usually called *soft page breaks* or *automatic page breaks*.) You can also force Word to break a page at a certain point by pressing the Ctrl+Enter key combination. This puts what is usually called a *hard page break* (or a *manual page break*) into your document. For example, many people like to have a separate title page for their documents, and hard page breaks are ideal for this. In Normal view, hard page breaks are indicated by a dotted line and the words "Page Break," as shown here:

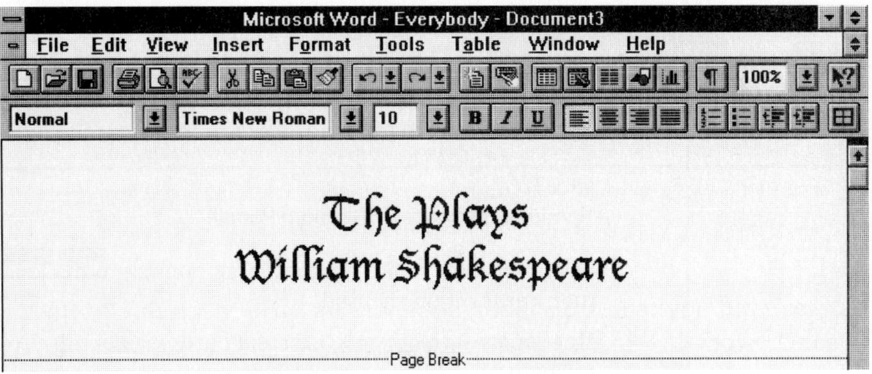

In Page Layout view, both hard and soft page breaks just show up as page boundaries, as shown here:

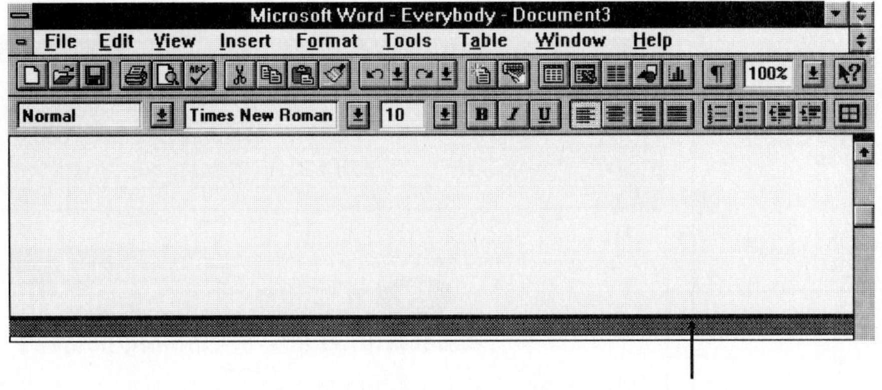

Page boundary

To delete a hard page break switch to Normal view and then:

▼ Select the page break you want to get rid of and press Backspace or Del.

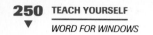

(If you don't remember on what page you added a hard page break, you can always use the Special button in the Find dialog box to find them. Chapter 6 describes how to use this feature.)

EXAMPLE

1. Type the following in a new document:

   QUOTES:
   Random Thoughts by Random People

2. Select the text, make the font large enough to make a good title, and then center it on the line.
3. Now press Ctrl+Enter to create a hard page break. Type the following to begin your book of quotations:

   Henry Adams (1836-1918): Practical politics consists in ignoring facts.

   The relevant parts of your screen will look something like this:

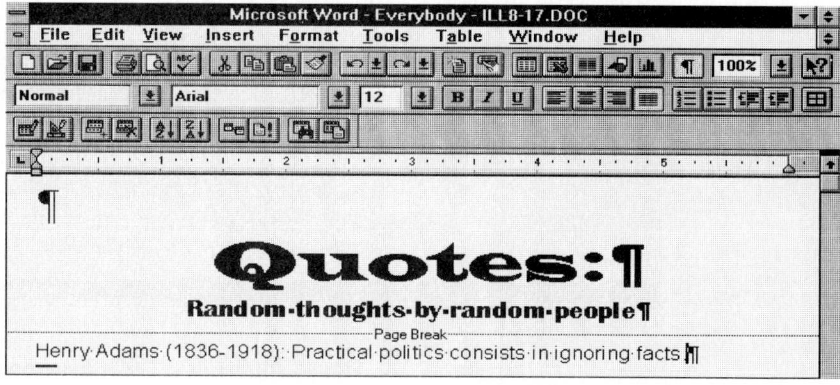

PAGE NUMBERS

Now that you know a bit about how Word handles pagination, you can learn how to add page numbers to your documents. To insert a page number:

1. Choose Page Numbers from the Insert menu (Alt I, U). You'll see this dialog box:

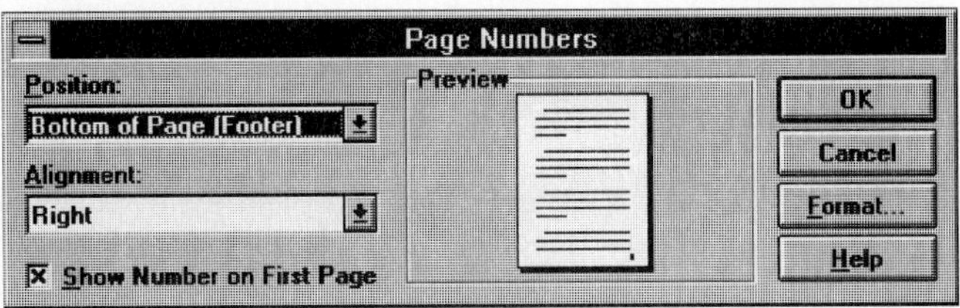

As you can see, Word lets you decide whether or not to include a page number on the first page. To leave the first page clear, make sure the Show Number on First Page check box isn't selected.

The Position drop-down list box lets you choose whether the page numbers appear on the top or bottom of the page. Once you have chosen the position for the page numbers, the Alignment drop-down list box, shown here, lets you control the placement of the page number. For example, a common choice is to have the page numbers centered on the bottom of each page or at the right margin of a page.

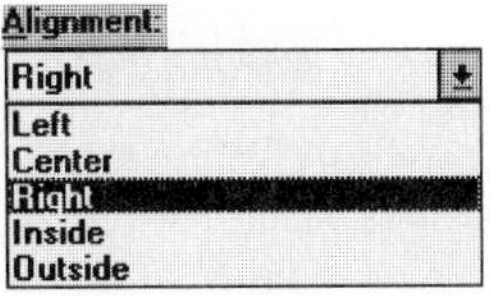

The only options in this list box that aren't self-explanatory are Inside and Outside. These options are most commonly used when you have set the Mirror Margins option (discussed earlier in this chapter). The point is that mirror margins are only used for pages that have text on both sides, so "inside" will be a different side on the odd and even pages. For example, choosing Inside puts the page number close to the inside edge of each side.

Finally, choose the Format button to open up a dialog box that lets you choose how you want the page number to appear. For example, you can decide to use Roman numerals for page numbers. You're most likely to change the format for page numbers with longer documents, which are covered in Chapter 11.

EXAMPLE

1. To use lowercase Roman numerals for your page numbers, choose Page Numbers from the Insert menu and click on the Format button in the Page Numbers dialog box. You will see the dialog box shown here.

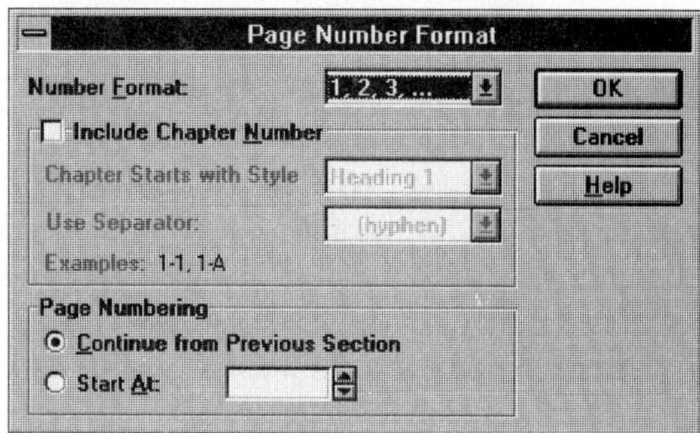

Pull down the Number Format drop-down list box. Choose i, ii, iii,... as shown here.

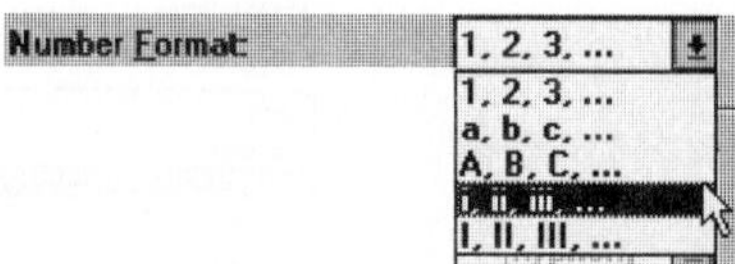

Click on the OK button to go back to the Page Number dialog box, and then click on OK to put the change into effect.

MORE GENERAL HEADERS AND FOOTERS

Headers and *footers* are text that is repeated at either the top or bottom of each page. A header or footer can be as simple as a page number or as complicated as one that gives the name of the author, the date and time the document was last edited, and a boldface **CONFIDENTIAL** in 36 point type at the bottom of each page.

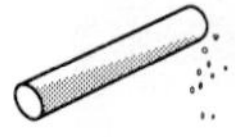

NOTE *The From Edge option on the Margins Tab in the Page Setup dialog box controls how much room you leave for headers and footers.*

If you want to add anything more complicated than a simple page number to your pages, choose the Header and Footer option on the View menu (Alt V, H). If necessary, Word switches to Page Layout view, and it presents you with a screen that looks something like the one shown in Figure 8-4. Notice the new Header and Footer toolbar in the center of the screen. Also notice that the original text is grayed. Finally, and most importantly, notice the dotted rectangular region marked Header in Figure 8-4. The word "Header" and the dotted rectangle won't print, but whatever you type inside this box will become the header for your document.

In Figure 8-4, the insertion point is inside the Header area. The idea is that you can enter and format header or footer text the same way you would any other text in Word. You can change the font, the point size, and so on—as you see fit. You can use the Tab key or the alignment button to position header and footer text as well. If you leave this area blank, nothing will be printed as a header.

You can't see the Footer area in Figure 8-4, but it will look almost the same as the Header area. You can get to the Footer area just by clicking on the Switch Between Header and Footer button on the Header and Footer toolbar, or by scrolling down through the document until you see the Footer area. Click inside of the boxed Footer area to set the insertion point where you want it, and then start adding the footer text.

REMEMBER *Although it may seem as though you're putting the header or footer on a specific page (for example, Page 1 as shown in the status bar of Figure 8-4), you are actually entering a header or footer that will (generally) appear on all pages of the document.*

Word makes it easy to add some standard items to a header or footer—including page numbers or the date and time. If you type the date or the time yourself, they will remain the same each time you print the document. On the other hand, when you place the date, time, or page number in a header or footer using one of the buttons on the

FIGURE 8-4

The Header area and the Header and Footer toolbar

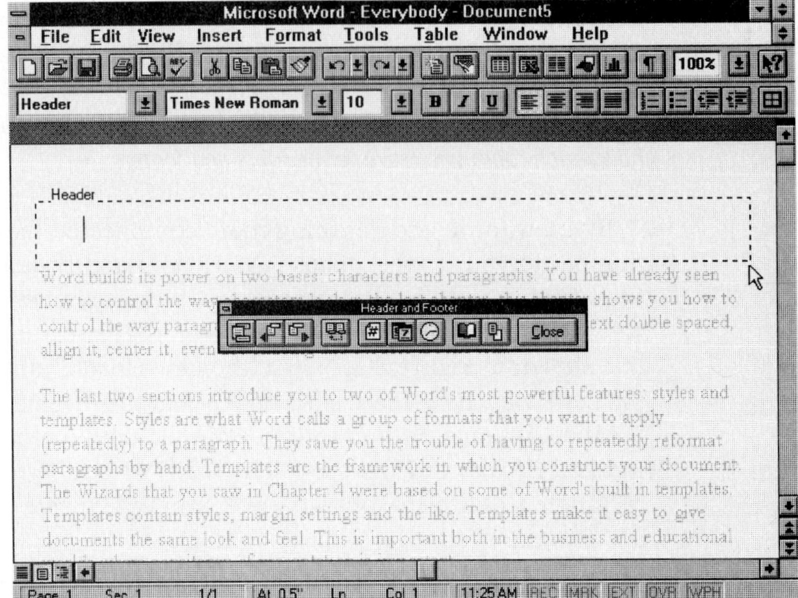

Header and Footer toolbar, Word actually places a special code in your text called *a field code*. This field code allows Word to change the information (in the jargon this is called *updating the field*) on request. You update all fields in your document by pressing F9. (You can insert field codes anyplace in a Word document by choosing Field on the Insert menu and working with the dialog box that pops up. Field codes are especially common when you are using form letters—see Chapter 14 for more information on them.)

To use the date, time or page number tools on the Header and Footer toolbar, first decide whether you want this information to be inside the header or the footer. Then place the insertion point inside either the Header area or the Footer area. Now:

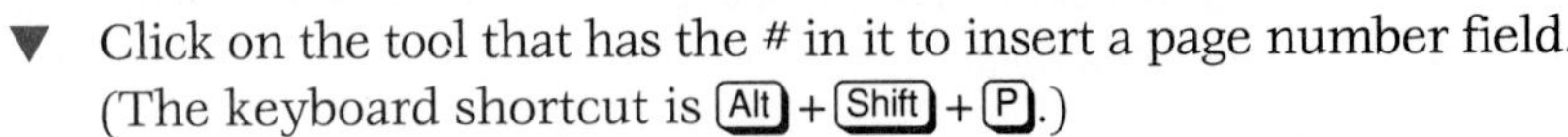

- Click on the tool that has the # in it to insert a page number field. (The keyboard shortcut is Alt+Shift+P.)

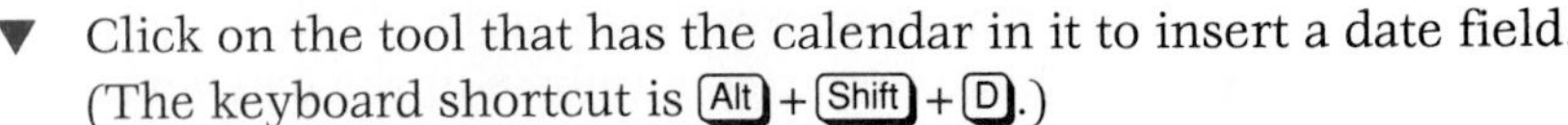

- Click on the tool that has the calendar in it to insert a date field. (The keyboard shortcut is Alt+Shift+D.)

- Click on the tool that has the clock in it to insert the time field. (The keyboard shortcut is Alt+Shift+T.)

To see the field codes rather than the results, make sure the insertion point is inside the header or footer and press Shift+F9. To go back to seeing the results rather than the codes, make sure the insertion point is inside the header or footer and press Shift+F9 again.

TIP *Since the Tab key moves a specific distance independent of the font you are using, use it rather than the Spacebar for more accurate positioning of items inside a header or footer.*

When you are happy with the information in the header or footer, click on the Close button. When you are inside the document in Page Layout view, you'll be able to see the header or footer text, although it will be grayed.

In Page Layout view, you can switch between the main document and the header or footer by double-clicking in the other area. If you are in the main document, double-clicking on a header or footer lets you edit the header or footer. If you're in the Header of Footer area, double-clicking on the grayed document text hides the Header and Footer toolbar, and lets you resume editing the document.

Finally, if you need to delete information in a header or footer, move the insertion point inside the header or footer area. Then the easiest way to delete the information is to select it and press Backspace or Del. You could also use the Backspace key alone but this will not work with field codes. In particular, if you have added a date, page, or time field code to your header or footer, you will have to select the whole field to delete it rather than trying to backspace through the item. If you need to clear the header or footer make sure you delete everything.

EXAMPLES

1. Create a document called QUOTES.DOC that will store your favorite quotes. You want the page number, the word "QUOTES", and the date to appear in the footer of each page. To do this:
   a. Choose Header and Footer from the View menu.
   b. Press the ↓ once to move to the Footer area.
   c. Click on the Page Number button on the Header and Footer toolbar.
   d. Press the Tab key and then type **QUOTES**.

e. Press Tab again then click on the Date button on the Header and Footer toolbar.

f. Click on the Close button.

2. It is quite common to have separate headers on the odd and even pages—as in this book for example. If you need to do this, it's easy to put a different header on odd and even pages.

    a. First create your document.

    b. Then click on the Page Setup button on the Header and Footer toolbar—it looks like this:

    c. Choose the Layout tab from the Page Setup dialog box, select the Different Odd and Even check box, and then click on the OK button.

    d. Look at the current page number on the status bar. If the current page is odd, you will be entering the header or footer information you want to appear on the odd page first. If the current page is even, the header or footer you enter will appear on even pages.

    e. Since you need to move to the next Header or Footer area in order to place the header on the remaining type of page, click the Show Next button. Type the header or footer you want to appear on the other kind of page (odd or even).

EXERCISES

1. Open MYMEMO2.DOC.
2. Select Headers and Footers from the View menu.
3. Change the font size on header text to 24 point.
4. Flip to the Footer using the Switch Between Header and Footer button on the Header and Footer toolbar.

5. Change the font size on footer text to 24 point.
6. Remove the date and page number from the footer. (Remember, you will have to select the whole date to delete it as this is actually an embedded field code, not the text for the date; the same goes for the page number.)
7. Insert a hard page break (Ctrl+Enter) into your memo text and enter some text on the second page.
8. Edit the second page header or footer.
   a. View the first page header or footer, whichever you changed.
   b. Choose Page Setup from the File menu, select the Layout tab, and examine the state of the Different First Page check box.
9. Create a third page and edit its header. (Check the second page header to see if it changed too.)
10. Close MYMEMO2.DOC, saving your changes.

8.4 FOOTNOTES AND ENDNOTES

This section is obviously only for people who need to use footnotes or endnotes in their documents. If this is not true of you, there's no reason to read any further. But if you *do* need footnotes or endnotes, you will be pleasantly surprised at how easy it is to create them in Word. If you insert a new footnote or endnote, Word automatically renumbers the other ones—ditto if you delete one. If you don't like the standard numbering of 1, 2, 3, Word makes it a cinch to use custom footnote and endnote numbers.

To insert a footnote or endnote:

1. Choose Footnote from the Insert menu (Alt I, N). You'll see this dialog box:

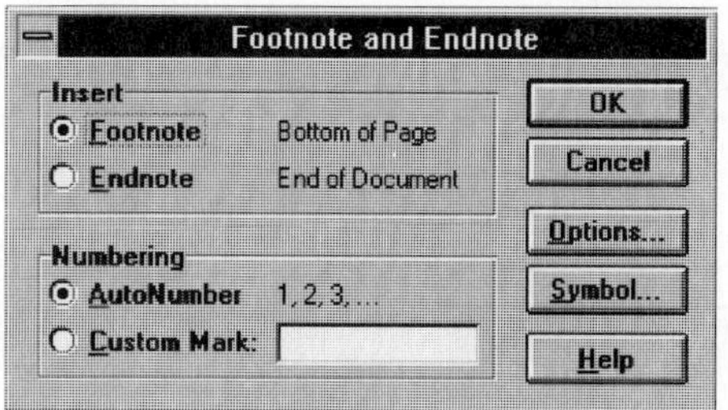

2. Choose what you want to create, either a footnote or endnote.
3. Now choose how you want the numbering to appear, either the standard 1, 2, 3 notation as a reference mark or a custom symbol like # or *. *Reference marks* show up as superscripts in your document immediately to the left of the insertion point.

Let's assume you choose to enter a footnote (the procedure is essentially the same for endnotes). When you click on OK, Word automatically adds the reference mark to the left of the insertion point. If you are using the default numbering, Word automatically adds one to the previous reference number. Now, if you are in Page Layout view, Word moves the insertion point to where the footnote (endnote) will end up, as shown here for a footnote:

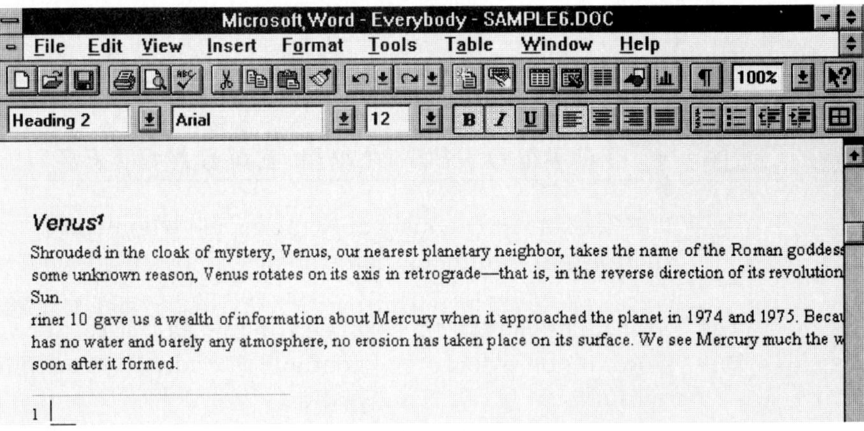

Now you can type your footnote (endnote) and, when you are finished, just move the insertion point back to wherever you want inside the document.

If you're working in Normal view instead of Page Layout view, Word opens a *footnote pane*, as shown here (the endnote pane looks similar):

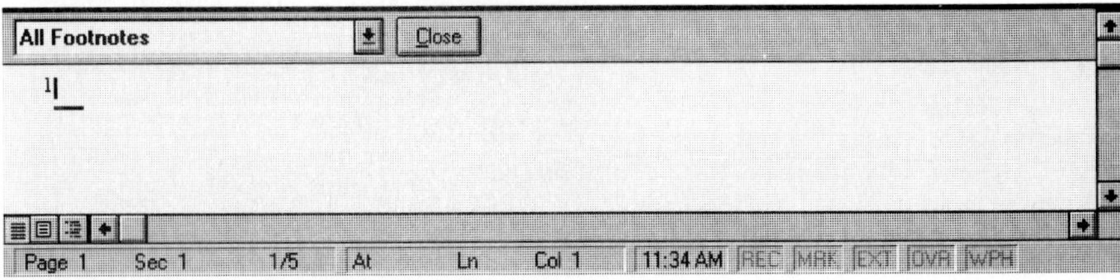

Now you can type whatever you want inside the footnote (endnote) pane. When you are satisfied, click on the Close button to return to your original location inside the document.

If you already have placed footnotes (or endnotes) in your document, you may want to look at them again. After you study their contents you may decide to revise, move, or delete them. Word makes all of these operations a snap:

- To view the contents of an existing footnote (or endnote), double-click its reference mark.

  If you are in Normal view, Word pops up the footnote (endnote) pane again; if you are in Page Layout view, Word moves the insertion point to the footnote (endnote).

- To delete a footnote (or endnote), select its reference mark and press Del.

  If you are using numbered footnotes (endnotes), Word automatically renumbers any subsequent footnotes (endnotes).

- To move a footnote (endnote), select its reference mark and drag it to the location you want.

  As always, if you are using numbered footnotes (or numbered endnotes), Word automatically renumbers the footnotes to take into account their new location.

EXAMPLES

1. Footnotes (and endnotes) are commonly used to give the source of quotes. Suppose you wanted to give the correct citation for this Shakespeare quotation:

   Words, words, mere words, no matter from the heart.

   Enter the quotation, choose Footnote from the Insert menu, and then enter

   Troilus and Cressida, v, iii [109]

In Page Layout view, you can just enter the citation and move back to the document. In Normal view, the footnote pane would look like this:

Now click on the Close button.

2. Suppose you use very few footnotes in your documents and want to use a custom reference mark. Word lets you choose from any symbol in its repertoire. Choose Footnote from the Insert menu and, when the Footnote and Endnote box pops up, click on the Symbol button. This takes you to the usual Symbol dialog box shown here:

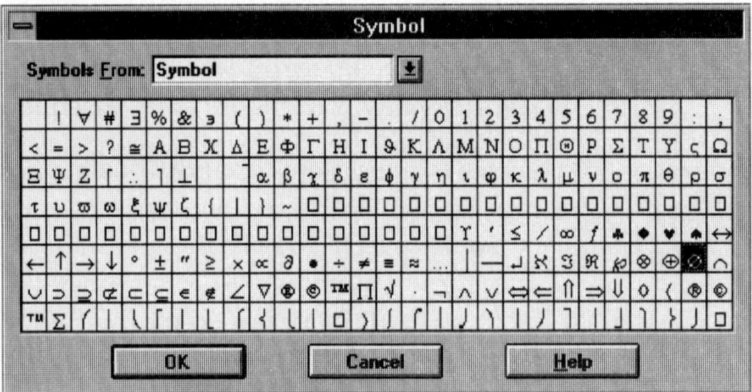

Now choose the symbol you want. Click on OK to go back to the Footnote and Endnote dialog box. Notice that the new symbol is shown in the Custom Mark box, as you can see here. Click on OK to use this custom reference mark. This mark will be used for all footnotes until you change this dialog box again.

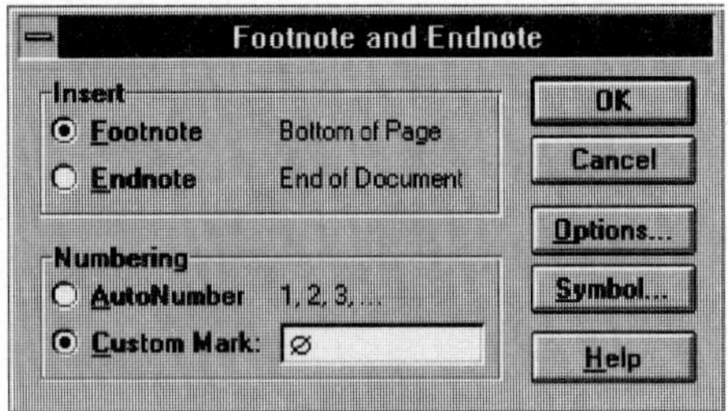

EXERCISES

1. Open MYMEMO2.DOC.
2. Add two footnotes to your memo text.
3. Select Insert, Footnotes and click on Options.
   a. If you want to see something neat, enter the year of your birth in the Start At field and select Roman numerals for the Number Format.
   b. Change your Number Format to symbols.
   c. Scroll through the Start At field to see the progression Word uses for symbols.
   d. Reset the Start At field to one.
   e. Return to your document by clicking on OK.
4. Zoom in enough in Page Layout view to easily see the footnote marks.
5. Enter a few footnotes above the footnotes you entered before.
6. Double-click on the footnote reference marks in both the body text and the footnote section to see what happens.
7. Close and save MYMEMO2.DOC.

mastery skills check

1. Type around 50 words in a new document and switch to page layout view. [8.1]
2. Zoom the text to 150% and to 200%. Switch between Page Layout and Normal view. [8.1]
3. Add a footer at the bottom of the page with a page number horizontally centered on the footer. [8.3]
4. Enter **Page One** and a blank line. Now enter a hard page break in front of the blank line and enter **Page Two**. [8.3]
5. Enter a header on page two with the text **The Header Entered On Page Two**. [8.3]

6. Use Page Setup and allow for a different first page header. [8.3]
7. Edit the header on page one and add **Different Page One Header**. [8.3]
8. Add a third page and edit the header, changing the "Two" to a "Three." View the page two header and notice it is now the same as the page three header. (They will be the same until we learn about sections in Chapter 11.) [8.3]
9. Select Footnote from the Insert menu and click on the Endnote option button in order to place an Endnote after the text "Page One" and after the text "Page Two." [8.4]
10. Switch to Page Layout view, change to Full Screen mode, and locate the endnote reference mark and the endnote itself. [8.1]
11. Close the document without saving your changes. [2.3]

cumulative skills check

1. Open the MYMEMO1.DOC file created in the last chapter's Cumulative Skills Check. [2.4]
2. Open the MYMEMO2.DOC file created in this chapter. [2.4]
3. Add headers and footers to MYMEMO1.DOC using MYMEMO2.DOC as a model. [8.3]
4. Open the Style Gallery from MYMEMO1.DOC and select a different memo style. [7.3]
5. Use the cut and paste features to move the body text from MYMEMO1.DOC into MYMEMO2.DOC. [3.3]
6. Close MYMEMO1.DOC, saving your changes. [1.6, 2.3]
7. Close MYMEMO2.DOC, saving your changes. [1.6, 2.3]

9

Previewing and Printing Your Work

chapter objectives

After completing this chapter, you will be able to

9.1 Preview a document in a variety of ways before printing it

9.2 Print your documents in a variety of ways

9.3 Print envelopes

AT this point, you know quite a bit about Word and your documents are getting fairly sophisticated. The simple printing and previewing procedures that you learned in Chapter 2 may no longer completely meet your needs. This chapter describes the ins and outs of Word's powerful printing and previewing facilities. You'll even learn how to print addresses on envelopes in a way that—aside from saving time—may also save you money and make it less likely that your mail will get lost.

review
skills check

1. Use the Letter Wizard to create a business letter, on plain paper in the Typewriter style, and request that an envelope be created and attached to the document. [4.5]
2. View the letter you created, switching between Normal view and Page Layout view. [8.1]
3. Using the File, Page Setup command, look on the Page Size tab and check the orientation (Landscape or Portrait?) for section one (the envelope) and section two (the letter). [8.2]
4. Save your document for use with other exercises in this chapter. [2.3]

9.1 PRINT PREVIEW

As your documents get longer and more complicated you might want to get into the habit of using Word's *Print Preview feature* to see what your documents will look like before they are printed. Recall that to start Print Preview you choose Print Preview from the File menu (Alt, F, V), or choose the Print Preview button on the Standard toolbar. After repaginating, Word displays a screen resembling the one shown in Figure 9-1. As you saw in Chapter 2, the center of the Print Preview screen is a birds-eye view of the current page of the document, and the

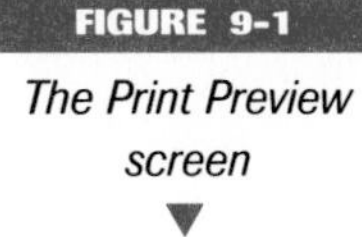
FIGURE 9-1
The Print Preview screen

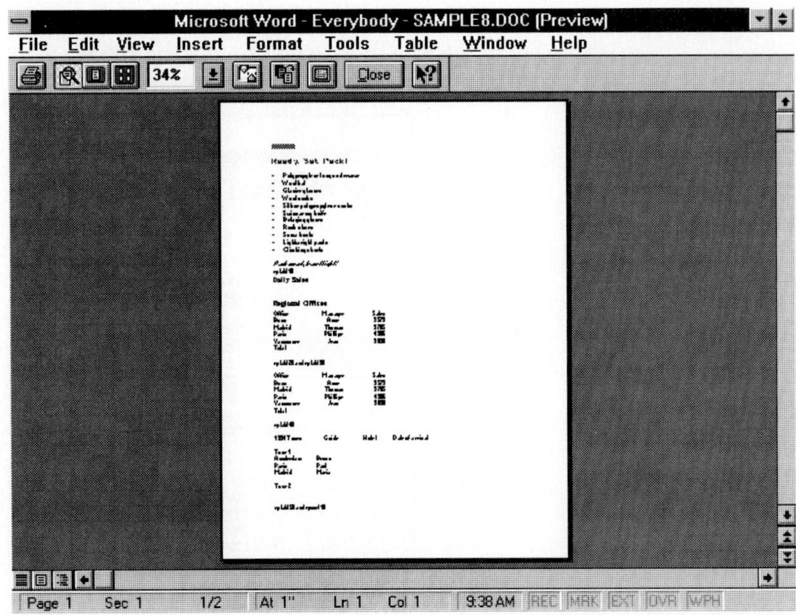

easiest way to move page by page through your document in Print Preview is to use Pg Up or Pg Dn as needed. Recall that unlike when you are editing a document in Print Preview these keys move you to the next and previous page respectively. You can also use the vertical scroll bars to move through the document. Click on the double-headed arrows at the bottom of the vertical scroll bar to move up or down a page at a time. Drag the scroll box to move through the document more rapidly.

To leave the Print Preview screen, Click on the Close button, choose Print Preview from the File menu again or just press Esc.

EXAMPLE

1. Retrieve the NEWS2.DOC supplied with Word by choosing Open from the File menu, going to the **wordcbt** subdirectory and double-clicking

on the file named NEW2.DOC. Then choose Print Preview from the File menu. Figure 9-2 shows what the screen will look like.

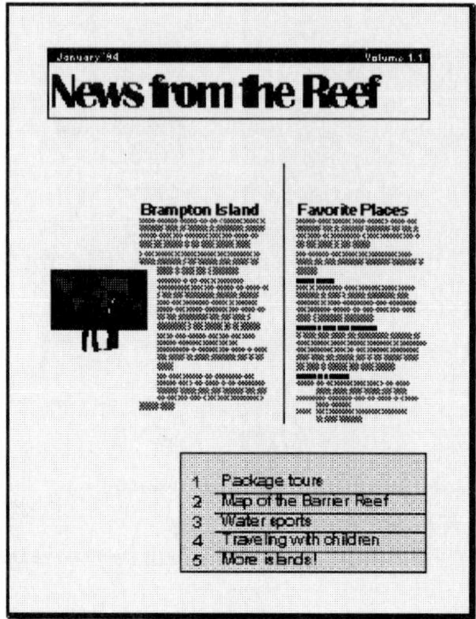

FIGURE 9-2 *NEWS2.DOC on the Print Preview screen*

THE PRINT PREVIEW TOOLBAR

You control the most important features of Print Preview from a special toolbar—shown here—located at the top of the Print Preview screen.

Let's go over the buttons on this toolbar one by one.

The Print Button The Print button is just like the Print button on the Standard toolbar that you've already used. Click here to have Word print the document using the current print settings in the Print dialog box.

The Magnifier Button The Magnifier button is a toggle that is on by default. If the Magnifer button is on (you can tell by looking to see if it appears pressed in), when you move into the Print Preview screen, the mouse pointer changes to a little magnifying glass, as shown here.

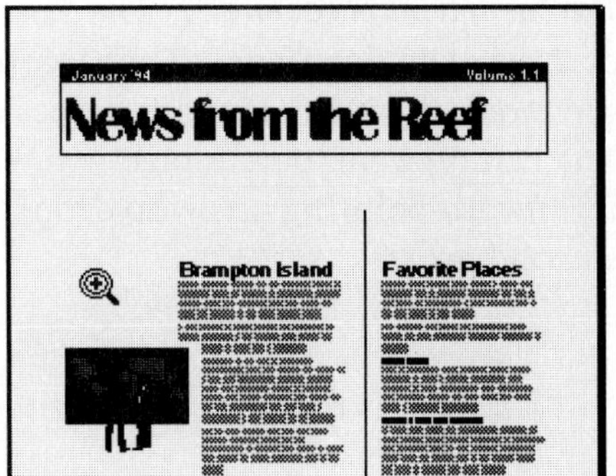

Click to magnify the region the magnifying glass is pointing to. Click again to return to the original magnification.

The One Page Button You can display a single page or multiple pages in Print Preview. Clicking on this One Page toolbar button produces a single-page display.

The Multiple Pages Button The Multiple Pages button is useful if you need a birds-eye view of your document. If you click on this button, Word drops down a box that looks like this:

You drag across this box to select the number of pages you want to preview, as shown here:

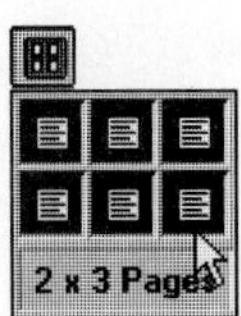

Click on the One Page button to go back to displaying a single page, or use the Multiple Pages button again to change the number of pages that are displayed.

The Zoom Control Feature The Zoom Control list box lets you zoom in or out on the document. The jargon usually says: use this control to see more of your document in less detail, or less of it in more detail. You can type the percentage you want to use or click on the downward-pointing arrow to drop down a list of common sizes, as shown here.

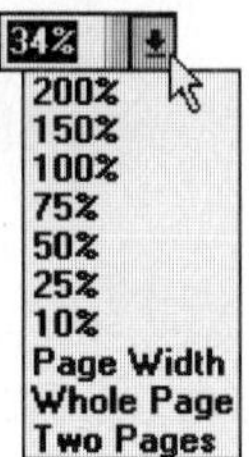

The View Ruler Button The View Ruler button toggles both the vertical and horizontal rulers on and off. Having these rulers showing is especially useful if you want to do adjust the margins or do any other editing in Print Preview mode (see the next section).

The Shrink to Fit Button Use the Shrink to Fit button when there's only a little bit of text left on the last page of your document. Word will try to adjust the text so that the material on the last page fits on the previous page.

The Full Screen Button Clicking on the Full Screen button hides all the features of the Print Preview screen except the toolbar and the pages themselves. Click on the Full Screen button again to return to the ordinary Print Preview screen or press Esc.

The Close Button Click on the Close button to leave Print Preview.

The Help Button The Help button in Print Preview works just like the Help button in the ordinary Word screen. When you click here, the mouse pointer changes into a help pointer with a question mark attached to it. Move the help pointer to the item you want help on and click to display a help screen (see Chapter 2 for more on the Help system).

EXAMPLES

1. Let's suppose you still are working with the NEWS2.DOC that you used in an earlier example. Preview this document and then click on the Full Screen button. Figure 9-3 shows what NEWS2.DOC will look like in Full Screen view.

FIGURE 9-3

NEWS2.DOC in a full screen Print Preview

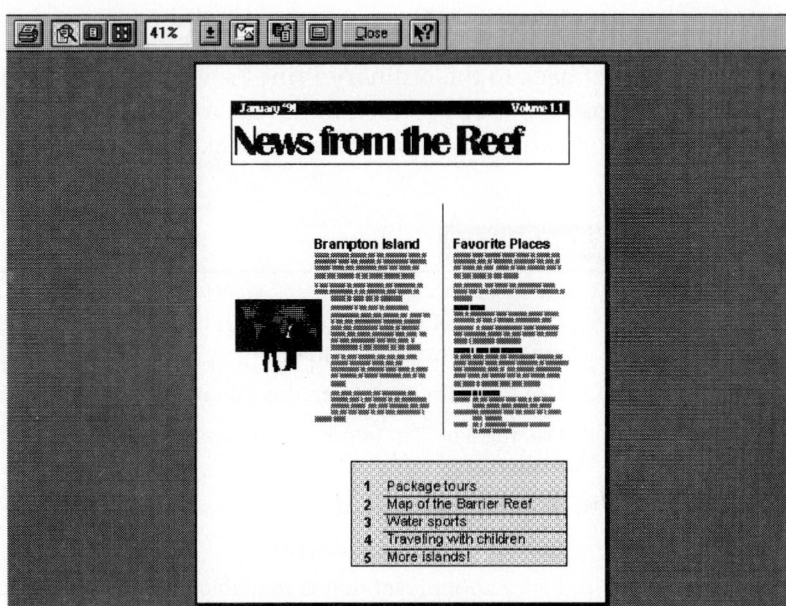

EDITING IN PRINT PREVIEW MODE

Word lets you edit in Print Preview mode. Although this is somewhat uncommon because of the extra steps needed, it can be a good way to make minor changes and get an overview of your document. It is also a good way to adjust margins and see where page breaks fall. To edit in Print Preview, first go to the page you want to edit. Then follow these steps:

1. Make sure the Magnifier button is selected (so the Magnifier button looks pressed in). You know you have the Magnifier

button in the right position if the mouse pointer changes into a magnifying glass inside the document.

2. Click where you want to edit, so the region is magnified and becomes easier to see.
3. Click on the Magnifier button again to turn it off. (The pointer should change back into the ordinary editing I-beam.)
4. Make your changes to the document.

To get back to the ordinary Print Preview screen, reselect the Magnifier button, go back to the document, and reduce the magnification back to normal by clicking again.

EXERCISES

1. Open BIGDOC.DOC (created in Chapter 3 Review Skills Check) or any other multipage document.
2. Use Print Preview from the File menu to view BIGDOC.DOC.
3. Use the ToolTip feature to review the buttons on the Print Preview toolbar.
4. Request a 2×3 page display.
5. Request a one-page display.
6. Pick a zoom level that is readable but shows as much of the page as possible.
7. Switch to edit mode (Magnifier button) and add another 50 words to BIGDOC.DOC. Insert a page break between the new text and the old text.
8. Close BIGDOC.DOC, saving any changes you may have made.

9.2 PRINTING

As you know, Word sends the printing directions for your document directly to Windows when you choose Print from the File menu or click on the Print button. This means that before trying to print a document you must install at least one printer into Windows. However, as you will see in the next section, if you have more than one printer available to you, you can choose which of these printers to use to print your document.

In any case, because Word doesn't do the printing itself, it's always a good idea to save the document before trying to print it. This way, if Windows freezes you won't lose any important information. (This rarely happens in Windows 3.1, but it's still a precaution well worth taking.)

You should also make sure you are satisfied with your document before you start printing it. Once you start printing, pressing Esc stops sending information to the printer, but your printer may keep on printing for some time. This is because most modern printers have large *buffers* (jargon for storage), so that they keep printing what's in the buffer even after you've tried to halt the printing operation.

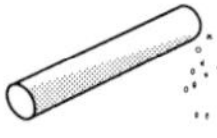

NOTE *Laser printers don't eject a page until they are finished. If you print only part of a page, you will need to eject the page manually. Check the directions that came with your printer for details on how to do this.*

EXAMPLES

1. Start printing a document and interrupt the printing by jiggling the cable (or do something else that some gremlin would be likely to do to your printer). In this situation (or when anything goes wrong with the printer), you will see a message box that looks like this:

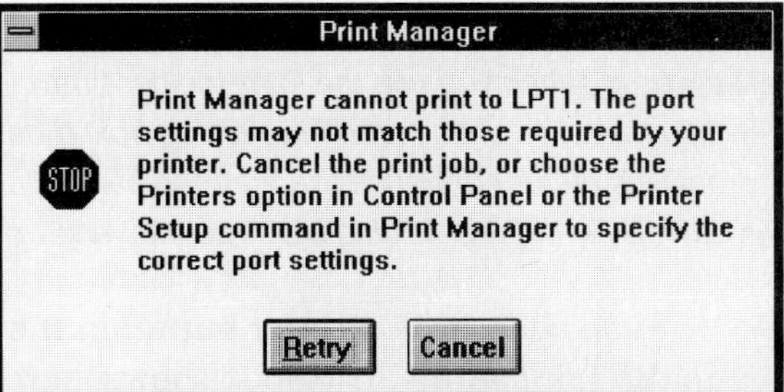

Correct the error and then click on Retry to restart the printing process.

THE BASIC OPTIONS IN THE PRINT DIALOG BOX

Suppose you start the printing process by choosing Print from the File menu. This pops up a dialog box that looks like this:

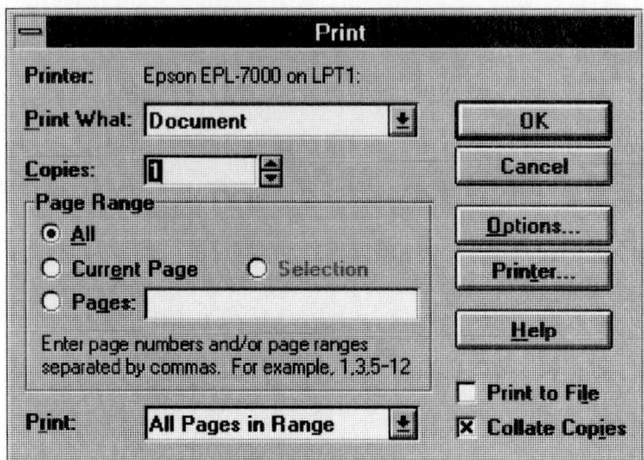

Many of the items in this dialog box are fairly straightforward. For example, you enter the number of copies that you want to print in the Copies box. And it's a snap to print the current page or a range of pages instead of printing all pages in your document. To print the current page only, just select the Current Page option button. To print a range of pages, choose the Pages options button. Then, if you need selected pages, separate the page numbers by commas. If you need a range of pages, separate the beginning and ending page number by a hyphen. If you need to print only a part of the text, first select it and then choose the Selection button in the Print dialog box.

REMEMBER *When you use the Print toolbar button, Word prints automatically using the current settings in the Print dialog box. It does not stop to display this dialog box. It's better not to use the Print toolbar button without knowing the current settings in the Print dialog box. You may end up with 30 copies of your document!*

If you choose the Printer button in the Print dialog box, Word pops up the Print Setup dialog box shown here. You can use this dialog box to select a different printer if any other printers are available. This, of course, depends on how Windows is setup for your machine (consult the documentation that came with Windows for more information on this). In the screen shown here there are three printers available that Windows knows about.

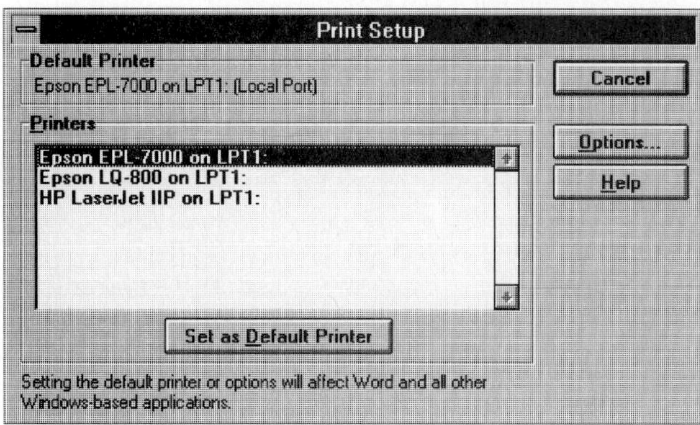

If you choose a new printer from the list and then click on the Set as Default Printer button, Windows will use the new printer as the default printer for all Windows applications.

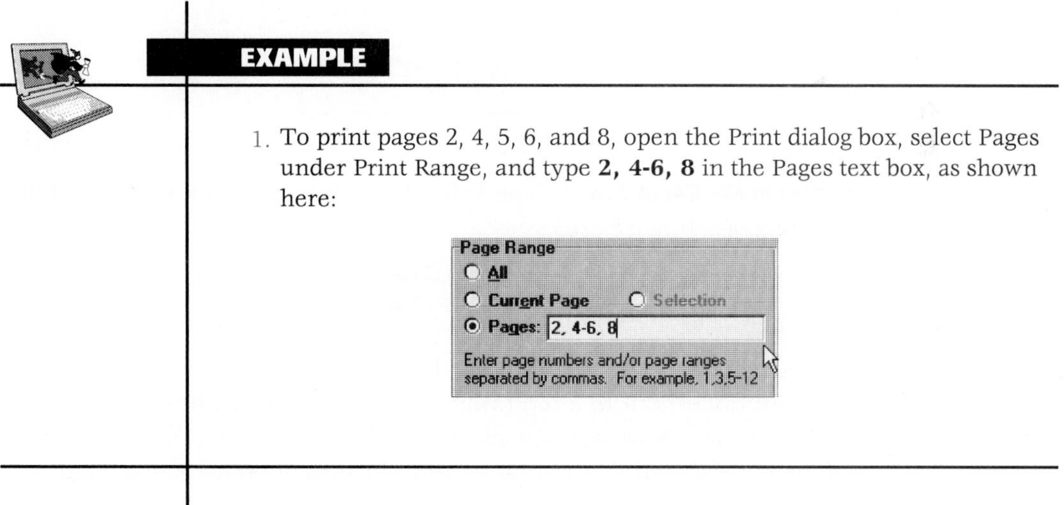

EXAMPLE

1. To print pages 2, 4, 5, 6, and 8, open the Print dialog box, select Pages under Print Range, and type **2, 4-6, 8** in the Pages text box, as shown here:

THE OTHER OPTIONS IN THE PRINT DIALOG BOX

Some of the remaining options in the Print dialog box will occasionally prove very useful. Here are short descriptions of these items.

The Print What List Box The Print What drop-down list box lets you choose what you want to print. Clicking on the downward-pointing arrow drops down this list box:

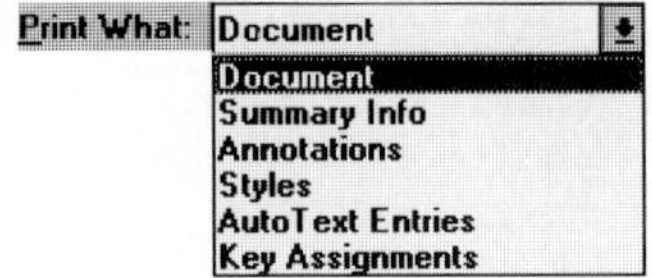

You can print the document, only the document's summary information (see Chapter 12), only the annotations (see Chapter 11), only the styles (see Chapter 7), or only the AutoText entries (Chapter 3), and the key assignments, which among other things gives you the shortcut keys you created for the current template (Chapter 7).

The Print List Box The Print drop-down list box shown here lets you choose which pages you want printed. You can choose All Pages In Range, the Odd Pages or the Even Pages. If you have a printer that can handle it, these options are useful for printing on both sides of the paper.

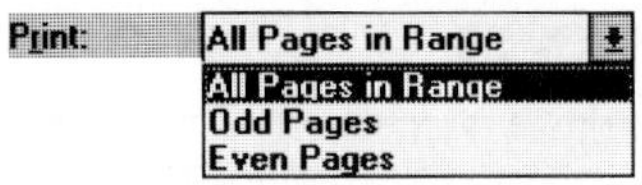

The Print to File Check Box The Print dialog box includes a Print to File check box, as shown here:

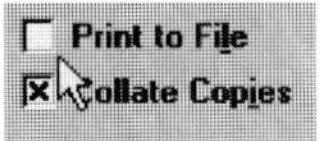

If you select this check box, Word sends the directions needed to print your document to a file rather than the printer. These directions are like a recipe: Now you can give the recipe for printing the document to someone else and they can print your document on their machine.

CAUTION *You must have selected the printer (or a compatible one) that will ultimately print the file before using the Print to File option.*

If you select the Print to File check box and click on the OK button, Word displays a standard Save dialog box so you can type a new file name. The file name you choose must be different from the original file name, or you must save the file in a different drive or directory.

The Collate Copies Check Box Make sure the Choose the Collate Copies check box is checked if you're printing multiple copies of a document and want Word to print a complete copy of the document before it begins to print a second copy of the document.

THE PRINT TAB ON THE OPTIONS DIALOG BOX

The Print tab on the Options dialog box—shown here—pops up when you choose Options from the Tools menu and choose the Print tab, or when you click on the Options button in the Print dialog box. This dialog box contains a few options that you will need to reset occasionally.

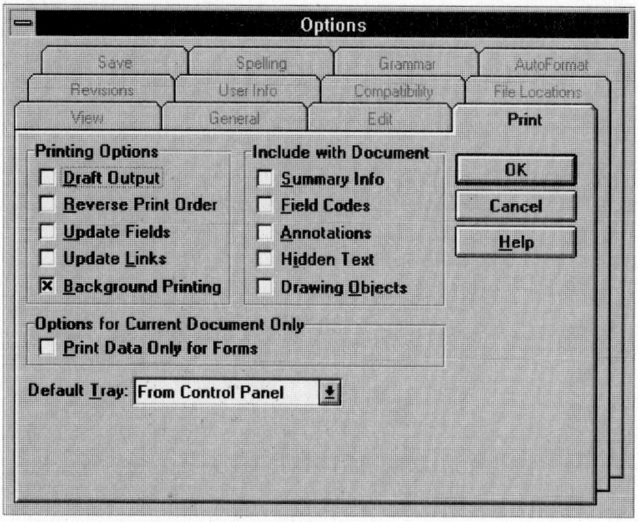

For example, Checking Draft Output prints a document with almost no formatting. The exact results you get depends on the printer. (For example, Hewlett-Packard LaserJet printers print formatted text but no graphics.) Choosing Draft Output greatly speeds up printing.

Choose Reverse Print Order to print the designated pages from last to first page. Don't choose this option if you are printing an envelope!

If you have used field codes (see Chapter 8) in your document for things like dates and times and want Word to update this information automatically, make sure the Update Fields box is checked.

The Background Printing option (which is on by default) allows you to continue working in Word while you print a document. Background printing can slow down your system if you don't have enough memory. If this happens, turn off this feature.

Choose the Hidden Text option to print any hidden text stored in the document. Word does not print the dotted underlining that appears on the screen under hidden text. (The other boxes in the Include with Document area are important when you work with larger or more complicated documents. See Chapters 11 and 12 for more on these options.)

Finally, if you are lucky enough to have a multitray laser printer, the Default Tray option is extremely useful. Click on the downward-pointing arrow to reveal a list like this one:

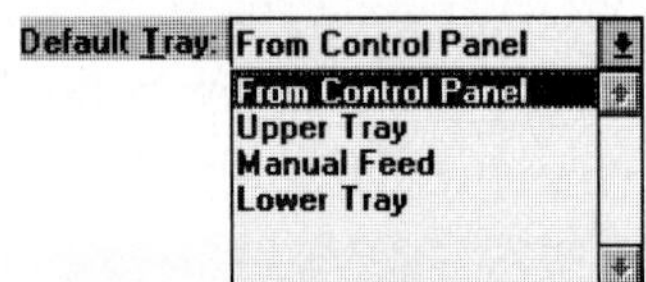

Choose the tray that contains the kind of paper you need.

EXERCISES

1. Open BIGDOC.DOC.
2. Set your zoom to a readable level and scan the document for something interesting. Set the Print dialog box to just print the page you are interested in.
3. Close BIGDOC.DOC.

9.3 PRINTING ENVELOPES

Printing envelopes used to be a pain; with Word it is now a snap. (Well almost: Envelopes not designed for laser printers have an annoying habit of jamming in the feed mechanism or getting sealed by the heat. Buy laser printer ready envelopes if you are going to use this feature a lot.)

To start the envelope printing feature in Word, follow these steps:

1. Choose Envelopes and Labels from the Tools menu (Alt T, E).

This pops up a dialog box that looks like this. (If the Labels tab is in front, click on the Envelopes tab so that your dialog box resembles this one.)

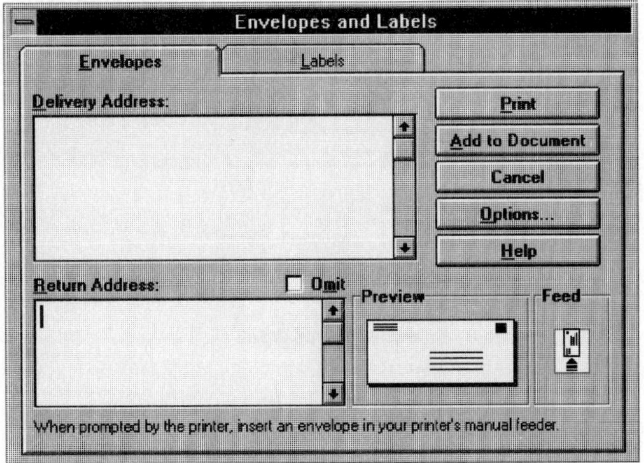

Word will actually scan your document for what it thinks is the delivery address and place it the Delivery Address box in this dialog box. If you disagree or Word can't find a delivery address, type a different one in this box. You can also select (highlight) the address you want to use in your document before you choose Envelopes and Labels from the Tools menu.

As for the return address, if you select the Omit check box, Word does not print a return address on the envelope. This option is useful if the envelope already includes a return address. Otherwise, Word will often propose a return address. If this one isn't acceptable, type the return address in the Return Address box.

Word allows you to use the same return address on all documents based on the current template. The first time you type an address in the Return Address area (or replace an existing return address), Word pops up a dialog box that looks like this:

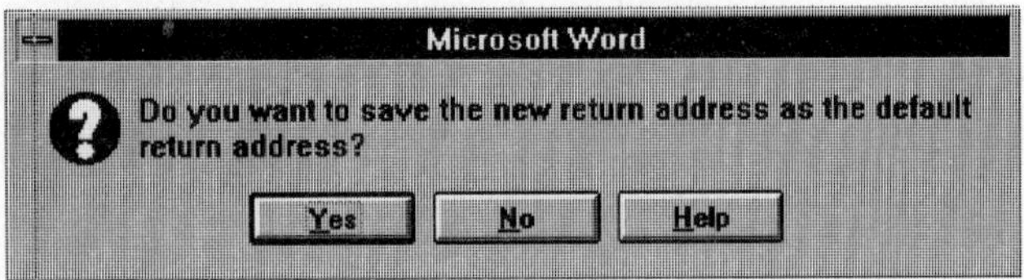

If you choose the OK button, Word stores the address on the User Info tab in the Options dialog box. Here's an example of this dialog box which you can get to by choosing Options from the Tools menu and clicking on the User Info tab.

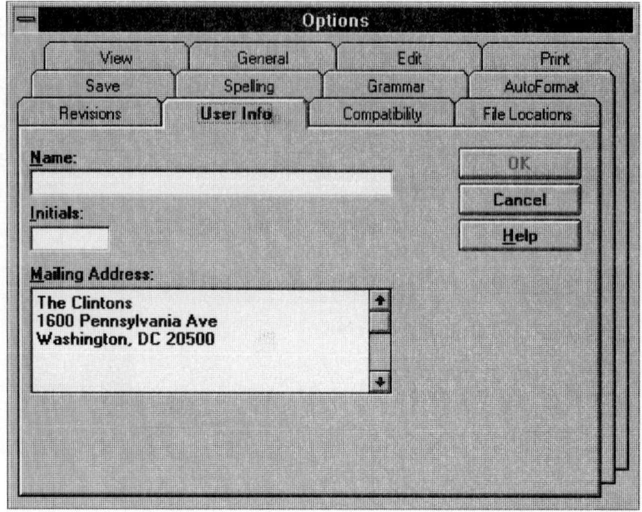

You can directly enter any data you want in this dialog box, of course.

The Preview section of the Envelopes tab on the Envelopes and Labels dialog box shows how the envelope will appear when it is printed. Clicking in this box takes you to the Envelope Options dialog box, just as if you had clicked on the Options button in the Envelopes tab in the Envelopes and Labels dialog box. This is discussed in the next section.

Finally, the Feed area on the far right of the Envelope tab of the Envelopes and Labels dialog box shows you how to place the envelope in the printer tray before you print it. If you click on this button, you are taken to the Printing Options tab of the Envelope Options dialog box, which looks like this:

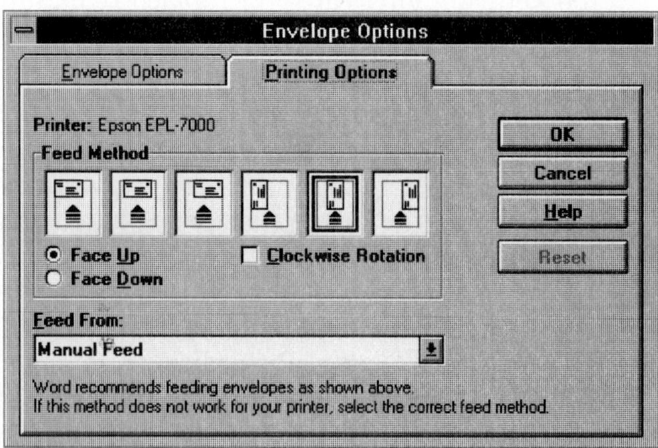

Notice the thumbnail envelopes. The feed method Word thinks will work best is boxed (in blue on color monitors) to indicate that it is currently selected. You can click on one of the other thumbnails to try a different way of feeding your envelopes into your printer if the method Word selected doesn't work.

THE ENVELOPE OPTIONS TAB

Click on the Options button on the Envelopes tab of the Envelopes and Labels dialog box to open the Envelope Options tab of the Envelope Options dialog box. This dialog box looks like this:

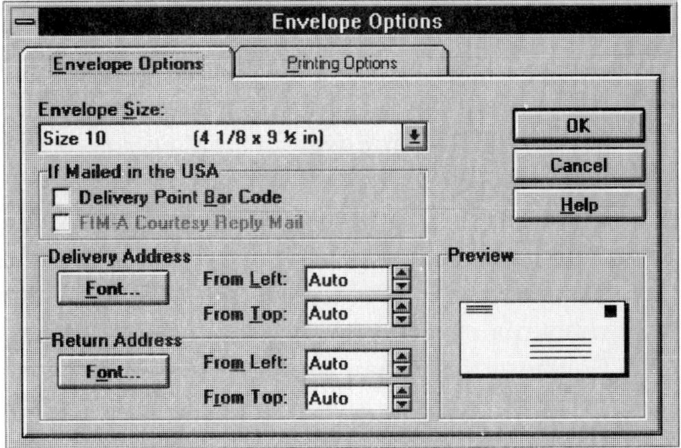

Now you can set the envelope size, and the position and default formatting of addresses. By choosing to add United States postal bar codes with zip codes to envelopes, you can sometimes save money and make it less likely that your mail will be lost. You can even select the printer tray and set the position of envelopes in the tray.

Let's go over the options in this dialog box:

The Envelope Size List Box Click on the downward-pointing arrow on the Envelope Size drop-down list box to see a list of standard envelope sizes, as shown here:

Envelope Size:

Size 10	(4 1/8 x 9 ½ in)
Size 10	(4 1/8 x 9 ½ in)
Size 6 ¾	(3 5/8 x 6 ½ in)
Monarch	(3 7/8 x 7 ½ in)
Size 9	(3 7/8 x 8 7/8 in)
Size 11	(4 ½ x 10 3/8 in)
Size 12	(4 ¾ x 11 in)
DL	(110 x 220 mm)
C4	(229 x 324 mm)
C5	(162 x 229 mm)
C6	(114 x 162 mm)
C65	(114 x 229 mm)
Custom Size...	

Now highlight the envelope size you want. If the size is not listed, select Custom Size from the bottom of the list. This opens a dialog box that looks like this:

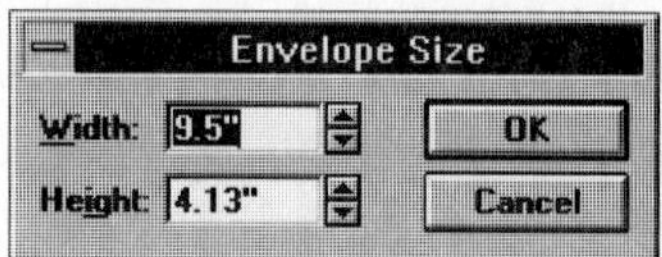

Now you can specify the exact size of your envelope.

The If Mailed in the USA Check Boxes The U.S. Postal service prefers to use automated sorters that depend on technology similar to those used in supermarket scanners. For these to work, you need to print *postal bar codes* on your envelopes. (Mass mailers and other businesses can sometimes get a discount for using these codes.) Choose the Delivery Point Bar Code option to print the *POSTNET* (Postal Numeric Encoding Technique) bar code. Choose the FIM-A Courtesy Reply Mail option to print a *Facing Identification Mark* (FIM), which is used on courtesy reply mail to identify the front of the envelope during presorting. Courtesy reply mail is preprinted with the sender's name and address.

The Delivery Address and Return Address Options These options let you change the font, size, and position of the address. A click on either one of the Font buttons brings up the usual Font dialog box (Chapter 6), from which you can choose the size and font of the address. The From Left and From Top boxes let you select the address's distance from the left edge and the top edge of the envelope. Most of the time, the Auto selection works best.

EXAMPLES

1. Suppose you want to print on #12 (4 3/4" × 11") envelopes. Pull down the Envelope Size list box and choose Size 12. Here's an example of what the dialog box will look like.

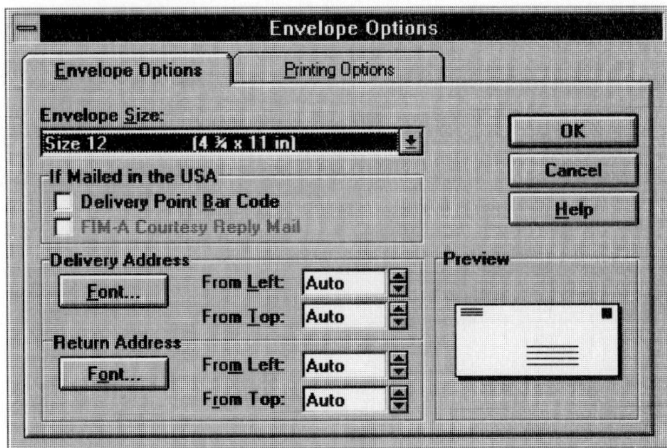

PRINTING THE ENVELOPE

Before you try to print an envelope, make sure that you have set the envelope size and the other important options discussed above. Once you have done this, to actually print an envelope, just make sure the envelope is positioned correctly in the printer (as shown in the Feed area on the Envelopes tab).

Now click on the Print button.

EXERCISES

1. Create a new blank document.
2. Enter the names and addresses of two friends or businesses you deal with. Leave the insertion point at the bottom of the document.
3. Choose Envelopes and Labels from the Tools menu and see which address shows up in which address box. Enter your proper return address if it's not correct.

4. Cancel the envelope request and then move the insertion point into the second address and request another envelope.
5. Click on the Feed icon in the lower-left corner of the Envelopes and Labels dialog box. Check that the settings are correct for your printer. Click on OK.
6. Click on the Preview icon at the bottom of the dialog box. Adjust the settings to your liking. Click on OK.
7. Print your envelope.

mastery skills check

1. Load the letter created in the Review Skills Check for this chapter.
2. Issue the Print, Preview command to preview the letter. [9.1]
3. Request a 2×1 multipage view. [9.1]
4. Zoom in on the letter and make some changes to the text. [9.1]
5. Print just the letter (note that printing page 2 won't work). [9.2]
6. Print your envelope and letter. [9.2, 9.3]

cumulative skills check

1. Use the Award Wizard and create an award. [4.2]
2. Switch to Page Layout view. [8.1]
3. Alter the fonts on the award. [6.1, 6.2]
4. Copy the award and insert the copy on a second page. [4.2, 3.3]
5. Issue the Print, Preview command to preview the awards. [2.5, 9.1]
6. Request a 1×2 multipage display. [9.1]
7. Edit the second award for a second recipient. [2.1]

10

Lists and Tables

chapter objectives

After completing this chapter, you will know how to

10.1 Create bulleted and numbered lists

10.2 Create and enter information into a table

10.3 Modify an existing table

10.4 Sort and calculate in tables.

IT'S important to organize the information in your documents. If you're organizing small amounts of information, you can always just use the Tab key after setting tab stops as you saw in Chapter 7. However, Word makes it so easy to number a list or organize tables of data that it's worth spending a little bit of time now learning these features in order to save yourself a lot of time later.

review

skills check

1. Create a new document and enter the following text using only Normal style paragraphs. [1.6, 7.3]

   To Do:

   1. Feed cat
   2. Feed horse
   3. Feed gorilla
   4. Go to town and see someone about a goat, bird, fish, and whatever other pets may be available to keep me company

2. Highlight item 3 and drag it to the front of the list. Then renumber the list. [3.3]
3. AutoFormat the document and see what styles are applied to it. [7.5]
4. Type **Feed dog** after item 3. Once again renumber the list. [2.1]
5. Save the document as TODO.DOC. (The first section of this chapter demonstrates how much easier it is to create and renumber lists with Word's list feature.) [2.3]
6. Create a new document and enter a list of about five names and phone numbers. Use the following headings and use tab stops to form columns. [7.1]

   Last Name First Name City Phone Number

7. Save the list as PHONES.DOC. [2.3]

10.1 LISTS

Numbering steps or calling attention to items by means of a *bullet* (the most common symbol for a bullet is a raised dot •) is so common that Word make this a snap. One way to create a bulleted or numbered list is to follow these steps:

1. Type the items you want to appear on the list, pressing Enter after you finish each one so that each item appears in its own paragraph (followed by the ¶ symbol).
2. Select all of the items.

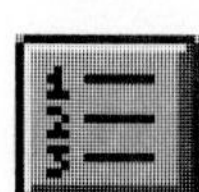

3. To place numbers in front of each item in the list, click on the Numbering button on the Formatting toolbar.

   To place bullets in front of each item in the list, click on the Bullets button in the Formatting toolbar.

That's it. Word automatically places numbers or bullets in front of the items in your list. By using this method repeatedly, you can create as many lists in your document as you want, each with independent numbering, or have some with bullets and some without.

There is one other way to create a numbered or bulleted list: simply click on the Numbering or Bullets toolbar button and then begin entering text. As long as one of these buttons is on, every time you press Enter to start a new paragraph, Word treats the next blank line as a new item on the list.

If you use this method to create a list, then you eventually get to the point where you need to tell Word to stop. In other words, you get to the point where you entered a paragraph and you *don't* want it to be numbered or bulleted—even though Word placed a bullet and number there. To remove the number or bullet from the last item on a list and therefore stop numbering or bulleting subsequent paragraphs:

▼ Make sure the insertion point is inside the paragraph to be affected, then click on the list button that you had been previously using.

To remove the bullet or numbers from the whole list, simply make sure the whole list is selected and click on the appropriate button again. To switch from bullets to numbers or vice versa, make sure the list is selected and click on the Bullets or Numbering button on the Formatting toolbar.

One common situation where you need to use the technique for removing the number or bullet from the last item on the list occurs when you are entering a list and hit Enter one time too many. For example, suppose you enter a numbered list that looks like this:

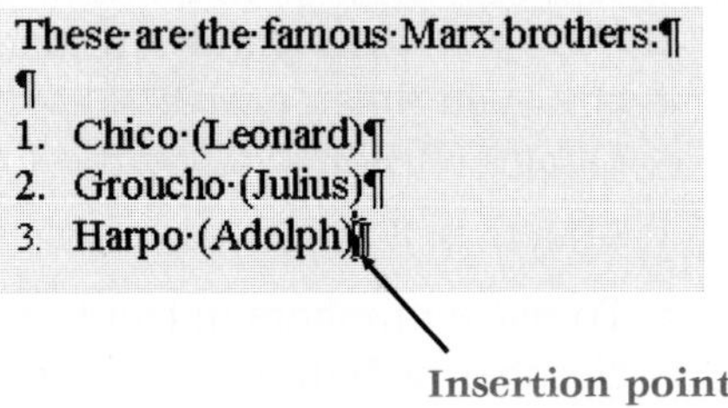

Notice that the insertion point is *still inside* the list (immediately to the left of the last paragraph symbol). Now, if you press Enter to start a new paragraph, Word treats the next blank line as a new item on the list. (This is because bullets or numbers are a type of paragraph formatting, and Word, as you saw in Chapter 7, stores such formatting in the paragraph symbol.)

By the way, if you have text in your document after the list, you can avoid this problem by remembering to move the insertion point past the end of the paragraph mark at the end of the last list item before you continue typing. Finally, another way to deal with lists to avoid these problems is to enter the text in your document and then convert items to lists afterwards. As you have seen, you can always do this by selecting the paragraphs and adding the bullets or numbering to them directly, using the appropriate button.

Word has a special *shortcut* menu for dealing with lists. Make sure the mouse pointer (the I-beam) is inside the list, then click on the right mouse button (or press Shift+F10 when the insertion point is inside the list). This opens up the List shortcut menu shown here:

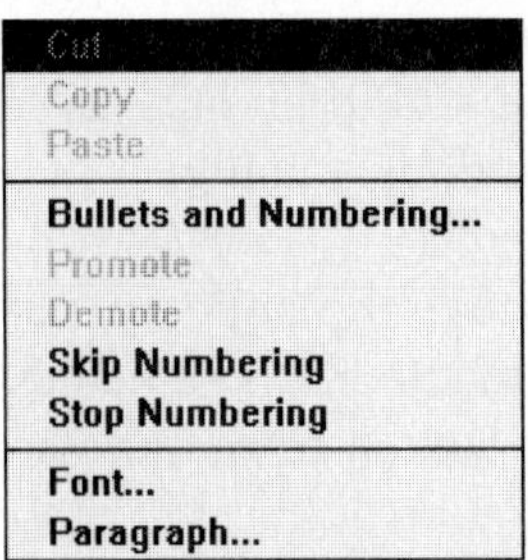

For example, you can stop the numbering (or bulleting—you see the same shortcut menu for lists or bullets) on a list by choosing the Stop Numbering item on this menu.

The Skip Numbering item on the List shortcut menu lets you have unnumbered (or unbulleted) items inside a list. Then Word can resume where it left off for any subsequent items in the list. To skip numbering (or bulleting) for items on an existing list:

1. Select the items (or make sure the insertion point is inside the specific item).
2. Then choose Skip Numbering item from the List shortcut menu.

EXAMPLES

1. Suppose you want to make a bulleted list out of the "five Ws"—the questions that should be answered in any news article. Type the following items hitting Enter after each one: **Who, What, Where, When, Why**. Select all five items and click on the Bullets button.

   To change this list to a numbered list, click on the Numbering button on the Formatting toolbar.
2. Suppose you wanted to make a list of the Marx brothers that looked like this:

   1. Chico
   2. Groucho
   3. Harpo
   Actually there were *five* Marx brothers; here are the two lesser known ones:
   4. Gummo
   5. Zeppo

   To do this, click on the Numbered List button and type the preceding text, remembering to hit Enter after each line. Word will number the items automatically—including the sentence we want to be just text. Now move the mouse pointer to the line that is supposed to be text, click the right mouse button to bring up the List shortcut menu, and choose Skip Numbering. Word will automatically remove the number from the text sentence and adjust the numbering of the last two names.

CUSTOMIZING YOUR LISTS

Suppose you want to build a list but are not satisfied with the basic list options you saw in the last section. For example, you may want to use Roman rather than Arabic numerals or a bullet character that's shaped like an arrow instead of the usual dot. You may even need a multilevel list. Word makes all these tasks a snap as well.

First, of course, select the paragraphs or list that you want to work with. Now turn to the Bullets and Numbering dialog box, shown in Figure 10-1, which pops up when you choose Bullets and Numbering from the Format menu (Alt O, N). The Bulleted and Numbered tabs on this dialog box let you control how lists are numbered or bulleted, and the Multilevel tab enables you to create multilevel lists. We will go over each of the tabs on this dialog box in the sections that follow.

THE BULLETED TAB

First, let's go over the items in the Bulleted tab of the Bullets and Numbering dialog box. The preview boxes in Figure 10-1 show your six basic choices, which range from a standard bullet (•) to an asterisk (*). If you have already selected the items to be bulleted, just click on the box that represents the type of bullet you want.

Clicking on the Remove button shown in this dialog box tells Word to remove the existing bullets. The Hanging Indent box is on by

FIGURE 10-1

The Bulleted tab in the Bullets and Numbering dialog box

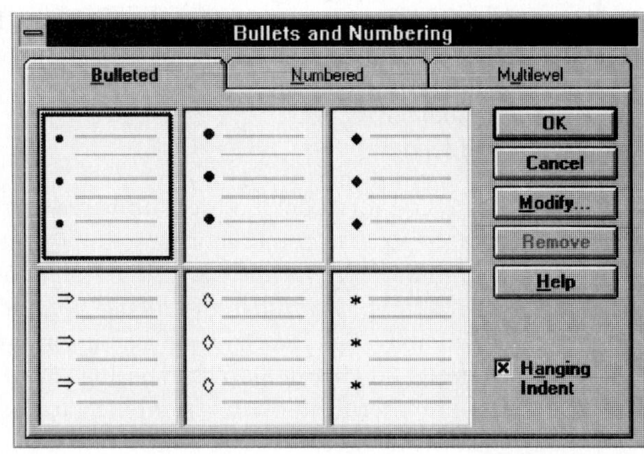

default. In a *hanging indent*, the first line of the paragraph sticks out to the left of subsequent lines (the exact opposite of normal paragraphs). In the case of numbered and bulleted lists, the idea is to have the number or bullet stand out in the margin all by itself, with no text directly underneath—this is why the hanging indent is on by default.

Clicking on the Modify button takes you to the Modify Bulleted List dialog box shown in Figure 10-2. This dialog box lets you modify the way Word puts together your bulleted list.

The Bullet Character boxes in the Modify Bulleted List dialog box show you the default bullet types. Clicking on the Bullet button displays the Symbol dialog box, shown in Figure 10-3.

If you see the symbol you want to use as bullet, click on it and then click on OK. If not, pull down the Symbols From drop-down list box and pick a different font to look for the symbol you want (the standard Windows Wingdings font is another good place to look).

The Point Size text box lets you enter a size for the bullet. The default setting is Auto, which means that the bullet character has the same size as the font used in the paragraph. You can use the Color drop-down list box to choose a color for the bullet. To take advantage of this feature, you need a color monitor to see the bullet and a color printer to print it. The various Bullet Position options let you change where the bullet shows up relative to the margins and the text. And, of course, the Preview box displays the effects of your choices before you click on the OK button to have them go into effect.

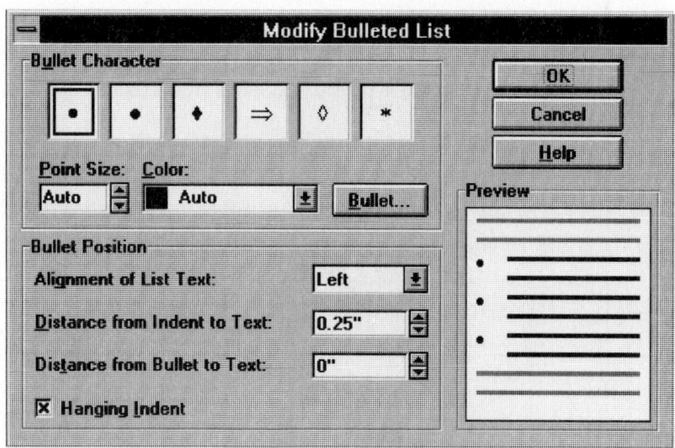

FIGURE 10-2

The Modify Bulleted List dialog box

FIGURE 10-3

The Symbol dialog box

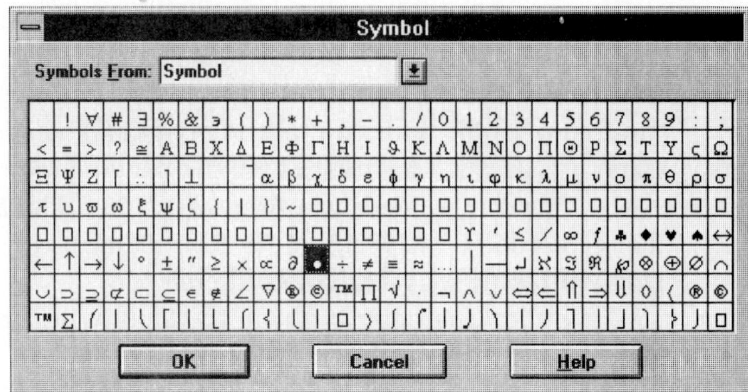

EXAMPLES

1. Suppose you wanted to change the bullet character in an existing bulleted list to a rightward-pointing arrow. Select the list, choose Format, Bullets and Numbering, and then choose the Bulleted tab from the Bullets and Numbering dialog box. Click on the fourth box under Bullet Character—the one containing the rightward-pointing arrow.

2. Suppose you wanted to use large hearts as bullets in the following list (with apologies to Elizabeth Barrett Browning):

   How may I love thee, let me *bullet* the ways:
   I love thee to the depth and breadth and height my heart can reach.
   I love thee to the level of every day's most quiet need.
   I love thee freely as men strive for right.
   I love thee purely, as they turn from praise.
   I love thee with the passion put to use.

   Enter the text, making each line that begins with "I love thee" a separate paragraph by hitting Enter. Select all the lines, and then choose the Bulleted tab from the Bullets and Numbering dialog box. Click on the Modify button, change the point size to, say, twice your current font size. Click on the Bullet button and choose the heart symbol from the Symbol font. Click on OK twice.

THE NUMBERED TAB

Figure 10-4 displays the Numbered tab in the Bullets and Numbering dialog box. As you can see, there are six basic types of numbered lists

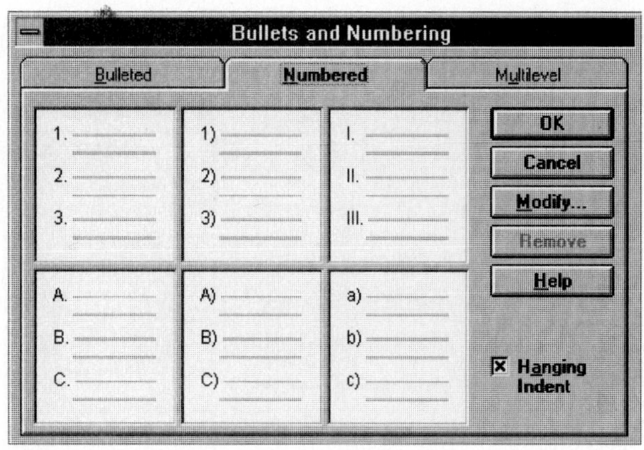

FIGURE 10-4

The Numbered tab in the Bullets and Numbering dialog box

to choose from. They range from Arabic numbers followed by a period to lowercase letters followed by an close parenthesis. The Remove button removes the numbering and the Hanging Indent check box controls whether the number hangs outside the text or not. (Refer back to the discussion in the previous section for more on hanging indents.)

Clicking the Modify button brings up the Modify Numbered List dialog box, which is shown in Figure 10-5. What follows are short descriptions of the most important of these items. As always, the Preview box illustrates the effects of the settings you choose.

The Text Before and Text After Text Boxes Use the Text Before and Text After text boxes to enter text that you want to appear surrounding each number. Most commonly, this option is used to add parentheses—as an example, to number the list with (1), (2), (3), and so on.

The Number Drop-Down List Box Pulling down the Number drop-down list box displays a list like this. Choose the numbering style you want for the list.

The Font Button Clicking on the Font button opens the standard Font dialog box you saw in Chapter 6. You can use any type of font you want for numbers in a list or for the text before or after the numbers.

FIGURE 10-5

The Modify Numbered List dialog box

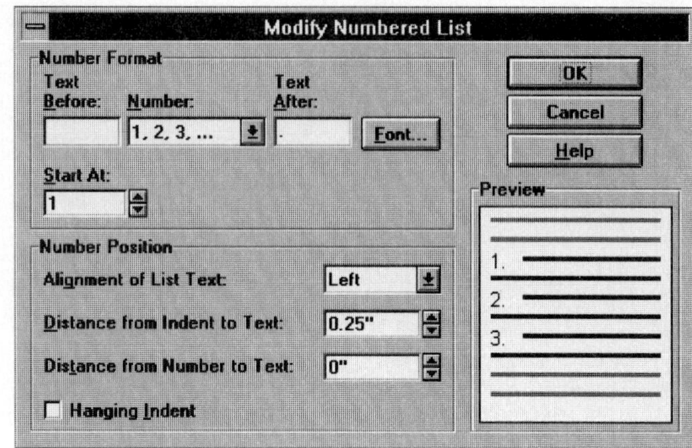

The Start At Text Box The Start At text box enables you to change the starting number of your list. Enter the number or click on one of the spin buttons to increase or decrease the number. (If you are just interrupting a list, use the List shortcut menu described in the last section.)

Number Position The various options under Number Position let you control how the numbers appear relative to the margins and to the text itself. For example, you can use the items in the Alignment of List Text drop-down list box to select the alignment you want for the list. The Distance from Indent to Text item controls the amount of space between the left indent and the paragraph. The Distance from Number to Text item, on the other hand, controls the amount of space between the numbers and the items in a list.

EXAMPLES

1. Suppose you decide to list the three fates from Greek mythology using Roman numerals. They are

   Clotho, who spins the thread of life
   Lachesis, who measures it
   Atropos, who cuts it

   Enter this text, select the list, and go to the Numbered tab on the Bullets and Numbering dialog box. Click on the third choice.

2. Suppose you want to number a list using (1), (2), (3), and so on. After selecting the list, go to the Numbered tab on the Bullets and Numbering dialog box and click on the Modify button. Fill out the Number Format part of this dialog box as shown here and then click on OK.

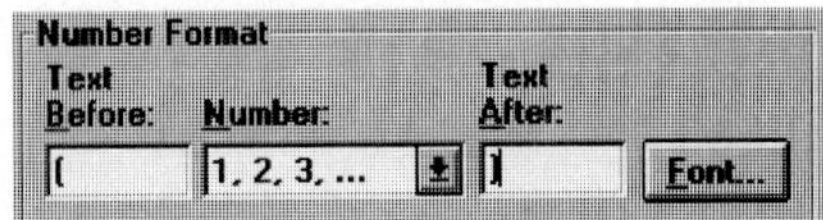

THE MULTILEVEL TAB

This tab controls whether Word will allow multilevels in your list. Multilevel lists allow you to see subsidiary relationships more clearly. For example, here is an example of a multilevel list:

1. The Beatles
    a) John Winston Lennon
    b) James Paul McCartney
    c) George Harrison
    d) Peter Best
        (i) Richard Starkey
2. The Dave Clark Five
    a) Dave Clark
    b) Lenny Davidson
    c) Rick Huxley
    d) Denis Payton
    e) Michael Smith

For some bands, if you placed the first player of the instrument in the band on the first level and then placed each subsequent player of the same instrument on lower and lower levels, then you might test Word's limits of 9 levels for its multilevel lists!

NOTE *You can use Word's multilevel list feature to build standard outlines. Multilevel lists work well for outlines as long as you do not intend to flesh out the outline into a document. If you do, it is probably better to use Word's outlining feature (described in the next chapter) for your outlines.*

To have Word build a multilevel list:

1. Open the Format menu and choose Bullets and Numbering.
2. Choose the Multilevel tab as shown in Figure 10-6. Select the desired format you want for your multilevel list and click on OK.
3. Enter the items that are to go on the multilevel list. Hit Enter after each item. At this point all the items are on the same level.

The next step is to work through the items, moving the items to lower ("demote") or higher ("promote") levels as needed.

1. To demote an item, make sure the insertion point is inside the item and use the right indent button on the Standard toolbar or press Alt+Shift+←.
2. To promote an item, make sure the insertion point is inside the item and use the left indent button on the Standard toolbar or press Alt+Shift+→.

Repeat these steps as often as you need to in order to move the items to the level you want.

You can also modify an existing list to allow multilevels. To create a multilevel list from an existing list, first select the list, then:

1. Go to the Multilevel tab in the Bullets and Numbering dialog box, as shown in Figure 10-6.
2. Click on the multilevel-list format you like and then click on OK.

Now you need to demote or promote items using the indent buttons or the Alt+Shift+arrow combinations mentioned above.

FIGURE 10-6

The Multilevel tab in the Bullets and Numbering dialog box

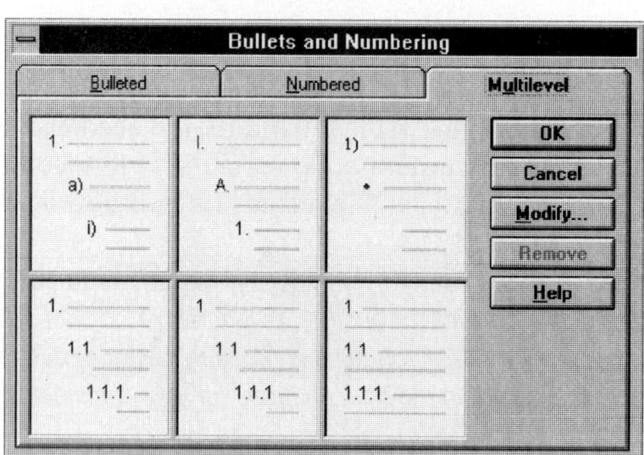

You can skip or stop numbering a multilevel list in the same ways as for an ordinary list. Click on the numbering button to stop numbering for example. Another possibility is to use the List shortcut menu discussed earlier. For example, to skip the numbering of the multilevel list:

1. Make sure the mouse pointer (the I-beam) is in the item (or that the insertion point is in the text).
2. Click the right mouse button and choose the Skip Numbering item from the List shortcut menu that appears. (Remember you can also press Shift+F10 to open the List shortcut menu if the insertion point is in the list, otherwise you need to have the mouse pointer in the list and use the right mouse button.)

(You can also make sure the insertion point is inside the item and press Shift+F10 to bring up the List shortcut menu.)

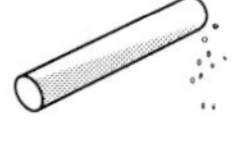

NOTE *If you need to have more than one format for a multilevel list in your document, you will need to insert a section break. Please see Chapter 12 for information on sections.*

EXAMPLE

1. Suppose you wanted to create the multilevel list of the (historical) membership of bands popular in 1964, as shown at the beginning of this section. First go to the Multilevel tab on the Bullets and Numbering dialog box. Click on the first choice.

   Enter the information given in the list. Demote the band members one level (except for Richard Starkey, who needs to be demoted two levels).

EXERCISES

1. Open TODO.DOC and format it as a numbered list by using the Numbering button on the Formatting toolbar.

2. A Latin student is doing the chores tomorrow; for his or her benefit renumber the list using Roman numerals.
3. Add **Feed frog** to the list and renumber the list using A, B, C.
4. Change "Dog" to "Dogs" and add **Rover** and **Fifi** under "Feed dogs." Then reformat the list as a multilevel list and indent the dogs' names one level.

10.2 FIRST STEPS WITH TABLES

Tables are grids made up of rows and columns. The intersection of a row and column is called a *cell.* Here's the way a typical table in Word might look before you enter any information into it:

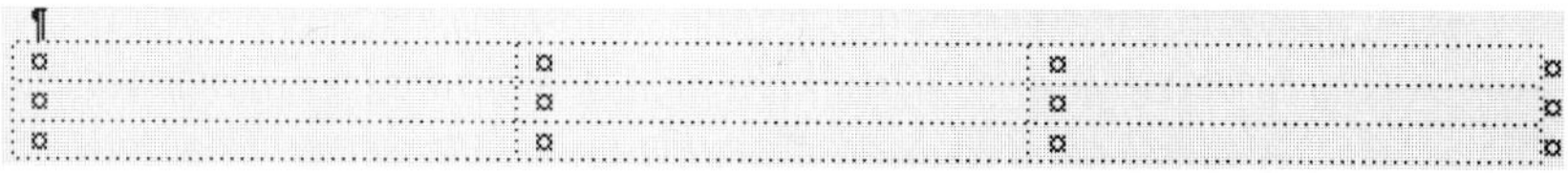

¶

¤	¤	¤	¤
¤	¤	¤	¤
¤	¤	¤	¤

Notice the dotted *gridlines* that mark the boundaries of each cell. These dotted gridlines don't show up when you print the document, but do make it very convenient when you need to navigate within a table.

Tables are convenient because, within each cell, text wraps and the cell normally grows *vertically* to accommodate new text. This makes it easy to keep your table neat. Think of each cell in a table as a specialized type of paragraph with its own tabs, fonts, and so on. (Of course, as you will soon see, you can also widen a specific column to give your table a different look if need be.)

There are many ways to create a table in Word. For example, one method is outlined here:

1. Choose Insert from the Table menu (Alt A, I). This pops up the Insert Table dialog box, which is shown here.
2. Enter the number of rows and columns of the table in this dialog box, and click on OK to generate a blank table of the specified size. (The limit on columns is 31, but there's no practical limit on the number of rows.)

By the way, don't worry if you create too many or too few rows and/or columns; you can always change it later. The Column Width text box in the Insert Table dialog box lets you determine the width of each column. Auto, the default setting, inserts columns of equal widths into your document that extend from the left to the right margin. You can enter a number directly or use the spin buttons to increase or decrease the number inside this box. You will soon see how easy it is to have columns of varying widths.

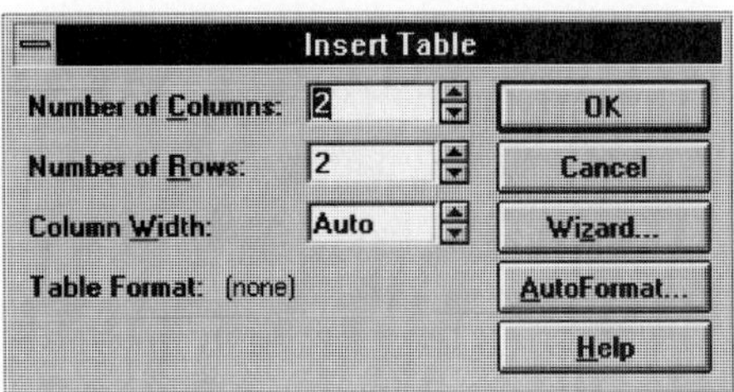

The next method for constructing the table involves the Insert Table button on the Standard toolbar. When you click on this button, Word pops up a little grid that looks like this:

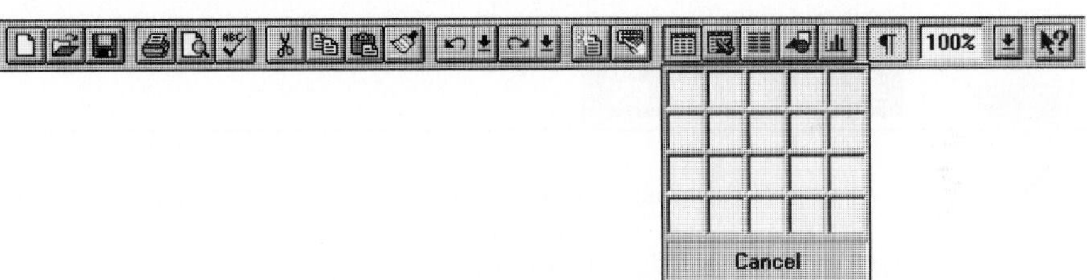

Now click in the first cell and drag across this grid. Word indicates the table size in the bottom of the box, as shown here:

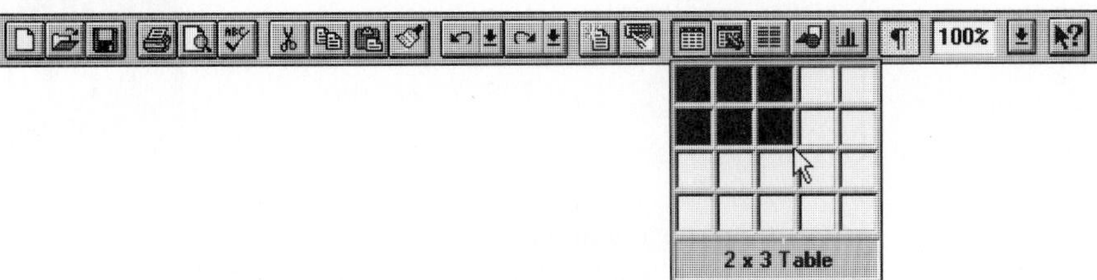

Release the mouse button when you are at the type of table you want.

TIP *The Insert Table dialog box is easier than the Insert Table button for creating very large tables.*

Finally, if you need to delete a table, the easiest way is to select the whole table, and cut it out of your document. To do this:

1. Make sure the insertion point is somewhere inside the table.
2. Select the whole table by choosing Select Table from the Table menu (Alt A, A). The keyboard shortcut is Alt+5 on the numeric keypad; the 5 on the ordinary keyboard won't work.
3. Choose Cut from the Edit menu (Ctrl+X).

This actually puts the table inside the Clipboard—where you can paste it inside the document somewhere else. You could also choose Copy from the Edit menu to make a copy of the table once you have selected it in order to make multiple copies if need be.

EXAMPLES

1. Suppose you want to create a three-row by five-column table using the Insert Table button. Click on the button and then drag through the box that pops down until it looks like this:

2. Suppose you want to create a three-column by five-row table using the Insert Table dialog box. Choose Insert Table from the Table menu and fill out the dialog box, as shown here:

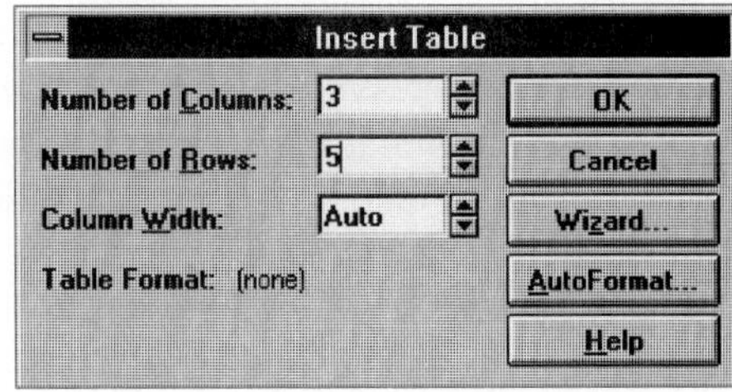

THE TABLE WIZARD

You can also create tables using the Wizard button in the Insert Table dialog box. This works much like the Wizards which were covered in Chapter 4. When you click on this button, Word leads you through a series of dialog boxes you fill in. Then Word processes the information you entered and constructs a table according to your specifications. The opening screen of the Table Wizard is shown in Figure 10-7.

Choose the type of table you want by selecting the desired Style button. Then click on Next to continue through the various Wizard

FIGURE 10-7

Opening Screen of The Table Wizard

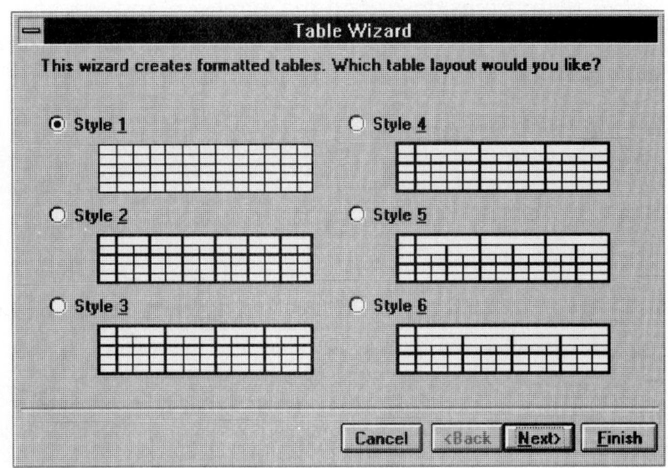

screens, entering the requested data. (Which screens you see depends on which type of table you chose.) When you finish with the last screen, Word displays the Table AutoFormat dialog box shown in Figure 10-8. This dialog box lets you control how the table looks, and is important enough that it has its own section later in this chapter (see "AutoFormatting a Table" later in this chapter).

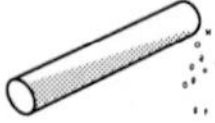

NOTE *The Table Wizard creates a new document. This means that you will need to copy the table created by the Wizard into the document you are working on.*

ENTERING DATA INTO A TABLE

Once you have created a blank table, the next job is to add the data to it. First, you need to make sure that the insertion point is in the cell you want to add the data to. A simple way to move the insertion point to a specific cell in your table is to click inside the cell you want. (You'll see more sophisticated ways to move around your tables in the next section.)

Once the insertion point is inside the cell you want, start typing the way you normally do. Word wraps text and enlarges the cell vertically as needed to accommodate the text you enter. You can press Enter to start a new paragraph inside a cell.

When you create tables, you can treat a cell like a microdocument. In particular, you can change fonts and point sizes using the techniques described in Chapter 6 and the shape of a paragraph using the techniques described in Chapter 7. For example, if you want to

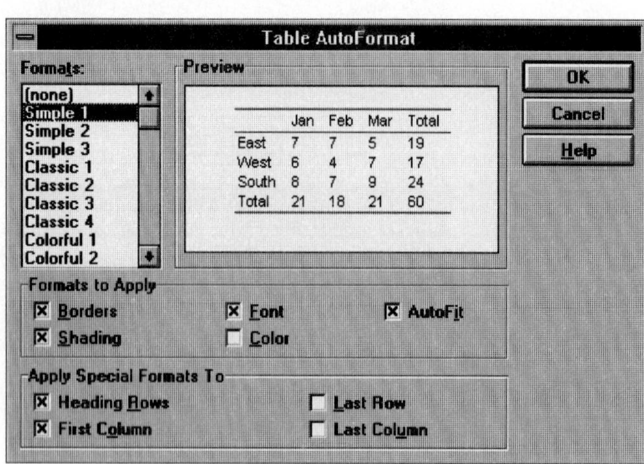

FIGURE 10-8
The Table AutoFormat dialog box

center text within a cell, make sure the insertion point is in that cell, and click on the Center button on the Formatting toolbar. If you want to place a border around a cell, make sure the insertion point is inside the cell and use the techniques from Chapter 7. Similarly, you can set indents, tabs, and the like for each cell independently.

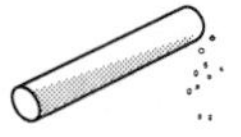

NOTE *The Tab key doesn't move you to a tab stop within a cell but instead takes you to the next cell (reading from left to right). Moreover, if you use the Tab key (or its backwards moving cousin Shift+Tab) to move to a cell that contains text, Word selects the text. If you press Tab when you are in the last cell in a table, Word adds a new row. Since the Tab key moves the insertion point into the next cell, you need to use Ctrl+Tab to move to the next tab stop within a cell.*

Just as the paragraph symbol (¶) marks the end of a paragraph, Word has a symbol that marks the end of a cell or a row. It looks like a box, as shown here:

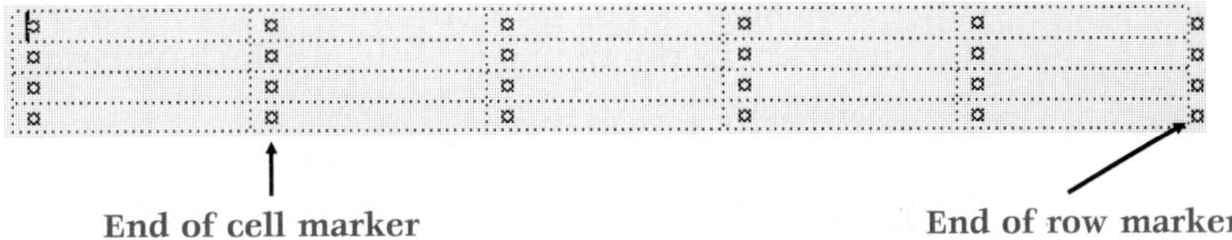

These little boxes represent the end of cell or the end of a row and are often useful for orienting yourself while entering data.

EXAMPLE

1. Suppose you want to create a two-column font table in Word. The first column will have the name of the font, the second will include the alphabet in that particular font. It might start like this:

Arial	ABCDEFGHIJKLMNOPQRSTUVWXYZ
Courier New	ABCDEFGHIJKLMNOPQRSTUVWXYZ
Times New Roman	ABCDEFGHIJKLMNOPQRSTUVWXYZ

Notice that the font name is centered in the first column, as is the alphabet in the second. Let's suppose you just have the three fonts shown here so that you need a three-row, two-column table.

a. First create a table consisting of two columns and three rows.

b. Now move the insertion point to the upper-left cell. Change the font to Arial, type **Arial**, and then click on the Center button.

c. Press Tab to move to the next cell, click on the Center button again, and type the alphabet. Continue until you finish the table.

MORE SOPHISTICATED NAVIGATION WITHIN A TABLE

To this point the only techniques you know for moving around a table are to click inside a cell or to use the Tab key (or Shift+Tab) to move to the adjacent cell. These are probably the most efficient methods for small tables. If your tables get too large to fit on a screen, you will need to turn to other methods for moving around them. Table 10-1 summarizes the methods for using the keyboard to navigate around a table:

You may have to press an arrow key more than once; for example, the ↑ key moves the insertion point up only one line. Word only breaches a cell boundary when you press the ↑ key enough times to

To Move To	Press These Keys
The next cell	Tab
The previous cell	Shift+Tab
First cell in row	Alt+Home
Last cell in row	Alt+End
First cell in column	Alt+Pg Up
Last cell in column	Alt+Pg Dn
The previous row	↑ as many times as need be
The next row	↓ as many times as need be

TABLE 10-1 *Navigating Inside a Table* ▼

have gone past the first line in the cell. Similarly, if you hold down the ← or → keys long enough, you will eventually move to an adjacent cell. (In contrast, the Home and End keys move you to the first and last character in the cell, respectively.)

EXAMPLES

1. Suppose you are in the lower-left corner of a table and want to get to the upper-left corner. All you need to do is press Alt+Pg Up.
2. Suppose you are in the lower-right corner of a table and want to get to the upper-left corner. All you need to do is press Alt+Pg Up and then press Alt+Home.

CONVERTING TEXT TO AND FROM A TABLE

Sometimes you will need to convert text into a table and vice versa. (It's quite common for a table in a document created by another application to show up in Word as text separated by tabs, for example.) Before you can create a table out of existing text, you need to make sure the items that are to go in each column in a row are separated by a common character. For example, you can have each item separated from the next item by a comma. (Another common possibility is to have each item separated from the next by a tab.) Also you must make sure that each group of items that is supposed to end up on a different row is separated from the next by a paragraph mark. (Remember, you must press Enter to insert a paragraph mark.)

There are two ways to make a table out of the text:

- You can select the text and click on the Insert Table button on the Standard toolbar.
- You can select the text and choose Convert Text To Table from the Table menu (Alt A, V).

The latter method opens this dialog box, which supplies some more options for the table:

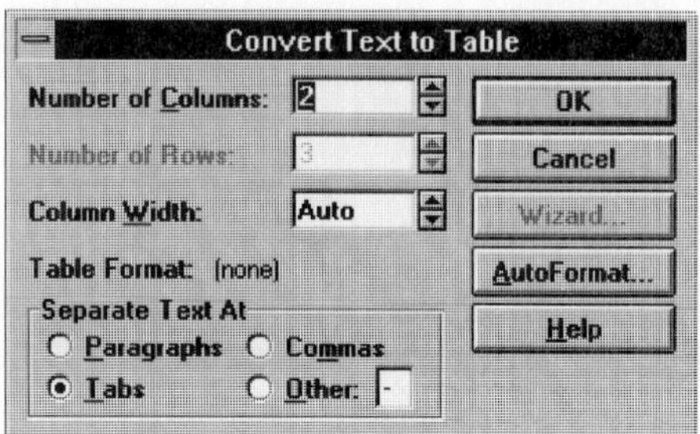

Most commonly you will need to work with this dialog box when you have text that mixes commas and tabs. You will need to tell Word where to separate the text into cells. You must choose one or the other: Word cannot use both commas and tabs as separators at the same time when converting text into a table. If the text mixes tabs and commas, for example, some of the information will not be separated in the table.

To convert a table to text, select the whole table (Alt A, A or Alt+5 on the numeric keypad) and then choose Convert Table to Text from the Table menu.

EXAMPLE

1. Suppose someone gave you a Word document that started like this:

   Dopey, the most popular dwarf, seems to be irresponsible. Doc, the leader, has a problem with the English language. Grumpy, hostile and paranoid, has a particular problem with women.

   You want to convert this information into a table to make it clearer what is a characteristic and what is editorial commentary about these important people.

   a. First, place each sentence in a separate paragraph by moving the insertion point right after the period and pressing Enter.
   b. Since the text is already separated by commas, choose Convert Text to Table from the Table menu.
   c. Now work inside the individual cells in the table to remove the periods and delete any extra spaces.

AUTOFORMATTING A TABLE

The AutoFormat option for tables is often useful once you have entered all the data in the table. This option lets Word automatically add borders, shading, or other formatting to your table according to certain standard styles. Word will even automatically resize a table if you ask it to.

To start the AutoFormatting process, make sure the insertion point is inside the table. Now:

1. Choose AutoFormat from the Table menu (Alt A, F)

This opens the Table AutoFormat dialog box, which was shown earlier in Figure 10-8. The Preview box in the center of Figure 10-8 shows what a table would look like in the style selected in the Formats list box. To remove any borders or shading from your table, make sure to select [none] from this list box.

Most of the items in Figure 10-8 are self-explanatory, For example, many of check boxes in Figure 10-8 prevent Word from applying the default table formats in the design selected in the Formats list. The AutoFit option may not be familiar. If you select this check box, Word automatically adjusts the size of the table based on the amount of text in the table.

EXAMPLE

1. Suppose you want to create a multiplication table for a child. This should be in a large font (try 16 point) and it should have borders around each cell. First, create the table as shown (partially) here:

	2	3	4	5	6	7	8	9
2	4	6	8	10	12	14	16	18
3								
4								
5								
6								
7								
8								
9								

Now choose Auto Format from the Table menu and pick the one of the Grid 1—Grid 8 table formats that you like the best and then click on OK.

EXERCISES

1. Open PHONES.DOC. Highlight all the text and convert it into a table.
2. Add a line of data to the end of the list.
3. Use Table, Auto Format and select an appropriate style.
4. Use the Insert Table button on the Standard toolbar and insert a two-column by two-row table below the existing table.
5. Enter **Prefix** and **City** in the two cells on the first row.
6. Fill in the table based on the data from the previous table.
7. AutoFormat the prefix table.
8. Save PHONES.DOC.

10.3 MODIFYING AN EXISTING TABLE

Just as few people have a perfect document, few people enter data completely correctly into a table (or format it perfectly) the first time around. You will often need to insert or delete rows and columns. You will also often need to change the width of a column or the height of a row.

Probably the most common modification to a table is to add or delete rows and columns. For this you first need to know how to select cells, rows, and columns.

SELECTING WITHIN A TABLE

When using a mouse to work with a table, note that there is a narrow selection bar in the far left side of a cell or immediately to the left of a row. When you move the mouse pointer into one of these selection bars, it changes into a rightward-pointing arrow, just as it does when you're selecting regular text. The following table summarizes how to select within a table using the mouse.

To Select	Do This with the Mouse
A cell	Click in the cell selection bar
A row	Click in the row selection bar
A column	Click the column's top gridline or border

To select multiple cells, rows, or columns you can drag the mouse pointer across the cells.

To select cells with the keyboard:

To Select	Do This with the Keyboard
The next cell	Press Tab
The previous cell	Press Shift+Tab
The whole table	Choose Select Table from the Table menu (Alt A, A) or press Alt+5 on the numeric keypad
A range of cells	Move the insertion point to the beginning of the range, hold down Shift, and use a navigation technique from Table 10-1

(A *range of cells* is a rectangular block of contiguous cells.)

For example, to select a whole column, move the insertion point to the top cell and either hold down Shift and press ↓ or press Shift + Alt + Pg Dn.

TIP *You can also place the insertion point inside a row or column and choose Select Row or Select Column from the Table menu.*

INSERTING ROWS, COLUMNS, AND CELLS

Now that you know how to select parts of a table, you can learn how to insert a cell, a row, or a column. Let's start with inserting rows and columns because you already know one way to insert a row: if you are in the lower-right cell in a table, you can insert a new row just by pressing Tab.

First off, you always need to keep in mind that Word inserts new rows above the rows you have selected and inserts new columns to the left of the columns you have selected. Because of this, you need to select all the end of row marks at the far right of a table if what you want to do is insert a column to the far right of a table.

Once you select the rows above which, or columns to the left of which you want to insert new rows or columns, proceed as follows:

- Choose Insert Rows or Insert Columns from the Table menu or click on the Table button on the Standard toolbar.

(The ToolTip for the Table button on the Standard toolbar switches from being Insert Table to being Insert Row/Column depending on whether you have selected a row or a column.)

TIP *If you need to insert more than one cell, row, or column, select that many cells, rows, or columns before starting the insertion process just described.*

Next, you might want to insert cells into an existing table. This requires telling Word how to shift the current cells. Here's what you need to do:

1. Select the cell or cells next to the ones where you want Word to insert the new cells.

2. Choose Insert Cells from the Table menu (Alt A, I).

Word pops up this dialog box:

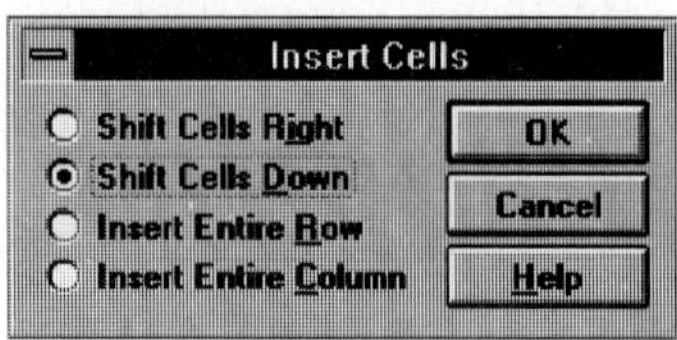

If you want to insert the new cells to the left of the selected cells,

- Pick the Shift Cells Right button.

If you want to insert new cells above the ones you have selected,

- Choose the Shift Cells Down option, then click on OK.

EXAMPLES

1. Suppose you want to insert two rows above the third row in a table. To do this select the third and fourth rows before starting the insertion process. Then choose Insert Rows from the Table menu.
2. Suppose you want to insert three cells to the left of the cell in the top row, second column. To do this select the first three cells in the second column before clicking on the Table button.

SPLITTING A TABLE

Another common modification you will make on a table is to split it into two smaller tables. To do this:

1. Make sure the insertion point is in the row where you want the new table to start.
2. Choose Split Table from the Table menu (Alt A, S).

Word inserts a blank line with a paragraph mark between the two smaller tables. You can now type whatever text you want to appear between the tables. If you want to rejoin the pieces, simply delete the paragraph mark.

DELETING, COPYING, AND MOVING PARTS OF A TABLE

As always the rule in Word is: Select, then do. For example, to move or copy a column or row, first select it (with rows, make sure you have selected the end of row marker). Then use the ordinary cut, copy, and paste techniques or the drag and drop techniques you learned in Chapter 2. If you need to delete a row or column, you can also select the rows or columns you want to delete and then choose the Delete Rows or Delete Columns items from the Table menu.

If you want to delete cells within a table, you must select the cells you want to delete. Then you have to tell Word how to rearrange the remaining cells. You do this via the following dialog box, which pops up if you choose Delete Cells from the Table menu (Alt A, D):

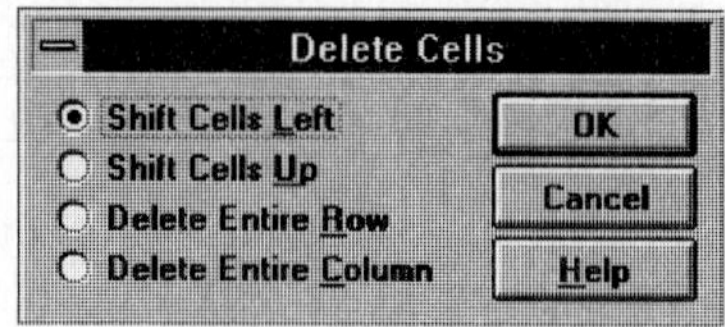

If you want to shift the remaining cells to the left, pick the Shift Cells Left option. If you want to move the remaining cells up, choose the Shift Cells Up option. Then click on OK. This dialog box also gives you another way to delete rows or columns from a table.

REMEMBER *Always keep in mind the difference between deleting the contents of a cell, column, or row and deleting the cell, column, or row itself. The former is done by selecting the cell row or column and pressing Del, the latter is done by the techniques introduced in this section.*

CHANGING COLUMN WIDTHS

As your tables get more complicated, you will rarely be happy sticking to Word's default table shapes. This section explains how to change the width of a column, and how to modify the space between columns. The next one shows you how to force Word to make all your rows a certain height instead of adjusting automatically to the text you enter.

Let's first suppose you want to change the width of a column. If you don't need absolute precision, it's probably easiest to use the mouse. To adjust the width of a column with the mouse, drag the boundary of the column to where you want it. The mouse pointer changes to a double-headed arrow separated by double bars, as shown here:

If you want to make any more precise adjustments to the width of a column, make sure the insertion point is in the column you want to work with. Now choose Cell Width and Height on the Table menu (Alt A, W). This opens a tabbed dialog box, whose Column tab looks like this.

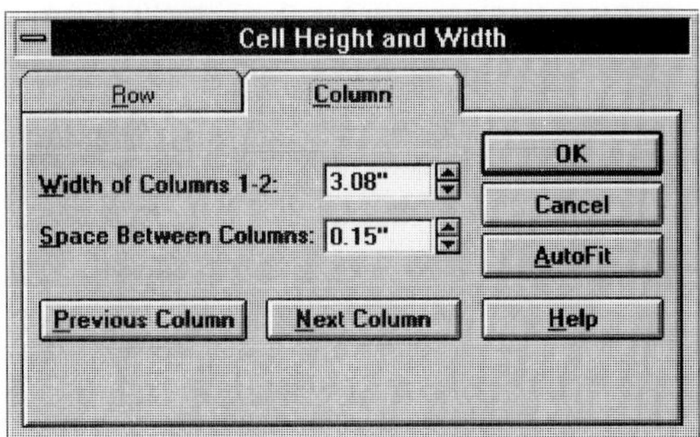

Just enter the width and space between columns that you want in this dialog box. Click on the AutoFit to have Word adjust the width according to the widest cell in the column. Now click on the Previous Column or Next Column buttons if you want to adjust any other columns in the table.

ADJUSTING THE HEIGHT OF A ROW

Now suppose that you want to adjust the height of one or more rows in your table. If you want to work with a specific row, first select it. (If you don't do this, Word assumes that you want to change all the rows in the table.) Again choose Cell Height and Width on the Table menu (Alt A, W), only now turn to the Row tab in this dialog box to adjust how each row looks.

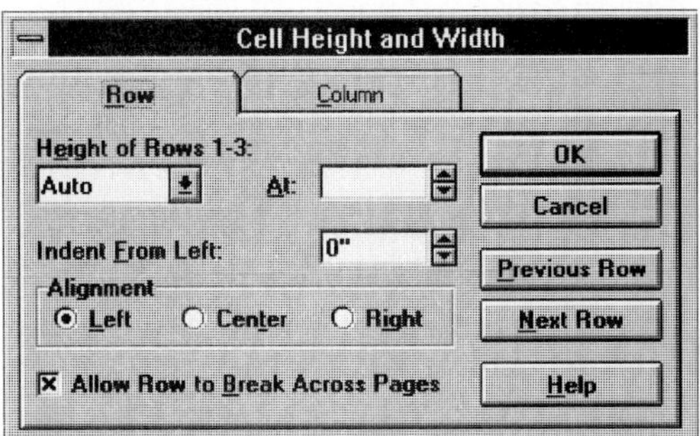

Let's go over the items in the Cell Height and Width dialog box more carefully. Some of its features can be very useful.

The Height of Rows List Box As you can see here, the Height of Rows drop-down list box contains three options:

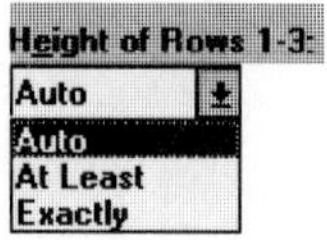

The default is Auto, which means that Word adjusts all cells in the row (or rows) to be the height of the tallest cell in the row or rows. In particular, as you enter more than one line of text, Word increases the height of the row.

The At Least option lets you specify a minimum row height. This is useful for making a row wider than the font size of the characters or the number of lines would make it. If cell contents are bigger than the height you chose, Word adjusts the height to fit the contents.

The third option, Exactly, lets you specify a precise row height. Word will not change this even if there is too much text to fit in the cell. (Word displays and prints only as much text as fits in the cell.) One use of this option is to add a somewhat narrower but completely empty row in your table in order to improve the look of your table.

If you chose the At Least or Exactly option button, fill in the height you want in the Height Of text box. You can use points, inches, or any of the other units of measurement that Word knows about.

The Indent from Left Text Box The Indent from Left box lets you specify the distance between the left page margin and the left edge of the first cell in the selected rows. Enter a number directly or click on one of the spin buttons in order to set or reset this distance.

The Alignment Buttons The Alignment buttons let you align rows (or the whole table) relative to the left and right page margins. Choose Left to align selected rows at the left page margin. Choose Center to center selected rows between the left and right page margins. Choose Right to align selected rows at the right page margin.

TIP *If you want to center a table inside the page, select the whole table and choose Center from this dialog box.*

The Allow Row to Break Across Pages Check Box If your table spans pages, you must decide if you want to let a row split across a page break. Make sure this box is not selected if you do not want the contents of a single row to appear on two different pages.

The Previous Row and Next Row Buttons Click on one of these buttons to go to another row so you can modify its height.

EXAMPLE

1. Suppose you want to create a three-column by five-row table with 1 1/2-inch columns. You also want to center this table in the page and never let rows break across pages.
   a. First, make sure the insertion point is where you want the table to be.
   b. Choose Insert Table from the Table menu and fill out the Insert Table dialog box as shown here:

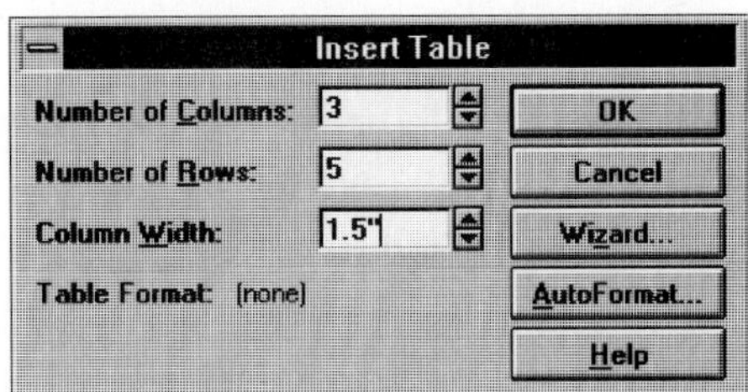

   c. Choose Cell Height and Width from the Table menu. Go to the Row tab and fill it out as shown here:

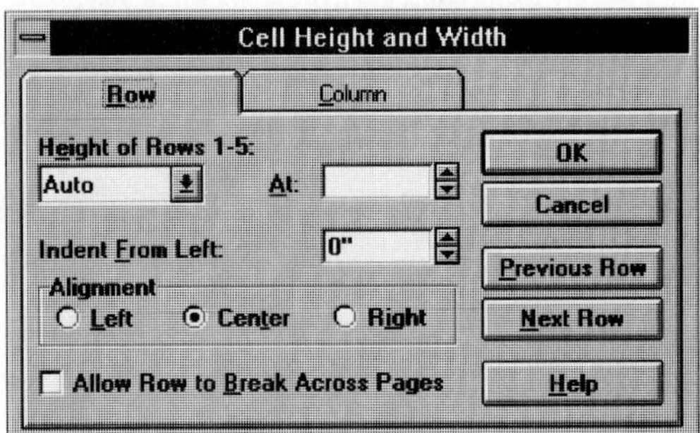

MERGING CELLS AND ADDING HEADINGS TO TABLES

As your tables get more complicated, you may need to add headings to them. A heading can just be the contents of the cells in the first row or it can be as complicated as you want. A very common type of heading for a table has a wide first row, an empty second row, and column headings in the third row.

Creating a heading that will extend along the length of a row requires *merging* cells—which is jargon for making adjacent cells into one larger cell. (You can only merge cells horizontally.) Merging cells is useful for other things besides creating headings: You may not want your tables to have uniform cell widths, for example.

Let's suppose you want to create a table heading like the one shown here:

The five faults of a leader (adopted from Sun Tzu)	
Recklessness	which leads to destruction
Cowardice	which leads to capture
Temper	which makes you easy to provoke
Delicacy of Honor	which makes you sensitive to shame and dishonor
Too much concern for your subordinates	which exposes you to worry and false economies

Notice that the cells in the top row have been merged to provide room for the long heading.

To merge cells:

1. Select the cells you want to merge.
2. Choose Merge Cells from the Table menu.

To split cells that you have merged:

1. Select the cells you want to split.
2. Choose Split Cells from the Table menu.

   This pops up a dialog box that looks like this:

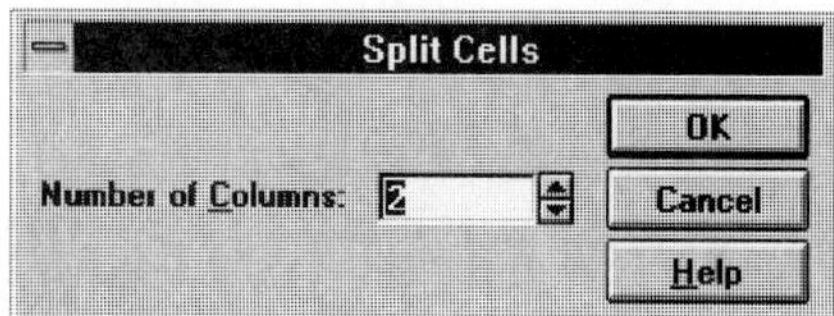

   If you don't agree with Word's suggestion,

3. Enter a different number of cells and click on OK.

TIP *Once you have added a heading to a table, Word lets you repeat the headings on the next page if Word has to insert a page break between rows in your table. To do this, first select the rows you want to be the headings for your table. Then choose Headings from the Table menu.*

EXAMPLE

1. Suppose you want to create a two-column by 13-row table whose first few lines look like this:

The Nine Muses (Daughters of Mnemosyne and Zeus)	
Muse	**Field of Responsibility**
Calliope	Muse of epic poetry
Clio	Muse of history
Erato	Muse of love poetry
Euterpe	Muse of lyric poetry

   a. First create a two-column by 13-row table.
   b. Change the width of the first column to 2 inches and the second column to 4 inches.
   c. Merge the two cells in the first row.
   d. Enter the headings and the names of the muses.

ADDING CAPTIONS TO TABLES

In addition to placing headings within tables, you will often want to add *captions* to them. To assign a caption to a table:

1. Select the table.
2. Choose Caption from the Insert menu (Alt I, I).
3. In the Caption dialog box that pops up, choose Table from the Label drop-down list box. You can enter anything you want in the Caption text box although Word automatically places the

word Table followed by what it thinks is the current number in the Caption text box.

4. Once you've established the desired settings, click on OK.

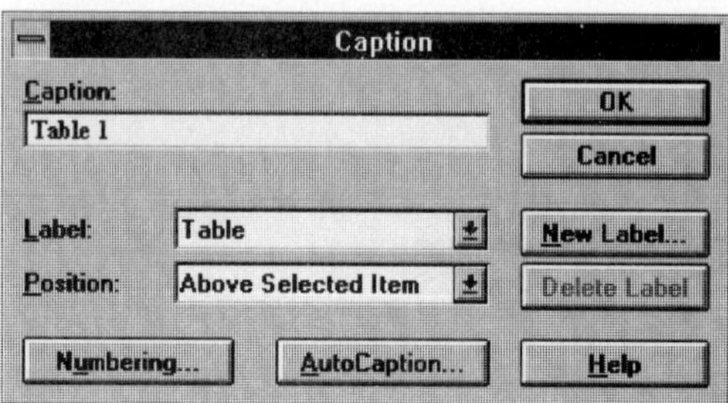

Of the other options in the Caption dialog box, the one you will most commonly use is the Position drop-down list box. This lets you control whether the caption will appear above or below the table.

EXERCISES

1. Open PHONES.DOC and add a few lines of data to the middle and the end of the list.
2. Highlight a row and press Del.
3. Delete the empty row.
4. Insert three rows in the middle of the table. Fill in the rows or delete them.
5. Add a column in front of City and enter **Address** in its first row.
6. Add two columns after City and label them **State** and **Zip** Code.
7. Fill in the data for the blank cells.
8. Select the Column tab of the Cell Height and Width dialog box. Select Auto from the Width of Columns list box to automatically adjust your column widths to fit the largest entry.
9. Save PHONES.DOC.

10.4 SORTING AND CALCULATING WITH TABLES

You may enter data into a table and then realize that it throws the whole table out of order. Word makes it easy to sort the information in a table. You can sort by a column containing alphabetic, numeric, or date information.

To sort a table, first select the rows that you want to sort. (If you want to sort all the rows, select the whole table.) Now choose Sort from the Table menu (Alt A, S). This opens the dialog box shown in Figure 10-9. The Sort By drop-down list box lets you specify the column upon which Word bases the sort. (The default is the first column). You may need to specify a "tiebreaker"—a column to use if two rows have the same entry. (If two people have the same last names, you'll then want to sort based upon their first names.) The Then By drop-down list box tells Word what to use for this tiebreaking column.

If your table had a heading (that is names for the information in the columns) in the first row, it is best to be careful not to include this row. However, if you inadvertently selected it, make sure the Header Row button in the Sort dialog box is checked. When this box is checked, Word excludes the header information from the sorting process. (For example, if the first column has the header of **Names**, you wouldn't want the first row to end up after the Ms!)

The Ascending and Descending option buttons in Figure 10-9 determine what order Word sorts in. If you turn the Ascending button

FIGURE 10-9

The Sort dialog box

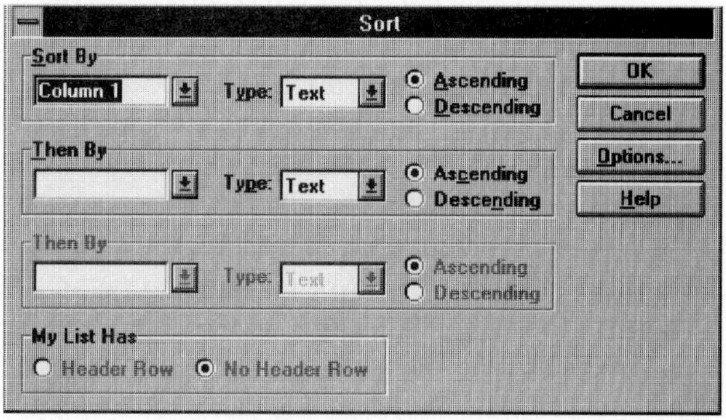

on, Word sorts from the beginning of the alphabet, the earliest date, or the lowest number to the highest. If you have the Descending button on, Word does the reverse.

Unless you change the case sensitivity of the sort, case is irrelevant and Word uses the following order for sorting text. (You control case sensitivity by working with the dialog box that comes up when you click on the Options button.)

- Items that begin with punctuation marks go first.
- Items with numbers go next.

For example, this list is sorted in ascending text order according to Word:

!Kung
e.e. cummings
Robert Frost

If you want to sort on dates or numbers, pull down the Type drop-down list box in the Sort dialog box, as shown here:

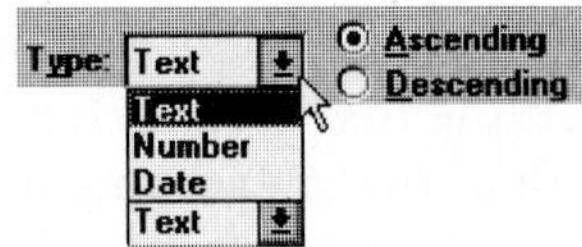

If you choose the Number option from the Type list box, Word ignores all the other characters except numbers and sorts by numeric order. If the Ascending button is on, Word sorts from the smallest number to the largest. (If the Descending button is on, Word does the reverse.)

Choose the Date option when you want Word to ignore everything but dates. You can use most standard formats and abbreviation for dates. For example, hyphens, forward slashes, commas, and periods are valid separators for dates. You can use a colon for the time. If a date is incorrect (such as 22/22/99), Word assumes the current date. If a time is incorrect, Word assumes that you meant midnight. Word puts any unrecognized entries at the top of the list for an ascending sort or at the bottom of the list for a descending sort.

Here's the Sort Options dialog box that appears when you click on Options in the Sort dialog box.

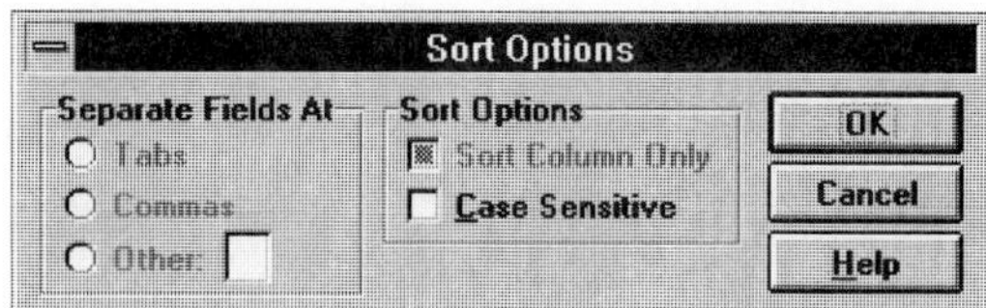

There are two important options in this dialog box. The first is Sort Column Only, which tells Word to sort only the selected column. Make sure this box is not checked if you want to sort the whole table. The other is the Case Sensitive check box. If this box is selected, Word sorts text so that capital letters precede the same letter in lowercase in a text sort. For example, suppose you have asked for a case sensitive ascending sort. Then *ZOO* precedes *apple*.

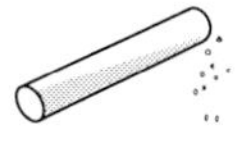

NOTE *You can sort a group of paragraphs or a list by selecting it. If you select text, the Sort item on the Table menu changes to Sort Text; sorting text works much the same as sorting in a table.*

EXAMPLES

1. Suppose you had the following table and wanted to sort the list according to the dates that T.S. Eliot wrote the "Four Quartets."

Quartet	Year Written
Burnt Orange	1936
Dry Savages	1941
East Coker	1940
Little Giding	1942

   a. Select the second column of this table.

   b. Select Date from the Type drop-down list box and make sure the Header Row button is selected under My List Has. Then click on OK.

DOING CALCULATIONS IN TABLES

It's pretty easy to add a row or column of numbers in a table.

1. Move the insertion point to the bottom cell in the column (or rightmost cell in a row).
2. Choose Formula from the Table menu (Alt A, O).

You'll see this dialog box:

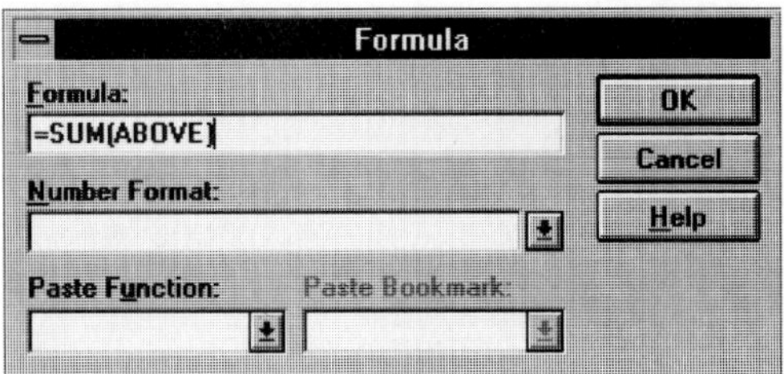

Make sure the Formula text box says =SUM(ABOVE), as it does here [or SUM(LEFT) if you are summing the entries in a row], and click on OK. Word adds the numbers and places the result in the current cell.

If you want to do any more sophisticated calculations within a table, you'll need to know how Word names table cells. Each column is assigned a letter (starting with A for the leftmost column) and each row is assigned a number (starting with 1, for the top row). Cells are specified with their column letter and row number. For example, A1 is the upper-left cell in any table, A2 is the second cell in the first row, B1 is the first cell in the second column, and so on.

Now suppose you want C3 to be equal to the results of dividing the value in cell A1 by the value in cell A2. Position the insertion point in cell C3, choose Formula from the Table menu and type **=A1/A2** in the Formula text box, as shown here:

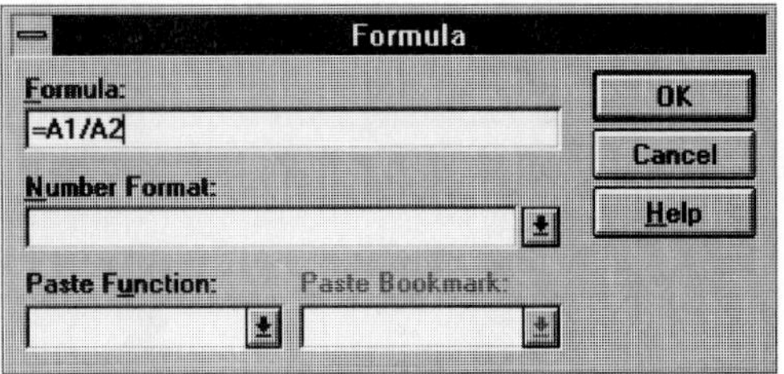

You can use a + (plus) sign for addition, a – (minus) sign for subtraction, a * (asterisk) for multiplication, and a / (forward slash) for division.

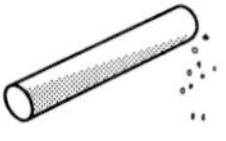

NOTE *Word can handle quite a few other arithmetic and logical operations on tables. Consult Mary Campbell's book,* Microsoft Word for Windows: The Complete Reference *(Osborne/McGraw-Hill, 1994) for more on these operations. This book also tells you how to take advantage of a spreadsheet like Microsoft's Excel in order to embed a spreadsheet into what looks like a Word table.*

EXAMPLE

1. Suppose you want to create a table like the one show here that lists the cost of a hamburger and french fries at a restaurant, assuming the prices increase at 5% a year. We will need a 10-row by four-column table.

The effect of 5% inflation on the cost of fast food			
Year	**Hamburger**	**French Fries**	**Total**
1993	2.00	1.00	3.00
1994	2.10	1.05	3.15
1995	2.21	1.10	3.31
1996			
1997			
1998			
1999			
2000			

   a. First create a 10-row by four-column table.
   b. Now prepare the table for the headings as shown above by merging the cells in the first row. Then fill in the heading in the first row and the column headings in the third row.
   c. Now place the following formulas in the cells. In the fourth column (under Total) we need to sum the two cells to the left. So you need formulas that look like this:

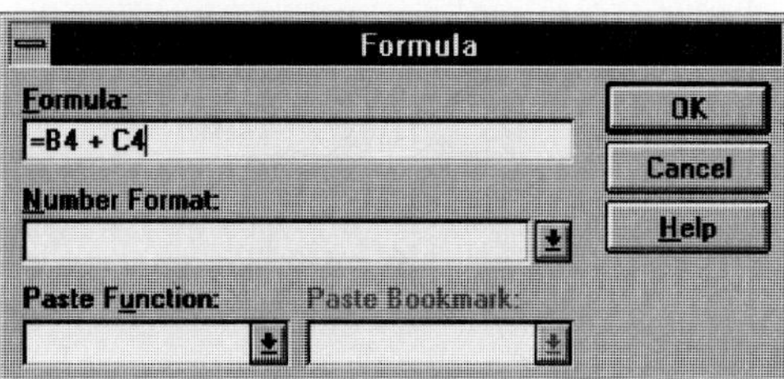

d. Select each cell, choose Formula from the Table menu and enter the formula.

e. In the second and third columns, you need a formula that multiplies the preceding cell by 1.05. (Inflation of 5% means every dollar costs 1.05 the next year.) The formula dialog box would look like this for cell B5:

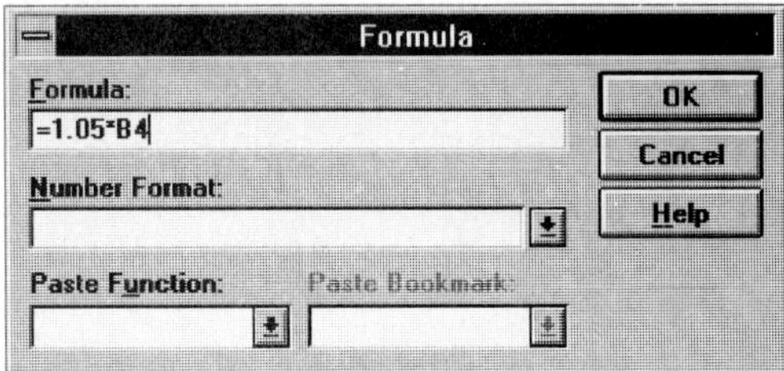

f. Choose Formula from the Table menu and fill it out for all the remaining cells as in the previous steps.

EXERCISES

1. Open PHONES.DOC and sort the phone list by last name.
2. If you don't already have one, add a record with a duplicate last name and a different first name.
3. Sort the table by last name in ascending order (make this the primary column), and by first name in descending order (make this the tiebreaker). View the results and then sort them again, this time sorting by first name in ascending order.
4. Sort the table by last name.
5. Delete the row containing the formulas.
6. Challenge Yourself! With the insertion point in the table, use View, Toolbars and bring up the Database toolbar.

   Experiment with the buttons on the Database toolbar. Close the toolbar when done. (This feature will be covered in Chapter 14.)
7. Close PHONES.DOC and save your changes.

mastery skills check

1. Create a new document and enter the following text or some other menu items more to your liking. (Enter a single tab between the item and it's cost.)

   Hamburger 2.85
   Cheeseburger 2.95
   Hot Dog 1.65
   Tuna Sandwich 2.15
   Chips .55
   Milk Shake 1.65
   Soda .85

   Select all the paragraphs and turn them into a bulleted list. [10.1]
2. To get rid of the bullets, make sure the list is selected and then click on the Remove button from the Bulleted tab of the Bullets and Numbering dialog box. [10.1]
3. Turn the text into a table. [10.2]
4. Add a row at the top of that table and add the labels **Item** and **Price**. [10.3]
5. Adjust your table using AutoFit for column width and center the table on the page. Right justify the paragraphs containing the prices. [10.3]
6. Add a few items in between others and at the bottom of the table. Readjust your table if necessary. [10.2, 10.3]
7. Sort the table by the Item column (this one is alphabetical), and then sort the table by the Price column (this would be a numeric sort). Then return the table to its original order by using the Undo feature. [10.4]
8. Add a column to the right side of the table. [10.3]

1. Open MENU.DOC (just created in the Mastery Skills Check). Choose AutoFormat from the Table menu and select the Colorful 2 format. [10.2]
2. Change the format of the first column to be Arial. [6.2]
3. Add a paragraph under Hamburger that says: **Lettuce, Pickle, Tomato, on a Sesame Seed Bun**. (Form a new line in the middle of the paragraph just before the word "Sesame.") [7.1]
4. Use the AutoFit feature, or drag the cell boundaries, to adjust the column widths. [10.3]
5. Format the paragraph you just entered under Hamburger so that it is indented and uses an 10 point italic font. [7.1, 6.1]
6. Define a new style for the paragraph you just formatted. [7.3]
7. Add a few notes under the other menu items using the new style you just created. [7.3]
8. Using the Borders toolbar, add a line between all the cells and add a thick double border around the whole menu. [7.2]
9. Add your new restaurant's name in a paragraph above the menu using a large font. [6.1, 7.1]
10. Select the menu table and perform a spell check. [10.3, 5.1]
11. Switch to Page Layout view and adjust the table shape or the fonts to improve the table's appearance. [8.1, 10.3, 6.1, 6.2]
12. Save your work. [2.3]

part three

Advanced Word

11

Working with a Single Large Document or Multiple Documents

chapter objectives

After completing this chapter, you will know how to

11.1 Open and work with more than one document at the same time

11.2 Use multiple document windows and split screens

11.3 Divide your documents into sections

11.4 Use Word's outlining feature

As the tasks you use Word for grow more complex, you will often need to work with more than one document at the same time. This chapter starts by showing you the techniques needed when you have several documents open at the same time. (How many documents you can work with concurrently is determined by how much memory your computer has—the more memory you have, the more documents you can work on.)

Then it's on to the techniques needed to work on documents like long reports or books. For example, you'll learn how to divide a document into *sections,* each of which can be formatted separately. (For example, if you want a document to contain two different sets of page numbers, you must break it into two sections at the place you want the page numbering to change.)

Of course, the larger the document, the more likely it is that you will want to outline it before you start the actual writing. So next you'll see how to use Word's powerful outline features. Word's outlining ability goes way beyond what you can do with paper and pencil because, after you create the outline and fill in the text, you can "collapse" the document so it again appears in outline form. When you have finished looking over the document in outline form, a click on a button brings the document back to its usual form.

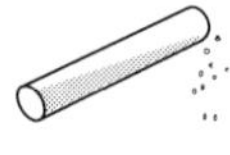

NOTE *Word has many specialized tools for dealing with indexes, tables of contents, or when a group will be working on different parts of a very large document all at once. For all this and more please consult Mary Campbell's* Microsoft Word for Windows: The Complete Reference, *Osborne/McGraw-Hill, 1994.*

review
skills check

1. Use the Letter Wizard to create a standard (prewritten) business letter on plain paper as well as an envelope. [4.5]
2. View the letter in Normal view and notice how the Wizard inserted a section break into the document. [8.1]
3. Move the insertion point between the envelope and the letter and notice the page and section numbers shown on the status bar. [1.4]

4. View the letter in Page Layout view. [8.1]
5. Zoom to Full Screen mode. [8.1]
6. Center the letter vertically on the page by selecting File, Page Setup, Vertical Alignment. [8.2]
7. Use File, Print Preview to preview the letter and envelope. [9.1]
8. Save the document for use later in this chapter. [2.3]

11.1 OPENING AND WORKING WITH MORE THAN ONE DOCUMENT AT ONCE

In Windows, the computer screen is meant to imitate an ordinary desktop. On a person's desk it is quite common to need to work with two things at once: you might need to compare a report on this year's sales to a similar report on last year's sales. For Word users the analogous idea is that Word has its own big window but this big window can have lots of little smaller windows inside of it. You can have one window for each document that you are working with—and you can switch between them very easily. (These smaller windows are called *subwindows* or *child windows* in the jargon.)

First off, it's worth keeping in mind the difference between *open* documents and the *active* document while you are reading this section. You can have many *open* documents but only a single *active* one. The active document is the one that is affected by your actions; the other (open) documents are waiting in the wings to be called so that they can get their turn on the stage.

When you start Word, you see Word's application window and a blank document entitled Document1 in the document area. As you create new documents or open existing documents by working with the appropriate items on the File menu or the New and Open buttons on the Standard toolbar, each additional document gets its own window. The windows for each additional document start out by totally overlapping. This means that at first, even if you have many open documents, you can only see the window for the last document you opened or created. However, it's worth keeping in mind that all the other windows are there; they just don't show on the screen at the moment.

EXAMPLES

1. Start Word and notice that Word has opened a blank document called Document1 based on the Normal style. Notice the document's name in the title bar at the top of the screen. Type **Document One** inside the document area to make it easier to identify the document.
2. Create a new document without closing the first document. Type **Document Two** to identify it. Notice the name of the new document in the title bar.

SWITCHING BETWEEN DOCUMENTS

If you followed the last example you now have two documents open at the same time. You could continue opening existing documents or creating new documents until you ran out of memory, but for now we'll just assume you are working with two open documents. We will call them Document1 and Document2.

There are two ways to switch between open windows. The first uses the Window menu (Alt W). The bottom of this menu lists all the open document windows. The document that is currently active (the one that you can type into or the one that will be affected by commands) has a checkmark next to its name.

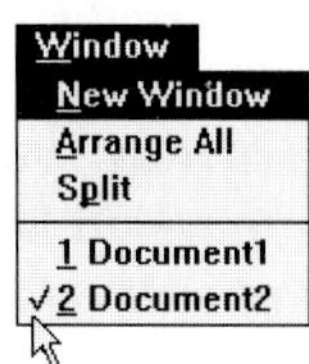

To switch to Document1 simply select Document1 from the menu (Alt W, 1).

The Ctrl+F6 combination is another way to switch between open windows. This method cycles through all open documents in turn, so if you have more than two open documents it may be quicker to use the Window menu.

TIP *To close the active document, use the Ctrl+W shortcut. To close* all *the documents, hold down the Shift key while clicking on the File menu. The Close*

item on the File menu changes to read Close All. Click on it to close all open documents at the same time. You can also use the Save All option on the File menu to have Word save all open documents.

EXERCISES

1. Open any existing document by selecting File, Open.
2. Open a second existing document by selecting File, Open.
3. Use the Window menu and bring the first file you opened into view.
4. Use Ctrl+F6 to switch back to the first document window.
5. Select File, Close once to close the first document; use the Ctrl+W shortcut to close the second.
6. Open more than one document at the same time and use the Close All method to close all the documents you opened.

11.2 USING MULTIPLE DOCUMENT WINDOWS AND SPLITTING THE SCREEN

Let's suppose you have opened more than one document using the techniques from the last section. As long as one window totally overlaps another, you really can't *work* with the documents at the same time. It's as if you have two folders on your desk but one always covers the other—not very useful. The jargon is to say you need to learn how to *manage your document windows*. Word's Window menu contains the items needed to do so; here again is a picture of this menu:

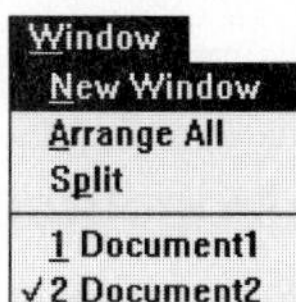

These items are important enough so that we will take them up one at a time in the following sections.

ARRANGE ALL

Let's experiment with the Arrange All item first. (You should still have two documents named Document1 and Document2 open in Word. If not, return to the first example in the previous section to see how to do this.) Open the Window menu and select the Arrange All option. The results should look like Figure 11-1. Notice that each document is now in its own window with its own title bar. You make a window active by clicking inside of it and then, as usual, its title bar is highlighted.

Notice in Figure 11-1 how the active window has its own control box, and minimize and maximize buttons. This lets you resize or move the active window by using the standard Windows techniques. To move or resize any of the other windows, you will need to activate it first by clicking inside of it—then you can use ordinary Windows techniques on it. (See Appendix A if you need to review these techniques.)

REMEMBER *As with any Windows application, you can recognize the active document window by checking which title bar is highlighted.*

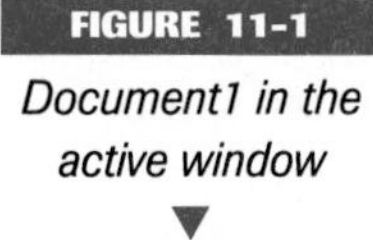

FIGURE 11-1

Document1 in the active window

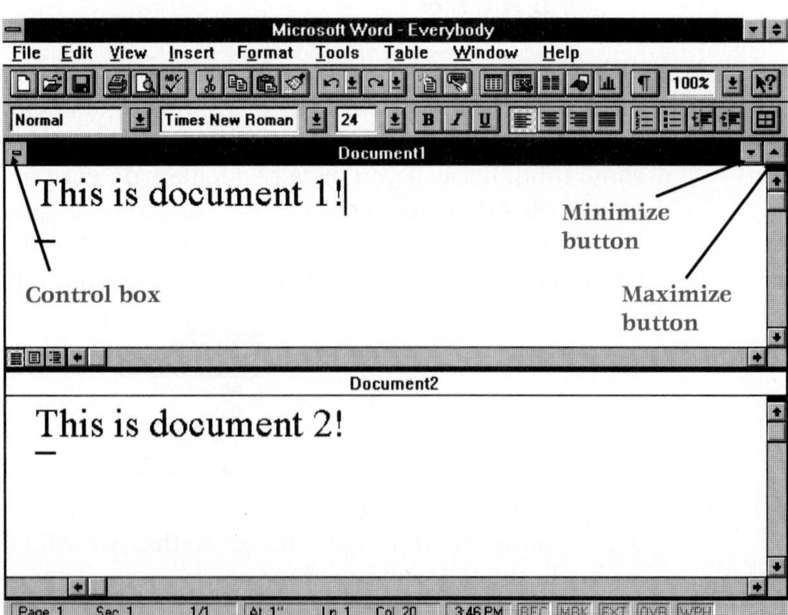

EXAMPLES

1. Make sure you have two open documents and choose the Arrange All option from the Window menu. Close the active document window using the Ctrl+W shortcut.
2. Notice the other document doesn't expand to fill the empty space. Use the Ctrl+F10 shortcut (or click on the maximize button) to maximize the remaining document window.

NEW WINDOW

Let's work a little bit with the New Window option on the Window menu. Choosing this item creates another view (window) into the same document. Note that when you use this feature only a *single* copy of the document is open. Use this feature when you need separate windows to see different parts of a document at the same time.

For example, suppose you say what you will cover in a chapter in the introduction to a chapter. You can use the New Window feature to see the introduction to the chapter at the same time you work with the part of the document that is supposed to deliver your promises. Another common use of the New Window feature is to display the same area of a document differently. For example, one window could show the document in Normal view in one font while the second window could display the document in Page Layout view zoomed in at some high level.

To see how New Window works, let's assume you have maximized one of the documents you have open at the moment. Now select New Window from the Window menu. Notice as shown in Figure 11-2 that each window has the (same) name of the document except that it is followed by a colon and a number. Each new window shows up on the list of open documents on the Windows menu.

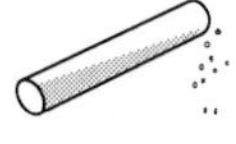

NOTE *If you use the New Window feature to get multiple views of the same document and want to close one of the views into your document, make sure that window is active and then use the Ctrl+W shortcut to close it.*

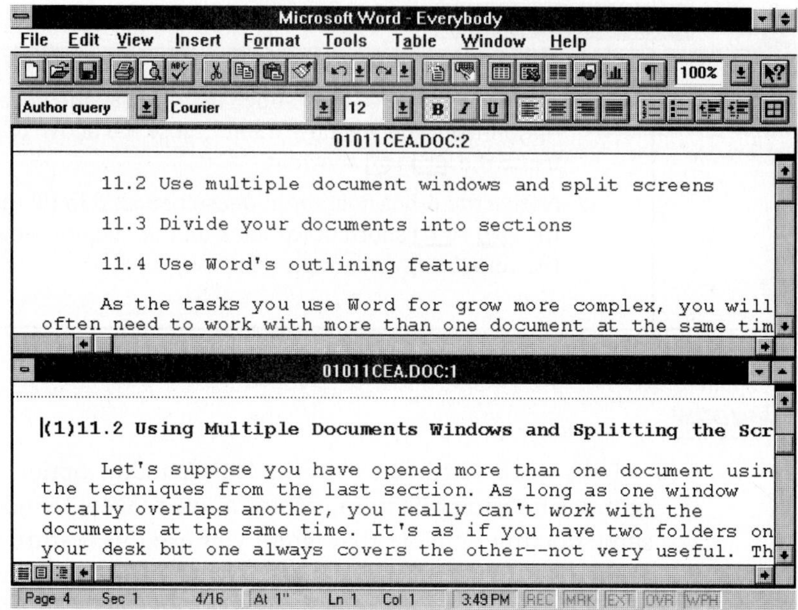

FIGURE 11-2 *Multiple documents displayed with Arrange All*

SPLIT

The Split option on the Window menu divides a single document window into two parts called *panes*. As with New Window, when you use this feature only a *single* copy of the document is open. On the surface, Split and New Window work pretty much the same. The difference is that when you split your screen there is a *linkage* between the two panes. The panes scroll horizontally together, for example. This is why splitting is more useful than opening a new window when you have a very wide document with column headings at the top of a table and data beneath it. If you split the document just below the titles, you can scroll the bottom pane from right to left, and the column headings will always remain in view in sync with your moving horizontally through the table.

To see Word's split feature at work:

1. Have one document open and maximized.
2. Choose Split from the Window menu.

   A narrow split line appears across your document, as shown in Figure 11-3.

FIGURE 11-3

A single document showing split line

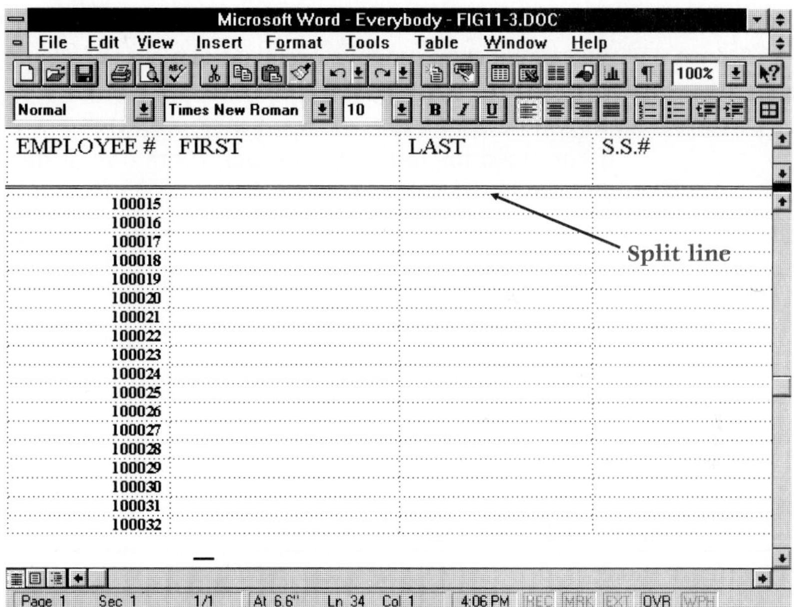

3. Drag the split line to where you want to split the window.
4. Click the left button to anchor the split. (You can also use ↑ and ↓ on the keyboard and press Enter to anchor the split.)

To return the window to a single pane, select Remove Split from the Window menu (Alt W, P) or use the mouse to drag the split line off the top or bottom of the window.

TIP *You can also create a split (and remove it) by dragging on the Split bar just above the up arrow on the vertical scroll bar as shown here.*

Once you split a window, any changes you make to the text in one pane are also made in the other pane. However, depending on how you split the screen, you may not see a change in the other window at the moment. (Remember that just one copy of the document is open at once; what you have is two different views of the same document.) As with setting up a new window, you can set the display modes differently in the two panes. For example, you could use Normal view on top and Page Layout view on the bottom.

If you need to change how much room one of the split documents is taking up on the screen:

1. Move the mouse pointer over the split boundary until it changes into the double-headed arrow split cursor.
2. Drag the split line to a new location.

EXERCISES

1. Open an existing document. Create a very wide table that goes beyond what fits on a screen. Add headings to the table.
2. Select Windows, Split to split the document area below the table headings.
3. Use the mouse to position and anchor the split, and then drag the split line to a new location.
4. Enter data in the table; notice how the parts scroll horizontally in sync.
5. Drag the split with the mouse using the split bar until it is above the ↑ on the vertical scroll bar and release it. Notice the Split bar is still above the ↑. Drag it down to form a new split.
6. Remove the split from the document area.
7. Select Window, New Window.
8. Open another existing document.
9. Select Window, Arrange All.
10. Close the second window into the first document.
11. Close all documents.

11.3 DIVIDING YOUR DOCUMENT INTO SECTIONS

Sections are used to break up your documents into logical portions where you want to format *the pages* differently from one another. For example, you might have a preface to the main document that needs different margin settings, page size, or orientation. Often you'll need to reset page numbers in different sections. You might even need to establish a different numbering style for the different sections—changing from Roman numerals to Arabic numbering. On the other hand, you would not use a new section to establish new paragraph indents—since that's *paragraph-level* formatting.

Here is a list of some document characteristics you may wish to vary within a document by using sections:

- Line numbering
- Changes in location of footnotes and endnotes
- Page numbering
- Page setup—such as page size and orientation
- Margins
- Paper source (which paper tray)
- Headers and footers
- Vertical alignment of text on the page

INSERTING SECTION BREAKS

To insert a section break in your document, make sure the insertion point is where you want the break to occur. Usually you insert section breaks between paragraphs—immediately after the paragraph mark (¶). Then:

- Choose Break from the Insert menu (Alt I, B). This opens the Break dialog box shown here.

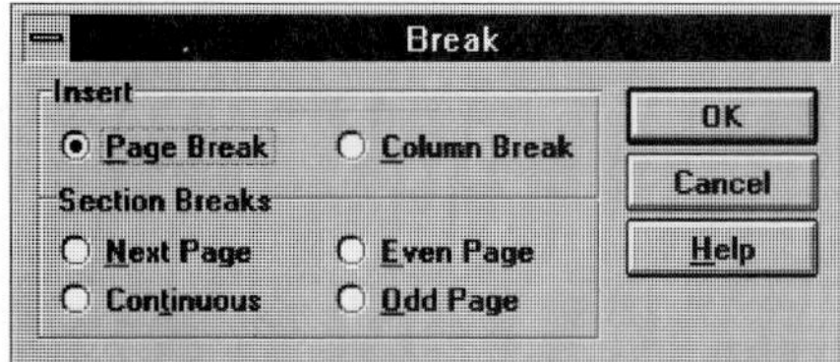

The options buttons for section breaks in the Break dialog box let you control where you want the new section to begin and the previous section to end. *However, Word will often insert page breaks when you make certain choices of section breaks*—so it is important to understand the effect on your document before actually inserting a page break by clicking on OK.

Here are short descriptions of the four possible types of section breaks and what they do to your document.

Next Page Choosing this type of section break tells Word to put a page break immediately after the insertion point, start the next section at the top of the next page and move the text after the insertion point to the next page. Word moves the insertion point to the top of the new page as well.

Even Page, Odd Page Use odd or even pages for section breaks when you are producing documents like a book where headers may need to appear in a particular way on each side. (Where Word inserts the page break depends on where the insertion point is.)

Let's suppose you choose an Even Page break and the insertion point is in page 5. Word immediately places a page break at the insertion point, moves any text after the insertion point to the next page and starts the new section at the top of page 6 (moving the insertion point to the top of page 6).

Next, let's suppose you choose an Even Page break and the insertion point is in page 4. Then Word inserts *two* page breaks leaving page 5 blank to start a new section break at the top of what will now be page 6, and moves all the text after the insertion point to page 6. Word also moves the insertion point to the top of page 6.

TIP *If you need Even and Odd Page breaks, wait until you have finished editing the document and are about to print the document before inserting this kind of break. The reason is that as you add text the section break will move and it may move so far that it is no longer on the right kind of page.*

Continuous Choose this option if you don't want Word to insert a page break into your document. Word splits the text at the insertion point and moves any text after the insertion point to the beginning of the new section. Word moves the insertion point to the beginning of the new section as well. An example of where you would use a

Continuous section break is when you need to create a page that has both two-column and three-column text (see Chapter 13). In this case you'd want to insert a section break *without* going on to the next page.

TIP *When you want to have different headers and footers, a different orientation for a page, or line numbers, choose one of the page-oriented section breaks rather than using a Continuous section break.*

Finally, to remove a section break, select it and then press Del.

EXAMPLES

1. Open a new document and select Normal view. Enter this text:

   This will be in Section 1. This will be in Section 2.

   Place the insertion point after the period in the first sentence. Insert a Continuous section break. Notice in the following illustration that the sentences are split and that the status bar shows we are still on page one, since we inserted a Continuous break. The status bar also shows that we are now in section two.

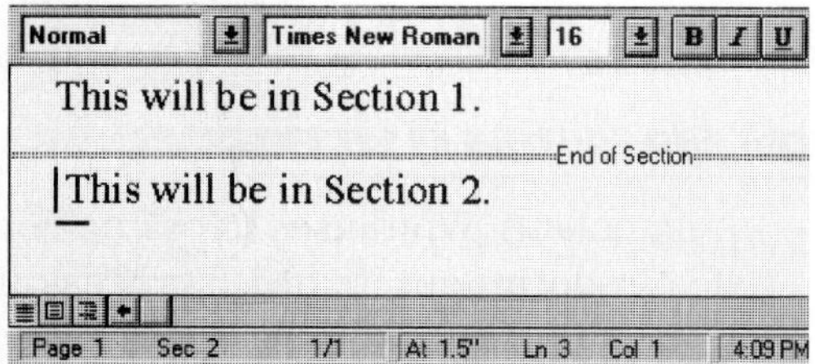

2. Now try inserting a section break that affects the page breaks. Make sure you are in Normal view, move the insertion point into the section break marker, and press Del to get rid of the existing section break. Then insert a new section break that starts a new section on the next page. Your page will still look like the one from the preceding example, but the status bar now reports that you are on page two when you move the insertion point onto the line that reads "Section 2."

3. If you repeat the preceding example but select Insert, Break, and insert an Odd Page section break instead of a Next Page section break, the line "Section Two" will still be in section two. However, you will now be on page three, the next odd page after page one.

USING PAGE SETUP IN SECTIONS

Whenever the insertion point is in a specific section, you can choose Page Setup from the File menu (Alt F, U) to modify the settings for that section. This lets you adjust the margins, page layout, paper size and orientation, and paper source settings for the text in the section containing the insertion point. (See Chapter 8 for more information on page setup.)

TIP *As long as you are not in the last section of your document, you can double-click on the End of Section separator and Word will pop up the Page Setup dialog box.*

Finally, remember that section breaks determine formatting of text above them, not of text below them. This means if you delete a section break, the text that used to be in the section will change to match the formatting of the text in the section following.

USING HEADERS AND FOOTERS IN SECTIONS

By default, Word uses the same headers and footers in every section of your document. In order to break the link between successive headers (or footers), follow these steps:

1. Insert a section break (most likely a Next Page, Odd Page, or Even Page break).
2. Move the insertion point into the new section.

3. Choose View, Headers and Footers and click on the Same as Previous button on the Header and Footer toolbar so that it is *off*. (It is on by default so that headers and footers are automatically the same as those in the preceding section.)

Once you turn off the Same as Previous button in order to break the link between the previous header or footer and the new header or footer, you can enter new header or footer text for the current section using the normal procedure for creating headers and footers, which was discussed in Chapter 8. This new header or footer stays in effect for all remaining sections in your document unless you repeat the previous procedure to break the link again in one of the following sections.

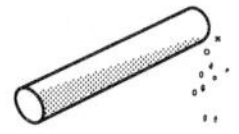

NOTE *Headers and footers have separate links. This means that breaking the Same as Previous link for a header does not break it for the footer in the same section.*

PAGE NUMBERING IN SECTIONS

To change the type of page numbering you are using (for example, to change from Roman numerals to Arabic) insert a section break using either the Next Page, Odd Page, or Even Page option.

Now there are two possibilities. Let's first suppose you set page numbering using Insert, Page Number from the Insert menu. In this case, follow these steps to change the page numbering:

1. Move the insertion point onto the page where you want to start the new page numbering format.
2. Choose Insert, Page Numbers to display the Page Numbers dialog box.

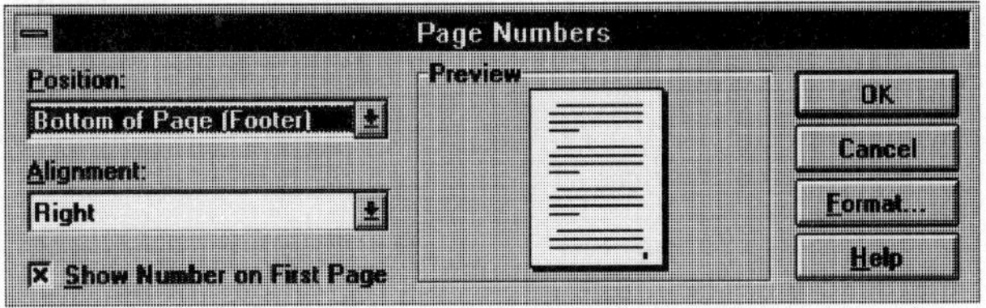

3. Click on the Format button to pop up the Page Number Format dialog box and pull down the list for Number Format on that dialog box shown here:

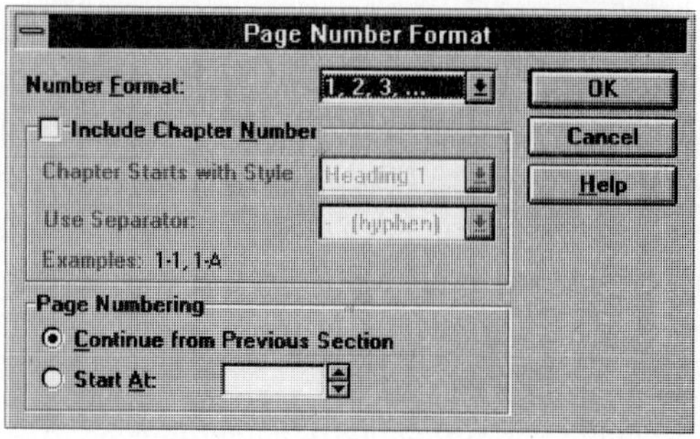

4. Now reset the number style or the numbering sequence in the Number Format list box to the one you want and then click on OK to leave the Number Format dialog box and then on OK again to leave the Page Numbers dialog box.

If the page number was inserted as a field (see Chapter 8 for more details on this) using the Header and Footer toolbar, you first have to break the link between the headers or footers of the previous section by turning the Same as Previous button off. (This requires opening the Header and Footer area—see the preceding section.) Once you have broken the link, keep the header or footer area open and follow these steps:

1. Highlight the page number you want to change in the header or footer.
2. Choose Insert, Page Numbers to display the Page Numbers dialog box.
3. Click on the Format button to pop up the Page Number Format dialog box.
4. Now reset the number style or the numbering sequence to the one you want and click on OK to set the format and OK again to leave the Page Numbers dialog box.

EXAMPLE

1. This example demonstrates how to number the first page with a Roman numeral, and then start over on the second page with Arabic numerals starting at the number one.
   a. Create a new document that contains the following text:

      Page One
      Page Two
      Page Three

      (Add New Page section breaks after each line.)
   b. Use Ctrl+Home to move to the top of the document. Now choose Insert, Page Number and click on the Format button. Select lowercase Roman numerals from the Number Format drop-down list box. (Notice that the page number on the status bar becomes a lowercase Roman numeral one.)
   c. Place the insertion point in front of the second line (you will be in the second section now), choose Insert, Page Number, and click on the Format button. Select Arabic numerals from the Number Format drop-down list box and set Start At to one.
   d. Place the insertion point at the end of the second line, as shown here:

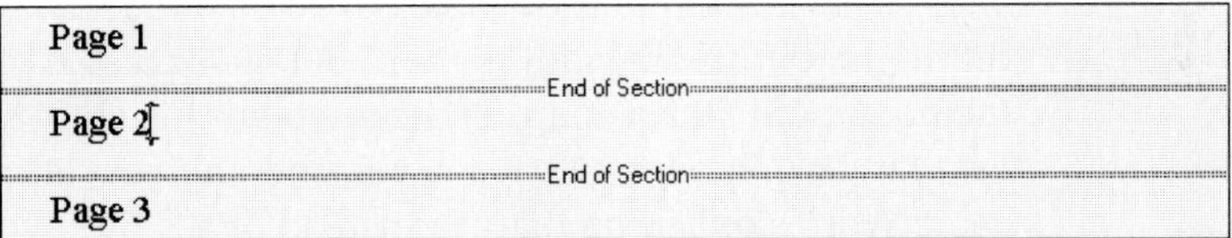

Notice the page number on the status bar is an Arabic numeral and that it has been reset to one. Finally, move the insertion point to the end of the document and notice on the status bar that we are on page two of section three and on page three of three total pages (3/3).

e. Move the insertion point from line to line and watch the status bar indications for page, section, and page number.

EXERCISES

1. Create a new document.
2. Enter text on two lines.
3. Insert a section break above the second line by selecting Insert, Break, Odd Page.
4. Move the insertion point between the two lines and watch the page number readout on the status bar.

11.4 OUTLINING

Outlining originally was simply a way of organizing your thoughts by jotting down main points/topics to be covered. Ideally, you would refine the outline by adding more details until the actual job of writing the document was a snap. You can do all this with Word's multilevel list feature (Chapter 10). However, the one very important benefit to using Word's outlining feature instead of a multilevel list is that you can "collapse" the outline to get an overview of the text and then "expand" it again to see the text. Word's outlining feature makes it easy to create full-length, fully fleshed out documents because you can move back and forth between the outline of the document and the text with the click of a button. In other words, Word's Outline view just gives you another way of *seeing* your document—one that lets you switch between seeing the forest, clumps of trees—or even individual trees—as needed.

Let's illustrate what happens by starting the process of making an outline for this book. First, start up a new document and choose Outline from the View menu (Alt V, O). Now enter this piece of the original *Teach Yourself Word for Windows* outline, hitting Enter after each line.

Introduction
Part I: Essential Features
Part II: Mastering Word
Part III: Advanced Features

These are the items at the highest level in the outline. One level below this will be the chapters, on the next level are the numbered sections within the chapters, and so on.

If you enter this text in Outline view, your screen will look something like Figure 11-4. Notice that there is a minus sign next to each item. This means that there is no text or lower levels below this line. (As you will soon see you can also have a plus sign next to a level. A plus sign means that there is another level of outline or text below the item.)

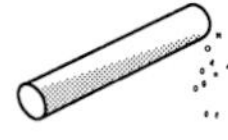

NOTE *The common terminology for the levels in an outline are* heading levels *or* level heads. *There is also a common shorthand for discussing outlines: people speak of items on the first level as being* 1-level heads *(or just* 1-heads*), those on the next level as being 2-level heads (or just 2-heads), and so on.*

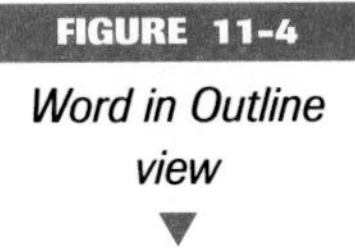

FIGURE 11-4

Word in Outline view

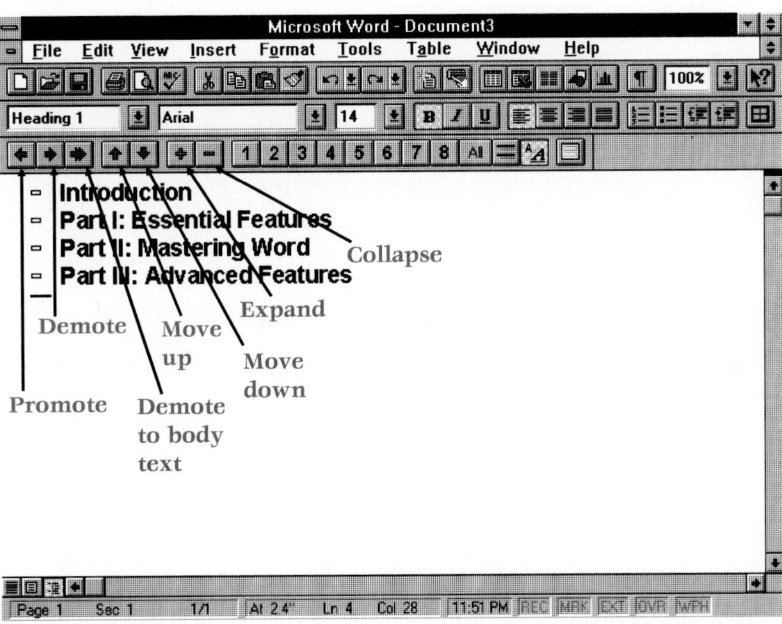

ADDING HEADING LEVELS TO YOUR OUTLINE

As you saw in Figure 11-4, when you have switched Word to Outline view, Word displays an Outline toolbar. You can use the buttons on this toolbar or keyboard shortcuts to change the level of items in your outline. (The jargon is that you *promote* when you raise the heading level and *demote* when you lower the heading level.)

It is a little easier to see how promotion and demotion of heading levels work if you enter all the text for the outline first. Edit the previous document so that it has the following text in it.

Introduction
Conventions
Part I: Essential Features
Chapter 1: Getting Started
1.1 What is Word 6.0 for Windows?
Chapter 2: First Steps with Text
2.1 Entering Text
Part II: Mastering Word
Chapter 5: Characters
Chapter 6: Using Word to Help Your Writing
Part III: Advanced Features

For example, we need to *demote* the chapter names down one level. To demote a paragraph in a document when in Outline view:

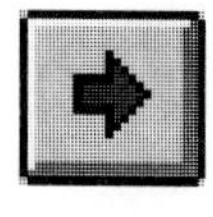

1. Make sure the insertion point is inside the paragraph.
2. Click on the Demote button or press Shift+Alt+→.

You can repeat this process to demote an item down eight levels.

If you make a mistake (or just need to change the level of an item) you can also *promote* items. To promote an item:

1. Make sure the insertion point is inside the paragraph.
2. Click on the Promote button or press Shift+Alt+←.

Figure 11-5 is a picture of what the completed outline will look like. Notice the plus signs that indicate that many of the items have levels below them. (Part 3 still has no items below it in this version of the outline.)

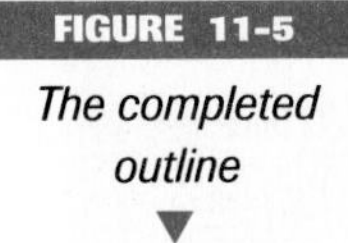

FIGURE 11-5

The completed outline

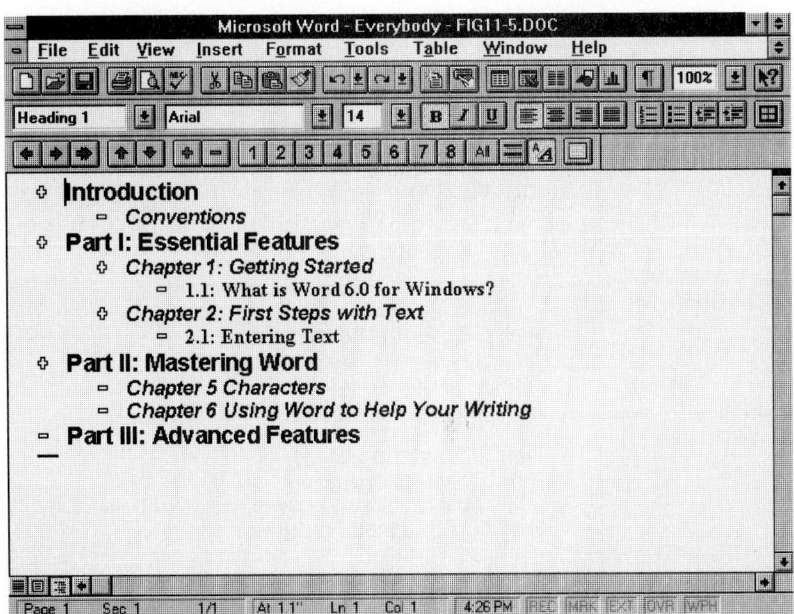

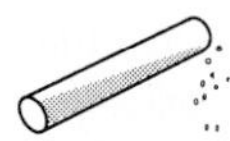

NOTE *We will be using this example extensively in what follows; you might want to save it as BOOKOUT1.DOC for future reference.*

Text that isn't at any of the heading levels in your outline is usually called *body text*. To enter body text into an outline:

1. Move the insertion point to the end of the item below which you want to enter text and press Enter.

2. Enter the text you want to be body text. Then click on the Demote to Body Text button (or press Alt+Shift+5 on the *numeric* keypad) to change the text you enter to body text.

(You can convert any heading level item to body text by clicking on this button.)

You can have body text below any level of an outline. For example, as shown in Figure 11-6, you might want to have body text below the Introduction to this book, although there is still an item one level below the Introduction for the Conventions used. Notice as well that there is a little square next to the body text—this is how Word indicates that text is body text.

FIGURE 11-6

An outline with body text

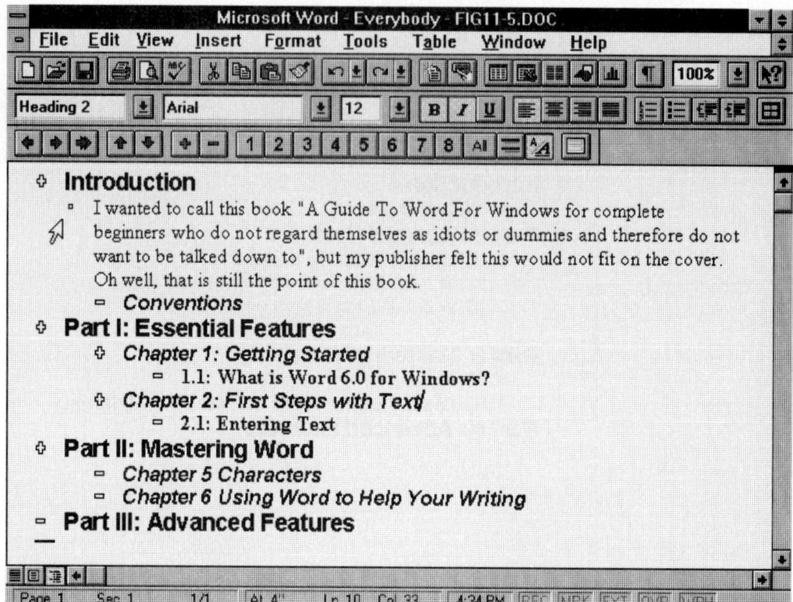

TIP *To make existing documents work right in Outline view, you only need to use the right styles (Chapter 7) for the various parts. In Outline view, Word automatically places paragraphs formatted with the Heading 1 style at the highest level of an outline, those paragraphs formatted with a Heading 2 style as the next level, and so on. Once the heading styles are attached to the right pieces of text in your document, you will have an instant outline when you click on the Outline View button.*

COLLAPSING AND EXPANDING AN OUTLINE

When you want to see items only at a certain level of an outline or higher, the jargon says you are *collapsing* the outline. When you want to see items at a lower level, you are *expanding* an outline. Outlines in Word get their power from how easy it is to collapse or expand them. Clicking on one of the buttons numbered 1 through 8 on the Outline toolbar shows all the levels at or above that number. For example, if you click on the button marked 2, you will see only the 1-level heads and the 2-level heads (items at the highest and second highest levels). Whenever any text (not only body text) is hidden because you collapsed a level, Word displays a dotted line under the heading level.

(There are also keyboard shortcuts for all these number buttons: Alt + Shift + the appropriate number on the *numeric* keypad.)

Clicking on the All button (Alt + Shift + A or just * on the numeric keypad) shows all the levels in the outline including any body text. Each time you click on the Plus button to the left of the level head (or press Alt + Shift + the plus sign on the numeric keypad), Word expands the outline by one level. If you double-click on the Plus button, Word shows all text under a heading. Clicks on the Minus button (Alt + Shift + the minus sign on the numeric keypad) do the reverse.

TIP *Whenever you see body text in Outline view you can have Word switch between displaying only the first line of each paragraph or all the body text by toggling the Show First Line button* (Alt+Shift+L).

This feature allows you to get a quick sense of the substance of each paragraph without running the risk of drowning in a sea of information.

EXAMPLES

1. Working with the outline for the book (BOOKOUT1.DOC) given earlier, click on the 1 button to see only the Introduction head and the Part heads.
2. Move the insertion point to after the Introduction, hit Enter and type the following text:

   I wanted to call this book *A Guide to Word for Windows for Complete Beginners Who Do Not Regard Themselves as Idiots or Dummies and Therefore Do Not Want to Be Talked Down to*, but my publisher felt this would not fit on the cover. Oh well, that is still the point of this book.

   Now click on the Demote to Body Text button
3. In the final version of this book, Chapters 5 and 6 were interchanged. You can do this by moving the insertion point to the line for Chapter 5 and then clicking on the Move Down button on the Outline toolbar.

WORKING WITH YOUR DOCUMENT WHILE IN OUTLINE VIEW

How Word will work with parts of your document while in Outline view depends on how much you have expanded or collapsed your outline. For example, Word features, like Find and Replace, only work on the outline levels that are currently visible. That is, using the book outline as an example, if you search for the word "Chapter," you will not find anything if all you have currently displayed are the 1-level heads.

Even more is true: *if a heading is collapsed, all items below it (including body text) move when you move the heading.* This gives you an incredibly quick way to rearrange your document.

TIP *You don't even have to collapse the item if you drag the plus sign that marks the item as containing lower-level items.*

For example, suppose you want to move all the items at or below a given item. Do the following:

1. Move the Outline cursor over the plus sign that marks the level of the item (and that indicates it has items below it).
2. Drag the plus item to its new location within the outline—Word moves *everything* below the item.

(Notice how Word automatically selects everything below the item.)

Finally, to print all or part of your outline:

1. Make sure only the levels you want printed are visible.
2. Print the document.

EXAMPLE

1. Select the 1 button on the Outline toolbar.
2. Using the Outline cursor, drag the Part I paragraph of the book outline to after the Part II paragraph.
3. Now select the All button to reveal all levels and to see that all the outline levels and text under Part I were moved.
4. Undo your moves using Word's Undo feature so that the book outline is back in its previous form.

EXERCISES

1. Start up a new document in Outline view and then enter the following lines into the new document:

   Title Page
   Table of Contents
   Introduction
   Part One
   Part Two
   Part Three
   Index

2. Move the insertion point to after the word "Introduction", hit Enter and type:

   This is where I am supposed to explain what I am going to say.

3. Demote this phrase to body text.
4. Type **Sub Part One** and **Sub Part Two** under Part One, and demote them to Heading 2 paragraphs.
5. Adjust the Outline view to show only Heading 1 paragraphs.
6. Show Heading 1 and 2 paragraphs.
7. Show all levels of headings and text. Print the outline.
8. Close and save the document as TESTOUT.DOC.

mastery skills check

1. Open two documents at the same time. [11.1]
2. Use Window, Arrange All to see both documents at the same time. [11.2]
3. Close the window into Part I. [11.2]
4. Maximize the remaining document window. [11.2]

5. Switch to Normal view and move the insertion point between the sections of the document and watch the status bar section number readout. [11.3]
6. Close all the open documents. [11.2]
7. Start a new document in Outline view. [11.4]
8. Enter an outline for the various parts of this chapter and demote or promote items as needed to reflect the organization of this chapter. [11.4]

cumulative skills check

1. Open BOOKOUT1.DOC. [2.4]
2. Add section breaks between all chapters in this outline. [11.3]
3. Switch to Outline view and move Chapter 5 to appear after Chapter 6. Edit the chapter numbers. [11.4]
4. Add some text under each Part. [11.4]
5. Insert page numbers using Roman numerals starting at the beginning of the Introduction. [8.3, 11.3]
6. Insert section breaks so that Parts I, II, and III all start on odd pages. [11.3]
7. Reformat the page numbers so that the beginning of Part I starts on page one and uses Arabic numerals. [8.3, 11.3]
8. Add different headers for Parts I, II, and III that say (for example): **Part 1 of Teach Yourself Word for Windows**. [8.3, 11.3]
9. Select File, Print Preview to preview the resulting document. [9.1]
10. Save the document as BOOKOUT2.DOC. [2.3]

12

Document Management

chapter objectives

After completing this chapter, you will know how to

12.1 Maintain summary information on your documents

12.2 Use annotations to add notes to your work

12.3 Use revision marks to keep track of changes

12.4 Use the Find File feature in Word to manage your documents

12.5 Use Find File's ability to search through the documents you have stored

THIS chapter teaches you about Word's document management features. If you (or a group of people) are ever repeatedly revising the same document, then the first part of this chapter will help you avoid the inevitable problem of confusing an earlier version of a document with a later one. The last half of this chapter shows you how to use Word's powerful built-in file-handling facilities.

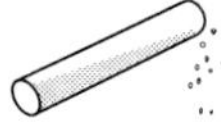

NOTE *If you are unfamiliar with some of the terminology used in the last half of this chapter (like "directory" or "subdirectory") refer to Appendix A. If you need more information than contained there, look at any book on DOS.*

In particular, the first section shows you how Word automatically maintains *summary* information about your documents. As the term suggests summary information gives you an overview of a document. Summary information can include a title for the document, information about the subject, the author, keywords, and even some general comments; you'll see how to modify this information to your best advantage. Then it's on to *annotations,* which are (generally) nonprinting comments that you can write to yourself or others. Finally, you'll see how to use *revision marks*. These features are ideal when revising more complex documents.

Word's Find File feature, covered in the last half of the chapter, is where to turn once your hard disk fills with hundreds of documents and you can no longer remember which document is which. It can also be a handy replacement for some of the features of the File Manager, which is covered in Appendix A. For example, you can rename, copy, or delete files without ever leaving Word.

review
skills check

1. Create a new document. [1.6]
2. Enter the following text: [2.1]

In all matters, before beginning, a diligent preparation should be made.

– Cicero, De Officiis

3. Reformat the text using a different font. [6.2]
4. Select File, Print Preview to preview the document. [2.5]
5. Save the file as CICERO.DOC. [2.3]

12.1 SUMMARY INFORMATION

When you save a document, Word keeps track of a lot more information than just the name you gave the file. To see the summary information Word is maintaining about your document, open the File menu and choose Summary Info. You'll see a dialog box that looks like this:

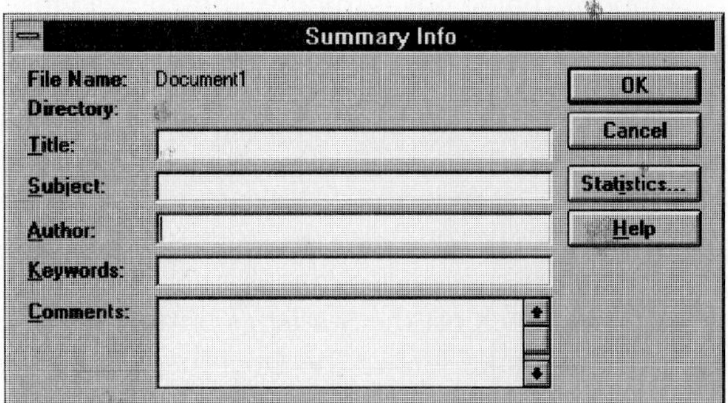

As you can see, besides the file name and directory, the Summary Info dialog box also has text boxes where you can add a title, subject, author, keywords, and comments about the document. In the Keywords text box, you might add words or phrases that you could use later to track down this document. Use the Comments box to "free associate" about the document. Information in this text box can help you if you are narrowing in on the search for a particular document and need a bit more information about it.

There are two reasons why you may want to put information in the Summary Info dialog box. The first is that you and anyone else who will be working with the document in the future might appreciate having a short overview of what's in the document. The second is that Word can use this information to quickly find a specific file. (Both these activities are a large part of what is usually called *document management*.) As you'll see in the sections at the end of this chapter, by filling in information in the Summary Info dialog box, you are building a searchable *database* about your documents. (A database is simply a collection of information that is stored in a way that makes it easy to search or work with.)

When you start a document and bring up the Summary Info dialog box, you will see that Word automatically inserts both a prospective author and a title. The title consisting of the first few words of the document. Word fills in the Author box using the information currently stored in the User Info tab in the Options dialog box (Alt T, O) (see Chapter 9, Section 9.3). Of course, you can change both these text boxes if the information Word automatically inserts doesn't match what you want.

To gain the most benefit from the Summary Info dialog box, you need to make sure this information is up to date. One way to do this is to turn on the Prompt for Summary Info check box on the Save tab of the Options dialog box, which is shown in Figure 12-1. (Choose Tools, Options and click on the Save tab to get to this tab.) When the Prompt for Summary Info check box is selected, Word displays the Summary Info dialog box for you to fill out whenever it saves a file for the first time.

DOCUMENT STATISTICS

If you click on the Statistics button in the Summary Info dialog box, Word will take you to the Document Statistics dialog box shown in Figure 12-2. As you can see in this figure, this dialog box shows:

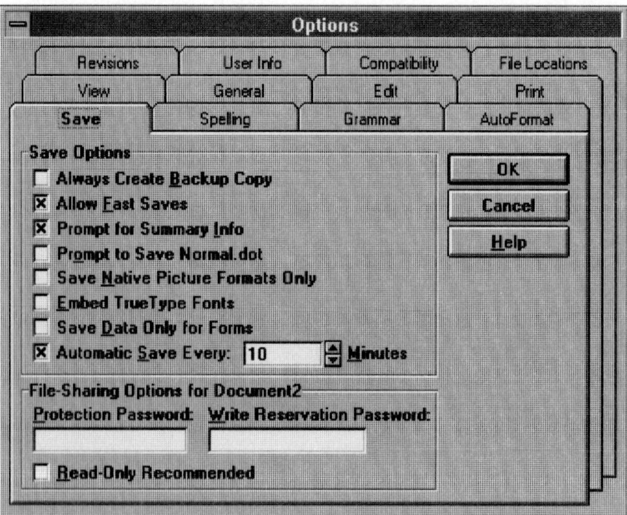

FIGURE 12-1

The Save tab on the Options dialog box

FIGURE 12-2

The Document Statistics dialog box

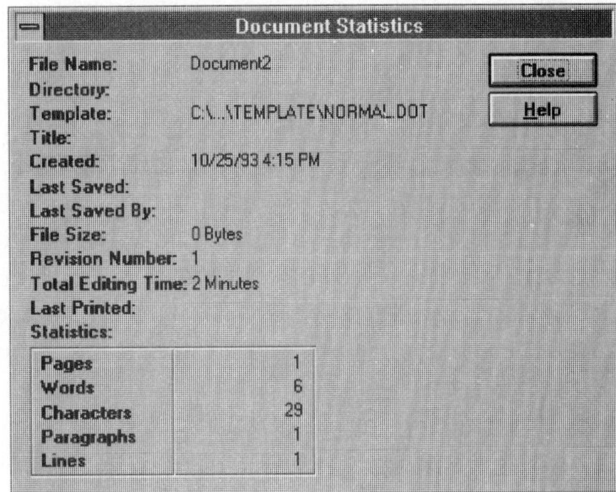

- Which template you based the document on.
- Timestamps indicating when you first created the document and when it was last saved.
- Number of characters, words, lines, paragraphs, and pages.
- The file's size.

Word also includes some miscellaneous information in the Document Statistics dialog box such as the time spent in editing, which revision number and so on.

EXERCISES

1. Select Tools, Options, choose the Save tab, and make sure the Prompt for Summary Info check box is selected.
2. Create a new document and enter a few lines of text. Save the file and fill in the Summary Info dialog box that appears. Type **Document Management** in the Subject field and include the word **Summary** in the Keywords field.
3. Open CICERO.DOC. Choose Summary Info from the File menu (Alt F, I). Click on the Statistics button in the Summary Info dialog box and check how long you worked on your document. Edit the document's Title and enter some data in the Subject, Keywords, and Comments fields. Enter the word **Summary** in the Keywords field.
4. Save the document.

12.2 ANNOTATIONS

Word's annotation feature allows you to leave notes to yourself or others inside your document. Annotations do not change the text of the document in any way—think of them as Word's equivalent of yellow post-it notes. You might use annotations in a document in order to leave comments for other readers of the document—or another reader can leave comments for you. Annotations also make it much easier to keep track of any changes suggested (or made). Once you annotate a document, you can keep the annotations from being displayed or printed.

You can add annotations from either Normal view or Page Layout view. To add an annotation, move the insertion point to where you want the annotation to appear. Then:

1. Choose Annotation from the Insert menu (Alt I, A). The keyboard shortcut is Alt+Ctrl+A.

As soon as you ask Word to insert an annotation, Word splits the screen and the annotation pane appears on the bottom half of the screen, as shown here:

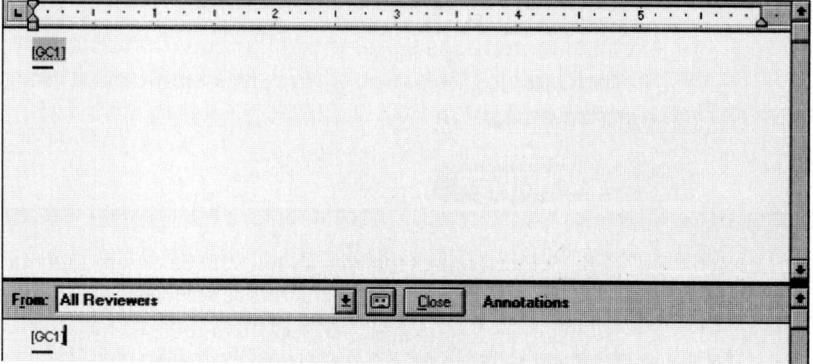

2. Now enter the annotation text and then click on the Close button in the annotation pane when you're done.

   Notice that at the insertion point in the document, Word:

- Inserts the author's initials followed by a number. (This shows up in the annotation pane as well.)
- Brackets it and then underlines it with dots.

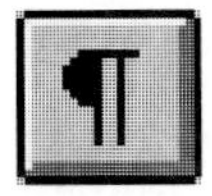

The dotted underline is Word's standard way of saying that both the brackets and the initials inside of them are formatted as *hidden text*. (This is text, like paragraph marks, that may or may not be displayed depending on whether you have set the Show/Hide button to be on or off.) Notice also that Word labels it GC1. The initials plus the number are usually called an *annotation reference mark,* or just an *annotation mark* for short. Word keeps track of the number of the annotations you make and automatically corrects the numbering whenever you insert a new annotation (or delete an old annotation as described below).

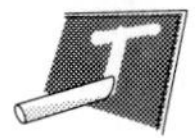

TIP *Word retrieves the initials from the User Info tab on the Options dialog box. To modify what Word is currently using, choose Tools, Options and pick the User Info tab on this dialog box. Now you can change the information contained in both the Name and Initial text boxes.*

By repeatedly changing the name and initials on the User Info Tab more than one person can annotate a document using the same copy of Word.

WORKING WITH AN ANNOTATED DOCUMENT

You can move quickly either to an annotation mark or its associated annotated text. If you double-click on an annotation mark, Word opens the annotation pane and moves the insertion point to the appropriate annotation text.

On the other hand, once you open the annotation pane (Alt V, A), you can quickly see the text where annotations were made. The idea is that as you move the insertion point through the annotations contained in the annotation pane, Word shows you the part of the document that contains the annotation mark. Since there are presumably fewer annotations then there are pages in your document, this can be much faster than scrolling through the document searching for annotation marks. Also note that since Word is showing you the part of the document with the annotation, you only have to click inside the document showing on the top of your screen to edit around the annotation mark.

If you have just opened your document and you want to quickly monitor whatever annotations have been made to the document, follow these steps:

1. Open the annotation window by choosing Annotations from the View menu (Alt V, A).
2. Now double-click any mark in the annotation pane to quickly jump to the text that was annotated.

TIP *When you look at an annotated document, it is easier to understand an annotation if you can easily distinguish the text it is supposed to apply to. Word can highlight the annotated text in a light shading while you are at the associated annotation mark in the annotation pane. To do this:*

1. Select the entire text you wish to annotate *before* you put the annotation mark there.
2. Place the annotation mark immediately after the selected text by making sure the insertion point is there and choosing Insert, Annotation or pressing Alt+Ctrl+A.

DELETING AND COPYING ANNOTATIONS

You can use Word's standard cut and paste features to delete, copy, or move annotations. All these tasks require that you first select the *mark* of the annotation you wish to work with. The easiest way to do this is to double-click the mark, which opens the annotation window and moves you to the relevant annotation. (Another possibility is to place the insertion point just in front of the mark and use Shift+← to select it.)

Once you have selected the mark, you can cut or copy it to the Clipboard (Ctrl+X, Ctrl+C) or use Del or Backspace to remove it from the document. If you cut or copied the mark, you can paste it into a new location (Ctrl+V). If you used Del or Backspace, you can use the undo feature (Ctrl+Z) to bring the annotation back to the same location.

Note that when you delete an annotation, or add one between two others, the marks are automatically renumbered to reflect their new position in the document. For this reason, you should not refer to particular annotations by their current numbering.

PRINTING ANNOTATIONS

You can print only the document's annotations by choosing Print from the File menu and then selecting Annotations from the Print What drop-down list box in the Print dialog box. When you ask Word to print annotations, it scans your document and then adds the appropriate page number before the annotation text.

If you want to print a document as well as its annotations (as opposed to the annotations alone) select File, Print and then click on the Options button in the Print dialog box. Then make sure the Annotations check box is checked in the Print options tab that Word pops up. When you have this box checked, Word first prints your text *with* the annotations marks, and then prints the *text* of the annotations on separate pages.

ADVANCED USES OF ANNOTATIONS

If you circulate a document among many people, then they might each add their own annotations—and Word keeps track of the initials they are using. You can see different initials either because they are annotating the document with *their* copy of Word or because they went in and changed the information on the User Info tab to reflect their initials. (Remember this is done by choosing Options on the Tools menu and then changing the initials text box in the User Info tab. One would hope they would be polite enough to change them back if they did this. If people are using your machine frequently you might check the state of the User Info tab periodically to see if it reflects what you want!)

Notice the drop-down list box labeled From on the title bar of the annotation pane. By selecting this list box, you can see annotations made by all reviewers or you can select only particular reviewers. If you select a particular reviewer, Word will hide all the other reviewers' annotations, in both the annotation pane and in the main document.

Let's end with a feature that will surely become more important as time goes by. At the top of the annotation pane is a button that looks like a tape cassette. If your PC has sound capabilities, then Word will enable this button. As you may have guessed, this feature allows you to attach a voice annotation to your document! To do so, begin by adding a regular annotation, and then click on the cassette button to insert a voice annotation. To play back the annotation, double-click on the microphone icon in the annotation text. (Some versions of Windows may display a cassette icon instead of a microphone.)

EXERCISES

1. Open CICERO.DOC.
2. Add the following annotation after "De Officiis":

   Research - What was the intent of this document?

3. Highlight "Cicero" and add the following annotation:

   Find out Cicero's full name, when he lived, and any other items of interest.

4. Close CICERO.DOC.

12.3 REVISION MARKS

Revision marks provide a way of keeping track of changes that are made to a document. Usually deleted text is marked by a strike through and Word changes its color as well. Additions are made in another color and underlined. Both deletions and additions are marked with revision lines in the margins.

To begin recording your revisions, select Revisions from the Tools menu (Alt T, V). (You can also double-click on the MRK indicator on the status bar at the bottom of the screen; it will turn dark instead of being grayed.) Word pops up the Revisions dialog box, as shown here:

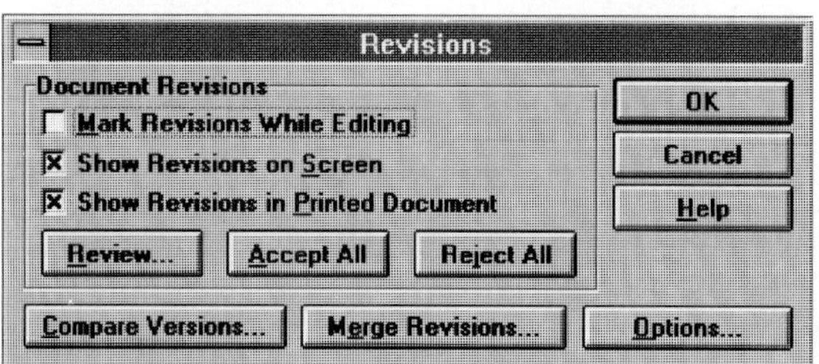

Once you select the check box labeled Mark Revisions While Editing, Word begins to record your changes to the document.

EXAMPLES

1. Open a new document. Enter the following sentences, hitting Enter after each period:

   This is an original line of text that has not been deleted or added to.
   This line has been deleted.
   This line used to say one thing.
   This is an original line of text that has not been deleted or added to.

2. Double-click on the MRK indicator and select the Mark Revisions While Editing check box.
3. Delete the second line.
4. Replace the third sentence with "Now it says another."

   Your screen will show the following:

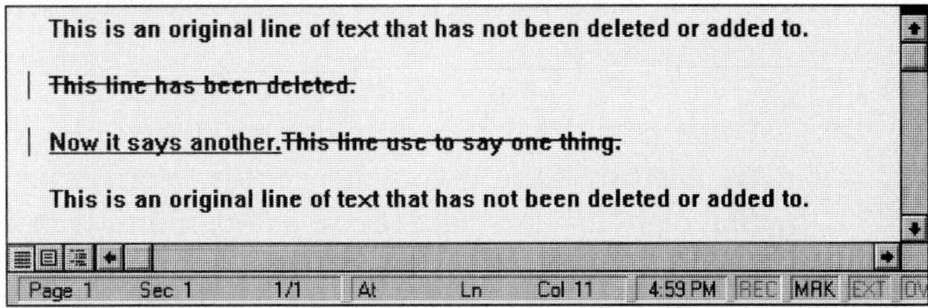

We can't show colors here, but you can see that the deleted text is struck through and the additions are underlined.

THE REVISIONS OPTION TAB

If you click on the Options button in the Revisions dialog box, Word displays the Revisions tab of the Options dialog box shown in Figure 12-3. This tab lets you control how Windows displays or prints inserted and deleted text and where the revision marks appear.

Here are short descriptions of the other options in this dialog box:

Inserted Text Options These two drop-down list boxes control how you want to display any text that someone adds to the document once revision tracking is turned on. The Mark drop-down list box gives you a choice from among bold, italic, underline, or double underline (underline is the default). The Color box gives you a choice of color.

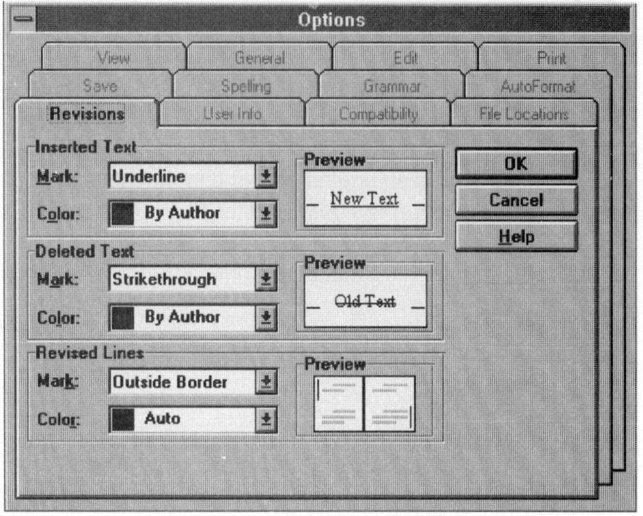

FIGURE 12-3

The Revisions tab on the Options dialog box

Potentially the most useful choice in the Color drop-down box is the **By Author** item. If you choose this, Word assigns unique colors to the first eight authors who revise a document. If more than eight authors revise the document, Word starts using the colors over again.

Deleted Text Options These two drop-down list boxes control how you want to display any text that someone removes from the document. The drop-down list boxes work similarly to those for inserting text except that you have only a choice between strikethrough text and hidden text. (Strikethrough is the default.)

Revised Lines Options These drop-down list boxes control how you want Word to mark the lines that contain any revised text. The Color box lets you pick the color of the revision line. The Mark drop-down list box controls where the revision lines appear in Page Layout view or when you print the document. (In Normal view, revision lines always show up in the left margin.)

The None choice prevents the lines from appearing. The Left Border choices tells Word to mark the lines containing revised text with a revision line in the left margin. The Right Border option tells Word to marks the lines containing revised text with a revision line in the right margin. The Outside Border option tells Word to mark the lines containing revised text with a line in the left margin of even-numbered pages and in the right margin of odd-numbered pages. (To use this option, you have to select the Different Odd And Even check box in the Headers and Footers area on the Layout tab in the Page Setup dialog box on the File menu. If this option is not selected, Word displays the revision lines in the left margin.)

REVIEWING REVISIONS

The whole point of turning revision marks on is so that you can look them over and see if you agree with the suggested changes or not. If you do, you will want Word to make the changes; if not, you will want Word to restore the text to its original form. Word lets you reject all the revisions, accept them all, or review them one by one and accept or reject each modification.

Once you tell Word to mark revisions while editing, the next time you choose Revisions from the Tools menu, Word will enable the Reject All, Accept All, and Review buttons on the Revisions dialog box. Reject All and Accept All are self-explanatory.

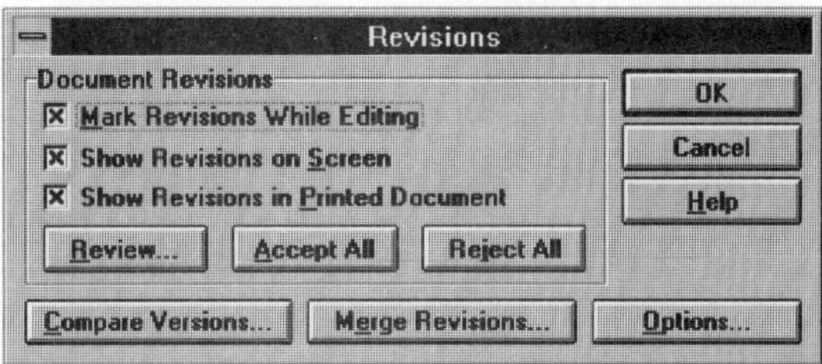

If you click on the Review button Word brings up the Review Revisions dialog box, an example of which is shown here:

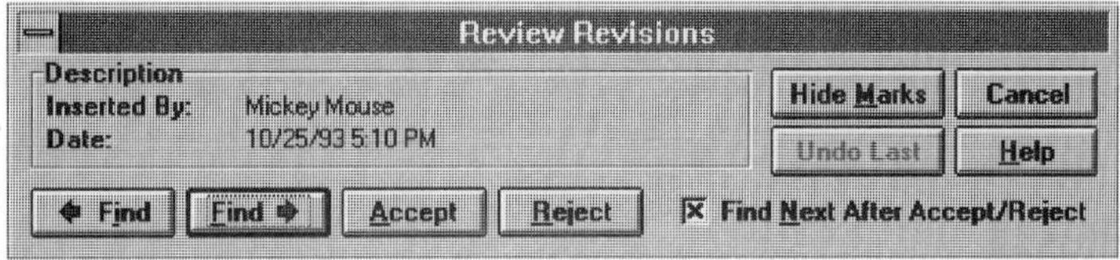

Notice that Word displays who made the revision in question and when it was made. (If a document has had multiple reviewers and you selected By Author in the Revisions options tab, then their changes show on the screen in different colors.)

The Review Revisions dialog box allows you to accept or reject each modification. Click the Accept button to make the change and click on the Reject button to cancel it. Click on one of the two Find buttons to move forward or backward through the various revisions in the document.

COMPARING VERSIONS OF THE SAME DOCUMENT

The Revisions dialog box (Alt T, V) has two other buttons that give you a way of working with two versions of the same document. (Make sure they have different filenames, are on different disks, or are in different directories on your hard disk.)

Let's suppose you have one version of the document on the screen and want to compare it to another version. If you click on the Compare Versions button in the Revisions dialog box, Word displays a dialog box for opening a file. Use this Compare Versions file box to choose the other version of the document to which you want Word to compare the version you currently have on the screen. Word regards the second document—the one you just opened—as the original one and the one you were editing earlier as the revised one. Word compares the document you were editing with the document you just opened and adds revision marks to the document you were editing based on the second document. (As you saw earlier, the defaults are underlined for new text, strikethrough for deleted text.) Now choose the Review button in the Revisions dialog box to see the differences between the documents using the techniques you saw in the last section.

If you click on the Merge Revisions button, Word pops up a dialog box that asks you for the name of the original document.

CAUTION *Word intends to merge any revisions from the document you have currently open into the document you are now opening.*

Once you choose the file and click on OK, Word will open the new document and *change it* based on the contents of the first document you were editing. (At this point you actually have two open documents, as a click glance at the Window menu (Alt W) would show.) Any changes Word made show up using the usual revision marks (underlined for new text, strikethrough for deleted text).

TIP *If you choose to merge revisions and are unsatisfied, click on the Undo button (Ctrl+Z is the shortcut) to go back to the unmerged version.*

EXERCISES

1. Open CICERO.DOC.
2. Turn on revision marks and display them while editing.
3. Move the insertion point before Cicero and type **Marcus Tullius Cicero**.
4. Add this line under Cicero's name:

   106 B.C. - 43 B.C.

5. Then add this line:

   Marcus Tullius Cicero was also know as Tully.

6. Hide your revision marks and make any formatting changes that may be required.
7. Scan each revision and reject the line about Cicero also being known as Tully.
8. Save CICERO.DOC.

12.4 FIND FILE

Word's Find File feature allows you to see lists of documents that share common properties. What the documents could have in common might be as simple as where they are located. For example, you could ask for a list of all documents in your C:\WINWORD\DOC directory. However, you could also list only those documents in C:\WINWORD\DOC that *you* have written. You could even have it list all documents on your hard disk no matter where they are stored.

Once you asked Word to generate a list of files with some common property, you can work with all or some of the files on the list. For example, you can ask Word to:

- Copy the files
- Delete the files
- Print the files
- Preview their contents

And, of course, you can ask Word to open the files for editing.

STARTING FIND FILE AND SIMPLE SEARCHES

To use Word's Find File feature:

- Choose Find File from the File menu (Alt F, F). The first time you do this, you'll see a dialog box like the one shown in Figure 12-4.

This Search dialog box controls Find File's searching ability. We will have a lot more to say about using Find File's searching ability in Section 10.5, but let's just go over the basics that you need to get started now.

The idea is simple: You enter the file name and location in these boxes (case is irrelevant) or pull down the list to see the most common possibilities and then choose one of them. For example, the drop-down Location list box shows you the drives on your system. You can also enter a path directly here and Word will look at files only in that path. Similarly, the File Name drop-down list box gives you the

FIGURE 12-4

The Search dialog box

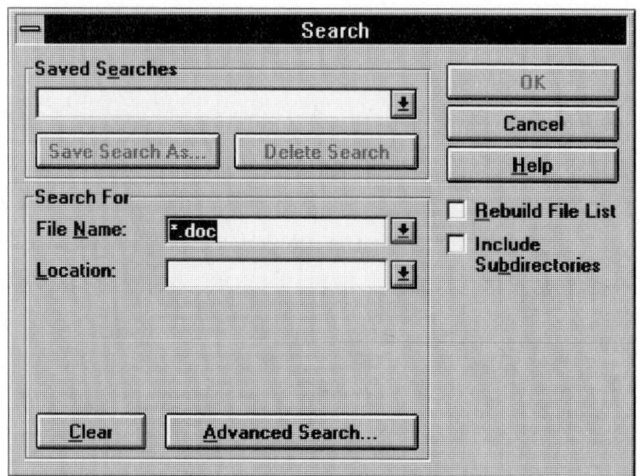

five most common choices for files that Word will look for. These five choices are:

- Word documents (files that end in DOC). Enter ***.DOC** in the File Name list box or pull down the list and choose the first item.
- Document Templates (files that end in DOT—see Chapter 7).
- Windows Bitmaps (files that end in BMP—see Chapter 13).
- Windows Metafiles (files that end in WMF—see Chapter 13).
- All files. Enter ***.*** in the File Name list box or pull down the list and choose the last item.

You can also enter any type of file using the pattern matching wildcards that you saw in Chapter 5. Recall these were a * to match anything or a **?** to match a single character. For example, CHAP?.DOC would find CHAP1.DOC but not CHAP11.DOC; CHAP*.DOC would find them both.

If the Include Subdirectories checkbox is on, Word will search all directories below the drive or path specified in the Locations box. For example, if you do not check this box and put C:\ in the location box and *.* in the File Name box, then all you will see is the files in the root directory—you would see nothing about most of the files on your hard disk.

The Rebuild File List check box should almost always be on. This tells Word to make sure the search is up to date whenever you click on OK.

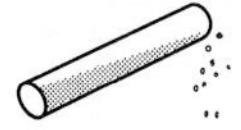

NOTE *To more easily follow the discussion in the rest of this section, you may want to make sure that your Search dialog box is filled in as follows:*

- The File Name drop-down list box in the Search dialog box shows ***.DOC**.
- The Location drop-down list box shows the directory that Word is stored on. (This should be simply **C:\WINWORD**.)
- The two check boxes on the right of the Search dialog box (Rebuild File List and Include Subdirectories) are both checked.

THE FIND FILE DIALOG BOX

Once you fill in the File name and Location boxes Word enables the OK button. If you have set up your Search dialog box as described above, then after you click on OK in the box, Word will let you know that it's building the file list. You will also see a little spinning disk icon in the upper-right corner of the screen as Find File scans your disk. Finally, you'll see something like Figure 12-5. (Your version of the Find file dialog box will look a little different than Figure 12-5 because the Listed files box on the left-hand side of your Find File dialog box reflects what you have on your own hard disk.)

The next two sections discuss the View drop-down list box and the Commands button on the Find File dialog box. The Search button brings up the same Search dialog box that you saw in the section above—you saw in Section 10.5 how to master the rest of its powers. However, before you can work with any of the features on the Find File dialog box, you need to always keep two points in mind:

- Directories show up on the left side of the Find File dialog box with either a plus sign or a minus sign next to them (similar to those in outlines as you saw in Chapter 11). If you click on the plus sign in front of the directory name, Word will expand what you see by bringing up all of the files and subdirectories below the directory. If there is a minus sign in front of the directory

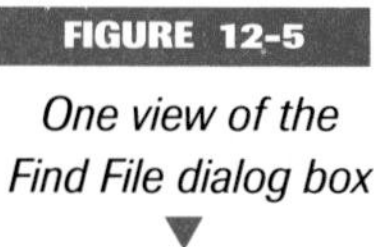

FIGURE 12-5

One view of the Find File dialog box

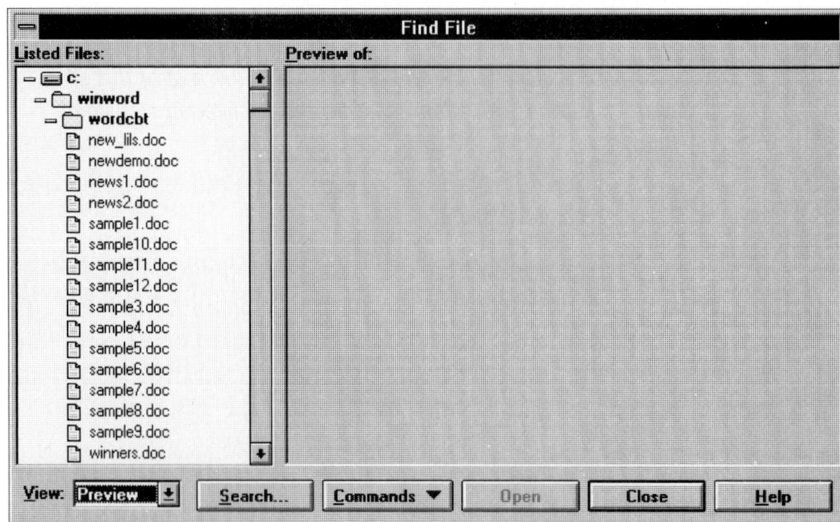

and you click on it, Word will collapse all the files and directories, showing you only the parent directory (with a plus sign next to it, of course).

- Files must be selected in order to see various information about the file or to work with the file. To do this, click on the file's name on the left side of the Find File dialog box (or move the highlight to it).

THE VIEW DROP-DOWN LIST BOX

The three choices in this drop-down list box control what you see in the big preview box on the right-hand side of the Find File dialog box.

Preview The Preview choice (the default) gives you a thumbnail view of the selected file—if Word can understand the contents of the file. If the preview convinces you that this is the file you are looking for, simply click on the Open button in the Find File dialog box. Word will then open the document for editing.

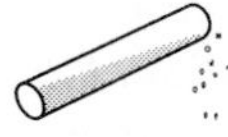

NOTE *Depending on the speed of your computer and the complexity of the document, previews may take a long time to generate.*

For example, Figure 12-6 shows a preview of SAMPLE1.DOC from the C:\WINWORD\WORDCBT directory.

Summary Info View If you have been maintaining summary information on your documents, select the Summary option from the View drop-down list box in the Find File dialog box in order to quickly learn more about a document. Figure 12-7 is an example of what you might see for the SAMPLE1.DOC file supplied with Word.

(As you can see in Figure 12-7, the people who worked on the document didn't fill in the Subject, Keywords, and Comments areas. However, you can see when Microsoft first created the document and when it was last saved.)

File Info View When you choose this option the Find File box changes its form to list items in columns. Each column contains different information about the files such as size, when it was created or last saved, and so on. What you see is determined by how you sort the file

FIGURE 12-6

The File Find dialog box in Preview mode

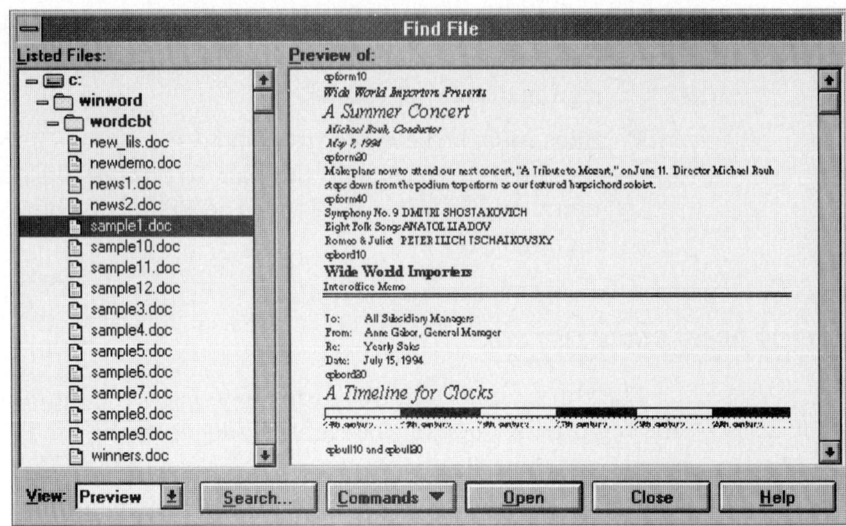

names (see the next section) but the far left column always contains the names of the files.

NOTE *When in this view you can adjust the width of the columns with your mouse. Simply move the mouse up to the dividers between the column names. When the mouse pointer changes to a double headed arrow, drag the divider left or right to change the column's width.*

FIGURE 12-7

The File Find dialog box in Summary mode

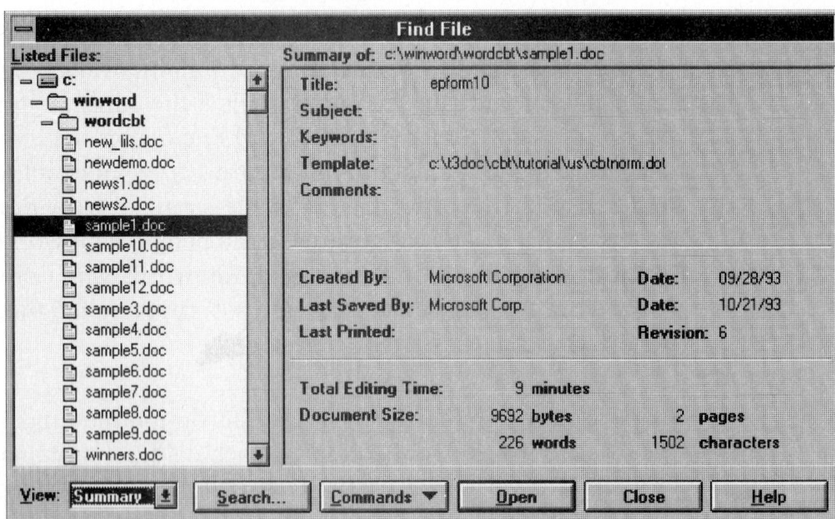

THE COMMANDS BUTTON ON THE FIND FILE DIALOG BOX

Most of the operations you can perform on files from the Find File dialog box are available via a click on the Commands button.

NOTE *These commands affect the files currently selected in the Files Listed box–it is possible to select more than one file at a time in the Files Listed box. This lets you apply the commands you just learned to more than one file at a time when you want to. See the next section for how to select more than one file at the same time.*

Here is what you see if you click on the Commands button.

Let's go over these important options one by one.

Open Read Only Choose this option and Word opens the selected file in *read-only mode,* meaning that you can read the document but cannot make any changes to it.

Print The Print option allows you to print the selected file without having to open it for editing. This selection brings up the standard Print dialog box (see Chapter 9).

Summary Choosing Summary brings up the same Summary Info dialog box that comes up when you issue the File, Summary Info command (Alt F, S).

Delete The Delete option lets you delete the selected file. (You can also press the Del key.) Word always pops up a message box asking you if you really want to delete the file.

Copy The Copy option allows you to copy the selected file to another directory. If you choose this option Word pops up the Copy dialog box, an example of which is shown here:

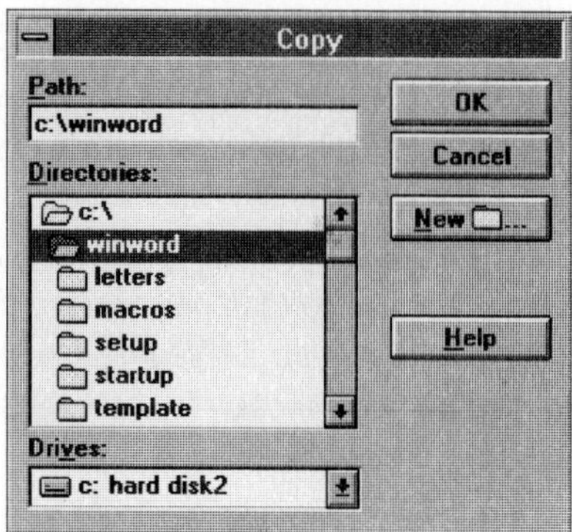

All you have to do now is click on the directory you want the file to be copied to. (When you click on a directory, Word puts the correct path in the Path text box in this dialog box. If you know the path you want to copy the file to, you could enter it in this text box yourself.) You can change to a different disk by pulling down the Drives drop-down list box in this dialog box and choosing the drive you want. If you want to create a new directory below an existing directory:

1. Select the existing directory below which you want to put the new directory.
2. Click on the New button.

A dialog box pops up asking you for the name of the new directory. Word creates the new directory and then copies your file into it when you click on OK in the Copy dialog box.

Sorting The Sorting option lets you determine the order Word displays the files on the left-hand side of the Find File dialog box. This also controls which information is shown when you choose File Info view. When you choose this option, Word pops up the dialog box shown here:

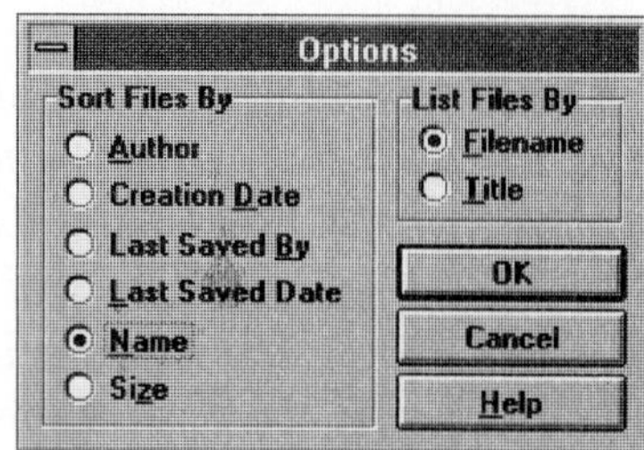

As you can see, you have six options as to how Word sorts (and therefore how it displays) the list of files in the left-hand side of the Find File dialog box. The following table describes what these options do:

Sort Option	Effect
Author	Word orders the files by the name of the author–from A to Z.
Creation Date	Word orders the files by the date the file was created–most recently created first.
Last Saved By	Also an alphabetical A-Z order by the name of the person who last saved the file.
Last Saved Date	Word orders the files by the date the file was last saved–most recently saved first.
Name	Also an alphabetical A-Z order by the name of the file or the title. (This is determined by the option buttons on the right-hand side of the Options dialog box. Most of the time you will pick the Filename button.)
Size	Orders from the smallest file to the largest.

SELECTING MULTIPLE FILES IN THE FIND FILE DIALOG BOX

As mentioned before you will need to select the file names in the Find File dialog box before you can ask Word to do anything to that file using the options available from the Commands button in the Find File dialog box. You can select a single file with the standard Word technique of clicking on the file's name in the Files Listed box or moving the highlight until you get to the name of the file. But suppose you want to copy a bunch of files at once? To take full advantage of the powerful options like copying or printing that are available by clicking on the Commands button in the Find File dialog box you need to know how to select more than one file at a time.

To select a group of files that are listed consecutively:

1. Highlight the first file.
2. Hold down the Shift key and then either click on the last file or press the ↓ until you reach the last file.

If you have a mouse, you can actually select multiple files that are not listed consecutively. To do this:

1. Click on the first file.
2. Hold down the Ctrl key and click on the next file name.
3. Continue step 2 until you have selected all the files you want.

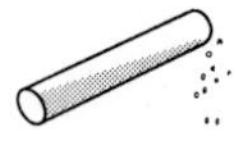

NOTE *This technique lets you select files in several different directories.*

EXAMPLES

1. From within the Find File dialog box, choose File Info from the View drop-down list box.
2. Choose the Commands button and then choose the Sorting option from the list of commands that appears.
3. In the Options dialog box, pick Creation Date under Sort Files By.

   Note that the last column in the Find File dialog box is now labeled Created and the files are listed from newest to oldest. Each sort order has a slightly different collection of columns. Try the others now and see what you get.

EXERCISES

1. Select File, Find File (Alt F, F).
2. Double-click on the directory containing Word's sample files (probably C:\WINWORD\WORDCBT) in the List Files box.
3. Use the View option in the Find File dialog box and experiment with the three view options: Preview, File Info, and Summary for the sample files that came with Word.
4. In File Info view adjust the width of the Title column so you can see more of the title.
5. Select two of the sample files that are listed together and click on the Open button.
6. Select two of the sample files that are not listed together and click on the Open button.
7. Close the four files you just opened.

12.5 MASTERING FIND FILE'S SEARCH CAPABILITIES

Earlier you saw a brief introduction to Find File's Search capabilities. This section describes the more powerful features that Word can offer you. To use Word's advanced search features:

1. Open the Find File dialog box and click on the Search button to open the Search dialog box if necessary.
2. Click on the Advanced Search button. This opens the Advanced Search dialog box, an example of which is shown in Figure 12-8.

On the computer used to produce Figure 12-8, the files of this book were stored on drive D in a directory called WINWORD6. To bring up the dialog box shown in Figure 12-8, I entered **D:\WINWORD6** in the Location box in the original Search dialog box (case is irrelevant) and *.DOC in the File Name box. I also made sure the Include Subdirectories box was checked and then clicked on the Advanced Search button.

The Advanced Search dialog box enables you to expand or narrow a search. As shown in Figure 12-8, this dialog box has three tabs: Location, Summary, and Timestamp. We will go over each of these tabs in the sections that follow.

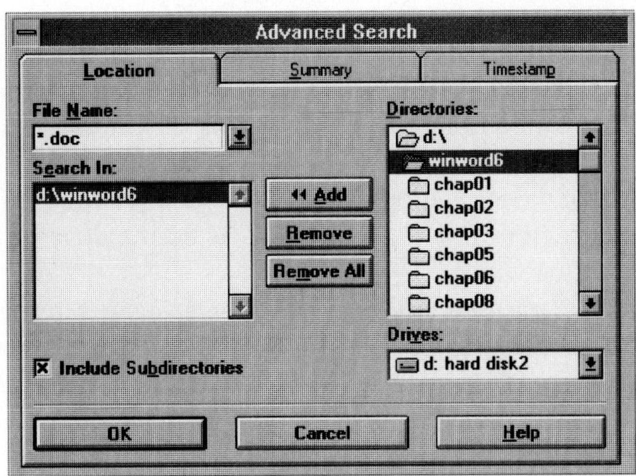

FIGURE 12-8

The Location tab in the Advanced Search dialog box

NOTE *The Clear button on the Search dialog box allows you to start a completely new search. You may want to select Clear before beginning a search to ensure that only the conditions you want are actually used.*

THE LOCATION TAB

The Location tab lets you add or remove places where you want Word to search through. For example, suppose you wanted to add C:\WINWORD to the search shown in Figure 12-8. To do this, make sure the Location Tab in the Advanced Search dialog box is visible:

1. Select C: from the Drives drop-down list box on this tab.
2. Select \WINWORD from the Directories list box.
3. Click on the Add button.

Word adds C:\WINWORD to the Search In list box and would now search both the C:\WINWORD and D:\WINWORD6 directories once you click on OK to return to the Search dialog box and OK again to actually start the search.

If you want to narrow the locations searched, reopen the Advanced Search dialog box, highlight the directories that you don't want Word to search through in the Search In list box, and click on the Remove button.

THE TIMESTAMP TAB

Figure 12-9 shows the Timestamp tab in the Advanced Search dialog box. You can enter dates in the text boxes under Last Saved or Created. Word automatically maintains this information on all documents. You can specify just a From date, just a To date, or both to establish a range of dates. The By text boxes enable you to limit your search to the person who created or last saved the document.

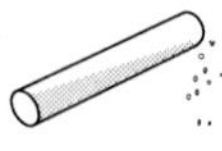

NOTE *Case is irrelevant in what you enter in the By text box and Word matches even part of what you enter. For example, suppose there were documents stored by both Bill Clinton and Bill Buckley on your hard disk. If you enter* ***bill*** *in the By box and click on OK twice, Word would list the files by both these people in the Find File dialog box.*

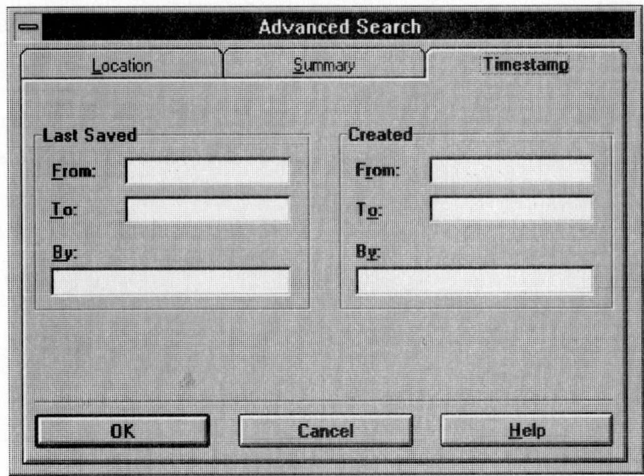

FIGURE 12-9
The Timestamp tab in the Advanced Search dialog box

EXAMPLE

1. Suppose you wanted to find the documents last saved by Mickey Mouse in any directory under D:\WINWORD6. First limit your search to D:\WINWORD6 using the Location tab on the Advanced Search dialog box. Then enter **Mickey Mouse** in the Last Saved By text box on the Timestamp tab. Then Click on OK.

THE SUMMARY INFO TAB

The last and potentially most powerful tab in the Advanced Search dialog box is the Summary tab shown in Figure 12-10. If you enter several items in one or more of the Title, Subject, Author, and Keywords text boxes in this tab, Word will only find the files that satisfy *all* these conditions. For example, if you enter both **Mickey** and **Donald** in the Title box, only documents whose titles contain *both* of those words will be found. Similarly, if you enter **Mickey** under Title and **mouse** under Author, Word will find only the files that have "Mickey" in the title and "mouse" as the author. Thus, Word will not find files that have "Donald Duck" as an author even if they have "Mickey" in the title. Finally, Word doesn't care about the order of the entries in these boxes. Searching with "Micky" followed by "Donald" in the Title box gives the same results as searching for "Donald" followed by

FIGURE 12-10

The Summary tab in the Advanced Search dialog box

"Mickey." Also, unless you select the Match Case check box, Word will ignore capitalization; MICKEY, miCKey, and so on give the same results.

Sometimes you need to find documents that contain either of two items (but not necessarily both). For example, to find documents that contain Mickey *or* Donald in the title (but not necessarily both):

1. First fill in **Mickey** in the title text box.
2. Pull down the Options list box and select Create New List.
3. Click on OK twice to run this search.
4. Click on the Search button again and click on Advanced Search. Fill in the Title box again in the Summary tab, this time with **Donald**.
5. Pull down the Options list box and select Add Matches to List in the Options box.
6. Click on OK twice to run this search. Word will add any new files found to the existing list in the Find File dialog box.

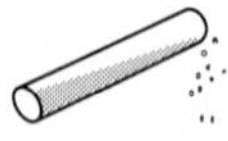

NOTE *Word does its best to keep Find File's list of files current, but it's possible that the list may not be absolutely up to date. For example, if you are working with files on a network, someone could add or delete a file after you started up the Find File dialog box. If you suspect that Find File's list may not be up to date, click on the Search button in the Find File dialog box and make sure the Rebuild File List check box is on before you click on OK to actually start the search.*

SEARCHING FOR FILES THAT CONTAIN SPECIFIC TEXT

Have you ever forgotten where (or under what name) you stored a document? If you have a hard disk filled with lots of documents, this unfortunate event seems to happen all too often. You might have thrown up your hands in disgust when this happened—or spent hours recreating the "lost" document. Find File's most powerful feature—and the biggest potential time-saver—is the one that can help you find "lost" files.

NOTE *For this feature to work perfectly, you cannot have saved your files using Word's Fast Save feature. If you think you will need to search for "lost" files, make sure the Allow Fast Saves check box on the Save tab on the Options dialog box is off when you save documents.*

Word can look through *every* file on your disk for text that it may contain. To use this feature, enter the text in the Containing Text box on the Summary tab in the Advanced Search dialog box as shown here. For example, if you enter the words **Word For Windows Version 6.0,** in the Containing Text box in the Summary tab, Word can search through your whole disk and find *all* the files containing this phrase. This happens once you click on OK once to leave the Summary tab and again to start the search.

TIP *As you can imagine, if you have a large number of files to search, or you have large files, this kind of search takes time. Plan ahead and narrow down the search by including the most specific (and unusual) text you can remember the document containing before you begin a search based upon text in file.*

If you aren't sure of the spelling or need to broaden the search, you can also use the same wildcards you saw for file names earlier in this chapter and used for the spelling checker in Chapter 5. For example, in the screen shown below the Containing Text box is set up to search for the term "wil*cox." Since the Use Pattern Matching box is checked, the asterisk will be interpreted to mean "find zero or more characters." Since the Match Case box is not checked, this means you will find files containing text like: "Wilcox", "Willcox" or even "We need a new coxwain, will you be the coxwain on this boat?"

SAVING SEARCHES FOR REUSE

If you have built up a complicated search using the advanced search facilities of Find File, you can save it for use another time. To do this,

1. Click on the Save Search As button in the Search dialog box.
2. Enter a name you want to save the search under in the dialog box that pops up and click on OK.

Once you have named a search, you can easily reuse it by:

1. Clicking on the Search button in the Find File dialog box.
2. Opening the Saved Searches drop-down list box.
3. Choosing which of the saved searches you want to rerun.

(Of course, you need to click on OK to actually rerun the search.)

EXERCISES

1. Open the File Find dialog box (Alt F, F), choose the Search button, and search for all files with the DOC extension. Include all subdirectories in this search.
2. Save the search as **My Document Directories**.
3. Select Advanced Search, choose the Timestamp tab, and limit your search to documents you created since you began to work on this chapter. Execute the search.
4. From the Saved Searches list box, select your My Document Directories search.
5. Select Advanced Search, choose the Summary tab, and create a new list limited to documents with the keyword "Summary." Execute the search.
6. Select Advanced Search, choose Add Matches to List from the Options list box, and enter **wilcox** in the Containing Text text box. Execute the search.
7. Review the files you've found and then save the search as **Advanced Search Test.**

mastery skills check

1. Using the advanced search feature, set up a search to find the documents with the Cicero and Wilcox quotations. [12.5]
2. Edit the summary information on both of the files and add **Quotation** to the keywords list for each file. [12.1, 12.4]
3. Open both quotation files. [12.4]
4. Enable revision marks and add **Ella W.** in front of Wilcox. [12.3]
5. Add an annotation **When did she live?**. [12.2]
6. Accept all revisions and close both files. [12.3]

cumulative skills check

1. Use Find File and use the Search dialog box to find all your document files no matter where they are on your hard disk. [12.4, 12.5]
2. Search through the list using whatever Find File tools you like and add **Quotation** to the keywords for all the files containing quotations. [12.4, 12.5, 12.1]
3. Use the advanced search feature and limit your search to files with "Quotation" in their keyword list. [12.5]
4. Sort your file list by creation date. [12.5]
5. Preview the quotations and open and edit any that could use enhancements (nicer fonts, visual balance, and so on). [12.4, 6.1, 6.2, 7.1, 7.2, 8.2]
6. Close all files and then use Find File to locate and print a few quotations without opening any files. [1.3, 12.4, 12.5]

13

An Introduction to Desktop Publishing

chapter objectives

After completing this chapter, you will be able to

13.1 Work with graphics (pictures) inside documents

13.2 Work with multicolumn documents

13.3 Position text and graphics exactly on a page using frames

THE term *desktop publishing* was invented to describe the whole process of doing at your desk what you used to have to pay professional printshops to do. Even in the early days of computing (and especially in the typewriter days), if you wanted a document to have anything other than 60 lines of text in a Courier-like font (see Chapter 6), you had to pay a printshop to do the job. With the advent of powerful computers and relatively inexpensive high-quality laser printers, it became practical to stylize in house. When companies (and people) stopped farming out work, they either saved lots of money or were able to make a higher percentage of their documents look professionally produced.

The Wizards from Chapter 4 made it easy to accomplish such specific desktop publishing tasks as preparing awards, calendars, resumes, and so on. This chapter shows you how to add graphics and columns to your documents directly—thus giving you far more power than the Wizards could. Unfortunately, the desktop publishing features in Word are so powerful and so vast, that to completely cover them would take a book at least as long as this one. This chapter will, however, get you started by teaching you the basics.

The first section covers the techniques needed to add graphics (pictures) to your documents, resizing and reshaping them as needed. The second section covers documents that use multiple columns. The third section covers *frames*, which are a way to position graphics or text at a specific spot on a page. (The drop caps you saw in Chapter 7 use a frame to position them exactly at the margins of a paragraph.) Among their other powers, frames let you wrap text around graphics automatically—an effect that was painful and expensive even for professional printshops to achieve in the old days. Figure 13-1 shows you many of these possible special effects.

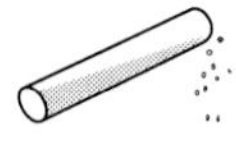

NOTE *Word comes with a Newsletter Wizard that you may want to experiment with to get you started in desktop publishing. However, you will almost certainly find that you need to use the techniques from this chapter to work with the document produced by this Wizard.*

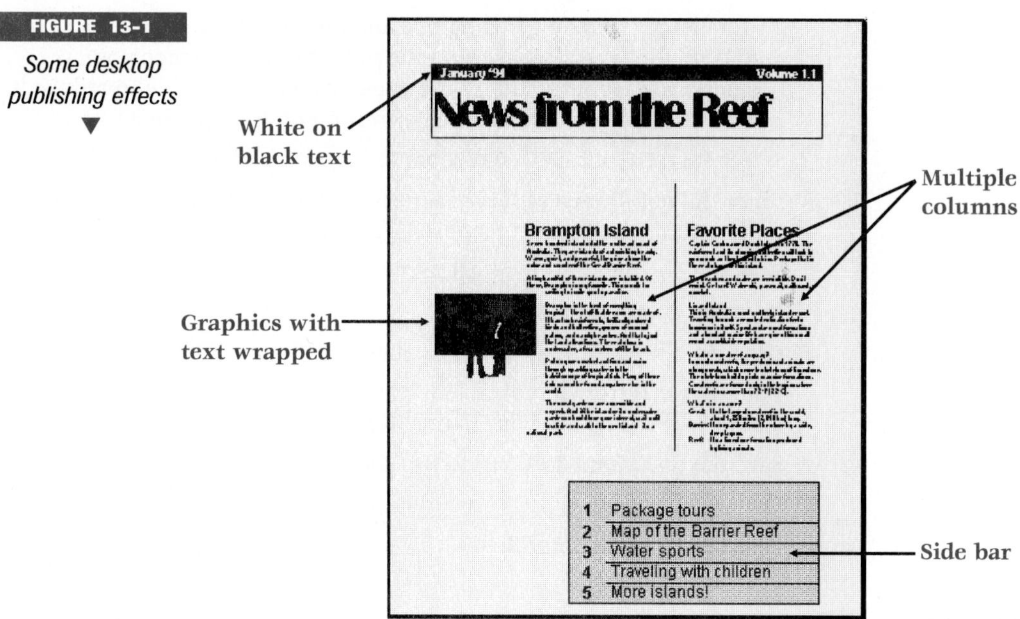

FIGURE 13-1

Some desktop publishing effects

review skills check

In this skills check we will create a basic business card and letterhead that will be enhanced during the other exercises and skills checks in this chapter.

1. Create a new document with the following Page Setup characteristics (we need .125" of white space between the text and the edge of the card, and the card itself will be the standard business card size of 2" × 3.5"). [1.6, 8.2]

   - Paper Size   Landscape, 5.5" Wide, 4" Height
   - Margins   1.125" all around (normal 1" margin plus .125 text offset from the edges)

   What we have done is create a structure upon which we will design a business card. Do not worry about needing this unusual-sized paper; we will print the card on standard 8.5" × 11" paper.

Challenge Yourself! During this and the rest of the exercises, double all the layout measurements so that when you take your business card layout to the printer, the printer will be able to reduce it by 50% thereby giving you a higher resolution final product.

2. Select Page Layout view and zoom to Page Width. [8.1]
3. Enter the text from a typical business card on the page. Hand select fonts and format the text to your liking. [6.1, 6.2]
4. Save the document as MYCARD.DOC. [2.4]
5. Print the document. [2.6]
6. Create a new document using normal Page Setup characteristics. [1.6]
7. Enter the text from a typical letterhead into the headers and footers and format the text to your liking. [8.3, 6.1, 6.2]
8. Save the document as MYLTRHD.DOC. [2.4]
9. Print the document. [1.6]
10. Close both documents. [2.4]

13.1 GRAPHICS

To use graphics (pictures) in Word, you have to have the file for the picture in a form that Word can handle. Potentially, Word can handle about 20 different types of graphics files. Word uses what are called *graphics filters* in order to handle the files that contain pictures. Filters for the most common types of graphics are supplied with Word and you can buy programs that give you even more filters if you need them.

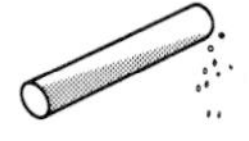

NOTE *To work with graphics, you may have to go back to the installation procedure in order to install the needed graphics filters (see Appendix B) if they are ones that you have not already installed.*

Once you have the proper graphics filter installed, inserting a picture into your document is easy.

1. Move the insertion point to where you want the picture to appear.
2. From the Insert menu, choose Picture (Alt I, P). This pops up the Insert Picture dialog box as shown in Figure 13-2.
3. Change drives and directories if you need to, choose the file name for the picture, and then click on OK.

FIGURE 13-2

The Insert Picture dialog box

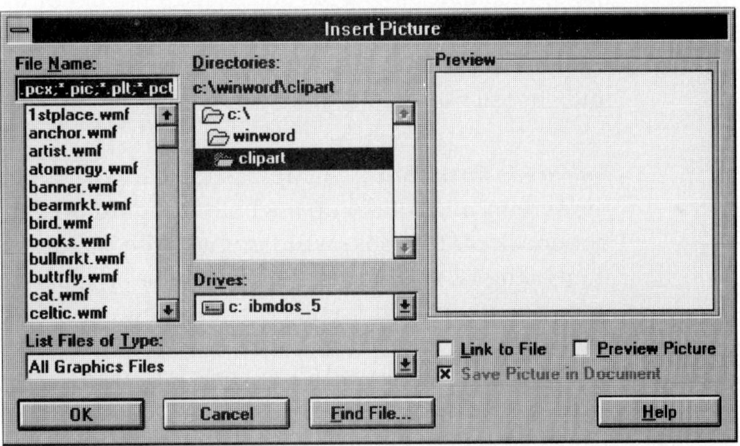

That's it. Word converts the picture using the right filter to the form it needs.

The Insert Picture dialog box is a little more complicated than an ordinary file handling dialog box. Let's go over its new features (or the ones that work a little differently than those you have already seen) one by one.

File Name The convention is that each type of graphic file has its own extension. For example, .BMP stands for *bitmaps*. Think of these as snapshots of your screen. Bitmaps have relatively low resolution compared to the other file formats, so they do not look as good as some of the other formats when printed. (A laser printer potentially gives much finer resolution than your screen.) A program like the Paintbrush program supplied with Windows generates bitmaps (.BMP) files. Another example is .WMF, which stands for *Windows metafiles*. These have very high resolution; Word comes with a lot of sample metafiles that you can use freely in your documents.

Most of the time it is not important to know what kind of graphics these file extensions stand for—the main exception is when you want to have Word resize the figure as discussed in the next section. Certain types of graphics respond better to resizing than other types. For example, bitmaps resize poorly and Windows metafiles resize well.

In any case, as with any file-handling dialog box, you can type or select the name of the file you want to open. You can change the extension selected in the List Files of Type drop-down list box to see a list of files that have a particular extension. For example, if you want to see only bitmaps, you will put *.BMP in File Name list box. However, it is easier just to drop down the List Files of Type list box and choose the type of files you want.

Link to File Check Box Graphics files are *big*. One multicolor bitmap of the screen might take up a whole standard 3 1/2" floppy disk! If you do not check off this box, Word embeds the picture file in your document, increasing its size proportionally. Put a couple of graphics files into your document and it will certainly no longer fit on a floppy, making backups difficult.

When you check off this box, Word creates a *link* between your document and the graphics file you want to insert. This is jargon for telling Word to search out the graphic when it needs to print or otherwise work with the graphics file. In order to have *only* this link saved instead of the whole picture (which is what takes up the space) saved, make sure the Save Picture in Document check box is off.

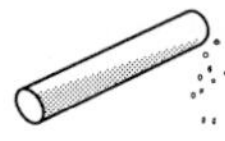

NOTE *To update this link when you want the latest version of the graphic, choose Links from the Edit menu (Alt E, K) and click on the Update Now button in the dialog box that pops up.*

Preview Picture Check Box If you check this box, you can see a preview of the graphic you select as you highlight different files in the File Name list box.

TIP *If you are working with another Windows program that generates graphics (a simple example is Windows's Paintbrush), you can usually paste that graphic into a Word document directly. You do this by selecting the graphic in the other program and then use the Copy or Cut items on that program's Edit menu—just as you copy information from Word into the clipboard using Word's Edit menu. Once it is in the Windows Clipboard, use the paste button (or Paste on the Edit menu) to insert the graphic into your text at the insertion point.*

(Windows actually allows you to have two programs running at the same time—consult any book on Windows for how to do this.)

EXAMPLES

1. The graphics supplied with Word for Windows metafiles are usually stored in the CLIPART subdirectory below where Word itself is stored. You may have to go back to the installation routine in Appendix B in order to place these on your hard disk.
2. Start a new document and look at the pictures supplied in this directory by choosing Picture from the Insert menu, checking the Preview Picture checkbox, and then highlighting each successive graphic.

   When you have decided on your favorite picture, double-click on its name in order to insert it into your document. (The author is quite partial to the butterfly. BUTTRFLY.WMF is the file name.)

EDITING IMAGES

Once you have a graphic in a Word document you can modify it extensively. This section only can cover the basics. (For example, Word comes with a full range of drawing tools that let you add lines and shapes to your documents: for more information on this and other drawing tools available in Word, consult Mary Campbell's *Microsoft Word for Windows: The Complete Reference* (Osborne/McGraw-Hill, 1994.)

To work with a graphic you first have to select it.

1. To select a graphic, click inside of it once.

This puts a dotted border around the graphic with eight *sizing handles* as shown here:

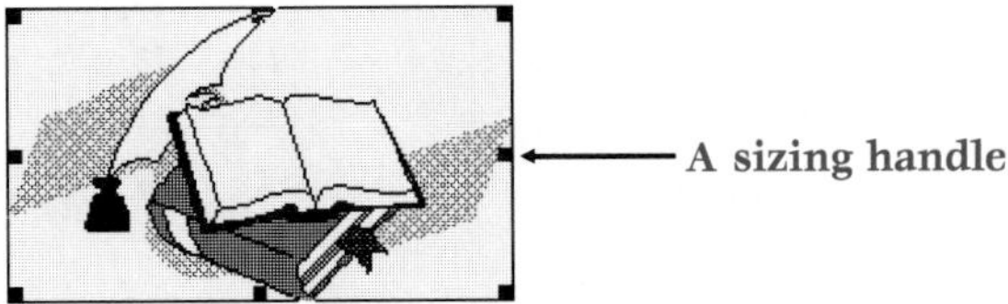

Now resizing the graphic is simple: drag on one of the sizing handles to resize it. Use the corner sizing handles to increase or decrease the size symmetrically; use the middle sizing handles to increase or decrease the graphic in only that direction.

You can also crop (cut off parts) or add space (*white space* in printer jargon) to a graphic. For this:

1. Select the graphic.
2. Hold down the Shift key while dragging the sizing handles inward to crop the graphic, outward to add white space.

Word displays the cropping measurements in the status bar, an example of which is shown here:

To reset a cropped graphic back to its original measurements:

1. Select the graphic.
2. Choose Picture from the Format menu (Alt O, R) and then click on the Reset button on the dialog box that pops up.

If you double-click on a graphic that you imported into Word, Word opens up another editing window. This lets you work with the graphic using a more uncluttered screen. Figure 13-3 is a typical example of a graphics window. Notice the new two-button Picture toolbar. You click on the Close button to return to the original Word document.

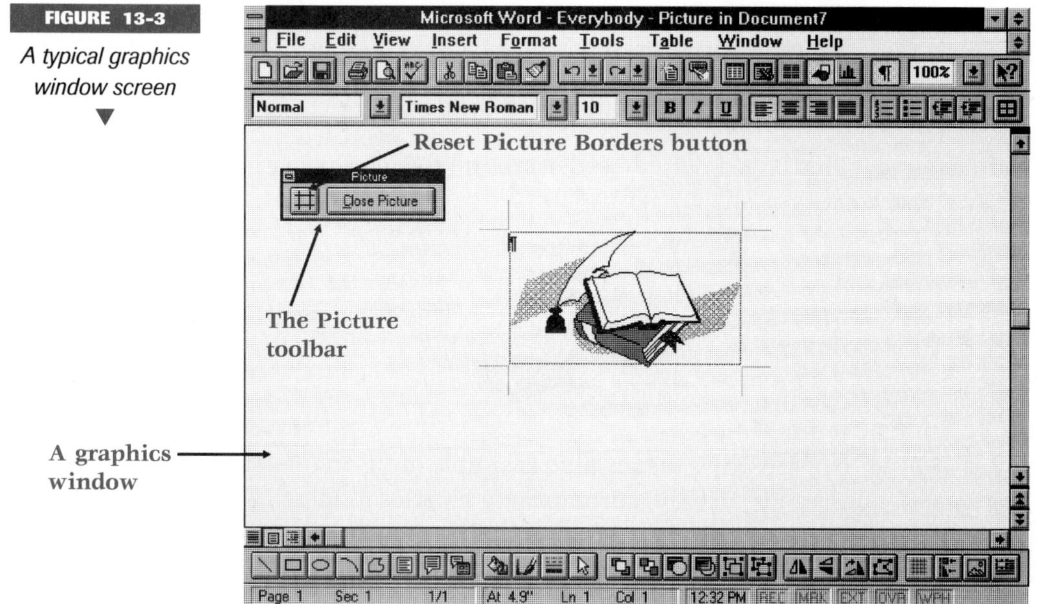

FIGURE 13-3

A typical graphics window screen

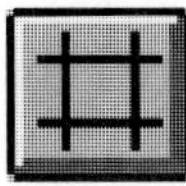

If you double-click on a graphic and then enlarge the graphic past the original boundaries, you need to click on the Reset Picture Borders button to retain the original boundaries when you return to the Word document (by clicking on the Close button).

EXAMPLES

1. Start a new document and load the butterfly graphic file (BUTTRFLY.WMF) from the CLIPART subdirectory, as shown here. Let's make the butterfly fill more of a page.

   a. Choose Full Screen from the View menu (Alt V, U) so that it is easier to see more of the graphic.
   b. Select the butterfly and drag the right corner sizing handles until the size fills the full screen.
   c. Drag one of the middle sizing handles to give the butterfly the look it might have in a distortion mirror, as shown here:

EXERCISES

1. Open MYCARD.DOC and insert a clipart image, storing the image in the document. Resize the art to fit your card. (Don't worry about exact positioning of the image. We will take care of that in the section on Frames later in this chapter.)
2. Double-click the imported image and customize the art. Make sure you reset the image's boundaries before returning to the document.
3. Select your customized image and copy it to the clipboard.
4. Open MYLTRHD.DOC and paste your art into the letterhead's header.
5. Close both documents, saving your changes.

13.2 WORKING WITH COLUMNS

When you produce a newsletter, you will often want to have multiple columns—say, one for each article. Word makes preparing multicolumn documents a snap. You can have some parts of your document use columns and others not by inserting section breaks (see Chapter 11) into your document.

NOTE *To work with columns in your document, you should be in Page Layout view.*

To add columns to your document,

1. Move the insertion point to where you want the columns to appear. (Remember to add a section break if you don't want the whole document to appear in columns.)
2. Click on the Columns button. This opens a box that looks like this:

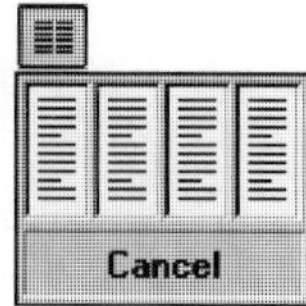

3. Drag to select the number of columns you want. This gives you columns of equal width.

Once you have added columns to a section, text automatically flows from the bottom of one column to the top of the next until the page is full. When a page is full Word continues to the leftmost column on the next page. You can apply all the formatting techniques you learned in Chapters 6 and 7 to the individual characters and paragraphs in a column independently.

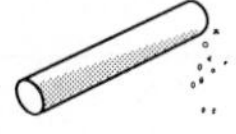

NOTE: *To end a column prematurely and move to the top of the next column, press* Ctrl+Shift+Enter.

One feature you may want to add to a section that uses columns is usually called a *banner heading*. This is a heading that covers all the columns—you see these frequently in newspapers, for example.

To create a banner headline:

1. Type the headline at the beginning of the top left column.
2. Select the text.
3. Click on the Column button and drag to make a single column.

Word automatically inserts a section break after the headline so you can center the headline, adjust the font and size, or do anything you want to it without affecting the remaining text that is already in columns.

EXAMPLE

1. Suppose you want to create a document that begins like the following.

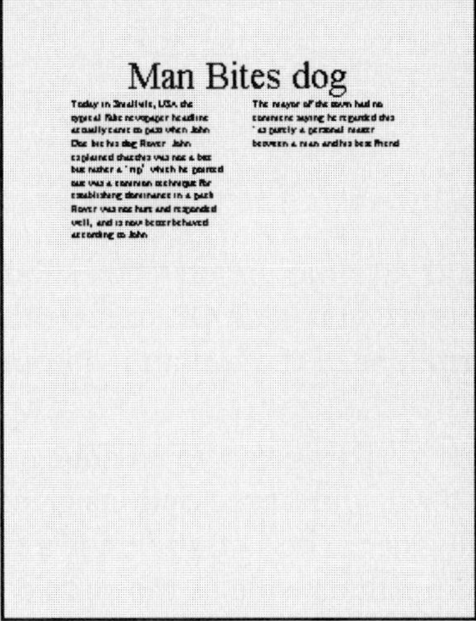

Man Bites dog

a. Start a new document, then click on the Columns button and drag to select two columns.
b. Now enter the text for the heading: **Man Bites dog**.
c. Select this text, click on the Column button and drag to make a single column.
d. Center the headline and change the font to 36 point bold.

SETTING COLUMN OPTIONS

If you want to have complete control over column width and spacing, turn to the Columns item on the Format menu.

Make sure the insertion point is in the section you want to work with.

1. Choose Columns from the Format menu (Alt O, C).

This pops up a dialog box that looks like this:

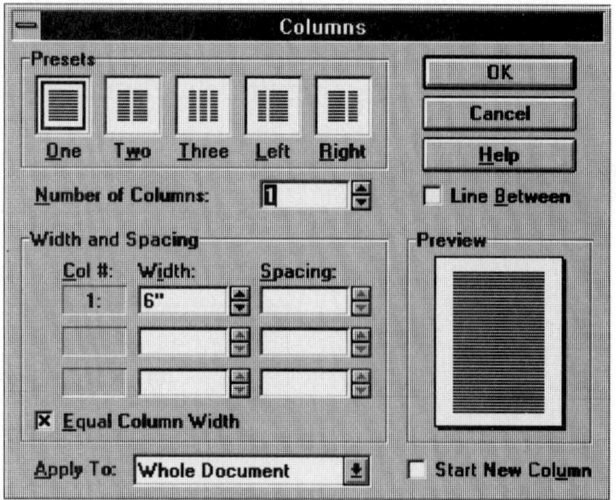

As always the Preview box shows you what your choices will look like before you click OK to have them go into effect. Here are short descriptions of the remaining items in this dialog box.

Presets This gives you a choice of five standard column sizes. The One, Two, and Three options gives you one, two, or three columns of equal width. The Left option is a two-column format with the left column half as wide as the right column. The Right option also formats the text into two columns but with the right column half as wide as the left column. Click on the kind of columns you want.

Number of Columns Text Box Here you can enter the number of columns you want directly. (With equal-width columns, four or five is about the practical limit.)

Line Between Check Box If you check this off, Word puts a vertical line between the columns. The line is the same length as the longest column on the page (or in the section). You can see the vertical lines between columns only in Page Layout view or when you do a print preview.

Width and Spacing Area This area lets you set the width of columns and the space between columns. The columns are numbered from left to right. You can only make the columns unequal width if the Equal Column Width check box is *off*. Enter the width of the column and then the spacing you want between the column and the next column to the right.

Obviously, if the Equal Column Width check box is on, then you can change only the measurement in the Spacing box; Word automatically calculates the column width.

Apply To Drop-Down List Box This drop-down list box lets you choose what portion of the document to which you want to apply the options you are currently setting. Here's what it looks like:

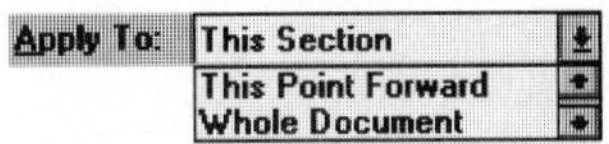

There are a couple of points you have to be aware of: if you choose the This Selection option, Word inserts section breaks before and after the selection. Similarly, if you choose This Point Forward, Word inserts a section break right before the insertion point, and then Word applies the column formatting you have selected to everything that follows.

Start New Column Check Box Check this box (it is off by default) and Word starts a new column at the insertion point by inserting a column break. This can leave you with a fair amount of white space.

EXAMPLES

1. Suppose you want to have two columns, the first column 2" wide and the second 3" wide with a 1" margin between them.
   a. Start by choosing Columns from the Format menu (Alt F, C).
   b. Now click on the Two column box, and also make sure the Equal Column Width box is not checked.
   c. Fill in the Width box for column one as 2", and the Spacing to be 1". Fill in the column two width as 3".

EXERCISES

1. Create a new document and enter three blank lines.
2. Switch to Normal view.
3. Select the second paragraph, click on the Columns button and make the selected text into three-column text. Note the automatic insertion of section breaks to mark the difference between the single-column and multicolumn text.
4. Enter a couple of sentences of text into the second paragraph (the three-column section).
5. Switch to Page Layout view.
6. Select just the sentences, not the paragraph mark, and copy the sentences to the clipboard. Then paste a couple of copies back into the three-column section of the document until the text spills into the third column.
7. Zoom to Full Page and add some paragraph marks in random locations to simulate text.
8. Copy and Paste some more text until the text spills into the next page.
9. Experiment with left-aligned and justified paragraphs within the columns of text. Experiment with first line indents to help better define paragraphs.
10. Select Format, Columns (Alt O, C), set the space between the columns to .2", and draw a line between the columns.
11. Close and save the document as COLTEST.DOC.

13.3 WORKING WITH FRAMES

When you hear the word "frame" in a free association game probably the first thing that comes to your mind is "picture frame". Word's frames, however, are far more sophisticated than passive containers for graphics. Think of them as containers that can hold *any* object that Word can handle: text, graphics, tables, and so on. Text automatically wraps within a frame and can be formatted by any of the usual Word techniques you saw in Chapters 6 and 7. You can use a frame to position a graphic between two columns of text, and Word will just flow the column's text around it as shown in Figure 13-4.

Frames show off their power most when you need to position objects in your document. For example, once you place the object in a frame, you can drag it to any location in your document—but since you can do that with the usual drag and drop techniques from Chapter 2, this doesn't sound so impressive. However, using a frame lets you position an object so that it is always a *fixed* distance from a margin or a *fixed* distance above or below a specific paragraph—regardless of any extra text you may add.

A good example of this is that Word lets you print a framed object on the bottom of the page that a specific paragraph falls on. (Think about

FIGURE 13-4

Text flowing around frames

all the work Word must do for this: every time you add text that changes a page break, Word *automatically* calculates on what page the paragraph you associated the frame with (*anchored it to* in the jargon) now falls on. Then it prints the framed object at the bottom of this new page.)

To put any Word object in a frame, first switch to Page Layout view, then:

1. Select the object.
2. Choose Frame from the Insert menu (Alt I, F).

Word places a little gray cross-hatched border around the selected object as shown here:

TIP *The frame around the object is actually stored in the paragraph marks within the frame. If you delete these (use the Show/Hide button), then the frame disappears.*

You can resize any framed object the same way you resize a graphic:

1. Select the frame (so its sizing handles are visible).
2. Drag the sizing handles inward or outward as desired.

Similarly, you can move any framed object around your document by selecting it and then dragging it to the new location. When you move a framed object, Word automatically anchors the frame to the closest paragraph.

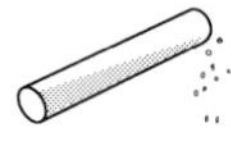

NOTE *A framed object always appears on the same page as the paragraph it is anchored to.*

To anchor a framed object to a specific paragraph so that the frame is always associated with that paragraph, regardless of whether you move the frame or add new paragraphs:

1. Make sure you are in Page Layout view with hidden characters showing and then select the frame. You will see a little anchor next to the frame, as shown here:

The·butterfly·image·is·currently·anchored·to·this·paragraph.¶

2. Drag the anchor to the paragraph you want to lock the frame to.
3. Double-click on the anchor icon. The icon changes, as shown here:

The·butterfly·image·is·currently·anchored·to·this·paragraph.¶

As you will soon see in the sections on positioning framed objects, you can control where on that page the framed object appears. For example, you can have the framed object always appear on the top or bottom of the page that the associated paragraph falls on.

When you work with frames a lot, certain operations come up time and time again. As is usually the case when this happens, Word has a shortcut menu for working with the object. Here's the one for working with framed objects:

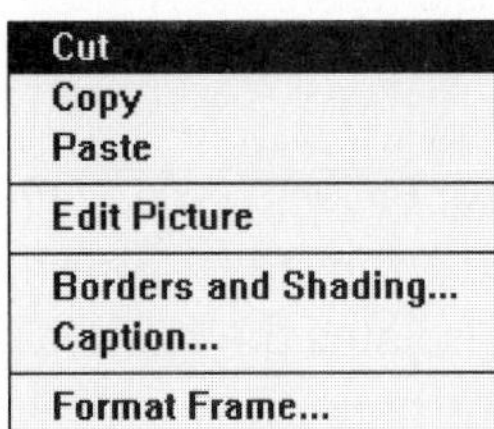

You can see this shortcut menu by selecting the framed object, then clicking the right mouse button (or pressing Shift+F10) when the insertion point is in the frame.

TIP *The borders around frames that contain graphics are just there to help you see the boundaries of the frame. If you want to actually place a border around the framed graphic (or modify the simple box that Word places around text that is in a frame), select the framed object and use the shortcut menu to bring up the Borders toolbar. Now proceed exactly as in Chapter 7.*

Finally, the power of frames comes from your ability to position them precisely on a page. For example, graphics are hard to position accurately just by moving the insertion point before you actually insert the graphic. Moreover, you can insert a frame and *then* tell Word what to do with the text that would normally be there. For example, do you want Word to wrap the text around the framed object?

To take advantage of all this power, you need to gain more control over how Word treats your framed object on the page. To do this:

1. First select the framed object you want to work with.
2. Then choose Frame from the Format menu (Alt O, M).

This brings up the Frame dialog box, an example of which is shown in Figure 13-5. Some of the options in Figure 13-5 are relatively straightforward to use. For example, if you click on the Remove Frame button in Figure 13-5, Word removes the frame from the selected object. (The elements in this dialog box that control the vertical and horizontal positioning of the framed object can be confusing—so we'll cover these elements in their own sections.)

Here are short descriptions of the other basic elements in the Frame dialog box.

Text Wrapping Boxes You click on one of these boxes to control whether or not Word wraps text around the frame. If you choose the None box, then Word isolates the framed object, and so does not wrap text around it. On the other hand, if you click on the Around box, Word wraps text around the sides of the frame, providing there is enough room to do so. For example, Word requires at least an inch between the frame and the margin, the column boundary, or any other framed object.

FIGURE 13-5

The Frame dialog box

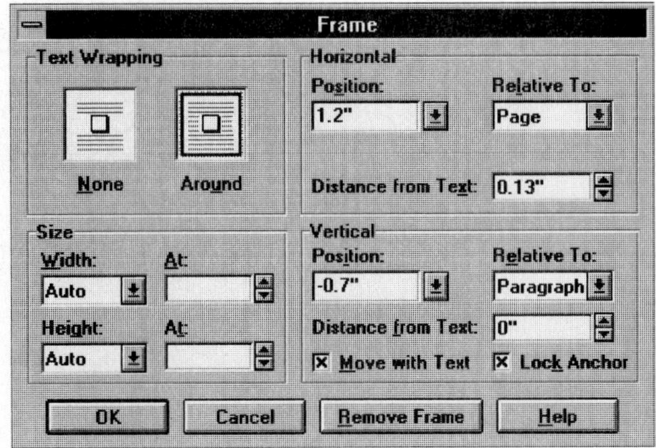

Size Boxes These boxes let you control the width and height of the frame if using the sizing handles wasn't sufficiently accurate. The Auto option in the Width box tells Word to automatically adjust the width of the frame to the width of what it contains. Use the Exactly option if you want to enter a specific measurement in the At box. Similarly, the Auto option in the Height box tells Word to adjust the height of the frame to be as tall as what it contains, whereas the At Least option lets you set a minimum height for the frame—as specified in the At box.

EXAMPLES

1. Start a new document. Type **Once upon a time** and add a drop cap to the O (see Chapter 7). Notice that the drop cap is in a frame.
2. Close the previous document and start up a new one. Type the following:

   Butterflies are truly among the most beautiful of creatures.

   a. Load the butterfly graphic image from the CLIPART directory as you learned to do in Section 13.1. Select the butterfly graphic and place a frame around it. Your screen will look like this:

Butterflies are truly among the most beautiful of creatures.

b. Select the frame around the butterfly and then drag the butterfly to a new location ahead of the quote as shown here. Notice the frame has disappeared. (It will reappear whenever you click inside the picture.)

Butterflies are truly among the most beautiful
of creatures.

c. Drag the framed butterfly so it is centered on the top of the page.

d. Finally, put a green-colored border around the centered butterfly by opening the shortcut menu, choosing Borders and Shading, and adding a green colored box around the butterfly.

3. To see text flow around a frame, start up a new document and type the following:

This will be the framed text. This text will flow around the frame if all goes well. We obviously want to have at least enough text so that a few lines can wrap around the frame.

a. Select the first sentence and place a frame around it. Choose Frame from the Format menu and check off the Around box. The screen will look like this:

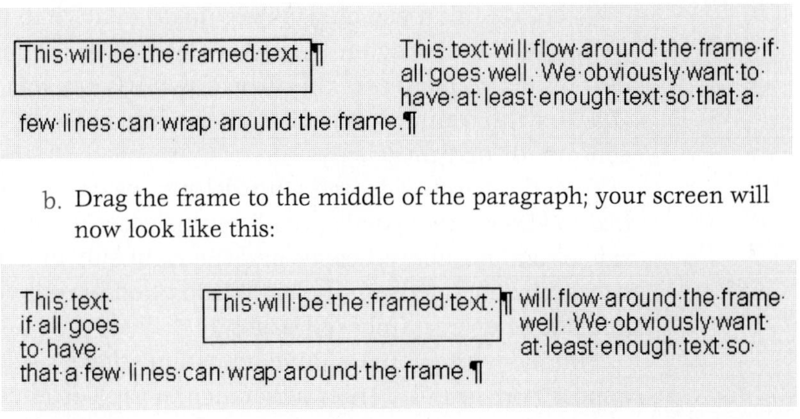
This·will·be·the·framed·text.¶
This·text·will·flow·around·the·frame·if·all·goes·well.·We·obviously·want·to·have·at·least·enough·text·so·that·a·few·lines·can·wrap·around·the·frame.¶
This·text·
if·all·goes
to·have·
This·will·be·the·framed·text.·¶
will·flow·around·the·frame·
well.·We·obviously·want·
at·least·enough·text·so·
that·a·few·lines·can·wrap·around·the·frame.¶

b. Drag the frame to the middle of the paragraph; your screen will now look like this:

Horizontal Positioning a Frame This group of drop-down list boxes in the Frame dialog box shown in Figure 13-5 controls how Word positions the framed object relative to the width of a page or the column. For example, do you want the framed object to sit centered on the page? Do you want it to appear flush with the left margin? Do you want it to appear on the right boundary of a column?

To exercise the possibilities above, it is usually easier to work first with the Relative To drop-down list box shown here:

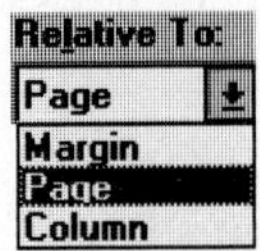
Relative To:
Page
Margin
Page
Column

Choose the option with respect to which you want Word to position the frame. For example, if you want to accurately position a frame on a page, choose Page from this list. If you want to position the frame with respect to the margins of an individual column, choose Column. Next, either enter a measurement directly in the Position box (you can use positive or negative numbers) or click on the arrow. This lets you choose from five standard choices shown here:

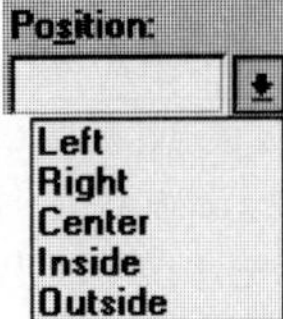
Position:
Left
Right
Center
Inside
Outside

Of course, all these choices are made relative to the page, column, or margin depending on what you chose in the Relative To drop-down list box. As you can see, this drop-down list box lets you control whether the frame is aligned with the left, right, or center of a page, column, or margin.

(Use the two Inside and Outside options only if you are binding the text to allow a two page spread. In this case the inside edge is the left side of odd-numbered pages and the right side of even-numbered pages; the outside is on the right side of odd-numbered pages and the left side of even-numbered pages.)

Finally, when you are done adjusting where you want the frame to appear horizontally, enter a distance in the Distance from Text box to specify the amount of space you want to appear between the frame and the surrounding text on both sides.

EXAMPLE

1. Suppose you want to position a frame in the center of a page. Select the frame and fill out the Frame dialog box. If you have a two-column text and want the frame to appear centered relative to the first column, make sure the frame is in the first column, the Position box in the Frame dialog box says Center, and the Relative To box says Column.

Vertical Positioning a Frame These drop-down list boxes work similarly to those for horizontal positioning. Usually you use these options to set the vertical position of the framed object relative to the top or bottom edge of the page, or top and bottom margins of the page. By choosing the Paragraph option in the Relative To drop-down list box, you can position the frame relative to the paragraph that the frame is anchored to. For example, you can always have it 1" above the paragraph.

The only new options are the Move with Text check box which tells Word to move the frame up or down on the page as you add (or remove) paragraphs on the page. This check box is defaulted to be on because you generally want the frame to move down the page as you add paragraphs to the document. (The Lock Anchor check box just gives you another way to lock the anchor of a frame to a specific paragraph instead of double-clicking on the anchor.)

Finally, since a framed object always appears on the same page as the paragraph to which it is anchored, you need a trick to get the framed object to be on a particular page. To do this, make sure the frame is on the page you want and:

1. Select the framed object and choose Frame from the Format menu.
2. Now make sure both the Lock Anchor and Move with Text check boxes are off.

EXAMPLES

1. Suppose you want to center a graphic exactly in the middle of the page and have text wrap around it. Select the frame and fill out the Frame box as shown here:

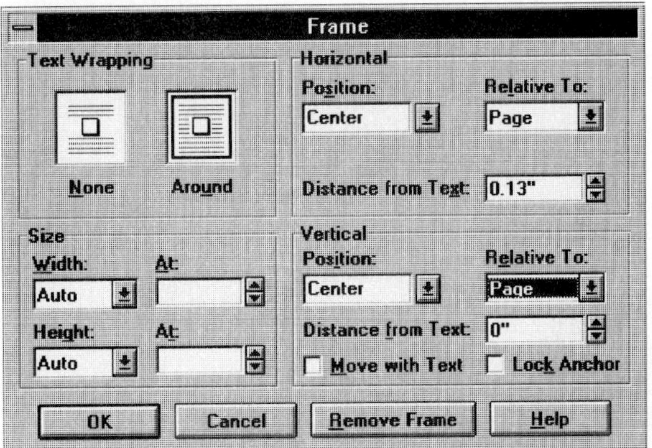

2. Boxed greyed text is an extremely useful tool for highlighting optional but still very interesting material. (These are sometimes called *sidebars* in printer jargon.) To create a sidebar, type the text that will make up the sidebar and frame it. Add grey shading to the paragraph via the Borders and Shading option on the shortcut menu (see Chapter 7). Choose Frame from the Format menu and lock the frame to the paragraph the sidebar pertains to. Finally, adjust the vertical position so that the frame is always positioned on the Bottom of the page that contains the paragraph that the sidebar is anchored to.

EXERCISES

1. Open COLTEST.DOC. Remove the first line indents on a few paragraphs and use Drop Caps from the Format menu to define the beginning of the paragraph.
2. Insert a frame into one of the columns and add a clipart image. Center the frame within the column and add some white space above and below the image (use Format, Frame to center and add white space in the Horizontal and Vertical portions of the dialog box).
3. Select some of your made-up text and copy it to the single-column portion of the document. Copy and paste until you have about a third of a page of text to work with. Insert a frame and add a clipart image within the new text.
4. Experiment with resizing, cropping, putting a border, or flowing text around the picture.
5. Open MYCARD.DOC and add a frame around the clipart image. Move the image around on the card and adjust the frame, art, and text to perfect your new business card. Save the document as MYCARD2.DOC.
6. Open MYLTRHD.DOC. Frame its clip art and adjust the frame, art, and text to perfect your new letterhead. Close and save the document.

mastery skills check

1. Create a new document and use Page Setup from the File menu to adjust the page for the development of another business card. (See Review Skills Check at front of this chapter for settings.)
2. Enter the text for one block of text for your business card (your phone and fax numbers for instance). To do this:
   a. Place a frame around the text and use Format, Frame to position the frame in the lower-right corner of the card.
   b. Repeat for the other blocks of text and any clip art on the card. Use Format, Frame to position each.

c. Save and print your final version of your new business card. [13.3, 13.1]

3. Create a new document and add your organization's title to the header. To do this:
   a. Add the organization's logo (or construct a nice layout for some personal stationery using ornate clip art to decorate the borders) high in the left margin.
   b. Save and print your new letterhead. If you think you might want to reuse the letterhead, save it as a template. [13.3, 13.1]
4. Create a new document and construct a newsletter.
   a. Use one thin column on the left for callouts, images, etc., and a second wider column for the news.
   b. Insert a frame and clip art image within the news text.
   c. Add a fancy header. [13.2, 13.3, 13.1]

cumulative skills check

1. Create a new file and insert a two-column by five-row table into the document. [10.2]
2. Set the column width to exactly 3.5" and the row height to 2". Center align the rows. [10.3]
3. In the first cell, build a business card. (You can use any tool you would like; however, you cannot insert frames into table cells.)

   Adjust all paragraph indents and space before and after paragraphs to make sure you have at least 9 points (0.125") of white space around text and art on the card. [7.1]
4. Add a clip art logo (or one that you have created) to the business card. [13.1]
5. Select everything in the first cell and copy it to the clipboard. [3.3, 10.3]

   You will have to make sure that there is a paragraph mark after the last paragraph in the cell to copy, otherwise you will lose the formatting of the last paragraph.
6. Paste a copy of the card into each of the remaining cells in the table. [3.3, 10.3]

7. Save your work. [2.4]
8. Print your new master copy for your business cards. [2.6]
9. Use the Newsletter wizard and create a newsletter. Review how the Wizard constructed the document. [4.1]

14

Form Letters, Envelopes, and Labels

chapter objectives

After completing this chapter, you will be able to

14.1 Create form letters

14.2 Create labels and envelopes for mass mailings

THIS chapter shows you how to create form letters using Word. Along the way, you will see how to maintain lists of addresses and names (or, for that matter, any data that needs to be organized) using Word's built-in data handling capability. Word lets you quickly sort or find specific information in a snap. Finally, you will learn how to print mailing labels and envelopes, which you'll need to get your mass mailing out the door.

At first glance, the information contained in this chapter seems to be most useful to businesses—business are, after all, the ones who prepare "personalized" form letters most often. On the other hand, Word makes it so easy to maintain address lists that you might find it worthwhile storing a copy of your personal address book in Word. That way you can get a new printout each time you update the list. Similarly, Word's label feature makes it easy to prepare your own mailing labels—much less expensively than you could buy them from a commercial printer.

review
skills check

In this skills check, we will convert a document you created in Chapter 10 into one suitable for use in this chapter as the names and addresses for a mass mailing.

1. Open PHONES.DOC, which you created in the review skills check for Chapter 10. [2.5]
2. Select the entire table containing the names, addresses, and phone numbers. [10.2]
3. Copy the table to the Clipboard. [10.2]
4. Create a new document. [1.6]
5. Paste the table from the Clipboard into the new document. [10.2]
6. If a caption was added to the table, delete it. [10.3]
7. Remove all formatting from your table. [10.3]
8. Update or add records to your phone list. [10.3]

9. Save the document as DB_PHONE.DOC. (DB is a common abbreviation for files used as a database.) [2.3]

14.1 GENERATING FORM LETTERS

You obviously need two things to create form letters:

- The text, which remains the same in each form letter.
- The names and addresses, which change for each form letter.

In Word the text that doesn't change is called the *main document*. The information (names and addresses most often) that will change is usually called the *data source*. *Mail merge* is the jargon for melding individual sets of information from a data source into a main document, most often for form letters or for mailing labels.

A typical main document might start out looking something like this:

1/1/1999

Dear

We are offering a special package for the new-year-to-end-all-new-years that will soon be upon us. The cost is a mere $2,000 per person. If you are interested, please e-mail your Visa, Master Card, or American Express card number to us ASAP.

Sincerely yours,

The Millennium Partnership
E-Mail Address: Really.Big.Show@World.Com

Notice that the recipient's name is left out after the salutation and that there is also room for his or her name and address right below the date. You can create main documents like this using all the ordinary Word techniques that you now know so well. Unfortunately, just creating a simple document with spaces for the names and address isn't enough. Before Word can actually *use* this letter as a form letter for a mail merge you have to fill in the blank spaces with markers that tell Word where to place the actual names and addresses. These markers are called *merge field codes* or *merge field names*. (Most people abbreviate this and say simply *merge fields*).

Since doing a mail merge can be confusing, it is worth keeping in mind that the usual order for doing a mail merge is the following:

1. Create a document that has universal text *and* space for the merge process.
2. Create the data source—i.e., the names and addresses that will change. (You can also use an existing data source, of course.)
3. Insert the specific merge field names into the document. Word uses merge field names to identify the places where information (like names and addresses that will change) will be inserted.
4. Tell Word to create all or some of the form letters by melding the information from the data source into the document. To do this Word uses only the part of the data source that corresponds to the specific merge field. (For example, if the merge field name was "last name", Word would successively paste last names from the data source at the spot in the document marked by the last name merge field.)

Note in particular that marking the places by inserting the merge field names is done fairly late in the game.

EXAMPLE

Let's suppose you wanted to prepare a mailing telling people that you have moved your business.

1. You will need to prepare a document and enter (something like the following) text into a new document before you can continue with the mail merge process. (Leave the blank lines as indicated):

1/1/94

Dear ,

Effective immediately my new address is:

1313 Mockingbird Lane
Hollywood, California

Sincerely yours,

FESTER ADAMS

THE MAIL MERGE HELPER

The easiest way to prepare a form letter is to use the Mail Merge Helper. The Mail Merge Helper lets you use the currently active document for the main document or create a new main document from scratch. (Don't worry if the current document isn't perfect; you will always be able to edit it again before Word actually prints those hundreds of form letters!)

To start the Mail Merge Helper:

- Choose Mail Merge from the Tools menu (Alt T, R).

This opens a dialog box like the one shown in Figure 14-1. Notice that only the Create button in Figure 14-1 is enabled (the others are grayed to indicate they are disabled). After the Mail Merge Helper is told what the main document will be (the currently active document or a new one that you will start from scratch), the second button—the one marked Get Data—will be enabled.

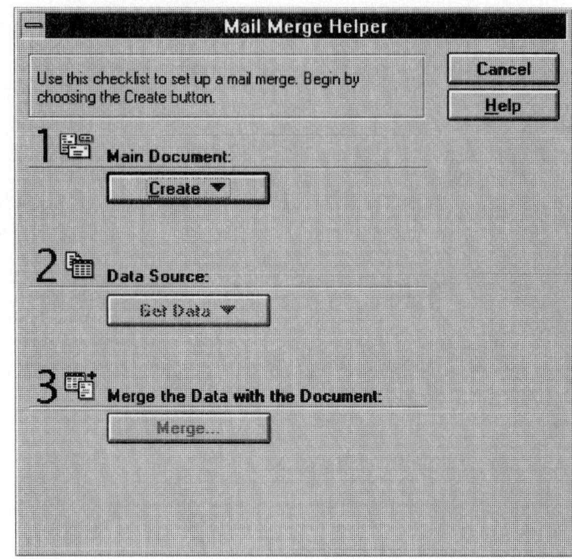

FIGURE 14-1

The Mail Merge Helper main screen

If you click on the Create button shown in Figure 14-1, Word drops down the list shown here. Choose Form Letters from this list:

Word pops up a message box that looks like this:

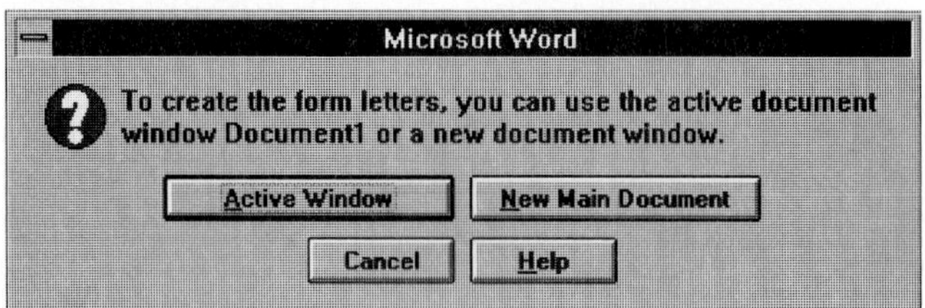

If you click on the Active Window button, you can use the current document as the main document for the form letter. If you want to create a main document from scratch, click on the New Main Document button instead. Regardless of which button you click on, you go to the same screen—a modified version of the original Mail

Merge Helper with a new Edit button for revising the main document, as shown in Figure 14-2. At this point you can click on the Edit button in Figure 14-2 to go back and modify the main document or you can go directly to getting (or building) the data source. Notice also how, in Figure 14-2, the Get Data button is now enabled.

If you need to edit the main document, click on the Edit button and then choose the name of the document from the list that drops down. When you are done with the main document, choose Mail Merge from the Tools menu to go back to the Mail Merge Helper screen shown in Figure 14-2.

TIP *If you want to have Word update the date when it prints the form letters, use the Date and Time item on the Insert menu (Alt I, T) to insert the date and time into a main document rather than typing it yourself. Remember to make sure the Insert As Field check box is selected in the Date and Time dialog box (see Chapter 8).*

Finally, once you have told Word what the main document is, you can put the mail merge process on hold and return to it later by saving the main document and then closing it. To continue the mail merge process at a later date, open the main document again using the Open command from the File menu, and choose the Mail Merge Helper once more (Alt T, R).

FIGURE 14-2

Modified Mail Merge Helper main screen

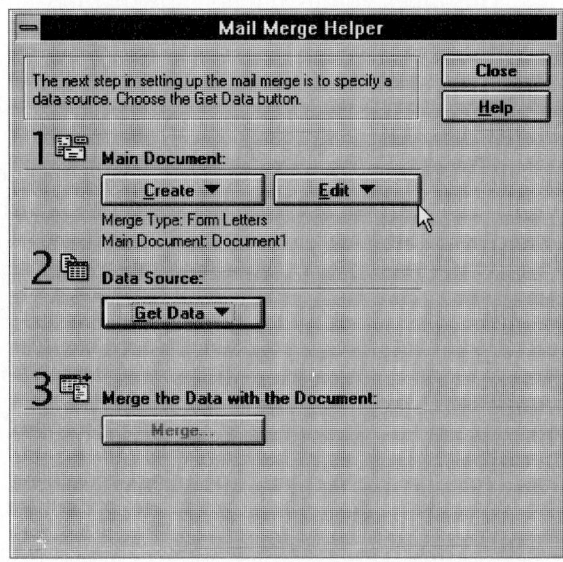

THE DATA SOURCE

Let's assume you are now satisfied with your main document for the moment (you can always go back and modify it later if you need to). You now need to tell Word the data source—the list of names and addresses that Word will meld into your document. You can create the data source from scratch or use one that you or somebody else has already created.

First off, you have to be aware that creating a data source is somewhat of an extended procedure. You need to first set up the structure of data source by determining which types of information it will contain. Once you've set up the structure for the data source, you still need to enter the data itself—the names, addresses, phone numbers, and so forth.

To create the data source from scratch,

1. Click on the Data Source button in the Mail Merge Helper dialog box.
2. Pick Create Data Source from the drop-down list box shown here:

This takes you to a dialog box that looks like Figure 14-3. This dialog box wants to know which types of information will be included in the data source. Will it have names, addresses, telephone numbers, etc.? However, as is often the case, there's a bit of jargon to be learned—we'll take that up next.

The Create Data Source dialog box may seem complicated at first, but don't be put off. You just need to keep three buzzwords in mind and you'll be ready to go. Two of these buzzwords you have seen before: field name and header row. A *field name* is what Word calls an identifier for common information in your data source. This is the information that Word uses to replace the *merge field names* that you use as placeholders in the main document. For example, you might be called Professor, Doctor, Judge, Lord, Mr., Mrs., or Ms.—but these are all *titles,* so Title is Word's choice for the field name for this common information.

Next, if you think of the information in the data source as being stored in a special kind of table, the field names are the identifying text

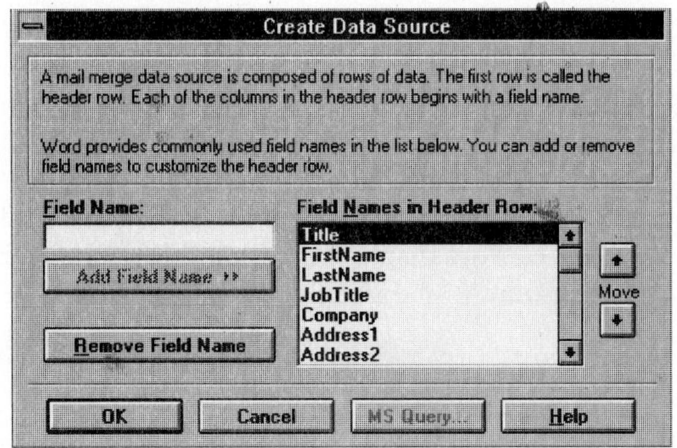

FIGURE 14-3

The Create Data Source dialog box

at the top of each column in the first *header row*. Finally, the new buzzword is record. Think of the rows that contain information in the table—each one of these makes up an individual record. A *record* is one complete set of information, such as name, address, and phone number.

The list box in Figure 14-3 contains most of the common field names used in preparing form letters. If you scroll through it, you will see another six possibilities. If you click on OK without making any changes in the Create Data Source dialog box, Word will store a table with *all* the column headings listed under Field Names in the Header Row. This is almost certainly more information than you need in your data source; it's a good idea to get rid of the field names you don't need. For example, if you don't need the JobTitle field, just highlight it and click on the Remove Field Name button. Continue this process until you have only the items you need for your form letter in the Field Name in Header Row list box.

You can also add field names in case what you need is not already listed. You can use any combinations of letters and numbers, but spaces are not allowed. What you choose for the field names doesn't matter but it is a good idea to use simple mnemonic ones. For example, DateOfBirth is a good choice for a field name, if you need this information. (Since we can't have any spaces, we have made it as easy to read as possible by using initial caps: DateOfBirth is easier to read for most people than DATEOFBIRTH.) To add a field name, enter some sort of descriptive name in the Field Name text box and click on the Add Field Name button.

You can also change the order of field names by using the two Move buttons at the far right side of the Create Data Source dialog box. Keep in mind, however, that *the order of field names in this dialog box need have no relationship to the order in which you use the corresponding merge field names in the form letter.* (For example, you'll probably need a person's last name twice—once in his or her address and once in the salutation—but you only have to have it once in the data source.)

After you are done modifying the list of field names, click on the OK button. Word displays a standard Save dialog box so you can save the data source, an example of which is shown here:

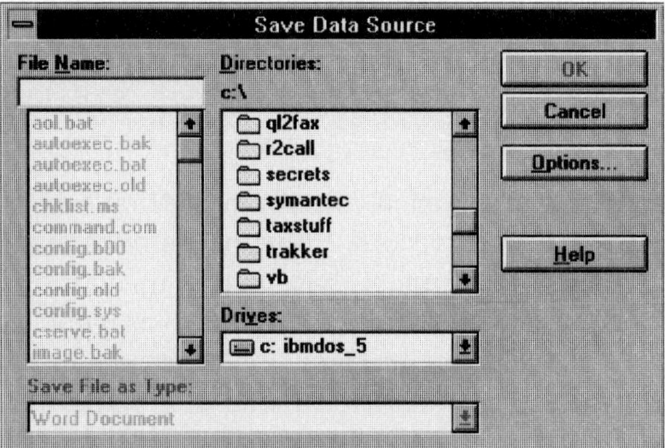

Choose the directory and drive where the data source will be saved, and give it a descriptive name so you can remember which mail merge it is associated with. Then add a three-letter extension if you want to. (Since the data source is a Word document, the default is .DOC). When you are done saving the data source, Word pops up this dialog box:

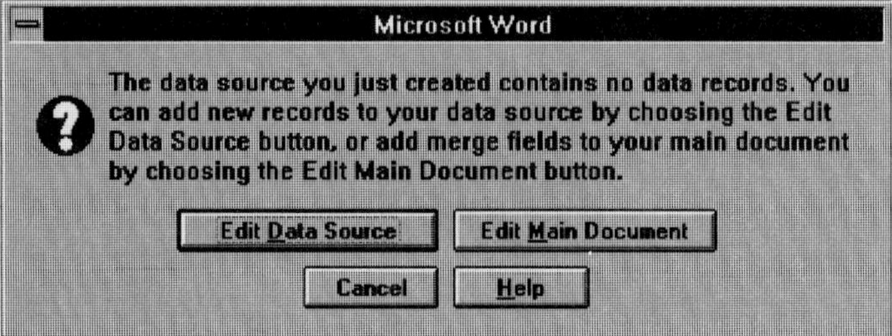

As you can see, this message box indicates that your data source "contains no data records." (In plain English, you have created a table with column headings, and now you need to fill in the rows.) Filling in the rows—adding the data records—is covered in the next section. To move on to this step, click on the Edit Data Source button in this dialog box.

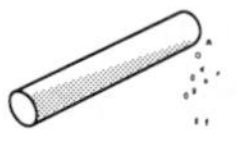

NOTE *You do not have to fill in the data source at this time. If you return to the main document by clicking on the Edit Main Document button, you can return later to fill in the data source by:*

1. Choosing the Mail Merge Helper again (Alt T, R).
2. Clicking on the Edit button and choosing the name of the data source.

You can stop the process of doing a mail merge at this time and return to it later by saving the main document and then closing it. To continue the mail merge process at a later date,

1. Open the main document again using the Open command from the File menu and choose the Mail Merge Helper once more (Alt T, R).
2. Now you can click on the Get Data button and choose Open Data Source to tell Word the name of the file for the data source.
3. Click on the Edit button and choose the data source to start adding records again.

ADDING DATA TO THE DATA SOURCE

After you have saved the document that contains the initial information for the data source (the names of the fields), you need to fill in the data. This is exactly what you told Word you wanted to do when you clicked on the Edit Data Source button a moment ago. When you do this, Word takes you to the Data Form dialog box, which looks like the following, if you still had all the fields. (In general, it would show only the fields you have left.)

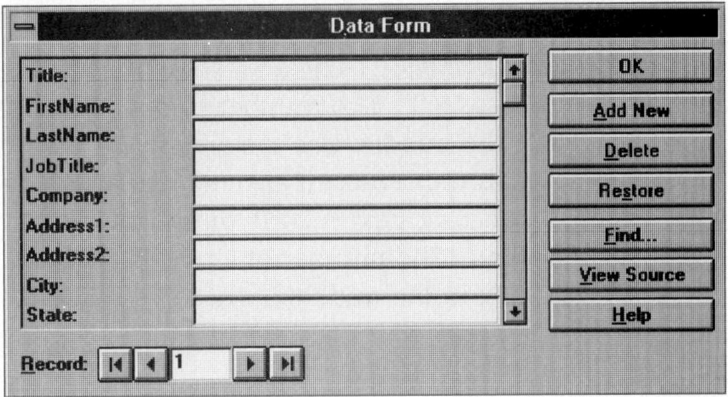

The Data Form dialog box has a line for each field name you have in your data source. In other words, this dialog box has blanks where you can fill in the information needed to fill in one row of your data table. Word created the data form by looking at the field names (the column headings) that you created earlier. Remember each (completed) row of your data table will be called a record. For example, each title, name, address, and so on for a single person would be considered one record.

Enter the information needed to fill out the record and then click on the Add New button to add a new record. You can move around this dialog box using the mouse or the Tab key, and you can use ordinary Word editing techniques to correct mistakes. (If you have a lot of field names, you may need to scroll down through the list box to see them all.) You repeat the process (enter data and click on the Add New button) for each record (set of data) to be included in the data source.

NOTE *If you are in a main document you can always add new data to a data source by:*

1. Choosing Mail Merge from the Tools menu.
2. Clicking on the Edit button and choosing the name of the data source from the list that drops down (or opening the file containing the data source if it is not already open).

OTHER OPTIONS IN THE DATA FORM DIALOG BOX

You have already seen how the Add New button adds new information to the data source. It's worth becoming familiar with the other elements in the Data Form dialog box; they make it easy to review and revise what you have already entered. Here are short descriptions of most of the other options in the Data Form dialog box.

The Record Buttons The area shown here looks a little bit like the buttons on a VCR. The number of the record (the row in the table) is shown in the middle. Use the arrow buttons to review what you have already entered. You can also use them to move to the first record, previous record, next record, or last record in your data source. You can also enter the number of a record that you want to go to directly in the text box in the middle of these VCR-like controls.

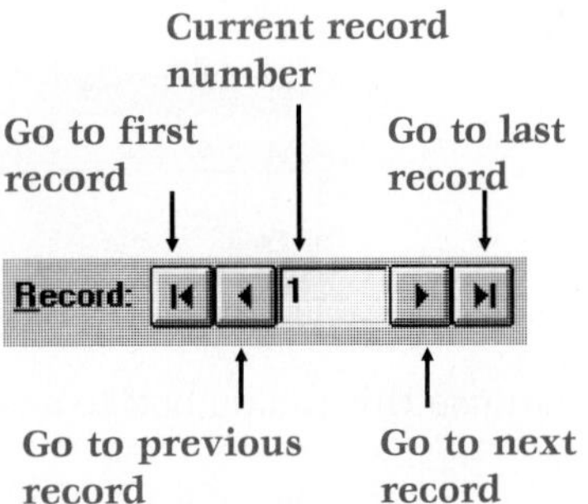

When you use the VCR-like buttons to review records you must be careful: clicking on one of these VCR buttons replaces the original information in the record with what is *currently* shown in the Data Form dialog box. Do not modify information in the text boxes in this dialog box and then click on one of these VCR-like buttons unless you really want to modify the information in that record.

On the other hand, if you do want to modify an existing record, use this feature as follows:

1. Move back to the record you want to modify using the VCR-like buttons; Word displays the information you have already entered in that record in the Data Form dialog box.
2. Make the changes you want.

At this point you need to tell Word to record these changes. You can click on any of the arrow buttons to do this. However, because of the danger of accidently overwriting existing records with bad information, it is safer to use the "go to last record" VCR button to go back to the end of the table. This way you are less likely to inadvertently modify an entry that you don't want to.

The Delete Button Click the Delete button and Word removes the current data record from the data source. (The current data record is the one that is showing up in the Data Form dialog box.)

The Restore Button Click the Restore button if you have made a mess of editing a record and want to restore it to the way it was before you started editing it.

The Find Button The Find button pops up a dialog box that looks like this:

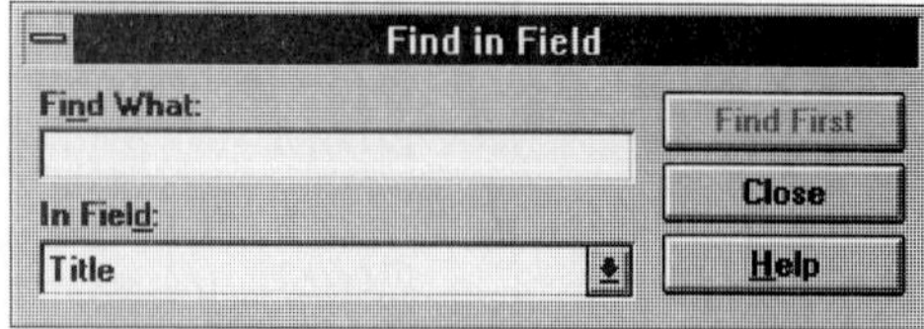

You can use this dialog box to search the data source.

1. Enter what your searching for in the Find What text box and pick the field name from the In Field drop-down list box. You don't have to enter the complete contents of the field. For example, Word will search using only part of a name.
2. Click on the Find First button to display the first matching record it finds. (Of course, Word may not find anything. It would then pop up a message box telling you "the search item was not found.") If Word does find a record that matches your search criterion, you can then modify the record if you need to by using the techniques you saw earlier.

EXAMPLES

1. Suppose you write a letter to a senator that looks like this:

   1/1/94

   Big Talk
   The Senate Of The United States
   Washington DC, 20515

   Dear Senator Big Talk,

   You have done a lot of silly things during the years you have been in Congress, but your vote on S93-1055 takes the cake. This is sure to remain one of the stupidest bills to be approved by Congress for the remainder of this century.

   Sincerely yours,

   Unfortunately, you decide that you need to make this into a form letter for future use. To convert this document into a form letter, follow these steps:

a. Remove the name of the senator and the number of the bill; leave the space they occupied intact. Then call up the Mail Merge Helper and click on the Create button. Choose Form Letters from the list that pops up and then click on the Active Window on the message box that pops up.

b. The form letter for the senators will need to change only the following information:

First Name
Last Name

Click on the Get Data button, choose Create Data Source and then remove all the fields except FirstName and LastName.

c. To enter all 100 senators names now, click on the Edit Data Source button that pops up and fill in the information. Otherwise, you can always return to the Mail Merge Helper at a later point when the main document is open, click on the Edit button, and add the information. An example of how you need to fill in the Data Form dialog box is shown here:

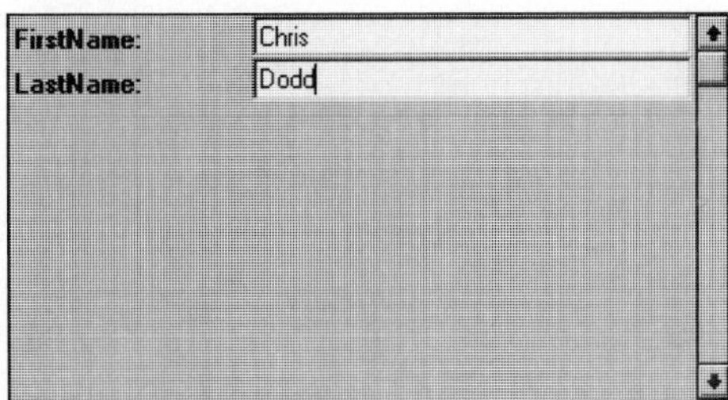

2. You now have filled in all 100 entries and Senator Feinstein is appointed to the Supreme Court and will be replaced by Barbara Streisand. You want to find her record in order to edit it. Choose Find from the Data Form dialog box and fill in the Find in Field dialog box as shown here:

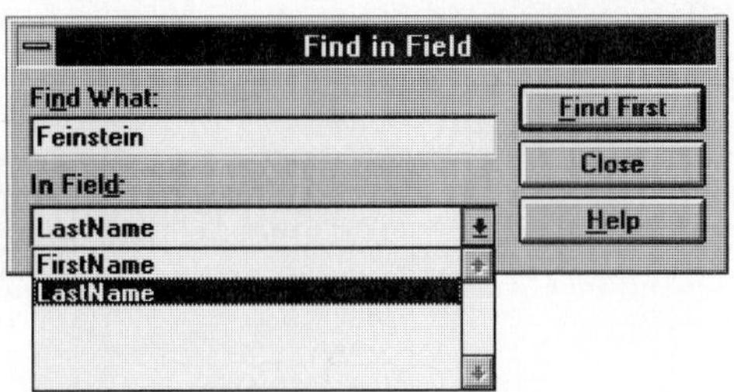

Click on the FindFirst button and then change the information in the data form and then click on one of the VCR-like buttons to make this change to your table.

THE VIEW SOURCE BUTTON AND THE DATABASE TOOLBAR

When you click on the View Source button in the Data Form dialog box, Word pops up a document screen that contains the data in your data source in the form of a table. The title bar of this document shows the data source name. Many people prefer to work with their data in tabular form, using the buttons on the Database toolbar (shown here) as needed.

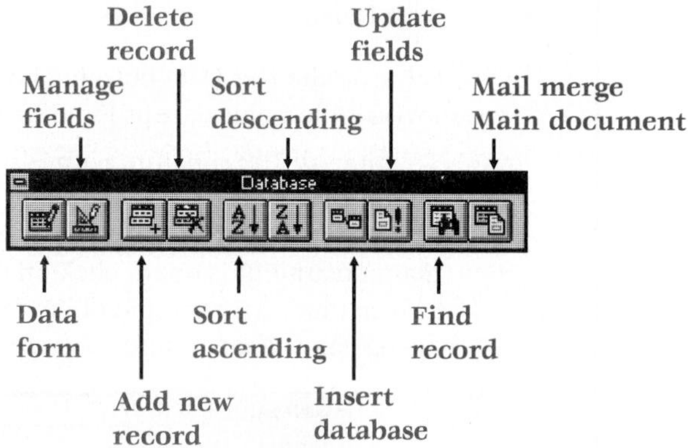

If the Database toolbar is not visible, choose Toolbars from the View menu (Alt V, T) and make sure the Database Toolbar check box is selected.

The callouts to these buttons describe their functions quite well. For example, the Data Form button brings up the Data Form dialog box, the Find Record button pops up the same dialog box as the Find button does in the Data Form dialog box, the Add Record button adds a row to the end of the table, and the Delete Record button removes the record where the insertion point is.

One useful button that gives you access to a power you haven't yet had is the Manage Fields button. If you click on this, Word pops up a screen that looks like this:

(In general, you will see all the fields in your data source.)

Highlight the field you want to remove, or enter the name of the field you want to add, and click on the Remove or Add button.

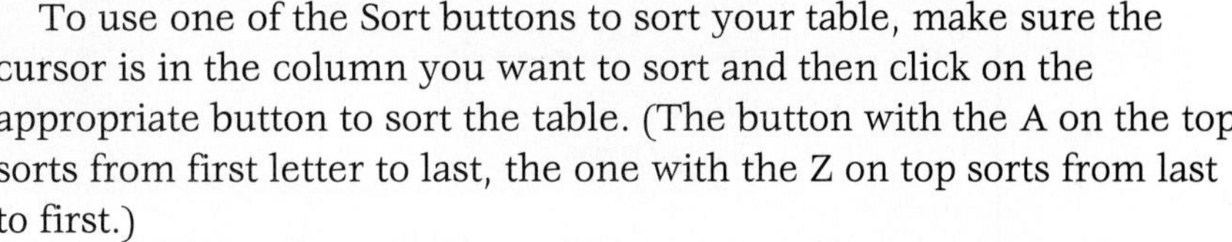

To use one of the Sort buttons to sort your table, make sure the cursor is in the column you want to sort and then click on the appropriate button to sort the table. (The button with the A on the top sorts from first letter to last, the one with the Z on top sorts from last to first.)

CONVERTING AN EXISTING TABLE TO A DATA SOURCE

As you might expect, if you already have made a table of names and addresses (see Chapter 10), you can use this table as a data source. For this:

1. Copy the table to a new document.
2. Make sure the insertion point is inside the table.
3. Choose the Data Form button from the Database toolbar.

When you save the document containing the (converted) table, you can use it as a data source for any mail merge document.

TIP *If you keep a simple database of names and addresses in a table in Word, you can use the Sort buttons on the Database toolbar to keep them organized. If your list grows too long to easily find a name, you can use the Find button on the Database toolbar to find a specific name.*

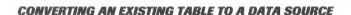

EXAMPLES

1. Let's assume you made up a form letter to mail to all the senators and you originally had a title field for each senator. You had already filled in the information in the data source and used the View Source button on the Data Form dialog box to see the information in the form of a table. You now decide that it would be more politic to call them all Senator rather than Mr., Ms., or Mrs. To do this, click on the Manage Fields button in the Database toolbar and fill in the dialog box as shown here:

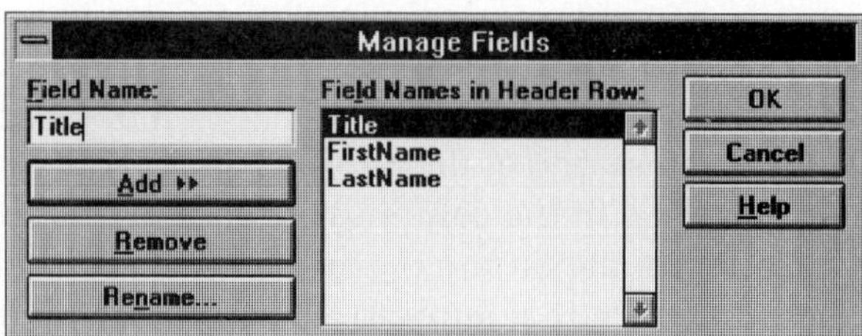

2. Again suppose you are looking at the information about the senators in tabular form. You now decide you want to sort the names in your Senator table by last names from last to first. Make sure the insertion point is in the second column and click on the Sort Descending button (the Z to A button).

ADDING FIELD NAMES TO A MAIN DOCUMENT

It is certainly a long road before we can actually carry out a mail merge but we are getting near the end. Let's assume you have long since added the text that will be the same in all the form letters to the main document. You have also created the data source. You now need to tell Word where to place the "personalized" information in your form letter. In Word, this is called placing merge fields into your main document. (Remember, a merge field is nothing more than placeholders for the data Word will eventually place in your document.)

First you need to go back to the main document. If you have used the View Source button to see the data source in tabular form, click on the Mail Merge Main Document tool on the Database toolbar. If not, choose Mail Merge from the Tools menu and click on the Edit button in the Mail Merge Helper dialog box. Choose the name of your main document from the list box that drops down.

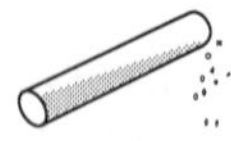

NOTE *You can also choose the main document from the Window menu (see Chapter 11) or reopen it from the File menu if need be.*

First notice that when you returned to the main document, Word added a new toolbar to the window containing the main document. This is called the Mail Merge toolbar, and it looks like this:

To insert merge fields in your document:

1. Place the insertion point where you want to put a merge field.
2. When the insertion point is where you want to merge information (such as first name) from the data source, click on the Insert Merge Field button on the Mail Merge toolbar.
3. From the list of fields that drops down, choose the field that you want to appear at the insertion point.
   Notice that the field name is surrounded by double angle brackets like this: < <first> >, < <last> >, and so on.
4. Repeat the procedure in steps 1 to 3 until you've inserted all the merge fields you need.
5. Now save your document.

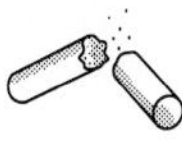

CAUTION *All fields must be inserted via the Mail Merge toolbar. You cannot just type their names and add double angle brackets (<< >>) around them.*

Finally, at what point you add the merge fields to your documents is just a matter of taste. Word will allow you to add them any time after you have specified the field names for the data source—you don't have to wait until you have entered all the data in the data source.

EXAMPLES

1. Suppose you want to add the merge fields for a form letter to the members of the senate.
   a. Enter the main document, which looks like this (leave a line above the address for the date and another line for the name of the senator):

      Senator

      The Senate Of The United States
      Washington DC, 20515

      Dear Senator

      Doesn't this steady diet of pork give you terrible hardening of the moral arteries? I am referring specifically to your affirmative vote on the bill to make the home of Deanna Durbin a national park.

      Sincerely yours,

b. Move the insertion point to the top line of the document and choose Date and Time from the Insert menu. Then choose the date format you like from the dialog box that pops up, making sure that the Insert As field check box is on in the Date and Time dialog box.

c. Move to the end of the line that says Dear Senator. Press the Spacebar once, and then insert a merge field for the Senator's last name. Then enter a comma after the merge field.

CARRYING OUT THE MERGE

Let's suppose you have finished creating the main document, added the field names as needed, and finished adding records to the data source. You are now ready to actually tell Word to do the merge! Word is quite flexible: you can merge only a specific record from your data source or you can merge all records from your data source simultaneously. You can even use Print Preview from the File menu to check whether what you will get is what you want.

To merge the data source with the main document:

1. Make sure the main document is the active document.
2. Click on the View Merge Data button on the Mail Merge toolbar.

Word shows you how the merged document will look by placing the information from the current record (shown by the number in the center of the Mail Merge toolbar) in the corresponding merge fields in the main document. (Remember, merge fields are placeholders!) Now you can print this merged document by choosing Print from the File menu. To preview other documents, click on the appropriate VCR-like buttons in the Mail Merge toolbar.

Once you are satisfied, you can print all the form letters in one fell swoop by clicking on the Merge to Printer button. However, it is probably safer to preview a random sample of the merged documents before doing this. You can also make one giant Word document out of the merged documents by choosing the Merge To New Document button; then you can print all the letters later on.

You can also continue to use the Mail Merge Helper to do the merge once you have set up the main document and the data source. After you have finished these tasks, the Merge button in the Mail Merge Helper will be active. If you click on the Merge button in the Mail Merge Helper, you are taken to a screen that looks like this:

The problem is that this gives you somewhat less flexibility in seeing what you are doing—checking what you have done. If you know you will be happy with the result, just make sure the All button is checked and then click on the Merge button.

EXERCISES

1. Create a new document.
2. Select Mail Merge from the Tools menu.
3. Select Create under Main Document and choose Form Letters.
4. Select Get Data under Data Source, choose Open Data Source, and then open DB_PHONE.DOC.
5. Return to the Mail Merge Helper (Alt T, R) and then choose the Edit button in order to insert the following merge fields and text:

   <<First_Name>> <<Last_Name>>
   <<Address>>
   <<City>>, <<State>> <<Zip>>

   Dear <<First_Name>>,

   I have your phone number down as <<Phone>>, is that correct?

6. Select the View Merged Data button from the Mail Merge toolbar and then use the VCR-like buttons to scroll through how the merged documents would look with the addresses in DB_PHONES.DOC.
7. Select the Mail Merge Helper from the Mail Merge toolbar and select Edit under Data Source. Edit the records currently in the data source if required and select OK when you are satisfied.
8. Select Merge to New Document from the Mail Merge toolbar, review the resulting document in Normal and Page Layout view, and then close and discard the document.
9. Challenge Yourself! Create a new main document but this time select Catalog.
   a. Open DB_PHONE.DB.
   b. In the main document insert a one-column by two-row table.
   c. In the first cell enter <<**Last_Name**>>**,** <<**First_Name**>>.
   d. In the second cell enter <<**Phone**>>.
   e. Select Merge to New Document and view the results. How is it different from the form letter?

14.2 GENERATING LABELS AND ENVELOPES

You can use Word's Mail Merge Helper to print addresses on labels or on envelopes using any data source, the ideas are the same. The methods are very similar so if you read one section carefully, you can probably skim the other.

GENERATING LABELS

Let's start with labels. Select Mail Merge from the Tools menu, click on the Create button under Main Document, and choose Mailing Labels. Choose whether you want to use a new document (New Main Document) or the current document (Active Window) from the dialog box that pops up. You now have to create (or use an existing) data source by clicking on the Get Data button and proceeding as you did before to create or modify an existing data source for a form letter. Let's assume the data source already exists. Choose Open Data source from the list that drops down. Then you'll see the Open Data Source dialog box, as shown here:

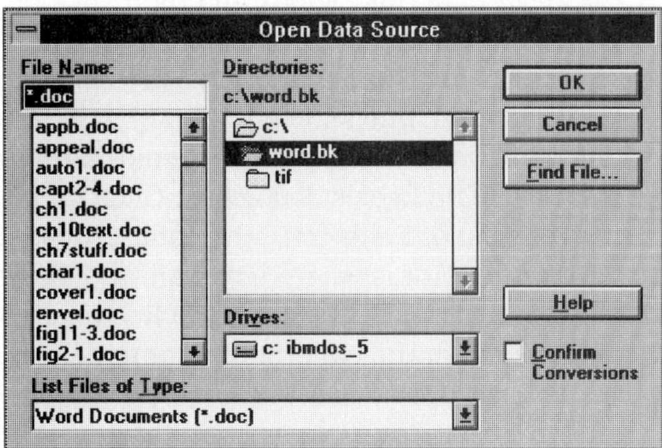

Choose the file that contains the data source and click on OK. Word pops up a message box that looks like this:

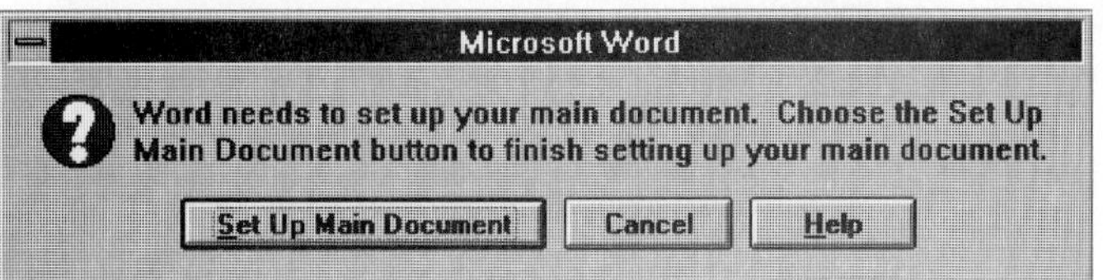

When you click on the Set Up Main Document button, Word will take you to a dialog box like the one shown here that lets you pick the type of label you have.

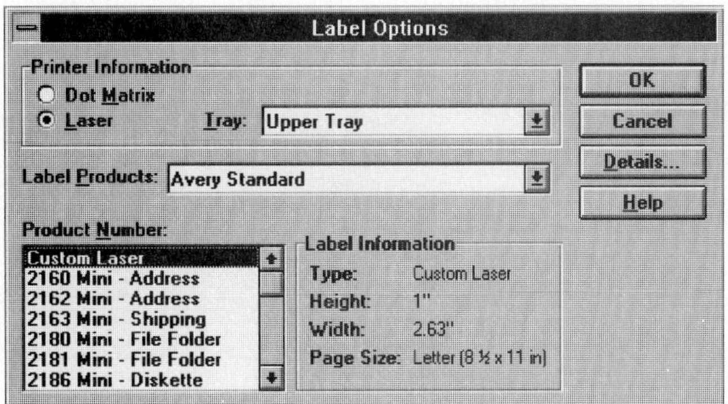

Choose the type of label you will use from the list shown in this dialog box. (Because Avery is the standard, most mailing label companies give the Avery equivalent somewhere on their package.) If you need to create a custom mailing label size, choose the Custom

Laser item in this list box and then click on the Details button to work with the dialog box that pops up.

After you click on OK, Word presents you with a dialog box that looks like the one shown in Figure 14-4. At this point you can add both merge fields and any text you want in the sample label in the middle of the Create Labels dialog box. Click on the Insert Merge Field button to get a list of fields from the data source and, as before, make sure the insertion point is where you want the field to be. Insert any common text you want on the label and click on the OK button when you are satisfied with the content of a sample label.

To insert postal bar codes to speed up your mailing, click on the Insert Postal Bar Code button. From the list of fields that drops down, choose the one that contains the zip code.

TIP *If you want to print a full page of labels with the same information on them, do the following:*

1. Choose the Envelopes and Labels option from the Tools menu.
2. Choose the Labels tab.
3. Fill in the address in the Address text box and make sure that the Full Page of the Same Label button is on.
4. Choose the Options button to go to the dialog box that lets you pick the type of label.
5. After you pick the label, click on OK to go back to the Label tab, put the labels in your printer, and then click on the Print button.

FIGURE 14-4

The Create Labels dialog box

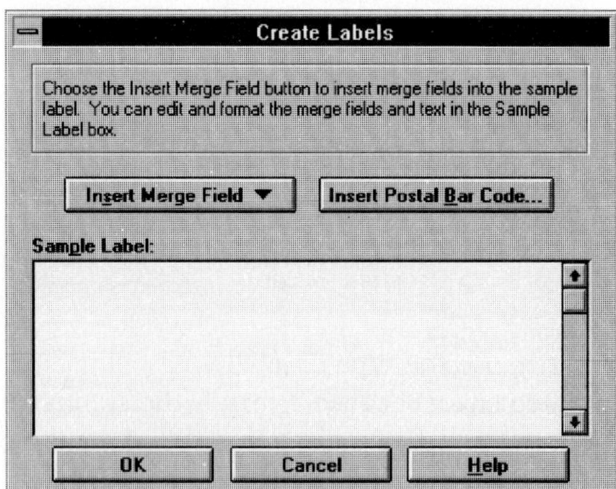

(Since Avery 5267 return address labels will cost you about $10 for 2000, you can save a lot of money printing your own return address labels by using Word's ability to print a full page of the same label. This is especially useful if you are having trouble with envelopes in your laser printer.)

EXAMPLE

1a. Suppose you want to print a mailing label with the senator's name in it. We will assume you already have a data source with the senators' names. Open the mail Merge Helper (Alt T, R) and click on the Create button in the Mail Merge Helper dialog box. Choose Mailing Labels from the list that drops down.

1b. After you choose which document should be your main document, click on the Get Data button to get the data source that contains the senators' names. Now, click on the Setup button and choose the type of mailing label you want. Fill in the fields and address in the label as shown here:

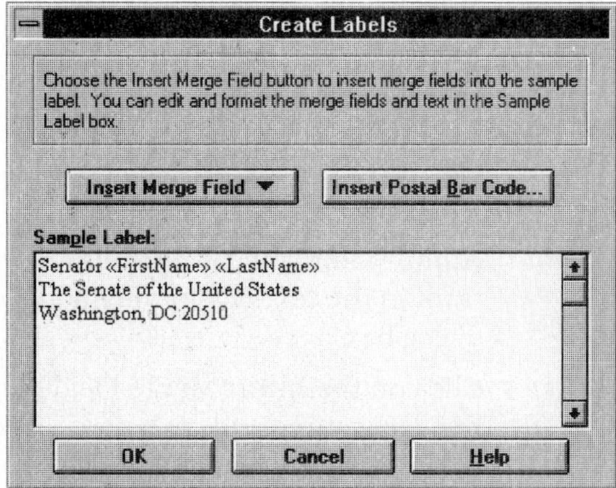

ENVELOPES

You can use the Mail Merge Helper dialog box to also print the names and addresses on the envelopes you will need. Of course, you may find it cheaper to use labels rather than envelopes that are designed for laser printers.

The procedure works similarly to that of printing labels. Let's start with labels.

1. Select Mail Merge from the Tools menu, click on the Create button under Main Document, and choose Envelopes.
2. Choose whether you want to use a new document (New Main Document) or the current document (Active Window) from the dialog box that pops up.
3. You now have to create (or use an existing) data source by clicking on the Get Data button. You can proceed exactly as you did before when you created a data source or modified an existing data source to use for a form letter.

   Let's assume the data source already exists.
4. Choose Open Data source from the list that drops down when you click on the Get Data button. Then Word pops up the Open Data Source dialog box.
5. After you tell Word to open the data source you want to use, click on the Set Up Main Document button to make the main document suitable for use for envelopes.

   Word now presents you with the Envelope Options dialog box.
6. Choose the type of envelope you're going to use by working with the Envelope Size drop-down list box; then click on OK.

   Now you'll see a dialog box like the one shown in Figure 14-5. At this point you can add both merge fields and any text you want in the text box in the middle of the Envelope Address dialog box.
7. Click on the Insert Merge Field button to get a list of fields from the data source and, as before, make sure the insertion point is where you want the field to be. Click on the OK button when you are satisfied with the contents of a sample envelope.

To insert postal bar codes to speed up your mailing,

1. Click on the Insert Postal Bar Code button.
2. From the list of fields that drops down, choose the one that contains the zip code.

FIGURE 14-5

The Envelope Address dialog box

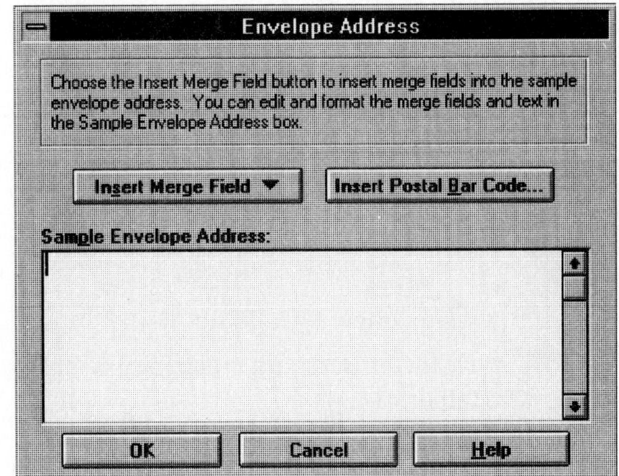

EXERCISES

1. Create a new document.
2. Select Mail Merge from the Tools menu.
3. Select the Create button under Main Document and request Mailing Labels.
4. Select the Get Data button under Data Source, open your DB_PHONE.DOC document, and proceed with setting up a main document by inserting fields for the first name, the last name, and the address and zip code.
5. Select your label options. Just use the defaults if you don't have any particular labels you want to use.
6. Insert a postal bar code on your label and use the Zip Code field from your database for the field where Word will print the zip code.
7. Start the actual mail merge process by Clicking on the Merge button in the Mail Merge Helper and working with the Merge dialog box that pops up. Choose New Document in the Merge To drop down list box in the Merge dialog box.
8. View the main document in Normal and Page Layout views.
9. Close the main document without saving your changes.

1. Create a new form letter. [14.1]
2. Select Get Data and create a new data source from the Mail Merge Helper. [14.1]
3. Create a data file of business addresses by telling Word to create a data source using the Create Data Source dialog box that pops up when you click on the Get Data button in the Mail Merge Helper and choosing Create Data Source from the list that drops down. Add FAXPhone and CellPhone as field names. [14.1]
4. Enter some of your business contacts into the database. When you complete your data entry, select View Source to look at your new data document. [14.1]
5. Edit the form letter you just created and add the following merge fields and text by using the Mail Merge toolbar. [14.1]

<<Title>> <<FirstName>> <<LastName>>
<<JobTitle>>
<<Company>>
<<Address1>>
<<City>>, <<State>> <<PostalCode>>

Dear <<Title>> <<LastName>>:

We enjoy having you as a customer. Thanks!

6. Select View Merged Data on the Mail Merge toolbar and see how the merged letters will look. [14.1]
7. Tell Word to actually merge all the data into one long document by choosing the Merge to New Document button on the Mail Merge toolbar. Preview the results. [14.1]
8. Develop a set of mailing labels from your business address data file. [14.2]

Use the Table Wizard to create a new document with the following characteristics by filling in the screens in the Table Wizard using the data supplied in the following list. (The lines correspond to the settings for successive screens in the Table Wizard.)

1. Choose Table Style 1.
2. Choose no column headings and two columns.
3. Set months in the row headings.
4. Left align the row headings.
5. Most cells will contain centered text.
6. The table will be printed in portrait orientation.

When the Table AutoFormat dialog box appears, just cancel it.

1. Delete the two empty columns and convert the remaining column to text. [10.3]
2. Used Edit, Replace and replace all paragraph marks (use the Special button) with the text **1994** and a paragraph mark. [3.5]
3. Select all the months and add two copies to the end of the document. [3.3]
4. Use Edit, Replace and replace 1994 with 1995 in the second set of months and replace 1994 with 1996 in the last group of months. [3.5]
5. Select all the text and turn it into a table. [10.2]
6. Insert a row at the top of the table, add the text **MONTH**, and use the Headings option on the Table to tell Word that you want the first row to be considered a heading. [10.3]
7. Close the file, saving it as MONTHS.DOC. [2.3]
8. Create a new main document for use in creating mailing labels. To do this,
   a. Open the Mail Merge Helper (Alt T, R) and use the active document as the main document.

   b. Click on the Get Data button in the Mail Merge Helper and tell Word to use MONTHS.DOC as the data source by choosing the Open Data source item.
   c. Choose Setup Document and then choose Avery Worksaver 8 - Tabs as the type of the labels.
   d. Insert the Month field into the Create Label dialog box.
   e. Finally, merge all the data in MONTHS.DOC into a new document. [14.1]

9. Switch to Page Layout view.
   a. Select the first label.
   b. Center the text in the label.
   c. Keeping the label selected, change the font used in the label to Arial.
   d. Start increasing the font using Ctrl+] until you are satisfied with the size of the characters.
   e. Finally, select all the labels (the whole table) and set the font and point size the same as in your first label. [8.1, 10.3, 6.2, 6.1]

10. Select Print Preview from the File menu and check out the results. [9.1]
11. Close the main document without saving it. [1.6]

A

A Ten-Minute Guide to Windows

PROGRAMS such as Word for Windows, which are designed for Microsoft Windows, are supposed to be easy to use—and they *are* once you learn a little jargon and a few basic techniques. This appendix explains the jargon, giving you enough of an understanding of Windows to get you started in Word for Windows.

Although Windows may seem intimidating if you've never used it before, you only need to learn a few basic techniques, which are covered right here. If you decide to go further with Windows, you might take a look at Tom Sheldon's *Windows 3.1 Made Easy* (Osborne/McGraw-Hill, 1992). This book covers what you need to master in order to use Windows for all your computing needs.

CAUTION *It's a bad idea to end Windows by just shutting off your machine. The section "Ending Windows" in this appendix explains how to end Windows properly.*

If Windows ends abnormally because of, say, a power failure, see the section "Abnormal Exits from Windows" for some tricks to try if your machine starts behaving strangely. Strange behavior after an abnormal exit from Windows is uncommon, but it can happen frequently enough to be annoying.

MOUSE POINTERS AND ICONS

When you use Windows, think of yourself as the conductor and Windows as the orchestra. The conductor in an orchestra points to various members, does something with his or her baton, and then the orchestra members respond in certain ways. For a Windows user, the baton is called the *pointing device,* and most often it is a *mouse.* The idea is that, as you move the mouse across your desk, a pointer moves along the screen in sync with your movements. There are two basic types of mouse pointers you will see in Windows.

Arrow The arrow is the ordinary *mouse pointer* that you use to point at various Windows objects before activating them. You will usually be instructed to "move the pointer to...." This really means "move the mouse around your desk until the mouse pointer is at...."

Hourglass The hourglass mouse pointer pops up whenever Windows is saying, "Wait a minute; I'm thinking." This pointer still moves around when you move the mouse, but you can't tell Windows to do anything until it finishes what it's doing and the mouse pointer no longer resembles an hourglass. (Sometimes you can press the Esc key to tell Windows to stop what it is doing.)

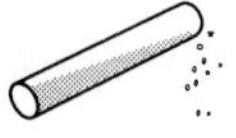

NOTE *The mouse pointer can take on many other shapes, depending on which program you are using and what task you are performing.*

Windows uses *icons* to indicate objects. Here are some typical icons:

File Manager

Paintbrush

As you can see, icons give both a pictorial clue and a textual description of the object.

MOUSE ACTIONS

When you get the (arrow) pointer to a place where you want something to happen, you need to do something with the mouse. There are four basic things you can do with a mouse.

TIP *You can pick the mouse up off your desk and place it in a new spot without moving the mouse pointer. This is useful, for example, when the mouse pointer is in the center of the screen but the mouse is about to fall off your desk!*

Pointing *Pointing* means moving your mouse across your desk until the mouse pointer is over the desired object on the screen.

Clicking *Clicking* (sometimes people say *single clicking*) means pressing a mouse button (usually the left button) once and then quickly releasing it. Whenever a sentence begins "Click on," you need to:

1. Move the mouse pointer until it is at the object you are supposed to click on.
2. Press and release the (left) mouse button.

An example of a sentence using this jargon might be "Click on the button marked Yes." You also will see sentences that begin "Click inside the." This means to move the mouse pointer until it is inside the boundaries of the object, and then click.

Double-Clicking *Double-clicking* means clicking a mouse button (usually the left button) twice in quick succession (that is, pressing it, releasing it, pressing it, and releasing it again *quickly* so that Windows doesn't think you single clicked twice). Whenever a sentence begins "Double-click on," you need to:

1. Move the mouse pointer until it is at the object you are supposed to double-click on.
2. Press and release the (left) mouse button twice in quick succession.

For example, you might be instructed to "double-click on the icon at the far left side of your screen."

NOTE *An important Windows convention is that clicking selects an object so you can give Windows or the program further directions about it but double-clicking tells Windows (or the program) to do something.*

Dragging *Dragging* usually moves a Windows object. If you see a sentence that begins "Drag the," you need to:

1. Move the mouse pointer until it is at the object.
2. Click the (left) mouse button *and hold it down.*
3. Now move the mouse pointer until the object moves to where you want it to be.
4. Finally, release the mouse button.

Sometimes this whole activity is called *drag and drop.*

STARTING WINDOWS

It's possible that, when you turn on your machine, Windows starts without your needing to do anything. If this is the case, you'll probably see a Windows copyright notice, an hourglass pointer while you wait, and then a screen that looks similar to Figure A-1. (Your screen might look a little different because one exciting feature of Windows is that you can change the way it looks to reflect *your* way of working.) What should remain the same is that the top line of your screen will say "Program Manager."

If you see an icon that says Program Manager in the left corner of your screen, double-click on it.

Finally, if instead you see something that looks like this:

```
C:\>
```

then you're at the (infamous) C prompt. This means that the much less friendly DOS program is in control. Type **win** and press Enter to start Windows. If your machine responds with something like "Bad Command," Windows may not be installed on your machine, in which case you'll need to get it installed before you can continue. If you know Windows *is* installed on your system and the above doesn't work, consult the documentation that came with it—or the guru who decided to set Windows up in a nonstandard way.

ENDING WINDOWS

To close Windows, hold down the Alt key and the F4 function key at the same time. (In this book we always indicate simultaneous keypresses with a plus sign. Our shorthand for the previous phrase is "Press Alt+F4.") You are presented with a *message box* that looks like this:

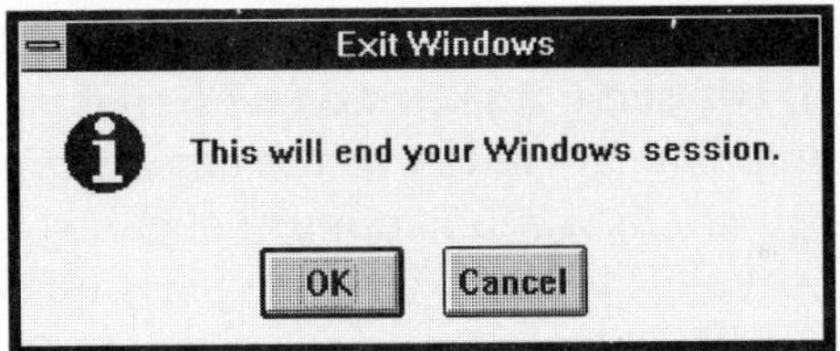

Click on the OK *command button* if you want to shut down Windows, or click on the command button marked Cancel (or press Esc) if you don't want to leave Windows.

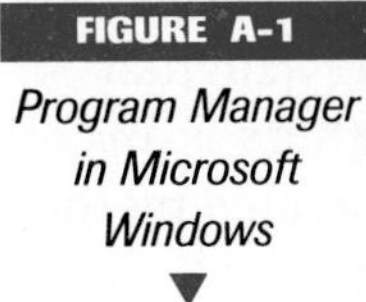

FIGURE A-1

Program Manager in Microsoft Windows

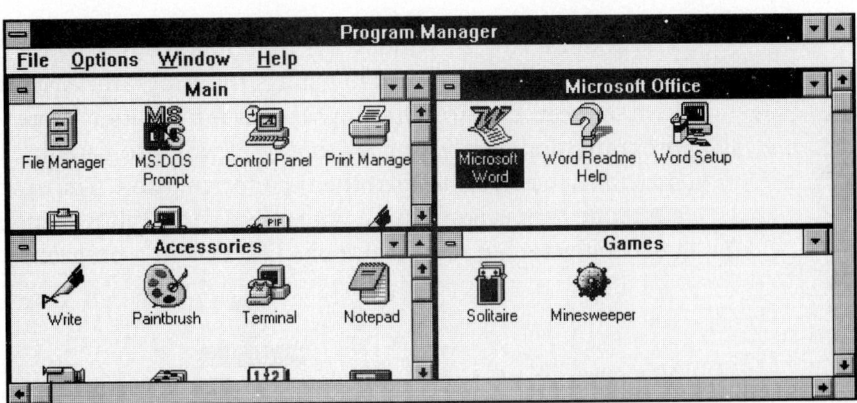

WINDOWS AND ITS LITTLE WINDOWS

Windows gets its name from the way it organizes your screen into rectangular regions. Each rectangular region in the Program Manager is called a *program group window*. The whole region is called the *Windows desktop.* When you run a program, the program runs inside a bordered rectangular box. Unfortunately, Windows jargon also calls all of these *windows*, so there's only a lowercase "w" to distinguish them from the program called Windows.

Think of a program group window as analogous to organizing your desk efficiently by grouping related piles together—as opposed to keeping all your papers in one unwieldy mess. The Program Manager in the Windows desktop starts out with four program group windows. When you install a program like Word for Windows, the installation procedure will usually add another program group window to the Program Manager for the program and its files.

Each rectangular program group window may contain icons. These icons represent files stored on your computer and are usually called *program items*. Some of these icons represent programs that you can run, and some represent *data* stored in your computer. You manipulate a window or the objects represented by the icons inside of it by various combinations of clicking, double-clicking, and dragging.

A typical window with the parts marked is shown in Figure A-2, which also shows the four basic program groups that Windows creates when it is first installed.

STARTING PROGRAMS FROM THE PROGRAM MANAGER

The general rule in Windows is that double-clicking on the icon that represents a program usually starts the program. Also, if there is an icon on your desktop that represents information (data) created by the program, double-clicking on that icon will also usually start the program and tell it to load the data for revision. For example, when someone writes something with Word for Windows and saves the file, you might see an icon that looks like this in a program group window:

FIGURE A-2

The typical parts of a window

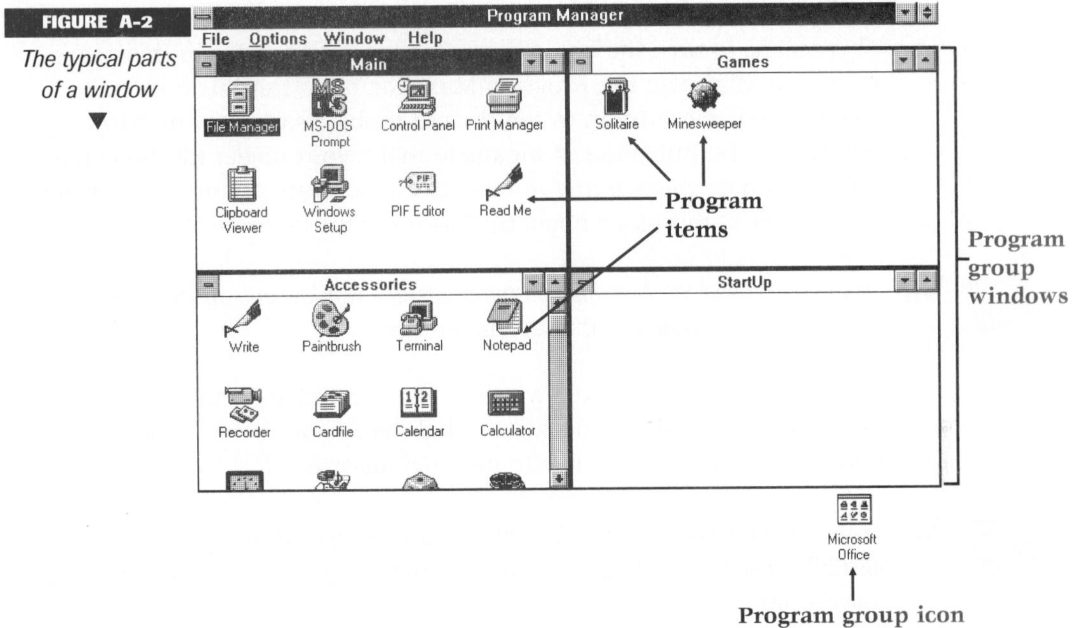

Double-clicking here would start Word for Windows and open that file.

THE TITLE BAR

When Windows' attentions are focused on a specific window, the *title bar* of the window is highlighted, and the window is said to be *active.* The active window is the only one that can be affected by your actions. An example of a sentence you might see is "Make the window active." This means if the title bar of the window is not already highlighted, click inside the window and at this point the (new) window will be responsive to your actions.

Many title bars contain little buttons that you can click to reduce the window to an icon (minimize it), make it fill up the whole screen (maximize it), or close it entirely. The following title bar shows you what to look for:

Typical jargon may include sentences that begin "Minimize the...." This means to turn the object into an icon. An example of this usage might be "Minimize the Program Manager." You minimize items to give yourself more room to see the other objects on your desktop. Similarly, "Maximize the..." means to make your object fill the whole screen. You do this when you want to concentrate on only that object. An example of this usage might be "Maximize the Program Manager."

TIP *If you have used the Minimize button to make a window into an icon, double-click on the icon to restore it to its previous size.*

If you have maximized a window, the Maximize button changes to look like a double-headed arrow called the *Restore button*. Click on this button to return the window to its previous size.

TIP *You can close any active window by double-clicking on its control box. You can also close the active window by holding down the Alt key and pressing the F4 function key.*

When you close the Program Manager window by double-clicking in its control menu box (or using Alt+F4), Windows itself starts to shut down. You are presented with the usual *message box* for shutting down Windows that you saw earlier.

Click on the OK button if you want to shut down Windows, and click on the button marked Cancel if you don't want to shut down Windows.

Finally, as long as the window isn't maximized, you can usually move a window around your screen by *dragging* the title bar of an active window. (Recall that this means to move the mouse pointer until it is in the title bar, hold down the left mouse button, move the mouse until the window is where you want it to be, and then release the mouse button.)

NOTE *You can also drag the icons inside a window to rearrange them.*

RESIZING A WINDOW

You can change the size of a window by minimizing, maximizing, or restoring it. In addition, you can change the size of most windows to exactly suit your needs. To adjust the size of any non-maximized window:

1. Move the mouse pointer until it is at the place on the boundary you want to adjust. The mouse pointer changes to a double-headed arrow.
2. Drag the border to the left, right, up, or down to make it smaller or larger. Which border you want to effect determines which one you drag.

When you are satisfied with the new size of the window, release the left mouse button.

SCROLL BARS

If a window or other Windows object contains more information than can fit on the screen, you need a way to move through this information so you can see it all. For example, you will certainly be writing documents in Word that are longer than one screen. You can use the mouse to march through your documents with small steps or giant steps. A *vertical scroll bar* lets you move from the top to the bottom of the Window; a *horizontal scroll bar* lets you move within the left and right margins of the window. Use this scroll bar when the window is too wide to fit on the screen. Figure A-3 shows the horizontal scroll bar.

As you can see, a scroll bar has two arrows at the end of a channel that also contains a little box (usually called the *scroll box*). The scroll box is the key to moving rapidly; the arrows are the key to moving in smaller increments. Dragging the scroll box enables you to quickly move long distances to an approximate location in your document. For example, if you drag the scroll box to the middle of the channel, you'll scroll to approximately the middle of your document.

MENUS

The jargon is to say that Windows programs are *menu driven*. This just means that you can control the features of the program by choosing items from menus. If you tried to close a window by double-clicking

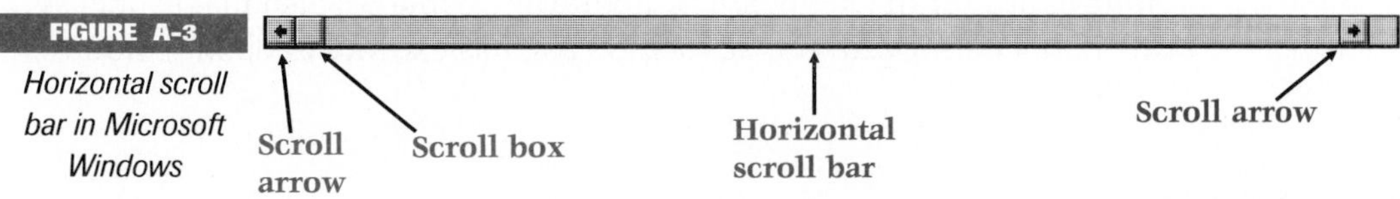

FIGURE A-3 *Horizontal scroll bar in Microsoft Windows*

but only clicked once on the control box by mistake, you may have seen the Control menu shown here:

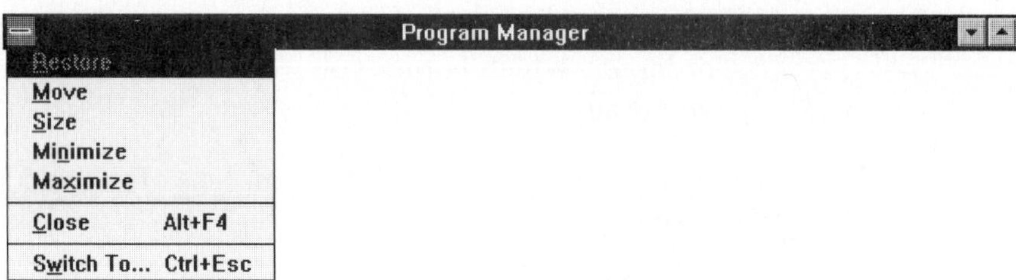

The jargon says "The menu is dropped down" (or "pulled down"). Once a menu is dropped down, there are two ways to pick a menu item (the jargon says "choose the item" or "activate the item").

- Click on the item.
- Use the ↑ and ↓ keys to move through the list of menu items. Each item is successively highlighted. Press Enter when you get to the item you want to choose.

For example, the jargon might say "An alternate way to close a window is to drop down the Control Menu box and choose Close."

Every Windows program has a *main menu bar* that runs right below the title bar; this is how you activate the program's features. (In contrast, the Control Menu box lets you manipulate the window that the program is sitting in.)

Here's an example of the menu bar for the Program Manager:

One way to open a menu is to move the mouse pointer to the name of the menu and click. This can be a disadvantage, especially when working with programs like a word processor because you have to take your hands off the keyboard temporarily. Windows also makes it easy to open a menu with the keyboard. The easiest way to open a menu using the keyboard is to look for the underlined letter of the desired option in the menu bar and then to press Alt and the underlined letter. We will underline that letter for you in this book for easy reference when we are talking about using that menu. Underlined letters are usually called *accelerator keys* or *hotkeys*. For example, if the Program Manager window is active, press Alt F to open the File menu, as shown here:

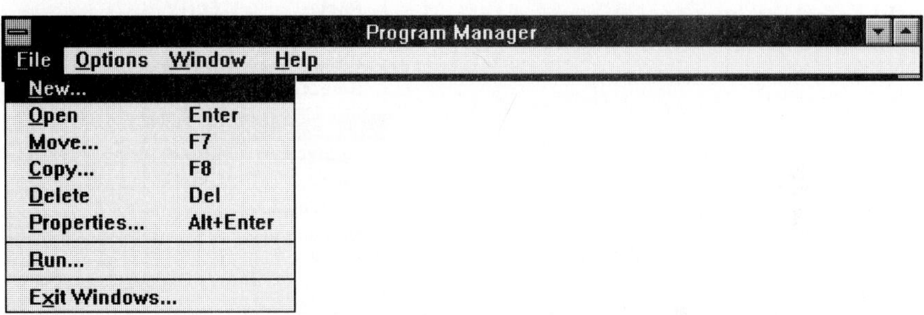

Notice that all of these menu items have underlined hotkeys. You can just press the letter while the menu is open to select the command. (For example, you can press X to exit Windows.)

TIP *You can activate a menu item in one step if you know its hotkey. For example, if you press the Alt key, the F key and the X key in quick succession, Windows opens the File menu and chooses the Exit item.*

In this book, successive key presses are indicated by a comma; Alt F, X describes the key combination described in the above tip.

Some items, like Move or Properties, have keys (or key combinations) listed to their right. These are called *shortcut keys*. A shortcut key is a key or combination of keys you can press to activate an item without opening a menu.

Some menu items have a three-dot *ellipsis* after their names (like Exit Windows in the screen above). The ellipsis indicates that choosing the item is not enough: You need to do more work. Usually choosing one of these options displays a *dialog box* that you will need to work with. Dialog boxes allow you to give the program a lot more information than a simple click on a button can do. We cover dialog boxes in the next section.

Finally, if you cannot use a menu item at the moment, it will appear grayed and clicking on it will have no effect. The jargon is to say that the menu item is *disabled.* Here is a typical example of a menu (from Word for Windows) with roughly half the items disabled and the other half *enabled*.

FINDING PROGRAM GROUPS FROM THE PROGRAM MANAGER'S WINDOW MENU

As you install more Windows programs, you may no longer be able to see the program group window that contains the program you want to work with. There is a surefire method of finding a program group window—if you remember its name:

1. Choose Window from the Program Manager's main menu bar (remember you can do this by pressing Alt W).

This drops down a (long) list of items that looks something like this:

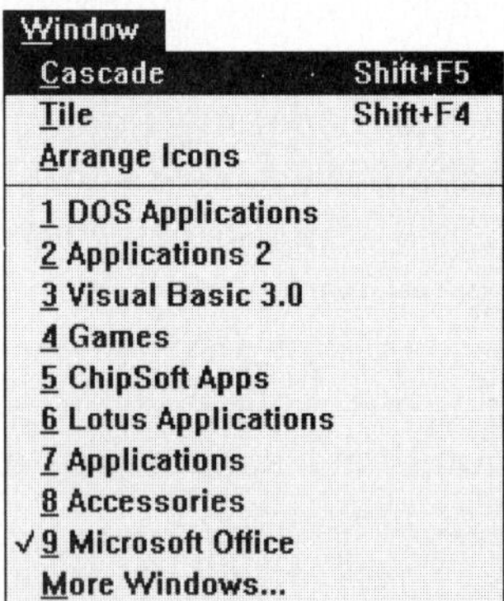

If the program group is listed on this list, click on it or type the number to the left of its name. If not, click on the More Windows item and look through the next list (and so on as needed) until you find the program group you want. Windows opens the program group window for the item you selected.

STARTING PROGRAMS FROM THE PROGRAM MANAGER'S FILE MENU

The general rule in Windows is that double-clicking on the icon that represents a program usually starts the program—but suppose you can't find the icon. As with program group windows, there is a surefire method of starting a program—if you can remember its name. To do this, open the File menu in the Program Manager and choose Run (Alt F, R). This opens a little dialog box that looks like this:

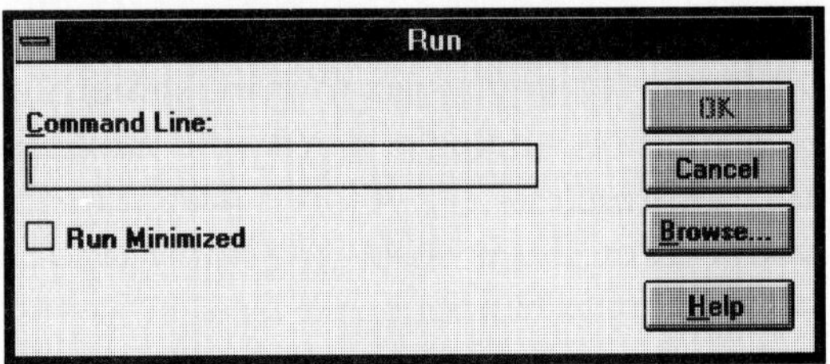

Now type the name of the program in the box labeled Command Line. (You will usually need the full name of the program in order for this to work; for Word for Windows this is usually C:\WINWORD\WINWORD.)

DIALOG BOXES

Working with a dialog box is probably the most common way for you to tell the program what you want it to do. If you read the previous section, you saw the Run dialog box which is available from the File menu in the Program Manager. Generally, you need to fill in the information requested in the dialog box or close it before you can continue working with the program. Almost all dialog boxes have a command button marked Cancel that you can click on if you decide you don't want to work with the dialog box. Often you can press the Esc key to achieve the same effect.

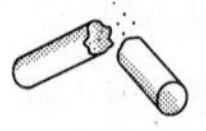

CAUTION *Dialog boxes frequently have a button that goes into effect when you press Enter. This is often but not always the OK button. You can tell which button will be activated when you press Enter by looking for the button with a bold outline around it. (The jargon calls this the default command button for the dialog box or just the default button.)*

Dialog boxes can contain many different elements. You have already seen three of these: the title bar, command buttons (usually "button" for short), and scroll bars. This section shows you the remaining common dialog box features.

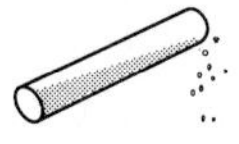

NOTE *If a command button has an underlined access key in its name, you can press Alt and then the access key to have the same effect as clicking on the button. This is useful when you don't want to take your hands off the keyboard.*

Figure A-4 is an example of the Print dialog box you see in Word for Windows when you ask to print something.

Note that a dialog box is an independent window with its own title bar. This means that you can drag it to a more convenient place on your screen if it is obscuring information you need to see. (Dialog boxes usually cannot be resized, however.)

You have already seen command buttons; you click on them to activate or cancel an action. Figure A-4 has five command buttons. One of the most important is the OK button, which tells Word to take the information you have entered and actually print the document. Notice the border around the OK button that indicates that it is the default button for the Print dialog box. If you press Enter when this dialog box is open, Word prints your document. The other important

FIGURE A-4

The Print dialog box

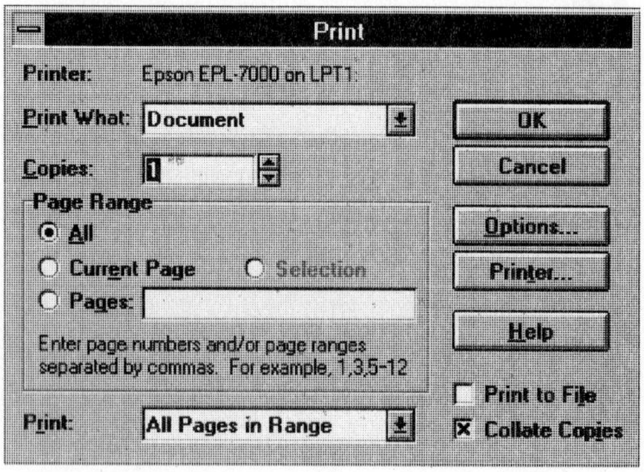

button is the Cancel button, which tells Word that you have decided not to print the document at this time. OK and Cancel buttons appear on almost every dialog box that requests information in a Windows program. Pressing the Esc key is always a shortcut for pressing the Cancel button.

Notice next that two of the command buttons (Options and Printer) have the three-dot ellipses indicating that they lead to dialog boxes requesting additional information. Here are short descriptions of the other items in this dialog box.

Option Buttons *Option buttons* are used to select mutually exclusive choices: Either you print all the pages, one of the pages, or a range of pages, for example. Option buttons generally are grouped within an identifying frame (in the illustration below it's called *Page Range*). To turn on an option button, click in it; this will place a black dot inside of it. If you click on one option button in a frame, the others are turned off. Notice the underlined access key for each option button; pressing Alt and the access key turns the option button on or off. For example, Alt and than an E, turns the Current Page button on if it was off and off if it was on.

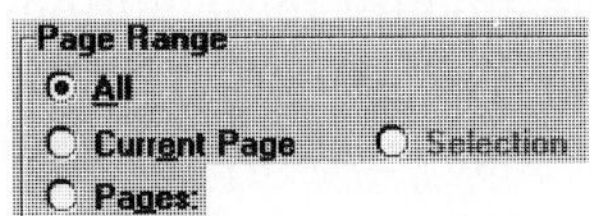

Notice that there is one option button that is currently *disabled*—it's the grayed Selection button.

Check Boxes *Check boxes* are used when there are independent choices. There are two check boxes in the Print dialog box shown in Figure A-4: Print to File and Collate Copies. You click inside the check box to turn that feature on (an "x" will appear); click again to turn it off (the "x" will be removed). If a check box has an access key, then Alt followed by the access key changes it from on or off and vice versa (*toggles it* in the jargon).

Text Boxes *Text boxes* are used to fill in information. In the Print dialog box, the Pages box is a text box. This is because if you wanted to have Word print a range of pages you would need to tell Word which pages to print. Before you can type the information in a text box, you need to point to it and click. Then type the information. A vertical bar (called the *insertion point*) tells you the text box has Word's attention, as shown here:

Insertion point

The jargon is to say that "you have moved the focus to the text box."

TIP *Text boxes often will have underlined access keys. For example, if you were working with the Print dialog box and used* Alt G*, Word would immediately move the focus to the Pages text box so that you could enter the needed information.*

Text Boxes with Spin Buttons The Copies box is another type of text box; you'll see this type of box whenever you can increase or decrease the quantity listed in the text box. Each click on the up arrow increases the number in the text box (by one in this case), and each click on the down arrow decreases the number in the text box (also by one in this case). The amount these buttons increase or decrease is determined by the designers of the program for what seems appropriate for the text box. These arrow buttons are usually called *spin buttons*.

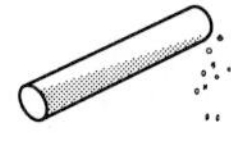

NOTE *Most of the time people just call these text boxes and do not give them their full name. If you see a text box with buttons like the ones described above while using Word For Windows, you will know you can click on them to increase or decrease the quantity that shows up in the text box.*

Drop-Down List Boxes The Print dialog box uses what are called *drop-down list boxes*, as shown here:

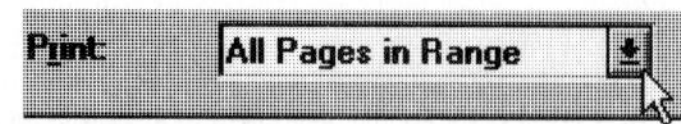

Clicking on the downward-pointing arrow "drops down" a list of possibilities, as shown in the following illustration. The jargon would say "Drop down the list of...." Once the list is revealed, click on the desired item to select it.

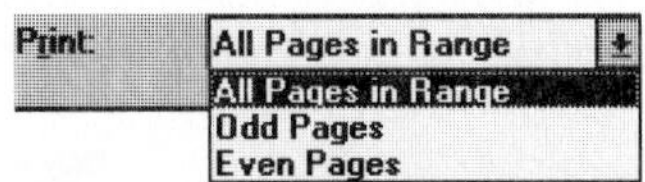

Drop-down list boxes can be sufficiently long that they need scroll bars to let you move through the list. For example, Word can handle so many types of files that if you drop down the List Files of Type drop-down list box, as shown here, Word has to add scroll bars.

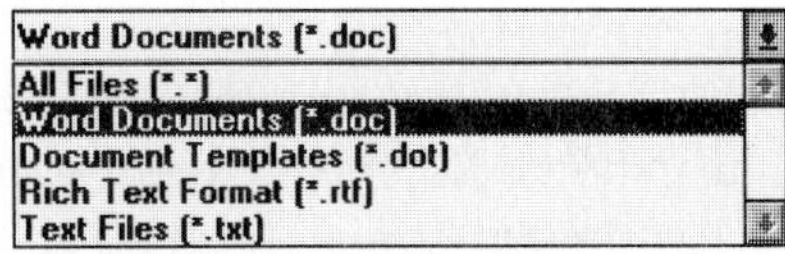

There are also ordinary list boxes that let you see the items without having to drop down. Examples of these boxes are shown in the next section.

FILE HANDLING DIALOG BOXES

In Windows programs, you will also encounter dialog boxes for working with files. Here is the Open dialog box from Word, which is typical of the dialog boxes you'll see when working with files:

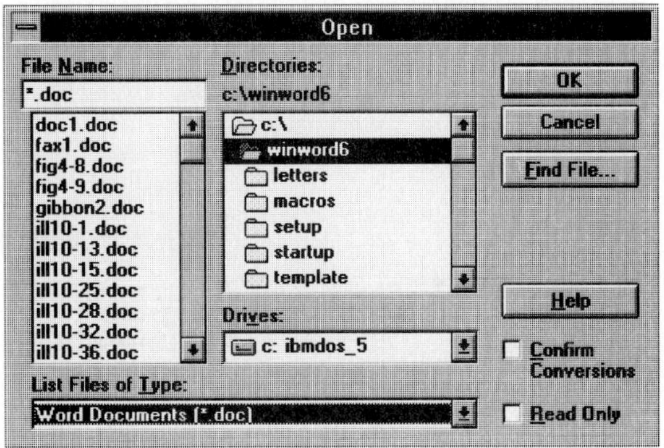

Most of the elements in these dialog boxes resemble those you saw in the previous section. There are command buttons, a couple of check boxes, drop-down list boxes for List Files of Type, Drives, and so on.

For example, if you click on the drop-down list box marked Drives, you see a list of the drives on your machine, as shown here:

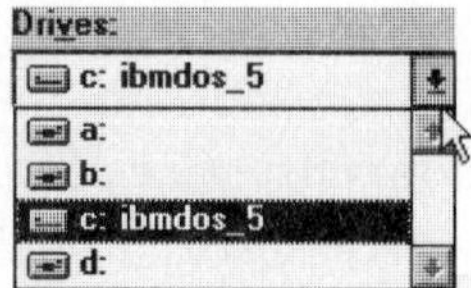

You would now click on the drive to tell Windows to look at the files contained in the new drive.

The one dialog box element you haven't yet seen is usually called an *ordinary list box*, or, simply, a *list box*. A list box works exactly the same as a drop-down list box—except you don't have to click on the arrow to see what the list contains. The list of file names on the left side of the Open dialog box is an example of an ordinary list box. The idea is you click once to select a file in this list box (it will then fill the text box marked File Name), or you can double-click to actually open the file.

REMEMBER *The Windows convention is that clicking on an item selects it; double-clicking activates it.*

Obviously, what "activate" means depends on the dialog box. In our example, double-clicking a file in a dialog box called Open would, naturally enough, *open* it.

The Directories list box in a file handling dialog box works a little differently than a regular list box. Here is an example of a Directories list box in the Open dialog box:

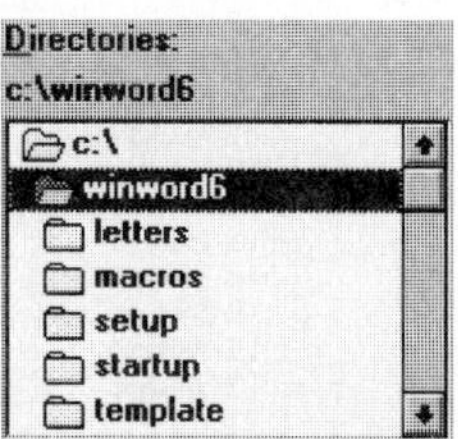

Think of a directory as a kind of file in a giant filing cabinet. These files are special in that they can contain other files—which can in turn contain other files and so on. The little icons next to the names of the directories makes this clear. The file icon is shown as open if Word is looking at files inside this "cabinet." You can have a whole chain of these open filing cabinets (also know as open directories).

When you see the directory you want the program to look for files in, *double-click* on its name. If the directory contains other directories, double-clicking forces the program to look at only those directories above and below the directory you clicked on.

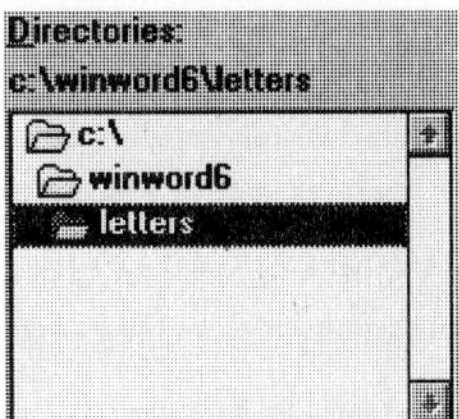

If the directory contains other directories, this forces the program's attention deeper into the cabinet. The jargon for this is "to move up and down the directory tree." You should also be aware that the jargon sometimes talks about *subdirectories*. This is simply a directory that is inside another directory. The directory that contains the subdirectory is called the *parent directory*. The top directory is called the *root directory*.

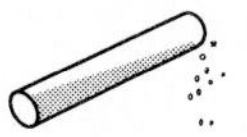

NOTE *All Windows programs automatically update the File Name list whenever you move up the directory tree by double-clicking or when you change drives via the Drives drop-down list box.*

HOW FILES ARE NAMED

Although this is not, strictly speaking, part of Windows, you do need to know the rules for file names to go further with Word for Windows. A *file name* is a way to completely identify one of the files in your giant filing cabinet described above—so you need to specify which filing cabinet and ultimately what the name of the actual file folder is. The jargon would say that a file is "identified by its path and its file name."

Think of the *path* as the name of the filing cabinet and the file name as the name of the folder.

Lets start with the rules for file names: A file name has two parts: The first can be up to eight characters, the second (called the *extension*) is optional. The extension consists of a period followed by up to three characters. No spaces are allowed, case is irrelevant, and you can use any characters except for these:

. " / \ [ ] : | <> + = ; ,

So SNAFU.MY is an acceptable file name with MY as the extension. SNAFU.MY! is also an acceptable file name, but MY.SNAFU is not acceptable as the extension is too long. "SNAFU" = MY is also not allowed for three separate reasons: It uses quotes, it contains an equal sign, and it is too long.

Extensions are like last names; it's customary to give related files the same extension. For example, files that you create with Word for Windows usually have the extension DOC (for document). CHAPTER1.DOC is the name I used for the first chapter of this book (which, of course, was written using Word for Windows). Notice that the (main) name is exactly eight characters long—so the file for Chapter 11 had to be called CHAP11.DOC (and not CHAPTER11.DOC) when this book was being prepared.

The path name consists of the names of the directories (which follow the rules for file names) separated by backslashes (\). The actual file name *does not* end in a backslash. For example, the name of the Word for Windows program after the usual installation is

C:\WINWORD\WINWORD.EXE

which means that the program is in the WINWORD subdirectory of the C:\ root directory. Many sample files that come with Word for Windows are stored in the C:\WINWORD\WORDCBT subdirectory and thus their actual file names would be something like:

C:\WINWORD\WORDCBT\SAMPLE1.DOC

FILE MANAGER

The File Manager is a special Windows program that you can use to copy files and disks, make new directories and so on. Mastering the

File Manager is probably the most important thing you need to do in order to master Windows. However, since this is not a book on Windows, what you'll see here is only a tiny sample of what the File Manager can do for you. We concentrate on three vital tasks:

- Formatting floppies in order to make backups

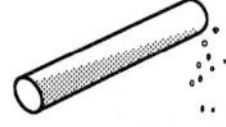

NOTE *Disks can't accept data if they haven't been formatted. If you format a disk you wipe out any data that was on it.*

- Making new directories to store information in a more organized fashion
- Copying disks

(You can also do these tasks directly from DOS if you know how, of course.)

STARTING THE FILE MANAGER

One way to start the File Manager is to look for an icon in the Main program group that looks like this:

Double-click on this icon to start the File Manager. The other way to start the File Manager is to fill out the Run dialog box that pops up when you open the File menu in the Program Manager and choose Run (Alt F, R), as shown here:

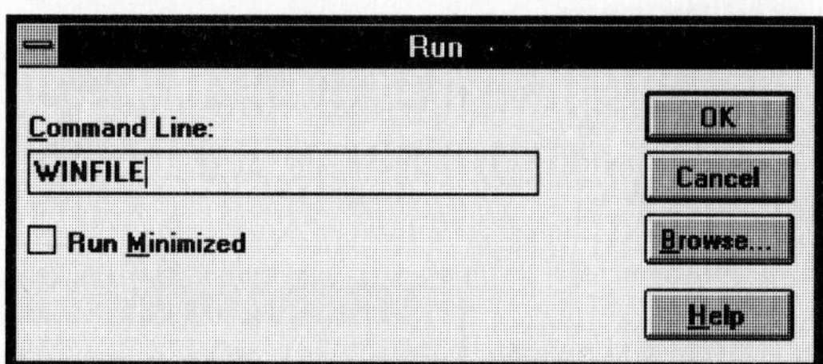

In any case, you will see the main screen of the File Manager, which is shown maximized in Figure A-5. As with any Windows program, you control the File Manager from its menus. Notice the *directory tree* shown in the far left side of Figure A-5. The right side of the File Manager screen shows you the files (and directories) in the directory that is highlighted on the left. Directories are always indicated in the

FIGURE A-5

The File Manager in Microsoft Windows

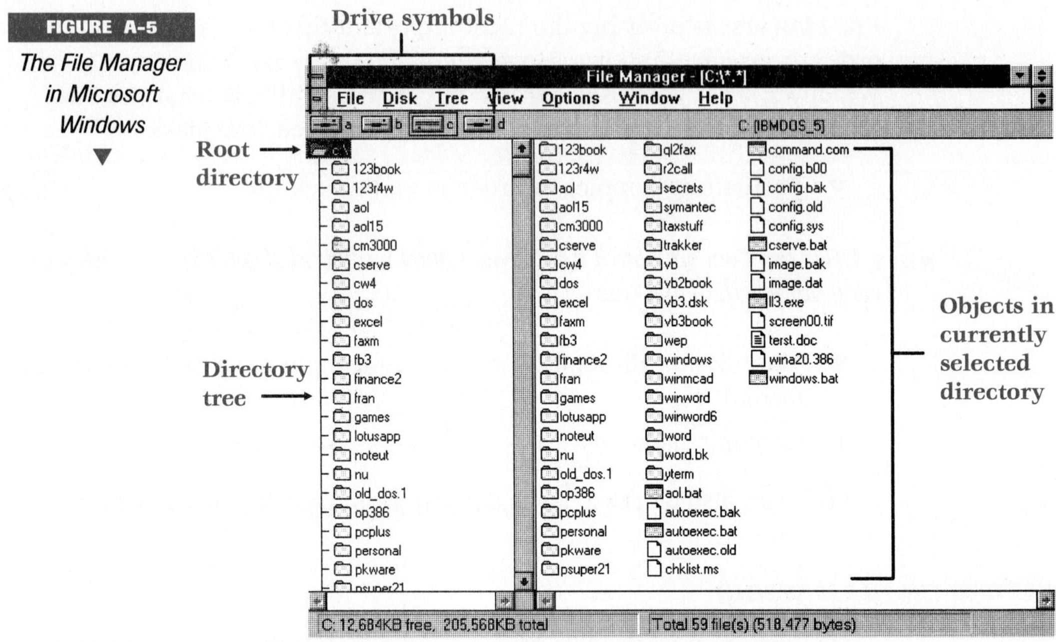

File Manager by icons resembling file folders. Use the scroll bars to move through the directory tree if it is very long.

To switch Windows's attention to the directory and files contained on a different drive, double-click on the drive symbols near the top of the File Manager screen (in Figure A-5 there are four possible drives). Finally, to leave the File Manager, make sure its title bar is active and then press Alt+F4.

FORMATTING A FLOPPY DISK

To format a floppy disk from the File Manager, open the Disk menu and choose Format Disk (Alt D, F). This opens a dialog box that looks like this:

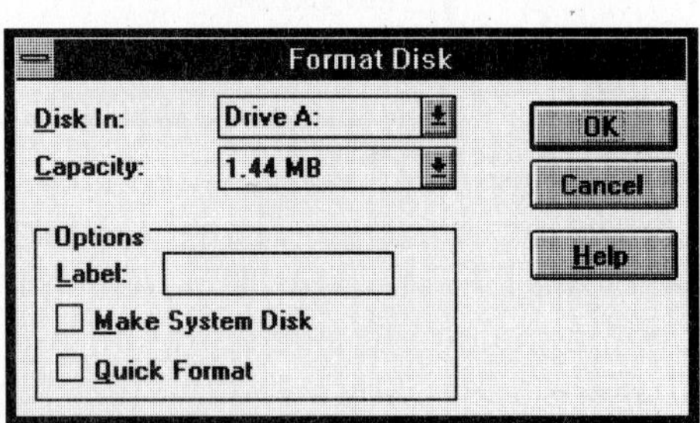

If you are satisfied with the defaults that the File Manager presented you with, click on OK. If not, scroll through the Disk In drop-down list box and choose the drive you want to format the floppy in. Similarly, scroll through the Capacity drop-down list box and choose the right capacity for your disk. When you click on OK Word pops up a message box that looks like this:

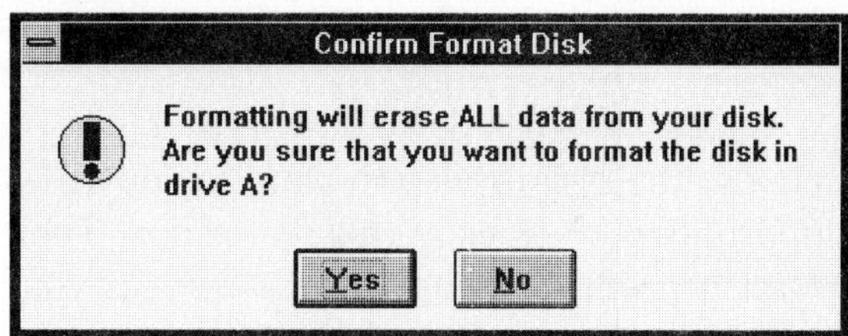

Click on OK again to actually start the formatting process.

CREATING A NEW SUBDIRECTORY

The easiest way to create a new subdirectory is to first find the directory you want to add the new subdirectory to. Scroll through the directory tree on the left side of the File Manager until you find the place you want the new directory to be and click there. Now choose Create Directory from the File menu (Alt F, E). This opens a dialog box that looks like this:

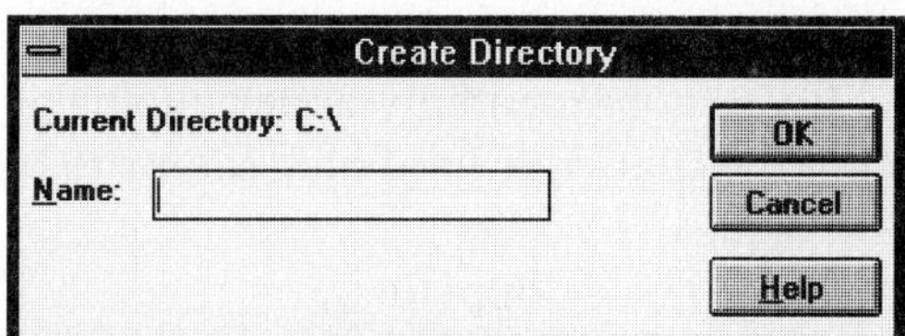

Now type the name of the new subdirectory. It will automatically be inside the directory you have highlighted.

COPYING A DISK

You will often need to copy disks (for example to back up the original disks that came with a program.) The jargon talks about copying "a source to a destination." The source is the original, the destination is the copy.

To copy disks, open the Disk menu in the File Manager and choose Copy. You will see a dialog box that looks like this one:

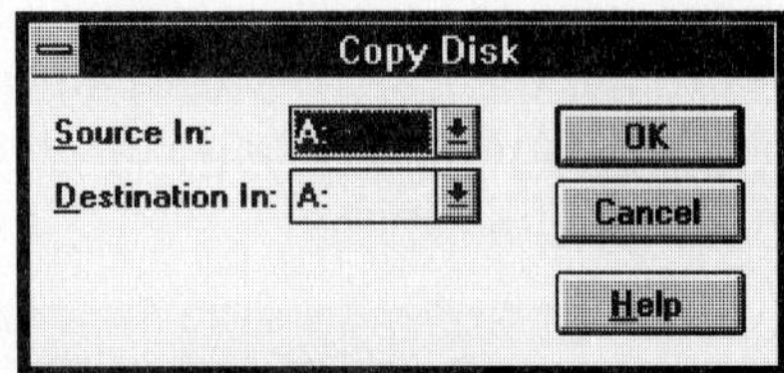

Choose the disk drive you want to copy the disk from and then choose the disk drive you want to copy the disk to by making the appropriate choices in this dialog box. Then click on OK. The File Manager will start copying the disk for you, and will pop up a message box when you need to place the destination disk in the drive.

ABNORMAL EXITS FROM WINDOWS

If you don't exit Windows normally, there is a very small chance that work you thought was saved wasn't saved. There's really very little that you can do if this happens. A much more common problem is that your hard disk, which you thought had plenty of room, no longer seems to have much room left. One possible reason is that Windows has filled your disk with temporary "scratch" files that it only needs while it is running. It automatically erases these scratch files when you exit it properly. Too many abnormal exits and you may discover that your hard disk is filled with these useless files!

If you are repeatedly experiencing abnormal exits from Windows and find that your hard disk seems to be filling up too rapidly, try the following:

1. Leave Windows (Alt+F4) and return to the DOS prompt.
2. Type the following at the DOS prompt:

   DEL C:\WINDOWS\TEMP*.TMP

3. Then press Enter.

There are no guarantees, of course, but this deletes all the temporary scratch files that Windows may have created while it was working and didn't get a chance to erase. (Since Windows needs some scratch files while it works and step 2 deletes them *all*, be sure not to try this from within Windows itself!)

B

Installing Word for Windows 6.0

THIS appendix shows you how to install Word for Windows 6.0 and how to add or remove features later on should that become necessary. This appendix assumes you know the basics of using Microsoft Windows as described in Appendix A. First off you need to always remember that because Word for Windows 6.0 is big and powerful, it is power hungry. You need at least 4 megabytes of memory. (Having 8 megabytes of memory makes Word for Windows 6.0 run much faster. If you intend to use Word for Windows 6.0 a lot, this is the first upgrade you should be thinking of.) You also need a lot of room on your hard disk: around 30 megabytes for a complete installation, 20 megabytes for a typical installation, and around 7 megabytes for the smallest system you can actually use—and these requirements give you only a little bit of space to store your work!

As far as power goes, the rule for Word for Windows 6.0 is this: the faster the machine you have, the better. However, if you have the needed memory, Word will run acceptably on almost any machine that has a 386-class processor. (It will nonetheless be somewhat slow on these machines.) A faster machine will give a much better performance.

NOTE *The way to tell if your machine has the right kind of processor is to look at the documentation that came with your machine—or even on the machine itself. If it says your machine uses a chip that has a 386 or a 486 in it (examples include 386DX33, 486SX25, 486DX33, and so on), and you have the right amount of memory (the buzzword is "megabytes of RAM"), then you should be okay.*

SETTING UP WORD FOR WINDOWS 6.0

As with all programs, the first thing you should do is make backup copies of the original distribution disks. Although the Word for Windows 6.0 files are compressed, the disks themselves are not copy-protected. You can copy the disks with the File Manager from Windows as described in Appendix A. (If you are familiar with DOS you can use the DISKCOPY command from DOS.)

Next, send in the registration card. It's true that you'll get a certain amount of junk mail as a result, but it also will be easier to get support and notices of upgrades from Microsoft.

RUNNING THE SETUP PROGRAM

The disks for Word for Windows 6.0 contain an automated setup program—however, Windows itself must be running for the setup program to run. The first time you set up Word for Windows 6.0, the setup program asks for your name and the name of the company that bought the copy of Word for Windows 6.0. It keeps track of this information and uses it to remind you to whom the program is licensed, every time you start Word for Windows 6.0 and every time you use the setup program.

NOTE *You can run the setup program as many times as you want, which means you are not tied into the options you choose the first time. (You'll see how to add or remove components in the last section of this appendix.)*

Setting up Word for Windows 6.0 is simple: once you start the setup procedure you are led through a series of dialog boxes. Fill in the information requested in each dialog box and click on the OK button to move to the next one. You can stop the process at any time but then you will need to start over from the first step to successfully install Word for Windows 6.0.

Start Microsoft Windows if it is not already running, then follow these steps to install it from the A drive. (You can install Word for Windows 6.0 from any floppy drive by substituting the name of the drive you're using in the instructions below.)

1. Place disk 1 in the A drive.
2. In the Program Manager choose Run from the File menu (Alt F, R).
3. Type **A:SETUP** in the dialog box that pops up.

   The dialog box will look something like the one shown here. Make sure that the Run Minimized box is not checked on this dialog box. (This shrinks any Microsoft Windows application to an icon when it starts.)

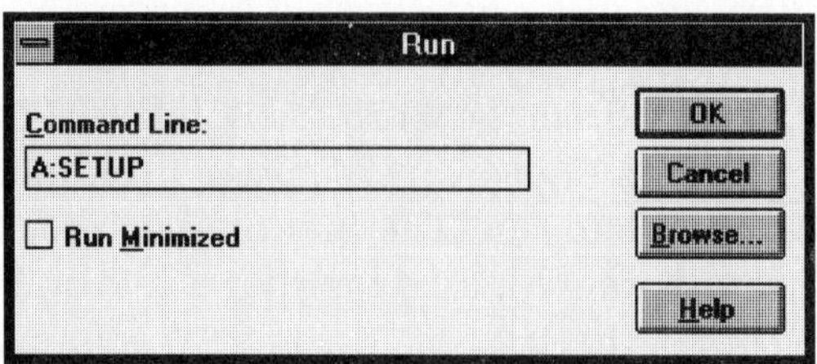

4. Press the Enter key or click on the OK button.

Next comes a short delay (you'll see the familiar Windows hourglass) during which you see a dialog box that says Word is starting the setup process. Then you are taken to the initial Word for Windows 6.0 setup screen, shown in Figure B-1. Click on the OK button to move on with the installation procedure.

Next, a dialog box appears asking for your name and company name. This information is copied to the disk you use to install Word for Windows 6.0. Another dialog box then asks you to confirm this information. The next dialog box shows you the serial number for your copy. You might want to copy this down in case you need to call Microsoft for technical support. Click on OK to move on to the next step. At this point, before Word presents you with another dialog box that you need to fill in. You will see a message box that says the setup

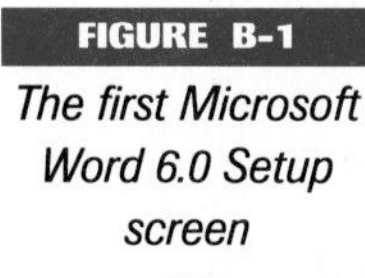
FIGURE B-1
The first Microsoft Word 6.0 Setup screen

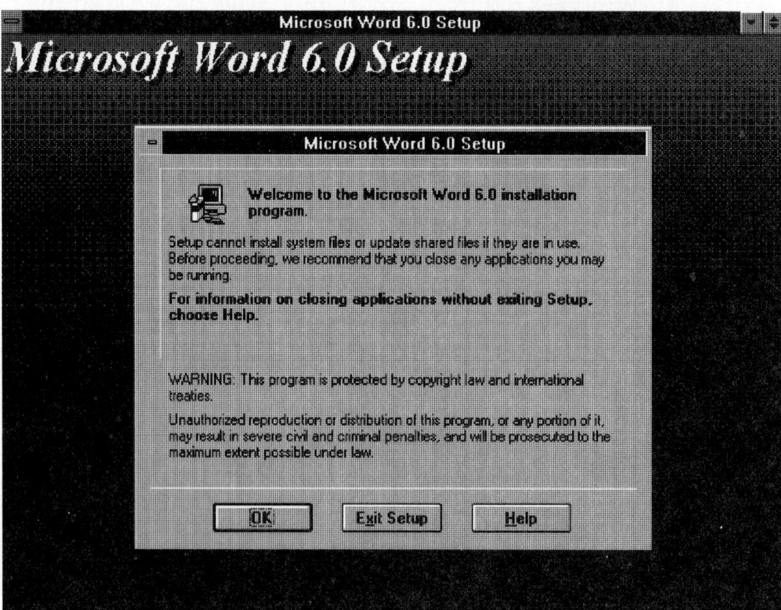

program is looking for "installed components." This just means that the setup program is looking for previous versions of Word for Windows.

If the setup program finds an earlier version of Word for Windows in the \WINWORD directory, it presents you with a dialog box like the one shown in Figure B-2. If you click on OK, then Word will overwrite the previous version of Word that you have. (This is usually not a problem since Word for Windows 6.0 works easily with files created by earlier versions of Word for Windows.) If you absolutely must have two versions of Word for Windows on your hard disk, click on the Change Directory button in Figure B-2 and work with the dialog box that pops up to find another directory for the earlier version of Word For Windows. In most cases, you will want to click on the OK button and overwrite the previous version in Figure B-2.

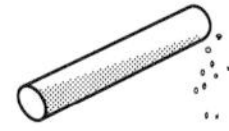

NOTE *Even if you do not have a previous version of Word for Windows installed, you will see a dialog box that looks similar to the one shown in Figure B-2. This is because the setup program wants to give you the opportunity of putting Word for Windows 6.0 in some place other than the C:\WINWORD directory. You can do this by clicking on the Change Directory button in the version of the dialog box in Figure B-2 that you will see, and working with the dialog box that pops up to find another directory for Word for Windows 6.0.*

Next, Word again tells you that it is searching for "installed components" and the hourglass pops up to tell you to wait. The next dialog box, shown in Figure B-3, is the key dialog box in the setup process. This dialog box lets you choose how many of Word for

FIGURE B-2

Dialog box when you have an older version of Word in the destination directory

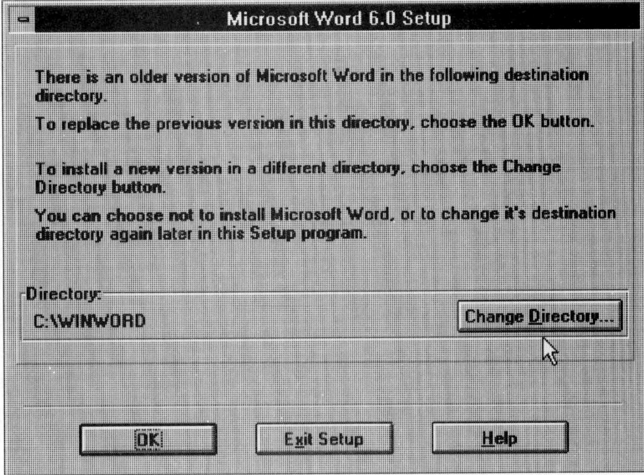

FIGURE B-3

The three possible types of installations

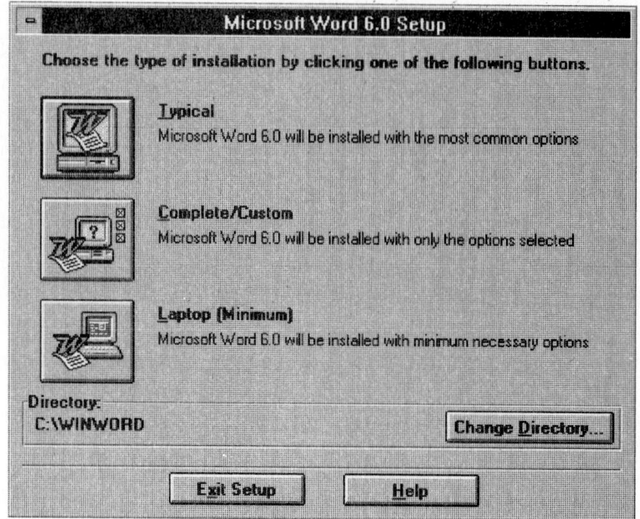

Windows 6.0 features you want the setup program to install. A complete installation needs around 30 megabytes of space, a typical installation needs approximately 20 megabytes, and the laptop version needs about 7 megabytes of free hard disk space. The laptop version gives you access to only a small portion of Word's powers.

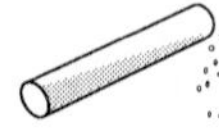

NOTE *The Laptop button is a misnomer: it should be called the Minimal button. Many laptops have more than enough hard disk space to install either the typical or complete versions of Word for Windows 6.0. It is the hard disk space available on your machine and not the type of machine that determines which button you should choose.*

Finally, once you are comfortable with the dialog boxes for a typical installation, then you will be comfortable with the similar ones that show up for a "laptop" (minimal) installation. In fact, even if you choose to do a custom installation, most of the dialog boxes you will see are similar to the ones for a typical installation. The only dialog box that is substantially different is described in the "Custom Installations" section that follows.

REMEMBER *You can install Word for Windows 6.0 as many times as you want. The rules are determined by the licensing agreement that comes with your package.*

A TYPICAL INSTALLATION

Suppose you click on the Typical button in Figure B-3 in order to do what the designers of Word call a typical installation. Choosing to do a typical installation gives you access to the most common features available in Word for Windows 6.0. After you choose the Typical button, Word pops up a dialog box that asks if you want to install the clip art for Word for Windows 6.0. *Clip art* is a name usually given to graphics images that you can use in your documents. (Chapter 13 shows you how to use them.) If you think you would like to incorporate pictures into your work, and have an extra megabyte or so on your hard disk, by all means click on the OK button. The next dialog box is for people moving from WordPerfect to Word; click on OK if you are, click on No if you are not.

The next dialog box asks you for the name of the Program Group into which you want to install Word for Windows 6.0 (see Appendix A for what these are). The usual Program Group is called *Microsoft Office.* Enter the name you prefer by typing in the text box or selecting a name from the list box that shows up in this dialog box. The next screen has a message box and the hourglass and tells you that the setup program is checking if you have enough disk space. After this check, the setup program starts copying the files. When it finishes with the first disk, you'll see a message box like the one shown here. As requested by the message box, put the disk numbered 2 into the floppy drive and click on OK. After Word finishes with the second disk it will ask you for the third with a similar message box. Continue this process until you finish with all the disks that the setup program requests. (The setup program takes about 10-15 minutes on most machines. While it is doing its job, you will see some advertising for what Word for Windows 6.0 can do.)

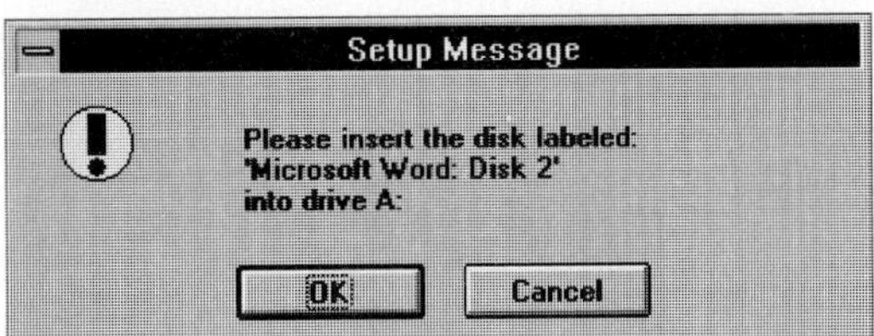

When you finish feeding in all the disks that the setup program needs, the setup program tells you to wait while it updates your system (this can take a couple of minutes). If the setup program has finished successfully, you will see a screen like this:

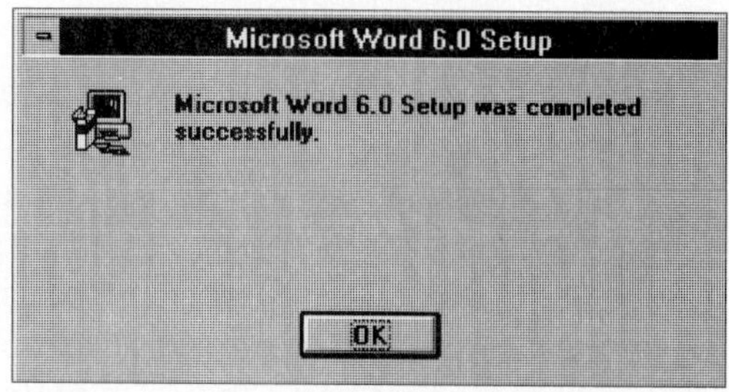

Click on OK and you are ready to start Word for Windows 6.0 as described in Chapter 1.

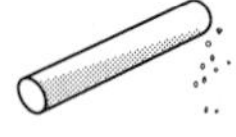

NOTE *In many cases the setup program tells you that you need to reboot your machine. You will need to look carefully at the final screen you see when the setup program finishes. Below is an example of a screen that instructs you to reboot your system in order to use Word for Windows 6.0.*

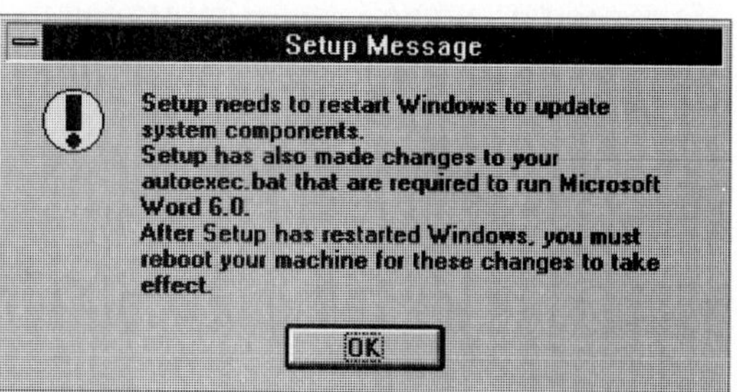

To leave Windows and reboot your machine:

1. Leave Windows one more time.
2. Hold Down the Ctrl, the Alt, and the Del keys simultaneously.
3. After your system returns (reboots), start Windows up again.

At this point, turn to Chapter 1 to see how to run Word for Windows!

CUSTOM INSTALLATIONS

If you click on the Complete/Custom button shown in Figure B-3, you will be taken to a screen like Figure B-4. This dialog box gives you a complete list of what Word for Windows 6.0 has to offer—as you can see by looking at the bottom of Figure B-4, a complete installation of

Word for Windows 6.0 takes a lot of space—close to 30 megabytes of hard disk space. (The setup program also tells you how much space you have left on your hard disk in order for you to plan.) If there is a component that you do not need and do not have room for, click in the check box (making sure the check box is off), to *not install* that feature. As mentioned before, if you have the space, there is no reason not to install everything; you can always remove components later (as described in the next section). Once you click on the Continue button in Figure B-4, the setup program leads you through screens, asking you to insert your installation disks in the floppy disk drive of your computer. Keep on following the directions, placing the correctly numbered disks in the floppy drive and clicking on OK. When you have finished you will either see a message box telling you Microsoft Word 6.0 Setup was completed successfully or you will see a message box telling you to reboot your machine and then restart Windows. (See the end of the previous section for the steps needed for this.)

INSTALLING AND REMOVING WORD COMPONENTS AFTER YOUR ORIGINAL INSTALLATION

If you did a typical installation, there may come a time when you need to install something you thought you didn't need originally.

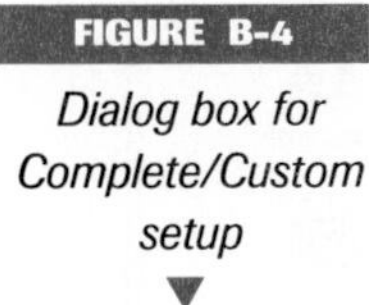

FIGURE B-4

Dialog box for Complete/Custom setup

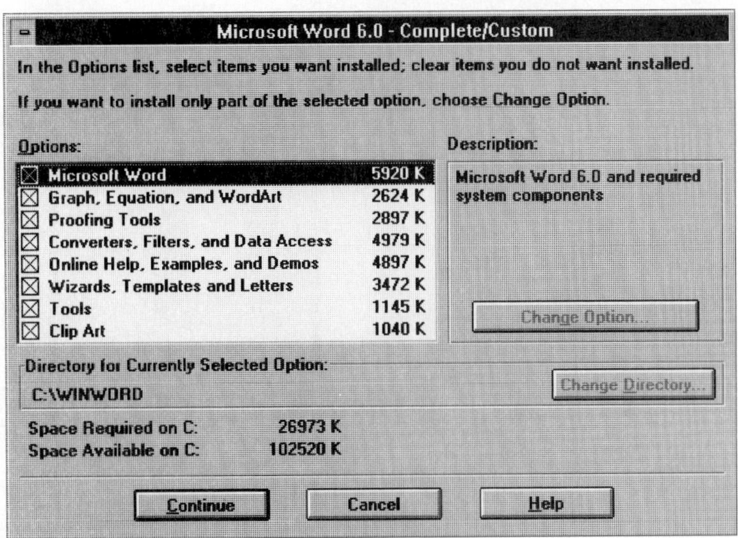

Conversely, there may come a time when you need to remove something you originally installed because you need the hard disk space it is using. Both these operations are done by activating the Word Setup program from the Program Manager. Look for the Word Setup program in the Program Group where you installed Word for Windows. If you installed Word for Windows 6.0 using the default Microsoft Office Program Group, look for an icon like the one pointed to in Figure B-5 and double-click on this icon. (If not, look for this icon in the group where you installed Word for Windows 6.0.)

After a short delay, this takes you to a dialog box like the one shown in Figure B-6. Click on the Add/Remove button in Figure B-6 in order to go to the dialog box that lets you add or remove components.

After a short wait, you are taken to a dialog box like the one in Figure B-7. To remove a component, make sure the check boxes are on *only* for items you want to keep. Figure B-7 shows a plan to remove only the clip art since that box is the only one not checked. Notice how in the right hand corner of Figure B-7, you are shown how many components you are asking to remove (one in this case). Click on the Continue button and Word pops up a message box that asks you to confirm that you want to remove this component. Click on Yes to

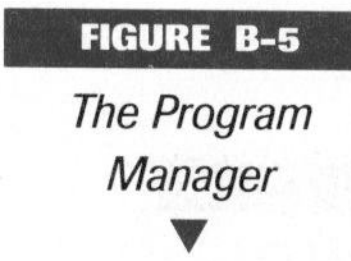

FIGURE B-5

The Program Manager

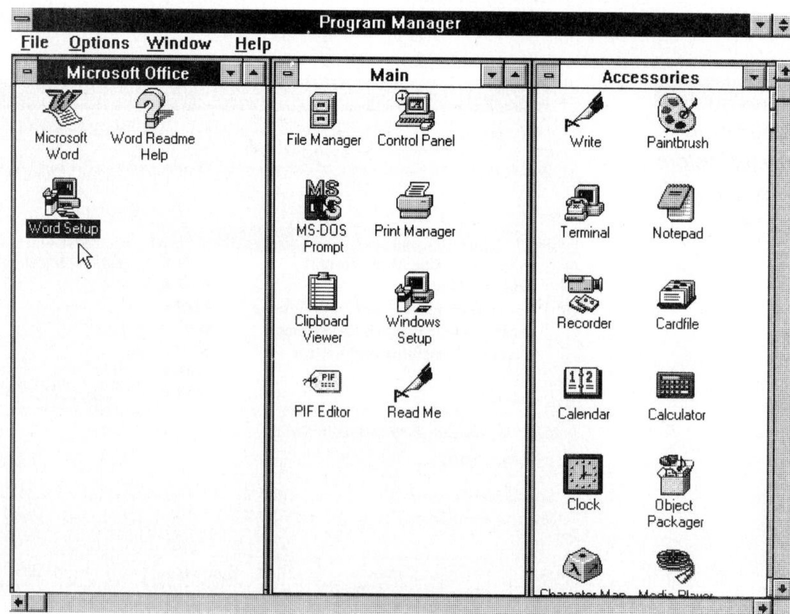

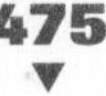

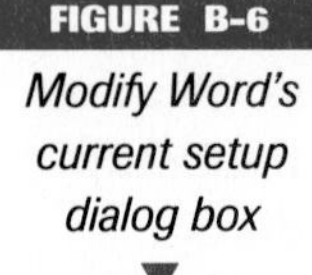

FIGURE B-6

Modify Word's current setup dialog box

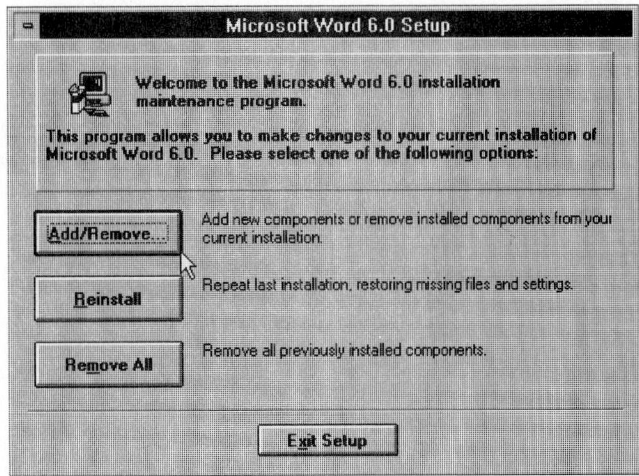

remove the component. After a short delay, the Setup program tells you that the changes were made successfully.

To install a component that isn't currently installed, you need to have the distribution disks for Word for Windows 6.0 that Microsoft provided. Choose the Word Setup program again and click on the Add/Remove button in Figure B-6, only now make sure the check box is on for items you want to have. Word keeps track of how many new

FIGURE B-7

Word's Setup Maintenance installation screen

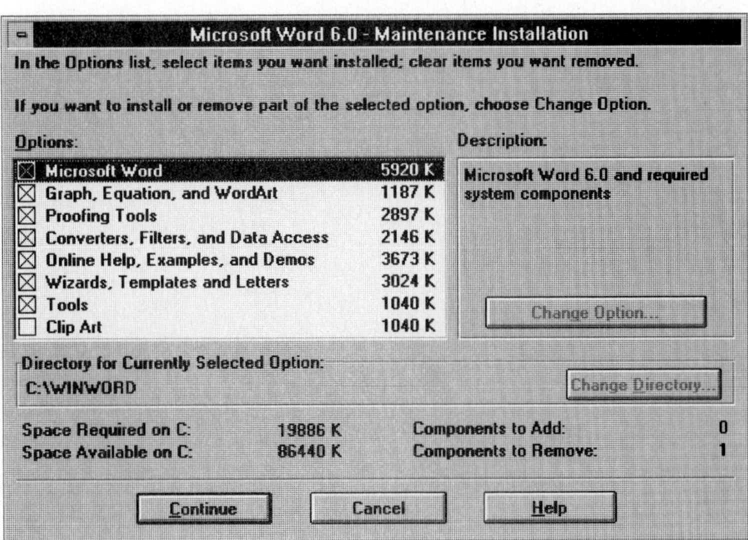

boxes you check. Now, when you click on the Continue button, Word pops up a message box that asks you to insert a specific disk. Put the correctly numbered disk into a floppy drive. Click on OK; the Setup Program copies the needed files (it may ask you for other disks periodically). When it is done with all the disks it needs, it will tell you the changes were made successfully.

Index

* (asterisk)
  as multiplication symbol, 321
  as wildcard, 79, 127-128, 369
(...) ellipsis on menu items, 15
= (equal sign)
  for calculating in tables, 320
- (minus sign)
  for calculating in tables, 321
  for levels in outlines, 345
  in find file dialog box, 360
¶ (paragraph mark)
  as end of paragraph marker, 23, 174
  as holder of paragraph formatting, 197
  colored for AutoFormat, 226
  finding and replacing, 174-175
  removing extra, *see* AutoFormat
+ (plus sign)
  for calculating in tables, 321
  for outlines, 345
  in find file dialog box, 360
? (question mark) as wildcard, 127-128, 369

A

Abnormal exits from Windows, 464
Accelerator keys. 14, 451
Active document, 329, 332
Adams, Henry, 250
Adding numbers. *See* Math calculations
Adobe fonts, 167
Agenda Wizard, 99-104
Aligning,
  frames, 405-407
  numbers using tabs, 189
  pages, 247
  paragraphs, 195
  text using tabs, 189, 197
All Caps, 159
Allow fast saves option, 48-49
  disadvantages for file searching, 381
Alphabetizing. *See* Sorting
Alt key and opening menus, 451
Anchoring frames, 400-401
Annotations, 358-362
  copying or deleting, 360
  displaying marks, 359
  going to, 359
  highlighting annotated text, 360
  inserting, 358
  multiple users and, 361
  printing, 361
  removing, 360
  user info tab and, 359
  viewing, 359
  voice annotations, 361-362
Antonyms. *See* Thesaurus
Arial font, 165, 209
Arrange All, 332-333
Arrow mouse pointer, 17, 442
  shape in selection area, 69
ASCII text files. *See* Opening Files; Saving Files
Asterisks
  as wildcards in file finding, 369
  as wildcards in spell checking, 127
  for multiplication, 321
Attaching templates to documents. *See* Templates
AutoCorrect, 26-27
  creating an entry for, 26
  dialog box, 27
  turning on and off, 26
AutoFormat, 186, 225-230 *See also* Table AutoFormat
  options for, 228-230
AutoFormat Options Tab, 228-230
Automatic backup, 38
Automatic saving, 38
AutoText, 122, 141-143
Avery labels, 433
Award Wizard, 93-98

B

Backspace key, 25-26
Backslash for directories, 459
Backup documents, 38
Bar codes for mailing. *See* Envelopes, Labels
Bierce, Ambrose, 75
Bitmaps for graphics, 399
Block. *See* Selecting text
Boilerplate. *See* AutoCorrect, AutoText
Bold text, 152
Border toolbar, 200
Borders, 200-204 *See also* Shading
Boxes. *See* Borders; Frames
Breaks,
  page, 249
  columns, 395
  sections, 337-339
Bullet and Numbering dialog box, 288
Bullet lists, 285-286, 288-290
  button, 285
  changing bullets used in, 289-290
  removing, 285
Bullet tab, 288-289
Burke, Edmond, 215
Byron, Lord, 399

C

Calculations, 320-322
Calendar Wizard, 105-108
Campbell, Mary, 171, 200, 321, 328, 391
Caps Lock key, 25
Captions, 315-316
Cells in tables, 296

deleting, 309
how numbered, 320
inserting, 308
merging, 314
selecting, 301, 307
splitting, 314
Center text
on page, 247
in a paragraph, 195 *See also* Aligning, paragraphs; Sections.
Centimeters. *See* Units of measurements,
Changing
case, 66
fonts. *See* Fonts
height and width in tables, *see* Tables
indents, *see* Indents
margins, *see* Margins
tab stops, *see* Tabs
Character attribute, *see* Character formatting.
Character formatting, 150-161 *See also* Fonts
keyboard shortcuts for, 160-161
removing, 152
searching for, 176-178
Character size, 154-156 *See also* Fonts
Check boxes, 455
Checking for repeated words, 125-126
Checking spelling. *See* Spelling
Child windows, 329
Clearing searches, 378
Clearing tabs. *See* Tabs
Clicking, 443
Clip art. *See* Graphics
Clipboard, 77
Closing,
all open documents, 330
the active document, 19, 330
cm (centimeters). *See* Units of measurement
Collapsing levels in Outlines, 348-349
Color,
for revision marks, 362, 363-364
for text, 158
Columns, 394-398
adding in tables, 320
breaks, 395
selecting in tables, 307
Command buttons, 445
default, 454
Comments. *See* Annotations
Comparing versions of same document, 366-367
Contents on Help menu, 48
Control menu box, 447, 448
Converting
files from another word processor, 43
files to another word processor, 35-37
tables to a data source, 427
text to a table, 303-304
Copying. *See also* Clipboard; Spike
disks, 463-464
files, 373
formatting, 180-181
shape of a paragraph, 180
text, 76-77
Copyright symbol, 173, 225
Count words, *See* Document statistics
Create a new directory,
in Word, 41
with the Windows File Manager, 463
Cropping a graphic, 392
Cursor. *See* Insertion point
Custom dictionaries, 131-134
Cut and Paste, 75-76
Cutting. *See also* Clipboard; Deleting; Spike
to the Clipboard, 73-74
to the Spike, 77
CV Wizard. *See* Resume Wizard

D

Dashes, 172
Data source, 413, 418-425
adding records to, 421-422, 423
converting tables to, 427
Database toolbar, 426-427
Date and time, 254, 417
inserting in headers and footers, 254
Default directory, 41
Del key, 25-26
Deleting. *See also* Cutting
annotations, 360
files, 373
text, 72
undoing, 73
words, 72
Demoting to body text, 345, 347
Desktop publishing, 5, 386-410
Dialog boxes, 451, 453-459
Dictionaries for spellchecking, 131-134
Directories, 458-459
creating, 41, 463
Disraeli, Benjamin, 165
Document,
active, 329, 332
area, 13
closing, 19, 330
comparing, *see also* Comparing versions
creating new, 19
management, 353-383
normal, 209
saving, 31-40
screen, 13
statistics, 356-357
switching between open, 330
templates. *See* Templates
Document statistics, 356-357
Document Windows, 331
arrange all, 332-333
new window, 333-334
splitting, 334-335
DOS text, *see also* Opening files; Saving files
Dot leaders. *See* Tabs
Double spacing. *See* Spacing between lines
Double underline. *See* Underline
Double-clicking, 444, 446
Drag, 444
Drag and drop for moving text, 74-75
Drawing boxes and lines in a paragraph. *See* Borders; Drawing; Shading
Drop-down list boxes, 456-457
Drop caps, 205-207, 386

E

Edit tab, 65-66
Ellipses, 15
Emerson, Ralph Waldo, 187
Endnotes. *See* Footnotes and endnotes.
End of cell markers, 301
End of row markers, 301
Ending a Word session, 9-10
Enter key, 23
Entering special characters, 170-171
Entering text, 22-30
Envelopes, 276-282
  addressing, 277, 280
  mail merge and, 435-437
  postal bar codes in, 280, 436
  printing, 281
  size, 279
  user info and, 277
Equation editor, 170
Error corrections, 25-26
  and AutoCorrect, 26-27
Exiting Windows, 442, 445
Exiting Word, 9-10
Expanding and collapsing outlines, 348-349
Extend selection mode, 71-72

F

Fast save, 38
  disadvantages of, 38, 381
Fax Wizard, 117-118
Field Names in data source, 418-420
Fields, 254-255
  deleting, 255
  entering, 254
  in mail merges, 418-420, 426
  switching between codes and results, 255
  updating, 254
File handling dialog boxes, 457-459
File Location for searches, 378
File Management, 367-382
  finding files, 368-369
  overview, 367-368
File Manager, 460-463
File naming, 31-32, 459-460
File Templates. *See* Template
File names, 31-32, 459-460
Find
  matching case, 82
  matching sounds, 82
  options for, 81-82
  records in a data source, 424
  special characters, 82-83
  text, 79-80
  text using sound alike, 82
  text using wildcards, 79
  whole words only, 82
Find File, 367-382
  advanced search abilities, 377-382
  by author, 381
  by file type, 369
  by time created or saved, 378
  by text within, 381
  by title, 379
  saving searches for reuse, 382
  search capabilities of, 368-369, 377-382
  specifying location for search, 378
Find File dialog box, 370-376
  directories in, 370
  different views in, 371-372
  file management commands available in, 373-374
  selecting single file in, 371
  selecting multiple files in, 375
  sorting in, 374-375
Finding files. *See* Find File
Fonts, 162-169
  bitmapped, 167
  changing, 163-164
  changing default, 168-169
  computer versus ordinary usage of, 150
  default, 164
  definition of, 5, 162
  disadvantages of using too many, 150, 165
  monospaced, 163
  non-serif, 163
  problems with overusing, 150-151
  printer, 167-168
  proportional, 163
  scalable, 167-168
  serif, 163
  sizing, 154-156, 157
  standard Windows, 166
  Symbol font, 166
  TrueType, 167-168
  Wingdings, 166
Footers, *See* Headers and footers
Footnotes and endnotes, 257-260
  creating, 257
  deleting, 259
  editing, 258
  marks for, 258, 260
  moving, 259
  reference marks, 258
  viewing, 259
Footnote pane, 258
Form letters. *See* Mail merge
Format Painter, 181
Formatting a floppy disk, 462-463
Formatting toolbar, 16
Frames, 386, 399-407
  applying borders and shading, 402
  inserting, 400
  positioning, 405-406
  sizing, 400, 403
  wrapping text around, 402-403, 404-405
Franklin, Benjamin, 73
Full screen mode, 237-238, 268

G

Gibbon, Edward, 65, 72, 80-81, 188, 196
Global search. *See* Find
Glossary. *See* AutoText
Go back, 63
Go To, 63
Grammar checking, 138-20
  options for, 140
  readability statistics, 139
Grammar Tab on Options dialog box, 140
Graphics, 388-393
  copying from another Windows program, 390
  cropping, 392
  filters, 388

linking into document, 390
size of documents and, 390
sizing, 391-393
Greyed items on menus
Gridlines in tables, 296
Gutter, 243

H

Hanging indents, 192-193, 288-289
Hard disk requirements for Word, 466
Hard page break, 249
Hard returns, 23, 187
Hardware requirements for Word, 466, 475
Headers and footers, 252-256
creating, 253
deleting, 253, 255
different for odd and even pages, 256
field codes in, 254
formatting page numbers in, 254, 342-345
inserting dates, page numbers or times into, 254
leaving room for, 253
linking and unlinking to previous, 340
switching between header and footer, 253
switching between main document and, 255
toolbar, 253-255
Header Row for a Data Source, 419
Headings in tables, 314-315
Heading styles, 209-210
in outlines, 348
Help, 46-54
accessing, 46, 52
button, 46, 268
context sensitive, 46
definitions via, 52, 54
different kinds, 52-53
how tied together, 52
jumps in, 52
menu, 47-50
moving between topics, 52
Quick Preview, 48-49
searching for topics, 48-49
on switching from WordPerfect, 40
Help Menu
Contents, 48
Examples and Demos, 49
Quick Preview, 48
Search for Help on, 48-49
Tip of the Day, 50,
WordPerfect Help, 50
Hidden text, 159
Highlighting text. *See* Selecting, text
Horizontal ruler. *See* Ruler
Horizontal scroll bar. *See* Scroll bars
Hotkeys. *See* Accelerator keys
Hourglass mouse pointer, 442-443

I

I-beam mouse pointer, 17, 61
Icons, 443
Importing graphics. *See* Graphics
in (Inches) *See* Units of measurement
Indents, 188-193
hanging, 192-193, 288-289
negative indents, 188
setting, 189-193
Ins key, 30
Insert mode, 30
Insert Table, 296, 297
Inserting,
annotations, 358
cells in tables, 308
columns in tables, 320
dates and times, 254
rows in tables, 301, 307-308
special characters, 170-171
Insertion point, 10
Installing Word, 466-476
default directory for, 469
hard disk requirements, 466, 473
hardware requirements, 466
new components after original installation, 473-476
updating Word, 469
Interrupting printing, 271
Italics, 152

J

Justification, 195 *See also* Aligning

K

Keyboard, 12

L

Labels, 432-435
creating page of same, 435
See also mail merge.
Landscape orientation, 105
Layout Tab, 246-247
Leaders, 197-198 *See also* Tabs
Left alignment, 195
Letter Wizard, 109-110
Level Heads in Outlines, 345
Lincoln, Abraham, 74, 153, 191, 193, 207
Line numbers, 247
Line spacing, 195
Lippman, Walter, 156
List boxes, 458
Lists, 285-295
bullet, 285, 288-290
multilevel, 293-295
numbered, 285, 290-292
removing bullets or numbers from, 285
shortcut menu for, 286
Locate. *See* Find and replace

M

Magnifier button, 266
Mail Merge toolbar, 428
Mail merge, 413-440
executing the merge, 430-431
merge fields in, 428-429
toolbar, 428
See also Envelopes, Labels.
Mail Merge Helper, 413-417
Main document, 413
Margins tab, 241-244
Margins, 187, 242
Marking revisions. *See* Revision Marks
Maximize, 447
button, 447
window, 447-448

Memo Wizard, 115-116
Memory requirements for Word, 466
Menu bar, 14
Menus, *see also* Shortcut menus
  accelerator keys, 451
  disabled items, 449
  ellipses in, 15, 451
  greyed, 449
  hotkeys and, 451
  opening via the keyboard, 450-451
  opening via the mouse, 450
  shortcut keys for, 451
Merge Fields, 414, 428-430
Measurement units of, 192, 242
Metafiles, 389
Microsoft Word: The Complete Reference (Campbell), 170, 321, 328
Minimize,
  button, 447
  a window, 447
Minus sign
  in Find File dialog box, 360
  for calculating in tables, 321
  for outlines, 345
Mirror margins, 243
Modify styles dialog box, 215-218
Monospaced fonts, 163
Most recently used file list, 41-42
Mouse,
  actions, 443-444
  copying text with, 76
  moving text with, 74-75
  pointer shapes, 17, 181
  selecting text with, 67-70
Mouse pointers, 17, 181, 442-443
Moving
  dialog boxes and windows, 448, 454
  text, 74-86
  the insertion point, 59, 61-62
  through the document, 59-64
Multilevel lists, 293-295
  promoting and demoting items in, 294

N

Naming files, 31-32, 459-460
Navigating through a Word document, 11, 59-64
New documents, 19
New line character, 187
New window, 333-334
Newsletter Wizard, 386
Non-printing characters, 23
Normal documents, 209
Normal template, 209, 214, 223
Normal view, 45, 235-236
NORMAL.DOT, 214, 223
Numbered lists
  ending, 285
  skipping temporarily, 287
  stopping, 285
Numbered Tab, 290-293
Numbering
  lists, 285, 290-293
  pages, 251-252, 254, 341-343

O

Open button, 41
Open dialog box, 42
Opening documents, 41-43
  converting from another Word processor, 329
  more than one document at once, 329
Option buttons, 455
Outline toolbar, 345-347
Outline view, 344
Outlines, 344-350
  adding outline levels, 346-347
  body text in, 347
  changing ordinary documents to support, 348
  collapsing, 348-349
  converting a document to an outline, 348
  expanding, 348-349
  heading levels in, 346, 348
  multilevels lists and, 293
  printing outlines, 350
  promoting or demoting outline levels, 346
  switching to outline view, 344
  toolbar, 345-347
  using to create documents, 349-350
Overtype mode, 30

P

Page,
  alignment, 247
  breaks, 249-250
  margins, 242-243
  numbers, 251-252
  orientation, 245
  printing selected, 272
  size, 244-245
Page breaks, 249-250
Page Layout view, 45, 92, 206, 235-236
Page numbers, 251-252
  adding to headers and footers, 254
  changing in multisection documents, 341-343
Page setup, 241-247
Pagination,
  background, 248
  hard page breaks, 249
  soft page breaks, 249
  turning off automatic repagination, 248
Paper size tab, 244-245
Paper source tab, 245-246
Paragraph dialog box, 191-196
Paragraph marks, 23, 174
  hidden character for, 23
Paragraphs,
  aligning, 195-196
  drop caps in, 205-207
  ending, 187
  formatting, 187-195
  spacing between, 194
  spacing lines in, 195
Pascal, Blaise, 240
Password protecting documents, 39-40
Pasting,
  from the Clipboard, 76
  from the Spike, 77
Path, 459-460
Picas, 192
Pictures. *See* Graphics
Point size. *See* Fonts, Font Size
Pointing, 443
Points (pt), 154 *See also* Unit of measurements.
Pope, Alexander, 399

Portrait orientation, 105
Positioning objects. *See* Frames
Previewing your work, *see* Print Preview.
Print button, 43-44, 266, 272
Print dialog box, 272-276
Print options, 272, 273-276
Print preview, 44-45, 264-270
  editing in, 269-270
  leaving, 45, 265
  moving through document while, 44, 265
  multiple versus single page in, 267
Print Preview toolbar, 266-268
Print Setup dialog box, 272-273
Printer fonts, 167-168
Print What drop-down list box, 274
Printing, 43-44, 270-281
  annotations, 361
  background, 275-276
  collate copies, 275
  documents, 43-44
  drafts, 275
  envelopes, 276-282
  hidden text, 275
  interrupting, 271
  laser printer problems, 271
  multiple copies, 272, 275
  odd and even pages, 274
  non-text parts of a document 274
  printer problems, 271
  specific pages, 272
  to a file, 274-275
  updating field codes before, 275
  without opening file, 373
Program groups, 446, 447
Program manager, 444, 446-453
Proportional fonts, 163

Q

Quitting Windows, 9-10
Quitting Word, 9-10
Quotation marks and AutoFormat, 229

R

Read-only documents, 40, 373
Readability statistics, 139
Record, 419
Redo button, 28
Redoing actions, 28
Removing
  annotations, 360
  footnotes and endnotes, 259
  formatting, 152, 161
  hard page breaks, 249-250
  numbers and bullets from lists, 285
  section breaks, 339
Repeating actions, 28
Replacing
  formatting, 177, 178-179
  special characters, 175, 180
  text, 84-86
Resizing windows, 448-449
Resume Wizard, 111-114
Revision Marks, 362-367
  accepting or rejecting all, 365
  adding while editing, 362
  after using AutoFormat, 226
  appearance of, 362, 363-365
  by author, 364
  reviewing, 365-366
  revision lines, 364-365
  undoing, *see* Undo
Revision options tab, 363-365
Right alignment, 195
RTF (rich text format), 36
Ruler, 16
  indenting with, 190-191
  setting tabs with, 189-190

S

Sans serif fonts, 163
Save As dialog box, 32-33
Save options, 37-38
Saving documents, 31-38
  as text only, 36
  automatically at intervals, 38
  backup copies, 38
  fast saving, 38, 381
  for the first time, 32
  in another word processor format, 35-36
  with a new name, 34-35
Scalable fonts. *See* Fonts
Scroll bars, 17, 60-61, 240, 449
Scroll box, 60
Scrolling
  defined, 59
  through a document, 60-61
Shaw, George Bernard, 181
Searching, *see also* Find, Find File
  by sound, 79
  for special characters, 174-175
  for text 79-80,
  using wildcards, 79
Sections, 337-344
  deleting, 339
  effect on pagination, 338
  headers and footers in, 340-341
  inserting section breaks, 337-339
  kinds of breaks, 338
  page numbering with, 341-343
  page setup with, 340
Selecting text, 65-71
  cancelling, 67
  entire document, 69, 200
  importance of, 58
  paragraph, 68, 69
  sentence, 68
  replacing it, 65
  typing replaces selection, 65-66
  vertical blocks, 69-70
  via selection bar, 69
  with the Extend key, 71
  with the keyboard, 67
  with the mouse, 67-70
  word, 68
Selection bar, 69
  in tables, 306
Serif fonts, 163
Shading, 201-202, 204-205
  applying to paragraphs and frames,
  applying to tables,
Shakespeare, William, 6, 228, 259
Sheldon, Tom, 165, 442
Shift key, 11, 25
Shortcut keys, 14-15
  creating for special characters, 402
  for menus, 451

for styles, 217-218
Shortcut menus, 76, 191, 286, 401-402
Show/Hide button, 23
Shrink to fit, 268
Sidebars, 407
Small capitals, 159
Smart cut and paste, 73-74
Soft returns, 23
Sort dialog box. *See* sorting
Sorting,
in tables, 317-319
text, 319
Sound annotations, 361-362
Spacebar, 10
not right way to indent paragraphs, 188
Spacing,
between lines, 195
between paragraphs, 194
Special characters,
changing shortcut keys for, 171-173
inserting special characters, 170-174
inserting symbols, 170
Spell Checking, 123-135
custom dictionaries, 131-134
dialog box, 123, 128-130
editing while, 124
for help with crossword puzzles, 128
Spell tab on Options dialog box, 130-131
Spike, 77-78
emptying, 77
Spin buttons in text boxes, 456
Split bar, 335
Split line, 334
Splitting a document window, 334-336
Splitting tables, 309
Starting Microsoft Windows, 444-445
Starting Word, 5, 8
from the DOS prompt, 9
Status bar, 16-17
Strikethrough text, 159
as revision mark, 362
Style area, 219
Style dialog box, 211-214
Style Gallery, 222-223
Styles, 186, 208-220
applying, 209, 212
creating, 214, 219-220
modifying, 212-214
Subscript, 159
Subdirectories, 459
Subwindows, 329
Summary Info, 354, 355-357, 373
prompting for, 356
Superscript, 159
Switching between open documents, 330

T

Tab key, 23, 188
hidden character for, 23
Tab stops, 189, 196-199
custom, 189-190
default, 189, 196-197
leader, 198
setting via ruler, 189-190
Table AutoFormat, 300, 305-306
Table Wizard, 299-300
Tables, 296-322
adding captions to, 315-316
adding cells rows or columns to, 301, 307-309
aligning entries in, 300-301
applying borders in tables, 301
calculating in, 320-322
centering a table, 312
changing column widths, 310-311
changing height of a row, 311-312
converting to and from text, 303-304
deleting cells, rows or columns from, 309-310
deleting text in, 310
deleting whole table, 298
end of cell or row markers, 301
entering data in, 300
formatting contents, 300-301
gridlines in, 296
inserting cells, rows or columns into existing, 307-309
inserting new table, 296, 297
headings, 314, 315
merging cells, 314
navigating in, 302-303
numbering cells in, 320
selecting parts of, 306-307
selecting whole table, 298
sorting in, 317-319
splitting merged cells, 314
splitting a table, 309
Tab key and, 301
using in Mail Merge, 427
Tabs, 23
Templates, 186, 221-224
attaching a new one, 222-223
to create a document, 222
Text boxes, 455-456
with spin buttons, 456
Text files, 36
Thesaurus, 135-137
Thumb, *see* Scroll Box
Time field inserting, 254
Times New Roman font, 164, 208
Tip of the Day, 6-7
Title bar, 13, 447
Toggles defined, 24
Toolbars, 15-16, 54
Border, 200
Database, 426-427
displaying, 426
Formatting, 16
Header and Footer, 253-255
Mail Merge, 418
moving, 200
Outline, 345-351
Picture, 392
Print Preview, 266-268
Standard, 16
ToolTip, 16
TrueType fonts, 167-168
Twain, Mark, 204
Typeface, 150

U

Underlining, 152,
dotted as mark of hidden text, 159
kinds of, 157-158
Undo button, 28
Undoing actions, 28

Units of measurement, 242
User info tab, 277-278
  and annotations, 359

V

Vertical scroll bar, 17
View options for documents, 45, 235-240
Vision impaired users of Word, 239
Voice annotations. *See* Annotations

W

Wildcards
  and find and replace, 79
  and file finding, 369
  and spelling, 127-128
Wilde, Oscar, 31, 240
Willcox, Ella, 87
Windows,
  maximizing, 447-448
  metafiles, 389
  minimizing, 447-448
  moving, 448
  sizing, 448-449
Windows 3.1 Made Easy (Sheldon), 442
Windows 3.1, The Complete Reference (Sheldon), 165
Wizards, 89-119
  starting one, 91-92
Word count. *See* Document statistics.
Wordperfect
  help in transition from, 50
  saving documents in format of, 35
Word window elements, 14
Word wrap, 4
Working with Word in a group, 39-40

Z

Zoom, 105, 239-240, 268